TODAY'S CHURCH
AND TODAY'S WORLD

with a special focus on
The Ministry of Bishops

The Lambeth Conference 1978
Preparatory Articles

TODAY'S CHURCH

AND

TODAY'S WORLD

with a special focus on
The Ministry of Bishops

CIO PUBLISHING
LONDON

ISBN 0 7151 4560 6.

Dramrite Printers Limited, Southwark London SE1

Contents

Contributors

AMIRTHAM,
Rev. Samuel

Principal, The Tamil Nadu Theological Seminary, Madurai, South India.
Other appointments, etc.: Member, T.E.F. Committee; Member, Board of the Ecumenical Institute, Bossey.

ASHBY, Very Rev.
Dr. Godfrey W. E. C.

Dean of Grahamstown, South Africa.
Other appointments, etc.: Assoc. Prof. in Old Testament and Hebrew, Rhodes Univ., Grahamstown, 1968-75.

BENNETT,
Rev. Gareth V.

Dean of Divinity, New College, Oxford University, England; Univ. lect. in Modern History.
Other appointments, etc.: Lect. in History, King's Coll., London 1954-59; Visiting Prof., Univ. of South Carolina 1975; Member, Gen. Synod of Church of England from 1975.

BONINO, Rev.
Dr. José Míguez

Dean of post-Graduate Studies, The Union Seminary, Buenos Aires, Argentina.
Other appointments, etc.: Minister of the Methodist Church in Argentina; Visiting Prof. at Union Theological Seminary, New York; Selly Oak Colleges, Birmingham. Member of the Presidium of the W.C.C.

CHADWICK,
Very Rev. Henry

Dean of Christ Church, Oxford University, England.

COMBER,
Rev. Anthony J.

Rector, St. Michael & All Angels, Farnley, Leeds, England. Part-time Chaplain, Leeds Industrial Mission.
Other appointments, etc.: Vicar of Hunslet, Leeds, 1969-77.

CONWAY,
Mr. Martin

Secretary, Division of Ecumenical Affairs, British Council of Churches, London, England. *Other appointments, etc:* Study Sec. World Student Christian Fed. 1961-67; Sec. for Chaplaincies in Higher Education, Church of England 1967-70; Publications Sec. W.C.C. 1970-74.

COVENTRY,
Rev. Fr. John, S.J.

Master, St. Edmund's House, Cambridge, England. Lect. in Christian Doctrine, Heythrop Coll. Univ. of London; Sec. and subsequent member of Roman Catholic Ecumenical Commission for England and Wales; member English ARC; Observer to British Council of Churches. *Other appointments, etc.:* Observer, Lambeth Conference 1968.

DEWEY,
Miss Margaret

A Vice-President, U.S.P.G., and author of its quarterly commentary *Thinking Mission.* *Other appointments, etc.:* Principal, Janet Clarke Hall, Univ. of Melbourne, Australia, 1959-63; Warden, U.S.P.G.'s Assoc. of Missionary Candidates, 1966-71.

ECCLESTONE,
Rev. Alan

Retired. *Other appointments, etc.:* Parish Priest in West Cumberland and Sheffield, England 1931-69.

ESCOBAR,
Mr. Samuel

Associate General Secretary at Large, International Fellowship of Evangelical Students. *Other appointments, etc.:* Gen. Dir., Inter Varsity Christian Fellowship, Canada, 1972-75; Pres. Latin American Theol. Fraternity; Ed. *Pensamiento Cristiano;* responsible for Training in Evangelical student movements of Latin America, linked to IFES.

FASHOLÉ-LUKE,
Rev. Dr. Edward W.

Senior Lect. & Head of Dept. of Theology, Fourah Bay Coll., Univ. of Sierra Leone: Sec. West African Assoc. of Theological Institutions. *Other appointments, etc.:* Dean, Fac. of Arts, Univ. Sierra Leone, 1972-77.

FRASER,
Rev. Dr. Ian M.

Dean of Mission, Selly Oak Colleges, Birmingham, England. *Other appointments, etc.:* Scottish Sec., S.C.M. 1945-48; Parish Minister, Rosyth, 1948-60; Warden, Scottish Churches' House 1960-69; World Council of Churches 1969-73.

FUGUI, Rev. Leslie
Parish Priest, St. Paul's Parish, Auki, Malaita, Solomon Islands.
Other appointments, etc.: Ex-member of Parliament; Asst. Adviser on Christian Education; Born of pagan parents, baptised when 14 years old.

GOMEZ, Rt. Rev. Drexel
Bishop of Barbados, West Indies.
Other appointments, etc.: Tutor, Codrington College, Barbados, 1964-68; Sec. Treas., Diocese of Nassau and The Bahamas, 1970-72.

GOODLAD, Dr. Sinclair
Senior Lecturer in Associated Studies (Literature and Sociology), Imperial College of Science and Technology, London, England.
Other appointments, etc.: Lect. in English, St. Stephen's Coll., Delhi; Lect. in Humanities, Massachusetts Institute of Technology.

GRANT, Rev. Prof. Robert M.
Professor, Divinity School, Univ. of Chicago, U.S.A.

HOWAT, Mr. Gerald M. D.
Sometime Principal Lect. in History, Culham College of Education, England.
Other appointments, etc.: Author of books and articles on history, education, biography.

HOWE, Rt. Rev. John W. A.
Secretary General of the Anglican Consultative Council.
Other appointments, etc.: Bishop of St. Andrews, Dunkeld and Dunblane, Scotland, 1955-69; Exec. Officer of Anglican Communion 1969-71.

JEFFREYS, Miss Irene F.
Fellow of Institute of Chartered Accountants; Chartered Secretary, Adelaide, Australia.
Other appointments, etc.: Member of General Synod of Australian Church; Co-opted member of Anglican Consultative Council, 1971-76.

JENKINS, Rev. Canon David E.
Director, William Temple Foundation, Manchester, England.
Other appointments, etc.: Fellow and Chaplain, Queen's Coll., Oxford, 1954-69; Canon Theologian, Leicester, England, from 1966; Director of Humanum Studies, W.C.C., Geneva, 1969-73.

KENNEDY, Rt. Rev. Dr. Donald M.
Bishop of Bombay, Church of North India.
Other appointments, etc.: Chaplain and Lecturer in History, Wilson Coll., Univ. of Bombay; Joint Sec. of Negotiating and Inaugural Committees on Church Union in North India.

KIRK, Rev. Prof. J. Andrew	Visiting Professor in the Catholic University of Buenos Aires and Member of Theological Community, *Kairos,* Buenos Aires, Argentina. *Other appointments, etc.:* Assoc. Prof. of N.T. in Union Theological Seminary, Buenos Aires; Member of Latin American Theol. Fraternity.
KOYAMA, Rev. Dr. Kosuke	Senior Lecturer, Phenomenology of Religion, Univ. of Otago, Dunedin, New Zealand. *Other appointments, etc.:* Lect. in Theology, Thailand Theological Seminary, 1960-68; Dean, South East Asia Graduate School of Theology, 1968-74.
MACQUARRIE, Rev. Canon John	Lady Margaret Professor of Divinity, Oxford University, England. *Other appointments, etc.:* Lect. in Systematic Theology, Univ. of Glasgow, 1953-62; Prof. of Systematic Theol., Union Theological Seminary, New York, 1962-70.
MONCREIFF, Rt. Rev. Francis H.	Retired. *Other appointments, etc.:* Formerly Bishop of Glasgow and Galloway 1952-73; Primus of Scottish Episcopal Church 1962-73.
MONTEFIORE, Rt. Rev. Hugh W.	Bishop of Birmingham, England. *Other appointments, etc.:* Dean of Gonville & Caius Coll., Cambridge, England, 1954-63; Vicar of Great St. Mary's, Cambridge, England, 1963-70; Suffragan Bishop of Kingston, Diocese of Southwark, England, 1970-77.
MORGAN, Mrs. Enid R.	Editor, Welsh Church Newspaper *Y Llan.*
NEILL, Rt. Rev. Stephen	Retired. *Other appointments, etc.:* Bishop of Tirunelveli, S. India, 1939-45; Director of Studies, etc., WCC, 1947-51; Prof. of Mission & Ecumenism, Univ. of Hamburg, Germany, 1962-67; Prof. of Philosophy & Religious Studies, Univ. of Nairobi, Kenya, 1969-76; Fellow of the British Academy.
NEWBIGIN, Rt. Rev. Lesslie	Lecturer, Theology and Ecumenical Studies, Selly Oak Colleges, Birmingham, England. *Other appointments, etc.:* Bishop in Madhurai, 1947-59; Gen. Sec., International Missionary Council & Associate Gen. Sec., W.C.C., 1959-65.

OOMMEN, Rev. A. C. Dean of Religious Work Department, Christian Medical College and Hospital, Vellore, India. *Other appointments, etc.:* Faculty of Bishop Tucker College, Mukono, Uganda.

POBEE, Prof. John S. Department for the Study of Religions, University of Legon, Ghana.

RAYNER, Archbishop of Adelaide, South Australia.
Most Rev. Keith *Other appointments, etc.:* Bishop of Wangaratta, 1969-75.

TALLEY, Professor of Liturgics, General Theological
Rev. Prof. Thomas J. Seminary, New York, USA. *Other appointments, etc.:* Prof. of Liturgics, Nashotah House, Nashotah, Wisc., USA, 1963-71.

TOMKINS, Retired.
Rt. Rev. Oliver S. *Other appointments, etc.:* Secretary of Faith & Order Commission of W.C.C. 1946-53; Chairman of F. & O. Working Committee 1953-67; Bishop of Bristol, England, 1959-75.

TRAYNHAM, Dean of the Tucker Foundation at Dartmouth
Rev. Dean Warner R. College, Hanover, New Hampshire, USA. *Other appointments, etc.:* Rector of St. Cyprian's Parish, Roxbury, Mass. 1967-72; Director of Black Studies for Boston Theol. Institute, 1972-74; Instructor in Pastoral Theology, Episcopal Theol. School and Weston College, 1972-74.

TUMA, Dr. Tom Secretary, Association of Theological Institutions in Eastern Africa, Nairobi, Kenya. *Other appointments, etc.:* Lecturer in African Church History, Dept. of Religious Studies & Philosophy, Makerere University, Kampala, Uganda.

VALENTINE, Bishop of Rupert's Land, Canada.
Rt. Rev. Barry

WARD, Fellow, Dean and Chaplain of Trinity Hall,
Rev. J. S. Keith Cambridge University, England.

WICKREMESINGHE, Bishop of Kurunagala, Sri Lanka.
Rt. Rev. C. Lakshman

Preface

This book of essays aims to help the Anglican bishops in their preparation for the Lambeth Conference of 1978. The Conference will engage in prayer and study, and in the sharing of experience. The main object will not be to make pronouncements, but to reflect on the gospel and ministry in which each bishop is involved, and which he shares with the whole People of God.

The members of this Lambeth Conference will, as in the past, be bishops. Naturally the starting point of many of their prayers and much of their thinking will be their own experience. Thus the title of these Preparatory Articles refers to a 'special focus on the ministry of bishops'. The ministry of bishops has its place as a part of the ministry of the whole Church. The Church exists for the sake of the whole inhabited earth. Thus the general title of the book is *'Today's Church and Today's World'*.

Following this approach the book consists of articles which may be found useful for preparation or discussion. A comprehensive survey has not been sought, nor was there any recommended point of view. The writers were asked for comparatively short articles that might be informative and stimulating, and if the author wished, provocative. Each writer has treated a subject as he or she thought best. One consequence is some diversity in the way material has been presented. There has been no attempt to edit this out. It has seemed more appropriate to preserve the individual manner than to impose an editorial uniformity. At times we may be usefully reminded too that English is not everybody's first language.

The contributors belong to different countries and cultures. While most are Anglican some are members of other Churches. We are extremely grateful to them all for accepting the invitation to write an essay for this book, and for the effort and time they have so generously given.

At the end of a number of the articles the writer has provided a short list of books for further reading. Other books are named in some of the notes.

In addition to the writers we wish to thank many people who have been consulted about the subjects and arrangement of articles for the book, and those who have helped by recommending contributors. Also we thank all who have participated in its production and printing.

Anglican Consultative Council
London, November 1977.

JOHN HOWE, Editor,
Secretary, Lambeth Conference 1978.

Introduction

These short essays, each by a person from a different country, give a preparatory glance at people, the Church and bishops as they currently appear to the eyes of the writer.

Only a few countries could be chosen, but there is at least one from each continent.

1 - As seen through African eyes

E. W. Fasholé-Luke, Sierra Leone

Modern Africa presents pictures of diversity, unity and variety. African peoples have come through periods of slavery, colonialism and now independence. Independent nations have had similar colonial experiences and Christianity has advanced largely through western missionary endeavours. Africa has a rich complexity of cultural, economic, political, linguistic, social and religious ideas, practices and rites. It is therefore not possible to speak of an African people. Rather, we should speak of African peoples.

Even in the same region the peoples are not homogeneous and modern national boundaries cut across ethnic groups, causing friction between States and frequent appeals to redraw the boundaries. There was a time when Africans did not know each other, but since independence, with the growth of the Organisation of African Unity and Regional Economic Associations, we are coming to know each other more closely. But in spite of the diversities there are also remarkable points of congruence; however it is difficult to define precisely who is an African. Canon Harry Sawyerr has suggested that the term African is a mythological term, indicating love for the continent and commitment to the ideals of the continent. This definition is useful because it is inclusive and not exclusive. It must be noted however, that there are those who would define the term African more narrowly and in South Africa where the problems of racism are now at their height, there is a tendency to limit the term to blacks: hence the production of Black Theology and the unwillingness of the blacks to allow whites to participate in that gigantic task. There are also quite a few Africans, who do not regard the Arabs in the North of the continent as Africans. These views point to the situation that in spite of the 'sloganeering' about African unity, and the formation of regional and continental Associations, Africa has the rich variety of *mores* already mentioned.

African peoples live in communities and these are thought to consist of the ancestors, the living and those not yet born. These communities however, are small and tend to be on ethnic lines. In some ways this has led to the fragmentation of nations and to the lack of unity. People's first loyalty is to their ethnic group, rather than to their nation. So,

3

for example, one would say, I am a Mende, a Yoruba, an Ewe, rather than a Sierra Leonean, Nigerian or Ghanaian. These situations have sometimes led to politicians in Africa demanding one-party states, because they claim that political parties tend to be formed on ethnic lines. One would not normally quarrel with this contention, except for the fact that one knows that these claims are meant to perpetuate particular parties in power against the wishes of the people and that corrupt one-party governments can only be removed by violence and are often replaced by military governments. The peoples of Africa therefore are living in situations of revolution, poverty, mass illiteracy and political instability. Modern technology is making great inroads on traditional societies and the old *mores* are breaking down, while new ones have not yet evolved. What the future holds is anybody's guess, we must just hope that with time mature counsels will prevail in the Independent nations of Africa.

One feature of life in Independent Africa today, is the tendency to criticise racism and the minority regimes in South Africa, Namibia and Zimbabwe and to make high–sounding resolutions demanding the liberation of these areas. It seems that these denunciations of inhumanity in Southern Africa would be more credible and gain greater force, if similar denunciations of oppression of blacks and imprisonment without trial are made of Independent nations in Africa.

Christianity in Africa is increasing rapidly and the forecasts for the future growth of the Churches in Africa are quite bright. Missionary methods and motives for evangelism are being subjected to critical scrutiny and review. Quite a few African Christians are criticising the activities and methods of western missionaries; but this is not because Africans are ungrateful or because they have failed to appreciate the significant contributions and the tremendous sacrifices that western missionaries have made towards the development of African nations. Rather it is because, we want to get the records straight and to move from the realms of hagiography to the field of sound Church history. When it is suggested for example, that there was a remarkable coincidence between Christian missionary advance in Africa and western colonial expansion, we are simply stating the facts of experience and not necessarily passing any value judgment on the activities of western missionaries. In any case, western missionaries have had opportunities to say what they think about African Christians and they have done this with remarkable frankness; all that African Christians now request is that we be allowed to speak about western Christians with the same frankness and clarity that Europeans have spoken about Africans in the past.

It is clear, that despite the political independence of many African nations, the Churches still operate on a dependence/domination axis and are still in many cases the agents of western colonial mentality and cultural imperialism. Too many of the mission-founded Churches are content with imported theologies, church structures, liturgies, spirituality and patterns of ministry. Perhaps the Anglican Church in Africa is most guilty of this. It is true that we must endeavour to maintain the tension between the particular and the universal, but what we are contending is that western theologies and culture must not be regarded as representing the universal, as was done by western missionaries before the dawn of political independence. It is precisely for this reason that the All Africa Conference of Churches Assembly, held in Lusaka, Zambia, in 1974, called for a moratorium on funds and personnel from Christians outside Africa. Even though this call was variously interpreted by African Churches, the violent reaction of western missionaries and Churches to this call, is nevertheless an indication that they have still to be liberated from the ideas of colonial paternalism and cultural imperialism.

The economic, political and social situations in Namibia, South Africa and Zimbabwe deserve special treatment and have produced myriads of Independent African Churches and distinctive black theologies of liberation, which have been defined as theologies 'of the oppressed, by the oppressed for the liberation of the oppressed'. But the point must be equally emphasised that African Independent States need theologies of liberation as much as, if not more than, the blacks in the occupied territories of Southern Africa. It is for this reason that we disagree with those who suggest that non-blacks must not participate in the creation of black theologies. We are convinced that the Christian gospel is for the oppressed and the oppressor alike; no one can be excluded from the Kingdom of God manifested in Jesus Christ.

In modern Africa today, we have to review the various possible patterns of relationships between Government, the Churches and African tradition. Often the churches are conservative and traditionalist, while African traditional religion may be innovative and progressive. Government may be either. But the significant point is that conservatism and radicalism run through every major segment of African culture.

Many African Churches are not grappling with the basic fears of African traditional society, mission-connected churches have stuck to a denial that witchcraft is a reality. But witchcraft accusations still continue and the tensions between the old and new, create problems at the pastoral and theological levels which must be realistically tackled by the Churches: unexplained illness, sudden deaths, barrenness, fear of spirits, all need to be carefully considered in the light of the various pastoral situations in Africa. For if African theologies must delve deeply into their traditional roots, they are equally challenged to look firmly at the contemporary state of African societies: ethnic conflicts, the increasing imbalance between the rich and educated ruling elites and the poor illiterate masses;

various species of modernisation and development policies. Zambian humanism, the different models of African socialism and Zairean implementation of 'authenticité' all need penetrating scrutiny. For it is possible that in the next couple of decades the significant point of division among African theologians will be between those who find the *raison d'être* of their endeavour primarily in the dialogue with African tradition and those who find it within a radical struggle for a new society freed from oppression and poverty.

Denominationalism is unashamedly practised in modern Africa. Many African Christians value a communion which extends far wider than their local church. Anglicans rejoice in their tradition and their link with Canterbury. They value the international bonds and full fellowship which are a strong feature of their communion. Equally they are pleased at the independence of the various Provinces. It is in this sense that archbishops and bishops are valued in Africa, because they form the link between local Christian communities and the universal Church. Even in large dioceses, bishops are not regarded merely as administrators; they are Fathers in God to their clergy and their people. Sometimes they have to represent their people and their views to the governments and in some cases to suffer for it.

Every society needs a structure, and the episcopal structure which Anglicans have inherited and maintained in Africa, prevents the Church from thinking and speaking about 'religious affairs' and turning people's attention to another world. The Church has been and is still involved in education, medical work and social work; she therefore has a right to claim to help in determining the political future of the State in which it is found.

African peoples, the Churches and bishops are still a poorly charted reality. It is the hope of this writer that this brief article will give new impetus to the quest of the Churches to discover how they can be authentically African and yet remain integral parts of the universal Church.

GUIDE TO FURTHER READING:
African Christianity, A. Hastings (London: Geoffrey Chapman, 1976).
Creative Evangelism, N. Sawyer (London: Lutterworth, 1968).

2 - As seen through Asian eyes

A. C. Oommen, India

The Church is called upon to bear its witness as an organism in living response to changing environments. Thus during the early centuries when it had to confront heresies from inside and persecution from outside, a defence mechanism was naturally formed. The formation of the Creeds, the proclamation of the Canon of the Bible and the episcopal structure of the Church were the expressions of this tendency for self-preservation.

The Creeds have a historic validity. They mark out for us the boundaries within which one may exercise his devotion. They are significant as demonstrating the widest Catholicity and unity in our belief. But apart from this they have only value as a pointer to the faith. Faith itself is based on events—the Life, Death, and Resurrection of Jesus Christ. Words are only approximations nearer and nearer to describe these events; events themselves cannot fully be verbalised; they are to be experienced. The challenge of the Christian faith is 'Come and See' not 'Sit and Discuss'. Here lies the essential weakness of dialogue as a method of evangelism in the Christian faith—unless the dialogue is existential. Thus the historic Creeds—though they embody for us the essence of the belief of the Church as a whole—should remain a pointer to the events they describe, exposure to which alone creates the responding Christian faith.

Again, the Scriptures contain the record of the experience of these events as witnessed by the early Church. In spite of all criticisms the credibility and the validity of these records still hold good. We have to fall back ultimately on the witness of those ordinary fishermen who tell us about that which they touched and heard. There is no question—that if we remove this ground of faith we fall into human fantasies. But does not the Scripture itself point out to us both through the Prophets of the Old Testament and through men like Stephen that we replace only at our peril the words 'Thus saith the Lord' by 'Thus it is written'. Stephen surely paid the price for his conviction by challenging the accepted notion that the Law and the Temple were the symbols of their faith. He showed that 'Come out' is the clue. The canon of the Bible again preserved at that stage of the history of the Church, for all time, the spring of divine revelation—something in which we can swim and enjoy without the fear

7

of undercurrent. Yet they should point to Him and out of the written word the Word should step out and confront us as a living reality.

We have to look at the structure of the Church from a similar point of view. At a time when it appeared as if the winds and storms thrashing against the ill-experienced little boat of the Christian Church would almost overrun it a strong anchor was needed to keep it on even keel. The ordinary man, often illiterate, a slave by status, who knew only with the reality of inner joy that he was blind but now he sees, could not stand by himself the penetrating and often disturbing questions of the world; he could then point to the elder or to the bishop who is supposed to be well versed in matters of debate and controversy to answer on his behalf. It was also necessary then that in order to avoid the destructive elements creeping into the fold a clear demarcation is made of the boundaries of the Church. There is no doubt that looking back historically the threefold ministry of the Church has contributed enormously in the shepherding of the flock and in preserving and handing down the purity of the faith. The question now is to see to what extent this has inclined the Church to lose its nature as a dynamic movement and turn it into a moribund institution—from being free to penetrate into the structures of the world to challenge and to capture, has it become a prison house—a ghetto, or a mission compound? Should the Christian Community always remain a socially recognisable people with its communal culture in confrontation with other communities but losing the opportunity to be the leaven in the lump?

In the formation of the Church of South India one of the four essential points accepted as a basis—known as the Lambeth quadrilateral —one of the most controversial of the four was Historic Episcopacy. While the Church as a whole agreed unanimously that episcopacy is the best system of church government and adopted it for the C.S.I., it was clearly mentioned that no theological interpretation of this will necessarily be unanimous. This model has been accepted by other Church union schemes also. Lambeth itself which was reluctant to acknowledge C.S.I. in 1947 because of what it called the 'anomaly' of the existence of some non-episcopally ordained presbyters shifted its position later by accepting 'episcopally ordered Churches' and not insisting on 'episcopally ordained presbyters'.

Thirty years have passed. Has the Church existed in a living response to the environment? Is the present system of episcopacy a help or a hindrance? The Church in Asia is confronting an explosive situation. The Roman Empire and the Gentile World seemed in the early centuries to engulf the Church. It was the renaissance and the revival of Greek thought that the Church confronted in the middle centuries. Today in the East, the Church has to face seriously the onslaught of religions

8

that have a long and rich tradition. What are the factors of this new environment?

First, the nature of the world in which the Church is. We are still in a missionary situation. Christians are minorities rooted mainly among the economically and culturally backward communities. Their richness is in their poverty, for they can say with Peter 'Silver and gold have we none'. They are called upon in their daily life to give account of their faith. Therefore it is highly necessary that they should be loosely organised to keep up the dynamism and be agile to experiment and to penetrate.

Secondly, these ancient religions have developed vehicles for the communication of their faith. Some of them have stood the test of time and adjusted to the Eastern climate. Wherever possible it is our duty to adopt them and baptise them into the Christian heritage. As religions both Hinduism and Buddhism have never been organised. The Sanyasis, the Gurus and the Sadhus are mendicant leaders and seldom conform to any rule or pattern. Ashrams were communities that appeared and disappeared. Continuity is assured more through persons or communities of persons than through institutions.

Thirdly, concepts of history, culture, secularism, development, etc., are not quite natural to the inherited faith in these countries. They have immense capacities for assimilation, even to the extent of synchretism. Today at the dawn of a new world with all the benefits of technology at their disposal, they look for a philosophy that is not world-denying. The Christian assertion of history as the sphere of God's dialogue with man has its relevance in this situation. Again our structures should show that the Lord is the Lord of history, that He is always involved in the movement of the Church and the world, and that we look forward and not backward for the fulfilment of His promise of the Kingdom of God.

Episcopacy expresses the nature of the Church. The image it creates ultimately makes the impact. What is the image of a bishop today in the newly independent and developing country? First he resembles an anachronism—a continuation of an authoritarian government, often foreign, which the nationalistic movement has thrown out. The Church often is slow to catch up with changing conditions and is still fighting the last battle. It has clung on till the last breath to the *status quo* and unfortunately bishops are often identified with the reactionaries as they have to safeguard the vested interests.

Secondly, they give the image of top administrators who are neither trained nor specially talented to do that job — chairmen of several committees, trustees of many funds and administrators of many institutions. In the modern world administration has developed as a speciality and to imagine that one merely because of his biblical studies is equipped for this task is not true. Thus often they get puzzled and frustrated and people on the other hand lose confidence even in their spirituality.

Thirdly, their special calling is to be the counsellors and pastors for the clergy and Fathers in God for the people. This aspect often gets pushed out of their busy programme. Since they often serve in an administrative capacity, others hesitate to confide their problems to them fearing legitimately that this may bias their opinion.

There is a biblical background for the ministry of the Church. St. Paul gives us a glimpse of what he considers as the significance of the ministry (I Cor. 12, Eph. 4). Each member of the Church is endowed with some gift or other of the Spirit. The duty of the leader is to supervise the employment of these gifts, so that along with the congregation he may move forward as a team, for the proclamation of the gospel. In this light the following images may be of some help towards a re-thinking and re-evaluation.

The honour and respect that a bishop receives should be based on his spirituality—not on the amount of temporal authority he can wield. Gandhi in India was an example pointing to this kind of authority. He was never an officer, not even a member of the Indian National Congress, but there was no significant step the Congress ever took without his full approval and blessing. We may have to empty ourselves deliberately of external authorities, so that the internal power may be more obvious.

An essential duty of the bishop is to push the movement of the Church forward when it gets entangled or stuck up with less important constitutional and organisational matters. He has to see that the end is not lost in the means. The great success of the work of Mother Theresa in Calcutta and in other parts of the world is that she wastes very little time or resources in plugging the loopholes of possible areas of corruption but inspires her people to go forward to show that their main duty is to provide love and care for as many needy as possible. The Church has an example in this. If we have to succeed on one front we may have to fall back deliberately on some other fronts. A duty of the bishop is to discover the priorities and stick to them even at the cost of being considered a failure or weakling.

In the developing countries the role of the Church has changed rapidly during the past decade and the bishops will have to represent the new image. The concept of Christendom has gone for ever. The 'servant' picture has come to stay, but first the servant of the Lord. In this capacity he can be the disturbing conscience of the Church and the nation. He should be the Sanyasi, detached from selfish ends, he should be the Guru, counselling and encouraging; and he should be the Sadhu, seeing the vision of tomorrow and living that today.

There is much in the words of the Lord 'Destroy this temple and I will rebuild in three days'. From institutionalism to movement—that is what bishops should help to do.

3 - As seen through Australian eyes

Irene F. Jeffreys, Australia

In thinking of people and Church in Australia, regard must be had for the foundations of the nation: it is a federation of separate States which started as British colonies with their own particular ethos and development, varying from the 1778 convict settlement in New South Wales to the new experiment of South Australia in 1836; the South Australian Colonization Act of 1834 made S.A. the only State to be settled entirely by free persons. One effect of this 'freedom' was the freedom of worship, so that State and University in S.A. are secular, with no established Church and no Chair of Divinity. In 1850, new Constitutions were granted to the Australian Colonies, and in New South Wales and Victoria provision was made for aid from the colonial revenues towards the support of clergy in connection with the various bodies of Christians, but not in South Australia.

Modern Australia's British origins have meant, however, that the Church of England has fairly consistently been the nominal adherence of one-third of the population who answer the census question on religion, but 12% now give no reply. The influx of war refugees and the planned migration of non-British peoples since 1945, have greatly influenced much of Australian life and reduced the high percentage of Anglicans—the C. of E. increase has fallen to 7.6% compared with Roman Catholic 27.1%. Although the country is nominally 90% Christian, according to census returns, the percentage of those listing themselves of 'no religion' is increasing. Many people do not know what the Anglican Church is, or how it is distinguished from R.C. and Protestant Churches. Approximately 9 to 10% of 'Christians' are church service attenders.

In such historical circumstances, the Christian denominations have had to rely largely on voluntary support. Children's education by the State is secular, so the Churches early founded their own schools which have had a great influence in character training and establishing Christian moral teaching. Christian teaching in State schools by outside instructors has had a chequered history in each State. In recent years there have been strong pressures by anti-Christian Humanists to eliminate religious instruction, whilst others have sought to have it enlarged to include all religions, not only Christianity.

11

It is distressing to many Christians that children can grow up in Australia knowing little, if any, of the foundation truths of Christianity and consequently ignorant of basic principles of law and order, without Christian standards to measure their own conduct and that of others. Churches seem to have found the work in the schools too hard, and given up in some States. Does it point to failure in example by the Church, that numbers of young people have been seeking a new life-style in 'caring' communes, some of Christian origin, others not?

In assessing comments made, it seems that the 'folk' understanding of Christianity is different from that of instructed Christians, and people see the visible Church in different ways, very often as an in-looking esoteric club, with (at least as regards Anglicans) a middle-class image. To say there is no class distinction in Australia is to ignore plain facts: inevitably one's education, natural abilities, and circumstances, create differences between people, even of the same over-all culture.

People generally no longer turn to the Church for guidance in their personal lives, but to specialised counsellors (e.g. marriage guidance, birthline, crisis centre, doctor, psychiatrist). Children are encouraged to 'do their own thing'; Christian doctrines and morals are taught only to a small percentage of the population. The voice of the Humanist is increasingly given more credence in the secular State schools than that of the Christian.

Social issues and sexual behaviour are much more freely discussed than say thirty years ago. The growing expansion of mass media like radio and TV has enabled it to alert people to population and food problems, the uranium issue, pollution in all its forms (but not, alas, the debasement of so many standards in work, language, and manners). Trade Unionists have refused to work on projects which have threatened a city's 'green belt'. But it is very difficult to discern what might be called the distinctive Christian concern and contribution in all these issues and debates.

There is more emphasis on rights than responsibilities, an inclination to want more money for less work. The average man is still concerned to retain his employment, to keep up his payments on house or car or the other household equipment which today's standards require. Australia is 13th on the world's list of wealthy nations, with a population of 13 millions; a growing number of homes have a swimming pool in the garden, and the number of boat owners goes on increasing; one in ten homes has a colour television set. Organised sport and racing occupy the thought and attention of a great majority of people.

As an offset to this picture of people seeking security, comfort, and pleasure, there is the large number who help the community voluntarily through organisations such as Red Cross, Women's Local Service organisations, and various service clubs such as Rotary, Soroptimists, Apex, Jaycee, Lions, etc., St. John Ambulance, Meals on Wheels, District Nursing Society. None of these are officially linked to a Church, yet they are carrying out the spirit of Jesus' teaching and his example of doing good to others.

Aside from the Churches, the more directly spiritual aspect of life is not so obvious. Some young people look towards Eastern mystical religions and transcendental meditation, so we have the phenomenon of Australian youths dressed in saffron robes and ringing the bell of the Hare Krishna devotee, in our streets. Others seek a 'back to nature' life, growing their own foods, looking for simplicity in a world which becomes more complex and frightening. The Christian Church does not attract these young men and women—the imposing building with its spire or tower, its respectably dressed people, is the last place where they feel like 'dropping in', according to one reporter.

The influence of the old-established Churches has declined as the number of people professing no religion has increased, but which is the cause and which the effect? Has the Church become too ingrown, too concerned with its own organisation and preservation? On the other hand, Pentecostal-charismatic type Christian assemblies are filling large halls with working class folk who come as families, enjoying a warmth of fellowship, singing, and simple worship which is not so easily found in the more formal Anglican church. Five thousand people from a variety of denominations gathered in Sydney in 1977 for the national Charismatic Conference; those who attended spoke of the loving care and concern for one another, of their growing awareness of their need of the Lord Jesus and of love.

Anglican churches, except for a few, are not filled like the Pentecostal halls: perhaps people do not see an obvious warmth and outgoing-ness which would draw them in. Anglicans have not been encouraged to demonstrate openly their joy in the Lord, so that others want to share it. Emphasis on personal spoken witness to one's faith has largely been left to the evangelical minority; apart from some individually concerned parish clergy, and the efforts of the Departments of Evangelism in Sydney and Melbourne, the laity have not been instructed very deeply in how to 'proclaim the Lord Jesus Christ,' nor the ramifications in today's complex society of loving one's neighbour as oneself. Part of the problem is that where, as in so many dioceses, the emphasis is on 'priestly' functions, rather than ministry, people are expected to seek out the Church: but Jesus went out where the people were and so should his followers today.

The movement of population is towards cities; 56% of Australians live in the seven capital cities, another 26% in smaller towns and cities. Shortage of low-cost land and housing is leading to a greater density of population, with more home units and high-rise flats: this may begin to

13

halt the suburban sprawl, with its problems of supplying water, electricity, roads and transport. In a country as vast as Australia, this imbalance of population frequently causes hardship to the rural community, e.g. an outback farmer may have to pay ten to twenty times as much for telephone connections (because of length of line) as the city dweller, yet the telephone is so much more vital to isolated country people.

These conditions create different problems for the Church in its ministry, and highlight the necessity for re-examination of the Anglican Church's structure. Is the present parochial system, with one ordained person solely in charge, and the laity leaving most of the responsibility to the priest, the best pattern for today, either in a mobile urban society, or in the sparsely-populated outback? At the third Anglican Consultative Council meeting in Trinidad in 1976, exciting examples were given of the ways in which the Spirit of God is provoking and providing new patterns of ministry around the world, 'involving the whole Body of Christ, and increasingly breaking the Church loose from its almost total dependence on the ordained ministry.' Examples are the 'house churches' in the high-rise apartments in Singapore, and the separation of the pastoral, teaching, and sacramental functions of the parish priest into a team ministry in Ecuadorian villages.

In Australia, one result of expecting the parish priest to be everything and meet all needs, has been Anglican women's involvement in Christian Women's International; this growing movement holds Bible studies and conventions for women all over Australia, and has sent 'safari teams' to Aboriginal women in North Australia; all the speakers are women, and their listeners testify to the great help these conventions are in their spiritual life. I doubt whether many women would be encouraged to undertake such a ministry *within* the Anglican Church, so it is heartening to note the emphasis laid on the principle 'every Christian a minister' (Eph. 4. 16) in the Report to General Synod 1977 of its Commission on Ministry.

This report, and that on *The Ministry of Women* issued by the Commission on Doctrine, should help to stimulate both men and women to a better understanding of how they can use the gifts which God has given them. Particularly does this apply to women: Australia has long been a male-dominated country, politically, socially and economically, as symbolised in the tradition of 'mateship' (restricted to males and whites). I personally know of nothing which the Church, as such, has done to redress such injustices to women; yet as John Stuart Mill wrote over a century ago (in his essay on the *Subjection of Women*) the improvement of women's social position goes hand in hand with general social improvement. I believe that implicit in 'that magnificent liberty which can only belong to the children of God' (Rom. 8. 21), is the allowing of every man and woman to undertake the work or service,

14

in home, society or church, for which God has fitted him or her, and not what public opinion, cultural pressures, or outdated traditions thrust upon them. The Church should be setting the example of men and women working together in true Christian partnership in *all* spheres of life, each encouraging the other.

Within the Church, bishops could give a more positive lead in the above. They could seek to draw out people's gifts, and delegate more of the jobs which take up so much of their time, especially administrative work. The Ordinal of the 1977 draft Australian Prayer Book states that the bishop is to give 'attention to reading, exhortation, and teaching'; to think upon the things contained in the Bible; to 'be to the flock of Christ a shepherd . . . to support the weak, heal the sick, bind up the broken, restore the outcasts, seek the lost'. How many Australian bishops consistently give teaching courses on biblical and social subjects I do not know, but I doubt if many do so consistently. And I question whether many take time off from innumerable committees, councils, and conferences to visit personally the weak, sick, broken, outcast, and lost, where they are to be found amongst our church-less communities.

In this regard, bishops of country dioceses have more chance to meet their flock as they travel around, visiting individual homesteads, where they can be known as ordinary persons, not remote dignitaries who only appear at Confirmations. Apart from 'the faithful', the average Australian would not know what a bishop did—if they think of a bishop at all, it would be of someone at the top of the ecclesiastical ladder, wearing robes and rings, remote from the ordinary person.

So often there is silence in public from church leaders, on moral issues such as pornography, drugs, alcohol, etc. Voluntary organisations like Right to Life Association, and Australian Festival of Light, have had to step in and fill the gap, but the public tends to see these keen groups as negative rather than positive forces. Bishops should be amongst the leaders in telling the community *why* Christians have the standards they have, otherwise Christianity can appear irrelevant and negative. From time to time when the Metropolitans do speak out forcibly on vital issues such as poverty, the media takes notice. Our Anglican Archbishops have won respect in the community by their own personal integrity and awareness of social concerns but more could be done.

As there is no Church Establishment in Australia, bishops do not have a right to seats in the Houses of Parliament, as they do in England, so they do not have a political arena in which to speak. They should therefore make more use of the mass media; TV reaches nearly everybody in their own home, people do not have to go out to a church building, and more and more are getting their ideas of religion from mass media, which has largely written off Christianity as a minority group, whilst the secular Humanists get disproportionate publicity. If a personable young

15

man can have a weekly 'cooking segment' on the national television, why not a bishop an evangelistic/emphatic 'need of the moment' spot?

Bishops, clergy, and laity, together need to examine our whole church structures; have they become too institutionalised, too bound up in real estate and buildings, with bishops having to give time to thinking what to do with non-viable parishes, and redundant church buildings, instead of to the priorities listed in the Ordinal? An increase in Anglican giving and membership would solve some of the problems, but this involves evangelism, which is not our strong point, as noted above. A Church without outreach is bound to perish, but how can we imbue Anglicans with the right motivation for evangelism? The bishops should give a stronger lead in evangelism, by encouraging their clergy to help congregations be evangelistic, and by influencing the theological seminaries to train ordinands for a practical evangelistic ministry in the world as it is today.

This should include a re-appraisal of the parochial system, to see how it could be helped become what is suggested in ACC-3 (Trinidad) Report, by the Church and Society section, viz. 'witnessing to the possibility, and even the bringing into being, of an authentic pattern of corporate life and social relationships . . . a kind of prototype community' . . . 'a pattern and a first-fruit of the reconciled community'. This cannot be achieved merely by coming to worship together, although the worship of God and response to the love of the Lord Jesus is the motivation for this corporate life; it begins in practice with loving care and concern for each other, as I am seeing in my own local parish: we are encouraged to share our spiritual experiences, our needs, and our prayers and praises, by meeting in each other's homes, at our monthly 'Parish At Homes', in a weekly 'prayer and share' fellowship in the home of a converted reconciled couple; at weekly Bible studies after church service, and in the rectory mid-week. Man, woman, child, married or single, are encouraged to feel a wanted part of diversified small community, and to use his/her gifts as fully as possible in worship and service. We have begun to realise that when in need, there will be concerned caring people ready to help. With this security, a person has courage to witness in daily life and work, trusting in the power of the Holy Spirit, and strangers can be asked to join such a fellowship without hesitation.

In the limit set to the length of this article, it is impossible to cover adequately the subject given, but I must not close without mentioning the devoted labours of Anglicans in a tremendous variety of official and voluntary work, in conducting homes for the aged and for neglected children, in serving Aboriginal communities in the tropical northern half of the continent; in diocesan social welfare bureaux; in supporting missionaries helping the Church in developing countries, or home

16

missioners in the Australian outback—just to list a few of their activities carried out in the name of the Lord Jesus, who said 'I am among you as he that serves', 'I came not to be ministered unto, but to minister.' This pattern of humble service, not of headship and rule (Christ alone is the Head), is His example to the whole ministry, ordained or lay.

GUIDE TO FURTHER READING:

A Changing Australia, by Professor Sol Encel: Australian Broadcasting Commission, 1971.

Reports of the Commission on Doctrine, Commission on Mission, and Social Responsibilities Commission, for 1977 General Synod of C. of E. in Australia.

Reports of the Anglican Consultative Council meetings 1971, 1973 and 1976.

4 - As seen through English eyes

A. J. Comber, England

For every Englishman there is a mass of visual, concrete evidence of the Church. Church buildings and their associated activities are seen everywhere. Every village has its church, associated mainly with history, traditional rites at life's turning points, and respectable Sunday worship. Towns and suburbs are prolific with buildings of many denominations, always having leisure activities, particularly for the young and elderly. In cities, cathedrals and prosperous civic churches are ringed by run-down or derelict 19th century structures sharing the inner-city malaise. Council housing estates have fewer and cheaper buildings, presenting a pale reflection of suburbia for a small section of the inhabitants.

There is a massive impact feeding deep English assumptions: the Church is associated with the past, with leisure activity for those who like the sort of thing it provides, and, where there is prestige, with the Establishment and its middle-class pillars. The Church with its active members, and particularly its leaders, is sensed in today's complex, global society, to be of decreasing significance, of selective social influence, to be withdrawing to the periphery of life, or even in an advanced state of decay.

For those who look harder there is evidence of meaningful growth. Worship is at the centre of church life: revised liturgies and a warmer personal approach in worship, with a welcoming, if small, congregation, have pleasantly surprised some occasional worshippers. A few churches are committed to opening up and deepening the issues within local bread-and-butter concerns: e.g. in education, with or without direct Church responsibility for schools and youth centres; in housing and social problems through community work; in industry and commerce through ecumenical industrial mission. But on balance, compared with its total resources, one is left asking: how much impact does the Church have, in this time of unprecedented speed of change, on debates and decisions deeply affecting English people's future way of life?

Almost all the resources of the Church of England are in parochial ministry. It accomplishes a vast amount of great good. But some of its best pastoral work suggests a deficiency in its vision of a good creation: there is a greater competency in promoting aid for victims of man's sin

18

and imperfection than in pointing to the light of Christ's gospel and His kingdom for our future; there is far greater emphasis on individual imitation of the good Samaritan than on living together as salt and leaven in God's world. The shepherd's work, however, does not begin by tending ailing sheep, but by leading the flock to good pastures to promote growth and health. Of course the Church ministers Christ's compassion to those who suffer, and Christians support all who work for their relief. This ministry is a sign of His kingdom, but not its central hope. Of prime importance is the vision of God's kingdom in Christ's life, death and resurrection, and of the guiding and healing power of the living, active Spirit for the whole future creation. This vision inspires the Church's true theology; from it stem our understanding of the hatefulness of sin, and our discerning of pastoral strategy to meet the alienations of our time with positive Christian hope.

Local churches do much to draw general attention to world-wide responsibilities, e.g. through Christian Aid Week. But the same pastoral angle is evident—emphasis on relatively minor aid. It is but slowly beginning to change towards positive development. The *Baptist Times* has reported evangelical Haitians in church 'praising God for rising coffee prices' which bring more justice to peasants than 'charitable' aid. The impact of the English Church leads one to associate action for world justice with leisure-time effort and surplus giving, rather than with the sacrifice and spiritual hope that a new economic order could bring.

The clergy going about their work are encountered often enough to influence people in England strongly, and there is a genuine friendly relationship. The same generous relationship exists with bishops when people meet them, but most folk rarely do. Outside the Church little is understood of a bishop's day-to-day life—it is rather the attitude of the ordinary man to top management, remote figures living in a different, unknown world. They are, however, rightly thought of as particularly responsible for the management of the clergy, and are often judged by what is known to happen to the circumstances of priests. They are known to be near the heart of the English Establishment and power centres, but thought not to wield much influence.

The church-centred activity of clergymen induces people to see them on the sidelines of real life. What is most important is the manner in which they minister. Our clergy are not so young (40% aged 55 and over) and almost all have been trained for the traditional English incumbency with a freehold in an independent parish. This has inevitably produced men with exaggerated individualism which is no part of the grace of holy orders. One of the strengths of the Anglican parish worshipping body, in contrast with a congregationalist fellowship, is that it can naturally represent a balanced local view, but there is a growing tendency towards urban congregationalism. This, together with clerical individualism, ill

19

serves the need for a truer pastoral ministry to all folk in society, and the token scale of the Church's ministry to institutions in society is minimal in its help. A growing number of younger priests are aware of labouring under two difficulties: first, the lack of team working and close understanding among clergy; and secondly, the lack of a serious tradition of laity and clergy working together with integrity to discover the ways for man's growth to Christian maturity in society and community affairs.

The mass media also present the Churches significantly to English people. From the broadcasting of hymn singing and special ceremonies, to the local reporting of bazaars and building problems, they not surprisingly reinforce expectations about the Church. When a religious subject recently gained a place in a current affairs broadcast, the continuity man passed from it with 'and now back to real life'—and who as much as noticed the significance of that?

Bishops surely have an opportunity here. Although it is not a main part of a bishop's task today to communicate directly to the public in major statements, there is the important challenge to be available on occasions to pinpoint clearly a crucial issue—to earn the right to counter current trivialising. The Archbishops' Call to the Nation of 1975 received much publicity and promoted worthwhile thinking; but remarks by Church leaders in interviews demonstrated a lack of awareness of industrial workers' frustrations and understandable prejudices, and elicited hostile reaction from many shopfloor representatives: for them, instead of an important lead from the Church for the whole nation, it was the middle-class Establishment at it again.

THE PART OF THE LAITY

The committed laity of the Church of England is a tiny proportion of those who are baptised and partake occasionally in Church rites. The borderline is very blurred at a time when all theological opinion, in and out of the Church, is confused and uncommitted to details. Regular worshippers inevitably share most of the assumed attitudes of their society, and this is especially so here, where the English Church is so much a part of the inherited tradition. For many years England and the West have been dominated by industry and commerce with their materialistically successful capitalist ethic—increasing competitive consumption, oriented to using things for individual self-fulfilment. More deeply, the western world is so overwhelmed by the scientific method that it persistently turns the question 'Why?' into the question 'How?' Our society has lost the capacity for discerning purpose in the world.

There are at present four currents moving in the Church. Laity, clergy and bishops must together choose which to encourage: —

1. To minister to individuals' private and family lives, and build up

20

fellowship in the Church. Movements emphasising churchmanship and charismatic gifts exaggerate this, and many lay folk are saying 'It's impossible to be Christian at work and in politics' and getting little help for their repressed consciences.

2. To continue to go along with whatever is the dominating influence in society. This is the besetting sin of the Established Church, and its inertia is immense. At present it largely accepts the capitalist ethic with a gilding of social concern, and encourages moderate compromise with social peace.

3. To challenge men by a counter culture based on certain biblical teachings. This current remains on the world's own secular plane, selective theology supporting the opposite of the western ethic— co-operative community, oriented to shared fulfilment. 'Lifestyle' movements and 'political theology' tend this way, and also industrial mission when it neglects traditions of liturgy and prayer.

4. To deepen awareness of Christ's kingdom, and of the fullness of biblical insights into God's justice and peace, and of His purpose revealed in Jesus Christ, and to hold this awareness in relation to all that our life meets in this world. Groups open to the world, who are also seriously struggling with theological understanding of creation and spiritual life, and its expression in worship, are attempting this way. Their success is limited, partly because most of our able theologians are distracted from men's real concerns by the academic rat-race.

Moltmann has stressed twin issues for Christian faith, which relate to the Church's choice of the way forward: that of relevance to the real questions man faces; and that of identity as the true way of Jesus. William Temple's understanding of men also held together two things: first, the importance of their relationships to God and each other; and secondly, the setting of their lives in God's creation; he rejected 'the idealism which assumes men to be so free spiritually that aims alone are decisive'. Their relationship to family, work, community and nature are to be understood as God-given constraints redeemed through Jesus Christ. Considering all these together may help the Church hopefully forward along the twin paths of paragraphs 1 and 4 above: but the balance needs urgently shifting towards the latter.

THE FUTURE

Leading the English Church into the future is a joint venture in synodical government. Bishops have a key role, and their precise relations with synods can work themselves out with the goodwill that exists.

A bishop is of the Church universal, and has opportunity and duty to consult internationally and ecumenically. Equally a bishop is of a

21

diocese, and is in touch with day-to-day concerns of men in given, local situations. Between these two they share in national policies. All this gives a breadth of understanding to bishops.

English bishops also contest with disadvantages. First, the State has a hand in their appointment. Perhaps our Church should be bolder in pressing for independence of appointments; some senior politicians hold that involvement by secular democratic government is very bad for the Church. Secondly, some suffragan bishops do not have true oversight. Area responsibility is the norm, but it could help to develop fuller ministry if some suffragans be charged with oversight of a sector ministry, e.g. industry and commerce, education and health—even on a multi-diocesan basis. Thirdly, bishops have a middle-class job. They could develop links with the working class by maintaining special relations with selected deanery synods; some may wish to live in a working class district and share its facilities.

The ministry of the whole college of bishops involves helping the Church equip itself to move forward. This requires attention to major issues and ruthless delegation of administrative minutiae. The strategic deployment of the clergy, and their in-service training, are crucial if the emphasis in ministry is to shift. Thinking out the meaning of the Auxiliary Pastoral Ministry in relation to the modern 'professional' ordained body gives opportunity for clarifying the priestly work of the whole Church in the world. More resources for bringing laity and clergy together for study are needed, and for appointing the best theologians to help; openness to learn from new work, and ability to appraise it, can be encouraged. This all requires synodical agreement to a major shift of resources. Much is being done: advances in synodical and ecumenical co-operation, in liturgical renewal and parish re-organisation, have prepared the ground for more adventurous mission.

A corporate commitment by bishops to stretch the Church's work in the fast moving current of history will raise the low degree of motivation towards the future more than any amount of individual pastoral care. The vision which alone will inspire it is God's, in the resurrection of Christ, who has moved ahead of all history, and in the power of His Spirit calls us to follow.

GUIDE TO FURTHER READING:

Built as a City: God and the Urban World Today, David Sheppard (Hodder and Stoughton, 1974).

Inflation and the Compromised Church, Charles Elliott (Christian Journals Ltd, Belfast, 1975).

Theology in an Industrial Society, Margaret Kane (SCM Press Ltd, 1975).

5 - As seen through North American eyes

T. J. Talley, U.S.A.

It is only with the greatest diffidence that one can undertake to speak to such a topic as this. While I know my eyes to be North American, I know equally well that they are not those of North America and so are not representatively North American even in the restricted English-speaking sense in which our Mexican brothers sometimes use the term. Further, in spite of close cultural similarities between the United States and Canada, it is only in the former of those nations that I have lived with the immediacy which seems requisite for such reflections as these. I must beg, therefore, to be allowed to speak as a priest of the Episcopal Church in the United States and, at that, one who is deeply conscious of the partiality of his vision.

Given that, it seems to me that the first thing that must be said of the people I encounter today is that their pains and problems, hopes and delights can hardly be understood or articulated save in reference to the preceding decade. The long nightmare of our involvement in Viet Nam and the erosion of popular identification with structures of authority which began in that period and reached its culmination in the unprecedented presidential resignation of August, 1974, left us with an unexpected need to celebrate our national identity on the 200th anniversary of the Declaration of Independence and surprisingly able to do that with honest joy and gratitude. Coming from that celebration as from a rite of mutual absolution, we find ourselves enjoying a mood of quiet toleration by comparison to the raucous confrontations of the past decade while still engaged by the serious questions of values so painfully raised in that period.

If it is so here in the 'silent seventies', it is not least because those value questions have been set in a broader context by the patent antinomy between our supposed need for constant economic expansion and the very evident limits set to that by our planet and its resources. Economic uncertainty and ecological imperatives (however deferred) form the frame within which other concerns must be set, and this has served to moderate their competing claims to priority. In the face of the frustration of great power, economic and political, the focus of popular concern seems more on the enrichment of personal life and away from ideological polarities.

There are still major public controversies, of course, and these in large number (abortion, rights of women, ways to racial integration, among many), but such issues seem to be engaged with more modest energy or at least with more measured method than was available or appropriate to the civil rights and peace movements of the sixties. Many such engagements in the public forum, further, seem more a dimension of, than an alternative to, that quest for personal fulfilment and enrichment which is doggedly pursued through a dazzling variety of techniques, serious or silly or both, ranging from psychotherapy to yoga, drugs, fad diets and jogging. More recently this quest has been further manifest in a hunger for the discovery of personal historical roots and, on the way to that, a fairly general taste for nostalgia.

Yet even when this spell is broken as by a recent failure of electrical power to the nation's largest city with a consequent serious breakdown of social order, the tendency today is to ask, 'what *went* wrong?' rather than, as was asked after the tragic assassinations of the past decade, 'what *is* wrong?'. Less frightened of ourselves than we once were, we prefer to think that the roots of our problems are technological and patient of adjustment if not correction. For the moment there is still fuel enough somewhere, and so surely we will consume it. Metanoia comes hard to a secular society, and we are that.

Apart from matters specifically 'religious', the attitudes and outlooks of even sincerely committed Christians today range over much the same spectrum as those of the surrounding culture. Consequently, it is difficult to identify distinctively Christian values operative in society except by reference to the historical origins of our traditions of justice and mercy and the value of the individual person. The Church is less a significantly discernible social force than the source of (again) personal fulfilment and enrichment. Larger concerns of Christians are held by them both as Christians and as citizens, and many matters of concern to society at large become agenda for the Church. This is nothing peculiar to our experience, of course, or even new to it; still it seems to some to be an influence from without. It is quite impossible, e.g., to view our recent decision regarding the ordination of women to the presbyterate and episcopate apart from the general emergence of women from the status of natural subjection in which they were seen by scholastic theologians. While little suggests that this development in the social status of women drew its impetus primarily from theological reflection, the same can be and has been said of that scholastic position. Such dialogue between sacred and secular ways of knowing is inherent in the theological enterprise. But when relatively mild public debates are brought into the ecclesiastical forum, those differences and disputes can appear as fissures in the deepest ground of our understanding and serious division can

24

result, division which reaches beyond the overt issues to strain our assurance of our fundamental unity in faith.

It was, therefore, with particularly acute gratitude that we saw the same General Convention of the Episcopal Church which had taken the grave and closely divided decision regarding the ordination of women adopt with a truly astonishing degree of unanimity the most sweeping revision of the Book of Common Prayer since 1552. This was the penultimate step in our own part in a long and difficult process shared in by virtually all the Churches, not only of the Anglican Communion but of the Christian west, a process which has amounted to nothing short of a concentrated review and reassessment of the founts of our spirituality. While liturgical change has been constant throughout the history of the Church to one degree or another, no moment of that history has seen such a total recasting of the forms of worship on such a broad scale as this which has occupied the western Church over the past decade and a half. Given the inherently traditional character of liturgy, such an enterprise is perilous indeed for it troubles the very roots of a worshipping community's experience of its identity.

While we in the United States can give thanks that our own moment of reform has brought such an extensive recovery of the whole sweep of Christian tradition and that the same seems true in many other places where the process continues, it must remain to the future to assess this greatest upheaval in the interior life of the Christian Church since the Reformation. It will be surprising, however, if that future does not recognise this time as one in which the Christian community in the western world—and in the Churches grafted from it around the planet—sought to step aside from ingrained cultural presuppositions, and will examine the tradition afresh, to organise it and the common life fed by it in order to lay the foundations for living the life of Christ in and for the salvation of a world from which Christendom has vanished.

However, while much of Anglican experience has suggested that common liturgical life can sustain at least external and formal unity in spite of underlying serious disagreements, we cannot delude ourselves that that is sufficient. Insofar as mutual recognition of ministries is a cardinal test of unity between ecclesiastical bodies, it must be confessed that we find ourselves in a seriously anomalous situation in which some ordinations to the presbyterate in our own Church, ordinations of undisputed canonical regularity, are viewed as invalid by some, bishops, clergy and laity. Both those who cannot accept the sacerdotal ministrations of women and those who rejoice in them are motivated by serious and honest devotion to significant principles and profound commitment to the unity of the Church. It would be easy to accuse one side of contempt for tradition or the other of male chauvinism (or some such) and such cheap shots have occasionally been taken in moments of irresponsibility, but no such accusations can withstand sober scrutiny. The simple fact is that devout and learned Christians (together with some less devout or less learned, no doubt) are of two minds in a matter which some consider crucial. If, as one suspects, this disagreement portends even deeper differences touching equally or more sensitive matters in the life of the Church and our address to the world, it is surely the task of our bishops to assess with the utmost care and concern the priority they assign to the unity of the Church and the moral force of such certitudes as would be preferred before that unity.

Here at this present it is this duty to guard the unity of the Church that must be the heaviest of the many responsibilities we lay on our chief pastors, for at best our diversity is of much more than gifts, and there seems every reason to believe that the years to come will manifest more rather than less diversity in the Church. In such circumstances the bishop must be deeply and critically and prayerfully immersed in sacred scripture and in the tradition flowing from it, not because these will afford easy answers or impregnable positions, but because in such immersion one discovers and becomes attuned to the motion of the Holy Spirit in history, and perceives that the communication of one gospel to an ever-changing history has been our concern all along. While such a perception will not always simplify the guarding of the unity of the Church, it can renew our resolve and, perhaps more importantly, liberate our imaginations.

Needless to say, such concern for the unity of the Church cannot be reduced to disinterested mediation, for the unity of the Church is not something other than its integrity; nor can unity under a bishop be isolated from his unity with the episcopal college or its unity with the Church all down history. At some point in all that it becomes gloriously clear that the unity of which we speak is nothing less than that of the Church with her Lord and His with the Father in the unity of the Holy Spirit. At such a point, we may pray, preoccupation with our perils will be converted to proclamation and, in that proclamation, the praise that is our end.

6 - As seen through South American eyes

S. Escobar, South America

At several points in the last five years bishops have hit the news in Latin America, in an unexpected way. We were used to the image of bishops—usually fat and old men—performing perfunctorily official duties at fixed dates of the year. We associated the image of bishop with a solemn figure extending his hand to be kissed by children, Indians and old women. Not so any more! Those bishops who hit the news are different characters. Like that lean, ascetic Spaniard, well-known as a defender of the Indians, whose life has been threatened several times in Matto Grosso, Brazil. Or like that Lutheran bishop who did his best to save some human lives in Chile, and was asked not to return after one of his trips. Or like that serious thinker and teacher whose weekly Sunday messages on the radio are heard all over the province of Santa Fe in Argentina, and read in many papers all over the country on Mondays. Or like those seventeen bishops from Latin America and North America who were gathered in Riobamba, Ecuador, when their meeting was interrupted by heavily armed military forces. They were rounded up, treated as common delinquents, taken to military barracks in Quito, after a rough trip in trucks, and then dismissed without any apologies.

Some of us, Latin American Protestants, were used to that kind of treatment from police forces ten or fifteen years ago, before the winds of religious freedom had blown around the world. But who would have dreamed ten years ago of Roman Catholic bishops being treated like that? Suddenly the average man on the street is watching the rise of a new kind of bishop in Latin America.

No one would have dreamed that university students, the intelligentsia and journalists would avidly wait to hear and read the latest pronouncement of a bishops' assembly. But that is what I have witnessed in Peru, Brazil and Argentina in the last couple of years. The pastoral role of these leaders of the Church—teaching, guiding, encouraging, defending— is suddenly being taken seriously by many more people than in the past in Latin America. The position of a bishop is not anymore the comfortable crown of a priest's career. It has become a dangerous position where every word and every move can mean attacks from left and right, problems with the government, and even the threat of an 'accidental' death; at least for some of the existing bishops, those who are shaping the new image that hits the eye of the average observer.

Of course, these are signs of change in the Church herself. Signs of a ferment which is running through the ranks of baptised people who are considered Roman Catholic and constitute the religious majority of Latin America. What course will this movement take? How will this ferment affect the daily life of the vast masses? All these are open questions. We have not yet seen enough to predict the answers.

TWO DIFFERENT HISTORICAL OUTLOOKS

The picture of the contrast between the old image of the bishops and the new one that we have sketched has to be complemented by understanding another contrast of the past that has shaped the personal outlook of this writer. It is the contrast between a 'Protestant' outlook, peculiar to Latin American Protestantism, and that of the pre-Vatican II Roman Catholicism.

From the middle of the last century Protestantism has grown at a surprising rate in Latin America. We usually recognise at least three streams of Protestant advance. *One* would be the ethnic or 'transplanted' communities that simply reproduced European Church patterns in Latin American soil. Usually they were not evangelistic of the native population. They even kept a foreign language in worship as a symbol of their 'separate' existence in our nations. Such were the Lutherans in Chile and Brazil, the Anglicans in several countries, the Waldensians in Italian or Swiss colonies of the River Plate republics. In the *second* place we have the communities that were formed out of the evangelistic effort of missionary-minded denominations, and interdenominational independent or 'faith' missions. These were Evangelical in their outlook and, in spite of their particular theological tradition, socially they adopted an Anabaptist or non-conformist stance. This can be understood as a reaction to established Roman Catholicism. In the *third* place we have the Pentecostal forces born out of local revivals, or as a result of Pentecostal missionary efforts from Europe and North America. This third group shares some elements of the Evangelical outlook and the Anabaptist stance that we have ascribed to the second group.

To a certain degree the first group kept an outlook of the relations between people and bishops that was similar to the Roman Catholic one. But it was considerably weakened by the simple fact that being expatriate communities, and minorities outside their own Constantinian milieu, the role of the bishop did not have the weight of social status that it had 'back at home'.

The other two groups shared an ecclesiology that we could describe as 'populist' using a modern political word. A strong emphasis on the local church or fellowship, on 'democratic' forms of church government,

28

on the Lutheran principle of the priesthood of all believers, and on the right and duty of every believer to be an active propagator of the Evangelical faith, created a dynamism and mobility which explains, at least in part, the amazing growth of the last hundred years. Here we see in action some of those elements that Roland Allen outlined as the condition for 'spontaneous expansion' of the church. Only after the fifties have Roman Catholic scholars and church leaders begun to recognise that this advance was not just 'sheep stealing', that the Latin American masses were pagan or de-Christianised, and that the Roman Church had not in four centuries developed the means and dynamics to minister to her baptised masses.

The encounter of these advancing forces with the Catholic Church accentuated in the latter at some points, the emphasis on authority of the hierarchy, social control of belief and practice, even use of the civil power to impose the official religion — all of these characteristics had become part of the Catholic Church pattern during the imperial domain of Spain in Latin America. We could also say that the Catholic reaction accentuated the 'populist' ecclesiology of Latin American Protestantism.

The change that at this point in time we witness inside Roman ranks, is partly the effect of this encounter and partly the result of Vatican II winds that were already in action at some focal points, even before the council. Closeness between pastors and people, mobilisation of laymen, the Bible in the hands of every believer, house meetings, joyful singing and spontaneous prayer, these are just some of the marks of Latin American Protestantism that are now being adopted by the Roman Church. It is true that sometimes the sanction and enthusiasm of a Dutch or Belgian missiologist has been necessary in order to have them accepted. But the Catholic believer knows that they were in existence, just around the block for decades, though only now are they imitated.

QUESTIONS AND CHALLENGES AHEAD

We live in a new stage of protestant life that challenges us with critical questions. It is my opinion that several protestant bodies in Latin America are experiencing now a need for bishops. To begin with, there is a desperate need for pastors. 'Populist ecclesiology' has its own limitations and we discover them as a second or third generation of Evangelicals grow up in our communities. There is need for pastors that will tend the flock, especially in times of crisis and transition, like the times we are facing right now. And then logically there is the need for shepherds to the shepherds. In critical hours we do not seem to have representative voices that can speak with an authority that comes from the Word and the Spirit, and is consequently recognised by a people that is sensitive to the Word and the Spirit.

The ecclesiological question is one of the most important items for theology in Latin American Protestantism. And an important aspect of it is precisely the way in which these pastoral needs can be met in a creative way, both biblical and contextual. The Free Church impatience with institutionalised patterns of church authority can sometimes give way to poor substitutes for the pastoral task.

The authority pattern of some Pentecostal Churches in Latin America has been studied, and it shows the existence of a strong 'caudillo' type of leadership, that is made up of a combination of father, boss and military commander. It seems adequate for migrant people who experience in the city the loneliness and the need for belonging of those who come from the rural areas. There are Pentecostal Churches which have an episcopal structure and bishops who are recognised as true 'caudillos' and followed. The lack of articulation and definition of this pattern makes it impossible to find ways to check natural trends toward authoritarianism and open abuse. The same could be said of some other Evangelical and Free Churches.

On the other hand, big and powerful interdenominational organisations impose, through the media and massive mobilisation, some popular and appealing figures that tend to fill the role of bishops especially in the teaching aspects of that role. But teaching has to be given by persons who live with the people of God day after day, who face with them the problems, tensions, suffering and joy of daily life in a nation. A 'star' that comes to a country for a week, fills a stadium during four nights, offers his opinions about everything and then moves on to the other end of the world to do the same, is not an authorised voice. However, the power of organisation, machinery and dollars give him the image of a bishop, and the platform to perform the role which is a poor substitute for real pastoral functions. Do not misunderstand me. We need the teaching ministry of the Word from people of God wherever they come from. But we should not impose on them the task of pastoring and teaching simply because they have a platform and we do not have bishops.

The bishops we need have to be Evangelical. This I understand to be people with a sense of mission, a clear idea of what the *evangel* is, and concern for the material and spiritual hunger of masses inside and outside the churches. Latin American Protestant Churches are advancing Churches. Their very existence comes from the Evangelical zeal of those who came to evangelise even when some official voices in Christendom dismissed them, as in Edinburgh 1910.

Protestants like myself have admiration and expectations for the new breed of bishops that is appearing in the Roman Catholic Church. We hope that the kind of 'disestablishment' process that this Church is experiencing in some countries will purify her and may even produce a New Reformation inside her. Meanwhile however we believe that we have a tremendous task of evangelising and discipling millions of pagans or nominal Christians, who show evidences of real spiritual hunger. And we also believe that there is more than ever a need to make clear through word and deed God's Word of judgment and hope for societies that have the exterior signs of Christianity but have lost the spiritual dynamism of it in social life. The ecclesiological answer to the pastoral needs of our churches that I have outlined, cannot be in contradiction with the missionary and evangelistic thrust that has marked our Churches.

Is this an impossible dream? No, a biblical pattern cannot be an impossible dream. It seems to me that as a process of disestablishment affects the Church of Christ in many areas of the world, Christians from the most varied backgrounds are starting to hunger for a renewed biblical vision of Church, people and bishops. We have seen some of them. Just some weeks ago I attended a conference of Anglicans from the diocese of the North of Argentina in Mision Chaqueña. Three hundred Christians from churches spread through four Argentinian provinces. Bishops and people sharing the same dust, the same poor food, the same risks, the same dreams, the same gospel, the same hope. Joyful in the fact of their growth, telling the miracles of God's grace saving people today, encouraging one another, these brethren in Christ were typical Latin American Evangelicals. And they were people, pastors and bishops.

GUIDE TO FURTHER READING:

Latin American Church Growth, William Read, Victor Monterrosa, Harmon Johnson (Grand Rapids, W. B. Eerdmans, 1969)

Haven of the Masses, Christian Lalive d'Epinay (London: Lutterworth, 1969).

Amidst Revolution, Emilio Castro (Belfast, Christian Journals Ltd., 1975).

The New Face of Evangelicalism. Ed: C. Rene Padilla (London: Hodder and Stoughton, 1976), Chapters VI, VIII, XII.

7 - As seen through South Pacific eyes

L. Fugui, Melanesia

People that dwell in the South Pacific today are mainly Melanesians, Polynesians, Micronesians and Whites and Yellow people. One can say that the Pacific region is a multiracial part of the world. Cultural backgrounds and different languages are many. Religious belief is also taken into account. Due to these many differences, the South Pacific people have some problems. There are racial tensions arising in some Territories, cultural mix-up is another, political unrest, communication difficulties due to many languages. Such things make our people very confused.

URBANISATION

Western influence is great in the South Pacific. Many of our young people are going from their villages to the urban areas. Many youngsters who have been to schools migrate to cities and towns in a very big way. They admire the attraction of the western civilisation.

UNEMPLOYMENT

Many of these youngsters that are going to urban areas are extremely disappointed when they find out that there is no job for them to do. This indicated very obviously that these people become very uncontrolled and of course tend to commit crimes of one sort or the other. Juvenile delinquency cases are growing higher every year. This is also low down the moral standard of the people. The world inflation has affected many people in the Pacific region. Due to these influences and changes our people are so confused how to budget for the families. Worse still is the fact that these unemployed people are feeding from those relations who are working. What does the Church do about this? In some territories in the South Pacific there is plenty of land lying idle; the Church should encourage the people to go to their lands and make a living. If the Church does not do this, it is a big shame. The Church should spend some of its money in rural development.

WITNESSING THE GOSPEL IN DAILY LIVES

Christians should be encouraged to participate more solidly in presenting Christ in their daily lives. The role of the laity in witnessing is needed in the South Pacific. Priests should release some of their responsibilities for the lay people to do. Functional leadership is needed. We should have worker priests, priests in politics and so on. By doing so, we are showing Christ in the world of work.

CHURCH IN THE SOUTH PACIFIC

The Church in the Pacific should be a uniting means of the South Pacific. The territories in the South Pacific are politically divided by our bureaucratic masters whether we have the choice or not. There is thinking of forming a South Pacific Region composed of the territorial provinces. The territorial provinces we have at the moment make a good starting point. The Church in the Pacific or anywhere should be an agent of change.

CHURCH INTERDEPENDENCE

The churches in the Pacific would honestly depend on overseas gifts, mainly finance for the next century. This is due to the undevelopment of the natural resources in the South Pacific territories. The Church's programme cannot be utilised to the fullest capacity without overseas grants.

LOCALISATION IN THE CHURCH

Localisation of the Church in the Pacific should have a different outlook from a political point of view. The Church believes that different people have different gifts, in spite of any race they belong. Such persons should stay on in any territories with the Church. Church employment should not be only restricted to certain countries, but throughout the whole Anglican Communion. There should be exchange of clergy within the Anglican Communion, if qualification is so fit.

ROLE OF THE BISHOPS

Due to the isolation and scatteredness of the territories and the islands in the South Pacific, I strongly believe that we should have some more Assistant Bishops. Occasionally many areas do not see a bishop for a long time. The work of the bishop is neglected in many areas, one man cannot cover the huge areas at one time. This would also train the Diocesan Bishops how to delegate authority more freely, would also give chance to the Diocesan Bishops to consult the Assistant Bishops and inform them of the Church affairs and so prepare them to go overseas for meetings as well.

The bishops in the South Pacific speak the prophetic voice in the field of politics. They should give guidance to political leaders so that the leaders would grow into Christian principles and attitudes.

ROLE OF WOMEN IN THE SOUTH PACIFIC

I think that the Church in the South Pacific should have women bishops and priests. This would minimise the superiority the men have

33

over the womenfolk in the Pacific. I believe there are some women in the South Pacific region who can become capable bishops or priests. Our world is a world of change therefore the Church should be a liberal avenue to initiate change in the lives of the people.

8 - As seen through Welsh eyes

Enid R. Morgan, Wales

'You Catholic then?' asked the rather snappish Ward-Sister as the Anglican Chaplain called one morning in a West Wales hospital.

'Church in Wales.'

'You mean Church of England.'

'No. It's the Church in Wales.'

'Well as far as I'm concerned it's the Church of England in Wales.'

'Me too', chimed in one of the orderlies.

Not a happy beginning to a pastoral visit! But these attitudes encapsulate well-rooted suspicions and prejudices.

Even now, 55 years after disestablishment and disendowment were forced upon the Church of England in Wales, it still cannot be said that the Church has found a role which matches the need of society in Wales. There are people, especially in anglicised Wales who have not come to terms even with the name. Some non-conformists still refer to her as 'Yr Eglwys Wladol'—the State Church.

Disestablishment came about as a result of a long and very bitter struggle. Those who lived through it were badly scarred and it was not surprising that for many years Anglicans closed ranks, concentrated on financial matters, on getting the new constitution to work, on reorganising the two South Wales dioceses into four.

The tremendous growth of radical non-conformity in Wales in the last century was boosted by factors other than those which caused the same phenomenon in England. In Wales the natural leaders of the people, the gentry, had long been estranged by their loss of the language. The Welsh-speaking population had to produce its own leaders. The growth of a more prosperous middle class and vigorous Victorian self-help led to the development in non-conformist circles of a vigorous folk culture with an ethos drastically different from that of the Church of England.

Since the connection of the Church with the State, with government and the gentry was perforce so strong, the ruling class in the Church was almost entirely English. This did not prevent heroic efforts being made by the bishops and some clergy as the nineteenth century wore on but the damage was done; 'Yr Hen Fam'—The Old Mother became

35

'Yr Hen Estrones'—The Old Foreigner. Meanwhile non-conformity was losing its spiritual vitality as its social predominance spread and the growth of liberal nationalism was channelled into the fight to disestablish the Church.

What has this history to do with the position of the Welsh Church, bishops and people today? Are not the difficulties which face us the same as those faced by the Church anywhere in Europe? Yet because of this background one particular problem will be concentrated upon in this article because, though not unique, it is very much our own problem in the Church in Wales. For Welsh-speakers in the Church in Wales the language is from time to time a matter of grief, for too often it is ignored or resented. On the other hand there are those who see the language as a purely marginal issue, a nuisance fussed over by people who are more concerned with culture than the saving of souls.

There is an element of comedy in this. Both sides are well aware that our particular problem must seem petty indeed to those who witness to Christ in circumstances of persecution, grinding poverty, starvation and war. It may well be a measure of our spiritual impotence that our small problem is papered over or ignored. This background in culture and politics accounts for several difficulties with which the Church in Wales is faced in the ecumenical sphere. One major difficulty for Welsh non-conformists is the fear not only of episcopacy as such, but of anglicisation and loss of identity. Yet the weakness of the various non-conformist institutions bodes ill for the cultural and spiritual welfare of Wales unless the Church in Wales can fulfil the role of mediator and healer.

This role was eloquently described by the late Archbishop Glyn Simon. On the very day of his election Dr. Simon declared his allegiance to the language and the particular role which he thought the Church could play in a society threatened by division and bitterness on the language issue. On May 6th, 1968, he said: 'It would appear that the Archbishop of a Church which is bi-lingual—one body with two languages —ought to have a most important healing and mediatorial role in the country if it is willing to play its part as the Church in Wales.'

The years following Dr. Simon's election were turbulent ones in Wales when the Welsh Language Society was active in painting out English-only road signs as part of a campaign for official status for Welsh. Headlines spoke of bombers being imprisoned, of searches for parcel bombs and of young people imprisoned for non-payment of fines imposed for sign-daubing activities. In April 1969 in a letter to the *Western Mail,* Dr. Simon declared his sympathy with the aims of the Language Society. Then on January 14, 1970, the Chairman of the Society, Dafydd Iwan, was imprisoned for non-payment of fines. This sparked off a series of protests throughout Wales. It was the Archbishop who visited Dafydd

Iwan in prison and persuaded him to allow the fines to be paid by a collection to which a significant number of magistrates had contributed. This pastoral visit and act of mediation earned for Dr. Simon a yet warmer respect than he had already earned from people who responded with delight and astonishment to his defence of the rights of the language.

The declaration by Dr. Simon which won for him warmest acclaim was the speech made to the Governing Body in September 1968: 'If there is not to be a division based on language there must be a genuine bilingual policy in Wales with parity of esteem and usage for both languages at all levels.'

Of the Church he added, 'Let her show herself to be a Church of understanding and sympathy for all her children. Let those who speak English only have a special and Christian care for the rights and grievances of the Welsh-speaking minority. Let those who speak Welsh only, or from choice, remember that majorities too have rights and grievances which deserve to be respected. Let both remember charity.'

This speech was greeted with astonished delight in Welsh Wales. It wasn't that the public was not well used to outspoken speeches from Dr. Simon, but concern for the language was not expected from an Anglican Bishop. The editor of the magazine of the Welsh Academy in December 1968 expressed the delight of Welsh literary circles: 'At long last we see at the head of the Church in Wales a man who knows his nation in a way that we have not seen since the days of Richard Davies, William Morgan and William Salesbury* a man with the honesty and courage to lead and express his opinion without fear. There is now hope that the Church as a whole will develop a truly national significance for every Welsh man and woman whatever their denomination, for here we see care for the nation raised to a Christian duty by our oldest Church.'

Such enthusiasm was touching but it was matched within the Church by a degree of silence if not consternation. Amongst non-conformists there was a readiness to embrace this man who in middle age had learned Welsh and abandoned his former sharp hostility.

Amongst the bishops of the Church in Wales Bishop Simon was a rarity. Other bishops, notably Timothy Rees and John Charles Jones— both from Welsh-speaking non-conformist origins like very many of the clergy—had made a tremendous contribution in their day. But Bishop Simon became Archbishop at a time of great ferment and in order to measure the surprise his attitude caused one must look back over ten years to the controversy which greeted the appointment of his predecessor Archbishop Edwin Morris in 1957.

Dr. Morris was an Englishman whose first appointment in the Church in Wales was as Bishop of Monmouth. There were protests

* The men who translated the Bible into Welsh in the 16th century.

when he was elected Archbishop, not because he was English, but because of his manifest lack of sympathy with the language. Dr. Morris whose considerable virtues of honesty and clarity did not include tact, made things worse by refusing to speak any word of reconciliation or appreciation of the value of the language and culture. His attitude recalled the severity and enmity of the first Archbishop of Wales, A. G. Edwards, to things Welsh.

In material and political terms A. G. Edwards served the Church well according to his lights but he heartily disliked any manifestation of nationalism, cultural or political. W. J. Gruffydd, Professor of Welsh at the University College of Wales, Cardiff, was his most incisive critic. When Archbishop Edwards declared, 'There is no room in the world for small and snarling nations', Gruffydd retorted, 'There is no room in Wales for small and snarling prelates'. Gruffydd was deeply suspicious of the new constitution of the Church in Wales and feared the influence of the gentry in appointments. He feared that there would never again be any Welsh-speaking bishops and urged the Welsh-speakers in the Church to form themselves into a party to withstand the attitudes of the Archbishop. Gruffydd's criticism was not confined to the bench of bishops and said that Welshmen would not forget 'that the Church more than any other religious organisation has betrayed the language; that the majority of priests today bring up their children to be English; that the churches have become English in hundreds of parishes where the chapels are still Welsh'. (This was in the twenties.)

Fifty years later things are in some ways greatly changed. Four of the present bench of six bishops are Welsh-speaking and Welsh is for the first time in centuries the language of bishops' homes. The Archbishop, Dr. G. O. Williams, is deeply committed to the language and Welsh is more widely used in his diocese of Bangor than in any other diocese in Wales. Dr. Williams has worked as mediator between protesting students and intransigent university authorities. He has worked quietly through committees and reports rather than by dramatic declarations of intent. He was one of three authors of a report on political devolution submitted to the British Council of Churches in the spring of 1977. Like all men of moderation he gets caught in the crossfire of the extremists.

Perhaps this will strike some as a peculiarly lop-sided view of the situation in Wales. But this is the only thing that makes our situation significantly different from the situation in England. It is one of the factors which lies behind the 'retrenchment and despair' which one young priest gave me as a reason for leaving Wales for a parish in England. Renewal is deeply needed in Wales and Christians involved in the language struggle are perfectly well aware of the spiritual poverty amongst Welsh-speakers. When renewal comes it must surely take account of this dimension of our lives and then the whole nation will be able to give thanks for all God's gifts which include 'the problem of the language' and turn it all into praise and glory. Welsh-speakers and non-Welsh Anglicans and non-conformists pray it may be so.

'Yn wir tyred, Arglwydd Iesu—Indeed come, Lord Jesus.'

GUIDE TO FURTHER READING:

A History of the Church in Wales. Ed: David Walker (Church in Wales Publications, 1976).

The Welsh Language Today. Ed: Meic Stephens (especially Chapter 4 'The Welsh Language and Religion' by R. Tudur Jones) (Llandysul: Gomer Press, 1973).

9 - As seen through West Indian eyes

D. Gomez, Barbados

The Caribbean is an area of great diversity composed mainly of island communities stretching from the southern tip of Florida to the northern tip of South America. The total region once formed one of the major battlegrounds for colonial mastery between the leading nations of Western Europe and several of the islands exchanged colonial overlords with some rapidity.

The advent of colonialism saw the virtual extinction of the indigenous Carib population which was replaced by the white colonialists and black slaves from Africa with the eventual result of a large black population and a small white ruling class in most of the territories. Although the cultural effect of the West European colonial experience is diverse the emphasis of this paper will be on the group of islands which have been the recipients of the British colonial experience and the version of Anglicanism which was its concomitant.

The Anglican presence in this region has for the last ninety-six years functioned under the aegis of the Church of the Province of the West Indies (CPWI), an autonomous province of the Anglican Communion containing until very recently eight Dioceses: Nassau and the Bahamas, Jamaica, Belize (in Central America), The Leeward Islands with its See in Antigua, The Windward Islands with its See in St. Vincent, Barbados, Trinidad and Tobago, and Guyana on the tip of the South American Continent. Recently the anachronistic cinderella Diocese of Venezuela was created with a very questionable future.

Although the territories of the Caribbean share a common colonial background they contain an extraordinary variety of cultural and geographic characteristics all of which contribute to the contemporary ferment in society which can be aptly depicted as a theatre of crisis. While the period of the 1950s and 1960s can be rightly described as exhibiting 'a search for identity' the present climate in the region can be more accurately defined as an attempt to affirm things Caribbean to be of worth and value in themselves. There is definitely a strong current of opinion in the entire region that there must be a re-definition of what life is all about in the identification of the aspirations of the peoples of the region.

While accepting the historical contribution of the mixed colonial experience and the 'rootlessness' which is part and parcel of being Caribbean there is undoubtedly a search for self-reliance and the establishment of values which are truly Caribbean. A basic part of this search is the current stress on regionalism among the ex-British colonies of the region. Despite the failure of the Federation of the West Indies in the early '60s the new Caribbean Common Market (Caricom) brought into being by the Chaguaramas Treaty of 1973 seeks to create a regional approach to trade and social services without political integration.

Among the peoples of the region there is a definite desire to correct the imbalance and deficiencies of the colonial past which created societies crippled by inequality of opportunity and disparity of wealth in which the masses, largely black, were both deprived and socially dispossessed.

It is only natural that political and economic forces should play predominant roles in this attack on the obvious deficiencies of the inherited past. The magnitude of the task of creating a new order with equality of opportunity to participate in the national life, coupled with the failure of the inherited capitalistic ideology, has led to an increasing interest in socialism. One must note specifically the influence of the socialist revolution in Cuba, the largest Caribbean territory. Both Jamaica and Guyana have opted for versions of socialism which have promised far more than they have been able to deliver.

The difficulty of creating a new order and a new ideology is accentuated by the failure of the modern prophets to reckon with the fact that there is still a large segment of the population of the region not prepared to adopt an attitude of uncritical acceptance of the mouthings of the secular prophets. This is especially so when it is evident that the new elite still gives the appearance of being 'privilege orientated' and is often oblivious to the inconsistency between the style of life proclaimed and that practised. Nevertheless the people of the region are definitely in need of a new order and are recognising the fact that they themselves must create this if it is to be authentically Caribbean. The effectiveness of the drive for self-reliance has been somewhat impeded by the fact that too much was expected from the politicians of the area. The colonial dependency syndrome conditioned the masses to expect someone to do the job for them without a sense of genuine involvement in the process. In addition the sectors of established privilege have not been too anxious to change the *status quo*.

Assistance in the promotion and expression of the aspirations of Caribbean peoples for self-determination and development has come from an unexpected source, namely, the Caribbean Conference of Churches (CCC) with special emphasis on its development agency (CADEC). The first Caribbean Ecumenical Consultation which took place in Trinidad in 1971, two years before the CCC came into being, provided the impetus for

41

an ecumenical approach to the transformation of Caribbean society from a non-political source. While many Christians in the region hold a negative view of the Churches' involvement in this process it is nevertheless beyond question that such involvement has contributed to the building up of an awareness for social justice in the region and has challenged the traditional attitudes of many Christians to the problems involved in human development.

The Anglican Church in the Caribbean (CPWI) in her composition and *modus operandi* displays a struggle to emerge from the dependency syndrome of the colonial period. This affects in varying degrees both clergy and laity in the Church.

The greatest success in the fight against the dependency syndrome can be seen in the area of Church finance. Although most of the dioceses are still in receipt of financial assistance from England, the United States of America and Canada there are definite indications that with the exception of Venezuela and Belize the remaining dioceses will shortly become financially self-supporting.

In the area of manpower there is a concerted drive for the indigenisation of the clergy. Twenty years ago the majority of the clergy were expatriates and mainly English. The House of Bishops only contained two Caribbean persons in 1968; today there is only one expatriate.

Manpower and style of life are integrally connected. It was only natural that a Church with a predominantly expatriate clergy would have its orientation slanted away from the region. Consequently a very English style of Church life has predominated the area with scant respect for indigenous cultural expressions. Anglican chant is still the order of the day and the standard edition of Hymns Ancient and Modern is almost as sacrosanct as the King James Version of the Bible. The Book of Common Prayer is still the predominant service book for services other than the Eucharist. The impression has certainly been created that nothing good can come out of the West Indian experience of Anglicanism. This is particularly evidenced by the strong reaction in some quarters to the 1975 Experimental Liturgy which was produced locally.

Although there has been a noticeable shift from a predominantly expatriate ministry this has not been accompanied by a similar shift in approach to ministry. Until very recently Caribbean ordinands received the same type of training as English ordinands and wrote the General Ordination Examination of the Church of England mainly at the Provincial Theological College at Codrington in Barbados. The College is now under local management and a deliberate attempt is being made to integrate theological reflection into a Caribbean context. Unless this process is accelerated the Anglican witness in the region will not bear the stamp of identification with the aspirations of the peoples of the region.

42

The specific role of the laity in today's Caribbean Church is also in a stage of metamorphosis. There are devout churchpeople who do not want changes in forms of worship because the Church is seen, in the wrong sense, as the one unchanging institution in the modern world. Those who have become accustomed to authoritarian and dogmatic teaching do not readily adjust to the challenge of becoming more deeply involved in the decision-making processes of the local Church, particularly where members of the clergy are themselves uncertain as to the way forward. On the other hand younger Anglicans, male and female, who in educational institutions in the region are being exposed to newer methods of teaching and are beginning to question and think for themselves, are often frustrated and sometimes angry at the lack of opportunities for service and participation within the Church family. Relationships between the clergy and laity need re-thinking and re-aligning and in this area the bishops of the Church are called to set a pattern for future development.

As both Church and Society in the Caribbean are in a process of change the bishops of the Church are involved in the creation of a style of episcopacy which relates to the Caribbean situation. The present holders of the office are pioneers in a very real sense as they are challenged to be the first group of Caribbean bishops both from an ethnic point of view and from performance. As the universal Church struggles with the inherent conflict between episcopacy and democracy the Caribbean bishops are in a state of ambivalence between two models of leadership. On the one hand there is the model of the leader who is involved in making decisions on his own initiative without reference to, or reliance upon, others and on the other hand there is the model of the leader who leads by motivating others towards a desired goal.

The former model has certainly pervaded the episcopal scene in the Caribbean with a strong tendency towards paternalism. It is noteworthy that for the greater part of the ninety-six years as a Province the House of Bishops met outside the Province!

The Partners in Mission process requires dioceses to think provincially. This poses peculiar problems in the Province of the West Indies where poor communications and lack of provincial machinery has militated against such a concept. The former can be overcome. Air travel has removed the physical barriers and the dioceses should share their problems and aspirations. With respect to the latter the Province has taken its first halting step in the appointment of a Provincial Secretary, but has not yet clearly defined his role.

The way forward is marked by a sense of urgency as Christians are challenged to awake to their task of searching out the mind of Christ in the present ferment and of interpreting this to the world of which they are part. The Caribbean bishop today is called to be a symbol of the quest for identity and for confidence in the worth of things Caribbean in which the whole Church is engaged; in a real sense to demonstrate a 'legitimisation' of this quest. As part of the Caribbean community he must speak from within it; sharing its sins and sorrows he must make the Word of God known to its diverse peoples. In this he must somehow carry with him his brother priests and the laity so that together they may provide the framework of leadership and stability in which real growth in Church and Society can take place and out of which a true Caribbean identity can evolve. A slight paraphrase of Archbishop Coggan's words in his General Synod Presidential Address sums it up: 'Perhaps this is the Caribbean's greatest need today—a band of men and women whose patriotism goes so deep that it leads them to pray, to criticise, to agonise; and out of that prayer, that criticism, that agony, to bear their witness, in season and out of season, to the truth of God as it has been revealed to them in Christ.'

Concerning the World Context

In this Section the essays variously refer to dominant influences affecting life-style, technology, traditional cultures, ethics, other faiths, nationalism and internationalism.

1 - Dominant influences in the current world

Margaret Dewey

The dominant influences at any given moment in history are like a seascape, in constant motion with conflicting cross-currents. The cult of contemporaneity (a very dominant influence) not only cuts us off from our roots: the up-to-date is soon out of date, and not all that is contemporary is of God. If we are not to be tossed to and fro and carried about by every wind of doctrine, it behoves us to be critically alert.

★   ★   ★

Three powerful currents still flow from the nineteenth century, associated with the names of Darwin, Marx and Freud. The idea of evolution burst upon the general public with Darwin's *Origin of Species*. A century earlier, the French historian Turgot had perceived the panorama of creation—hitherto seen as an unchanging, hierarchical 'great chain of being' from the lowest forms up to God—as witnessing to stages of human development through time. But in 1859 Darwin's theory reinforced a self-confident age's dream of limitless progress. It was soon seen as a universal law. The pioneer anthropologist Lewis Morgan applied it in his work of primitive societies, which was to influence Marx and Engels. It was the heyday of the industrial revolution and of Western expansion. Vast, supposedly 'empty' lands overseas provided a safety-valve for Europe's population explosion, food for growing cities, cheap raw materials and expanding markets. It was natural for the successful to see themselves as the crown of evolution.

Many Christians (taking the imaginative metaphysics of Genesis to be literal history have always seen evolution as an attack on religion, and man's supposed 'descent from the ape' as an assault on human dignity. Today even some scientists question Darwin's theory, but 'progress' remains a basic assumption of the Western way of life.

There were other assaults on human dignity. Herbert Spencer's phrase 'the survival of the fittest' aptly mirrored the market economy. Machines produced cheap goods, but reduced persons to 'labour' and 'consumers'. In 1790 Edmund Burke's *Reflections on the Revolution in*

France described the 'masses' into which people were being forced, not only by speculative commercial enterprise, but also by the levelling effect of democracy and the atomising effect of absolute power to remake society. Burke recognised the bureaucratic obsession with central power and passion for uniformity. In the 1830s, Alexis de Tocqueville's *Democracy in America* warned how the despotism of egalitarian mass society would crush real freedom. He saw the natural authority of social groups usurped by bureaucracy. And he saw how the French Revolution's successful alliance of intellectuals and politicians had brought into being the power-bemused intellectual, idealistically eager to manipulate people for their own good.

Marxism was born in 1848, when some European revolutionaries commissioned the young philosopher Karl Marx to write them a *Communist Manifesto*. (English socialism is pre-Marxist in origin, with deep Christian roots.) Marx, whose Jewish family had reluctantly accepted baptism under anti-semitic pressure, grew up despising religion. With prophetic indignation, he located man's inhumanity to man in the 'bourgeois' ruling class. The 'sinless proletariat' (an abstraction corresponding to no actual group) were a new Chosen People with a messianic vocation. (The 'matter' of Marx's 'dialectical materialism' is likewise not the solid stuff handled by engineers but the metaphysical principle of a secular Gnosticism.) Hebrew prophets of old, wishing to heal society, called the oppressors to repent; Marx, wishing to polarise society, called the oppressed to revolt.

Polarised opposites mirror each other. Marxism embraced the capitalist goal of material prosperity and the capitalist method of industrialisation. Socialist States are dominated by the same well-meaning but power-hungry planners as multi-national corporations. Marx and Engels were themselves solidly middle-class, the former supported (while writing *Das Kapital* in the British Museum) by profit from the latter's Manchester factory.

Marx and Engels idealised the 'classless' society they thought they saw in Lewis Morgan's account of the Iroquois Indians of America. But the model of primitive kinship groups is irrelevant to urban industrial societies. The 'dictatorship of the proletariat' in practice suggests Burke's 'masses' manipulated by a Party élite. Lenin welcomed this; his contributions were party discipline, revolutionary organisation, and ruthlessness in pursuit of power.

Ironically, the Communist Party resembles the Catholic Church in the heyday of the Inquisition, or the totalitarian theocracy of early Massachusetts. Marxism is basically a utopian *faith,* zealously missionary, with a dogmatic theology which precludes learning from experience (that is 'revisionism') and a this-worldly asceticism not unlike the 'Protestant ethic'. Its collectivism and inverted snobbery penetrate every area of

47

modern life, including the Church. It remains a major contender for the souls of men.

Christians ought not to have needed Marx to remind them that 'all our righteousnesses are as filthy rags' (Isaiah 64.6). But his most important insight is that our perception of reality is coloured by our 'class interests'. This of course discredits all claims to objectivity. Marxists fail to see that it relativises their *own* claims: such devastating knowledge must be repressed.

It was Freud who disclosed our unconscious repression of things we fear to know. (Significantly, he missed the real point of the Oedipus myth, which is not *what* Oedipus refused to see—parricide and incest—but *that* he refused to see.) The Victorian era was an age of repression, attempting to keep alive, in the form of bourgeois respectability, an ideal of Christendom badly shaken by the Enlightenment and French Revolution. Like Marx, Freud was less an innovator than a destroyer of illusions of the past.

Unfortunately he lost his nerve. There is a deeper ambiguity about motherhood even than the incestuous dimension of the 'bonds of natural affection' between parents and children. No villain of folklore is more feared than the devouring witch or wicked *stepmother*: not even the fairy tale can openly admit that one's *own* mother, the very source of life, is also a source of nameless terror. (The cult of the ambivalent Great Mother remains, in countless disguises, the most pervasive religious impulse.) Freud described the revolt against the father, yet clung neurotically to paternal authority in both his public and private life. He sensed the 'perils of soul', should the revolt against reason ever succeed. It was as a rational bulwark against this terror that Freud promulgated his celebrated dogma of repressed sex, in an attempt to reduce the unconscious to decayed consciousness. A living, autonomous unconscious—complementing, correcting, even guiding rational consciousness—was a threat to his materialist cosmos. Freud was interested in where things come from, not where they are going.

The real explorer of the creative unconscious was Jung, who ventured further into the depths and dared to live through the transforming encounter with what he met there. Much of his insight came from primal and Eastern religions.[1]

Jung's approach illuminates the perennially dominant tendency to polarisation. His recognition of extroverted and introverted personality types helps explain (for example) the 'activist/pietist' split in Christian commitment. Equally basic is his concept of a person's 'shadow', consisting of *all* the aspects of human nature one fears to acknowledge in oneself (not just sexuality). This repressed 'dark' side of ourselves is projected onto others and experienced, condemned and fought 'out there'. It is this hidden dynamic which makes racial or religious prejudice so intractable. Political dissension, too, is mostly 'shadow-boxing'.

Polarisation is an essential stage in the formation of a conscious ego strong enough to confront its own shadow. We cannot love our enemy without until we have agreed with our adversary within. Only after wrestling with his own shadow can Jacob see the face of God in the face of his alienated brother (Genesis 32.24-29 and 33.10). The transforming encounter cuts the nerve of our aggressions: no more crusades, 'class war', or seeking to 'improve' others (Matthew 5.38-48, 7.1-5). The opening of the eyes of the blind is the first of the Messianic signs, but our resistance to seeing our own shadow is prodigious. The natural man craves polarisation, and finds reconciliation 'subversive'. Dread of self-knowledge underlies today's insistence on politicising everything.

Jung's stress on the complementarity of opposites and the quest for wholeness, found in Judaism (Eccles. 33.14-15, 42.24-25) as well as in Eastern religion and alchemy, represents a more mature integration than the conventional quest for 'perfection' according to moral law. As our Lord saw, it alone makes true reconciliation possible. Erich Neumann spells this out in *Depth Psychology and a New Ethic*[2]—required reading for those who take discipleship in the current world seriously.

Depth psychology is hard for extroverts to accept. Most materialists prefer behaviourist psychology, which sees only from the outside and reduces personality to a mere product of biochemistry and conditioning. This accords well with the widespread positivist philosophy which restricts knowledge to the methods and findings of the physical or 'positive' sciences.

Early in this century, relativity was in the air. As the implications of Einstein's theory were perceived, time and space converged. 'Solid matter' was seen to be energy in motion. When it was realised that you cannot determine *both* the location *and* the speed of an electron, and that the very act of observing such tiny entities alters them, 'scientific objectivity' collapsed. (The myth lives on, in academic philosophy as well as in popular thinking.) Meanwhile, anthropologists' accounts of primitive cultures fed a growing sense of the relativity of all human values. Loss of nerve about moral standards and misinterpretation of Freud's warning about (unconscious) repression as an attack on (conscious) discipline still deprive countless children of the firm boundaries needed for the formation of personality.

Relativity is related to a general decay of *Logos* (reason, law, speech itself). It is the spoken word which creates the world around us out of the chaos of sensation, George Steiner's *Language and Silence* (Pelican, 1969) describes the 'retreat from the Word' since Milton's time. Confidence in language declined. Mathematics, once a shorthand for verbal description, became increasingly abstract and untranslatable. The sciences became steadily more mathematical; philosophy, too, until Wittgenstein declared that language can deal 'meaningfully' only with that very restricted segment of reality which is 'verifiable' by the scientific method: for the rest, including metaphysics and ethics, 'whereof one cannot speak, thereof one must be silent'. This is of course itself an unverifiable metaphysical assertion, but apparently unnerves theologians of little faith.

Respect for literature is undermined by critics more concerned with subconscious motives of authors than with the merits of their works. The lies of propaganda and advertising subvert rational speech and thought, while meaninglessly inflated jargon proliferates. Techniques of 'non-verbal communication' also take their toll. We are bombarded with images and deprived of the silence and solitude in which to assimilate them.

The impact of television is underestimated. (The debate about TV violence is superficial.) In the West, many a child spends more time with the 'electronic babysitter' than in school. Life itself becomes fiction, in which all problems must be effortlessly solved in sixty minutes. Real relationships with real people suffer. Passive dependence kills creativity, curiosity, self-reliance, perseverance. Childhood exposure to commercials induces (as the lies are perceived) cynicism and outrage at adult hypocrisy generally. There is evidence that extensive TV-watching (mainly a non-verbal 'right-brain-hemisphere' process) is especially damaging in early childhood, when the brain needs 'left-hemisphere' stimulation if cognitive skills are to be developed.

Parental abdication of responsibility leaves schools an impossible task, made worse by 'progressive' educational fashions. The cult of the unstructured is particularly inappropriate with younger children, whose formation and orientation call for firm limits and clear definitions. Graduate seminar methods are imposed from kindergarten onwards and sophisticated relativism on vulnerable children whose deepest need is certainty. It is a fallacy to suppose that the *preparation for* something (e.g. adult life in a pluralist and permissive society) should resemble the thing itself. Much wisdom about all this is to be found in Dorothy Sayers' *The Lost Tools of Learning*[3] and C. S. Lewis's *The Abolition of Man.*

Over a century ago, F. D. Maurice observed that the modern world was producing a kind of man to whom the gospel cannot be preached. When language itself decays, how can anyone hear the Word, or speak of God? The decline of English poetry and prose with the passing of the generation of Eliot and Auden marks the last decade or two as the worst of all possible times to have attempted liturgical reform or biblical translation. The appearance in 1961 of the *New English Bible* New Testament prompted Ian Robinson to wonder 'why the translators can't write English at all, and why so glaringly obvious a fact was generally missed by the literary critics who reviewed the version'.[4]

His second point exposes another potent influence: the desperate anxiety to be 'with it' (or whatever is the latest jargon for this immemorial human craving, vividly portrayed in the fable of the emperor's new clothes). In this age of public relations, innovations come packaged complete with the 'correct' reaction to them, and most folk either lack the criteria for independent judgment or are too timid to trust their own instincts. It takes courage to dissent from one's peers concerning the offerings of experts commanded by authorities.

Belief can be made impossible by the atrophy of its language, observes Robinson, but 'all hope need not be lost so long as we can see the situation more or less for what it is. The light by which to do so is given us by the language of the real English Bible and Prayer Book; they provide the standard in their record of a real religion which, such is their power, is always in danger of coming alive for any reader of goodwill who ventures unwarily into their pages'.

We are still dominated by the culture shock of two World Wars. Christendom was buried in Flanders' fields, though the older generation in the West grasped neither that fact nor its impact on non-Europeans and their own young. The blinding birth of the nuclear age at Hiroshima finally shattered the old continuities and certainties and the liberal assumptions about rationality and human goodness. Who now could define right and wrong? Permissiveness shook off all restraints. The young could see no possible future in the shadow of the bomb; their elders went on pretending. Angry young writers emerged from the newly articulate 'lower orders' to disturb and shock. Teenage barbarian tribes roared about on motorbikes. Rock music and psychedelic colours conveyed raw sensation. Writers and artists experimented with 'expansion of consciousness'. Responsible protest culminated in the Campaign for Nuclear Disarmament; its failure led to the despair of the drug subculture, with its nihilistic quest for madness and death.

But the technological 'imperative' went marching on. Exuberant optimism fed on cheap energy and the Keynesian illusion that money and 'credit' (meaning debt) could be limitlessly expanded to enable us all to live beyond our means. The Affluent Society arrived (for some), with its institutionalised waste and its meaninglessness and boredom. The despair of the young deepened, but for the dominant culture in the West the Sixties were a time of extroverted collectivism and the repression of self-knowledge and of God. It was the heyday of sociology. Electronic communication and jet travel created the 'global village', while the rise of the computer and data bank enhanced the power of a tiny élite to control the rest of us. 'Berdyaev pointed out that in the old days we used to read of utopias and lament that they could not be actualised', wrote Thomas Merton in 1968, 'Now we have awakened to the far greater problem: how to prevent utopias from being actualised.'[5] 1984 is just around the corner.

The one-sided rationality of technocratic consciousness was bound to evoke its opposite. Never before has mankind been so preoccupied with the irrational and abnormal, with sickness, deformity, crime, perversion, violence and terrorism. The under-culture has emerged into full view, and as civilisation confronts its collective shadow, out of the agony something new is coming to birth. A great new healing current is flowing in the depths: a quest for wholeness which can embrace the insights of all mankind, and a new understanding (not only among Christians) of the 'cosmic Christ' of Colossians 1.

There is a resurgence of religion (often in unconventional forms), with a hunger for awe and wonder and holiness, for imagination and the non-rational, for silence, for personal experience and individuality, for the disciplines of spiritual formation. Since these are seldom available nowadays in 'mainstream' churches, people look elsewhere. Eastern religions attract many. Neo-paganism is rife, complete with occultism and witchcraft.

There are also unmistakable signs of a recovery of the discerning, defining, ordering, creative *logos*. Already in 1968 Jeff Nuttall, after years inside London's schizophrenic 'bomb culture', wrote that 'it is now necessary to come back from inner space. Having revived the faculty of wonderment, it is necessary to apply it. . . . It is time that we gave power and body to the true music of the gods by cultivation of the craftsman in us. . . . It is time we asked ourselves what we are going to do with a future, should we now, after the sickness and the vision, gain one'.[6]

The declining literacy of school-leavers and growing awareness of the bankruptcy of 'progressive' education are leading concerned parents to demand a return to discipline and to structured teaching of 'basics' (reading, writing, arithmetic). Recently published results of a nine-year U.S. Office of Education study admit that in these matters the educationalists have been wrong.

There is a distinct cooling of public support for egalitarianism (despite the shrillness of its advocates) and a new appreciation of the complementarity of differing roles. In the U.S., the campaign for ratification of the Equal Rights Amendment has ground to a halt because women have suddenly awakened to what they and society as a whole stand to *lose* by it.

The Church would do well to pause before going any further with women's 'ordination'—to many, a transvestite charade. Father-figures and

52

mother-figures are not interchangeable. ('Fathers' speak the word with authority and lead the growing child out into the wider world; 'mothers' are regressive, reigning in the dependent pre-verbal layers of personality laid down in infancy.) It is no historical accident that our Lord reveals to us God *as Father*. Women (and lay men) ought certainly to share in preaching, theological teaching, retreat conducting, spiritual direction: a surer grasp of the office and work of a layman in the Church of God would clarify that of the priest. But the creative *logos* is masculine; all creation, including every soul of man or woman, is feminine to God. Our Lord sums up in his own person all humanity, womanhood as well as manhood, but the *logos*-made-flesh can only be a man. The archetypal *theotokos,* projected onto the historical person of our Lord's mother, is a type of the Church—the People of God who, overshadowed by the Spirit, bring forth the Christ. The Orthodox rightly see the priest as an icon of Christ the Bridegroom, preparing his Bride the Church for the marriage of the Lamb. Priestesses are pagan; 'women priests', a semantic impossibility.

The infantile craving for more and more is always with us, not only in profiteering and wage claims, but in all our inflationary demands for government benefits and subsidies whose true cost we refuse to pay in taxes. Over against this, however, a new awareness of limits improbably coincided with man's reaching the moon and looking back at his own tiny, fragile life-system in perspective. The Arab oil embargo and world-wide inflation have exposed the vulnerability of the whole technological dream. (Anyone who has not yet read E. F. Schumacher's *Small is Beautiful* should do so now.) The population problem is created by shortage of land for living space and food supply. The next shortage in the 'closing circle', already apparent from California to the African Sahel, is water.

Ecological awareness slowly penetrates the dense fog of human selfishness. The affluent are just beginning to perceive that they must live more simply so that others may simply live; that technology must be appropriate to genuine needs; that energy-intensive, capital-intensive mechanised agriculture (heavily dependent on chemical fertilisers and pesticides) will *not* solve the world's food problem. The old virtues of frugality, thrift, hard work, self-reliance and local co-operation are returning. Half the families in the U.S. now grow part of their own food; homes are being insulated and water and electricity consumption cut.

It is becoming clear that governments do *not* have all the answers. Self-determination at local levels is everywhere in the air (the jargon is 'participation in decision-making'). The bureaucratic juggernaut with its military/industrial/financial vested interests rolls on, but now meets informed and growing opposition, not least the campaign to put the nuclear genie back into the bottle and choose a less energy-wasteful way of life.

These things may as yet be a cloud no bigger than a man's hand, but in them (as in Elijah's cloud) is life. Now, as then, we need not serve the gods of the land: *we can choose*. John V. Taylor's *Enough is Enough* (SCM, 1975) and John Lawrence's *Take Hold of Change* (SPCK, 1975) contain much food for thought in this connection.

★   ★   ★

Westernisation remains a dominant influence, but the West is beginning to be disillusioned with 'progress' just as the Third World is discovering it. The cry for international justice tends to assume that 'developing' nations, given fair shares, could and should follow the Western pattern. (Encouraging others to duplicate our mistakes is certainly profitable for the purveyors of 'high' technology.) It has been noted that 'aid' to poor countries often only enriches a minority. In fact, the 'exploitation' popularly attributed to capitalism is inherent in all large-scale industrialisation: whoever owns such means of production, *somebody* must accumulate vast amounts of capital, and feed the urban masses from the countryside. Capital-intensive 'high' technology, providing jobs only for a highly skilled few, is a luxury the global village can afford only for very limited purposes. Obedience to God sometimes requires Adam to say 'No' to things in themselves good. But such Western hindsight will be heeded only when we ourselves begin to 'de-develop' and practise what thus far only a minority even preach.

In all revolutions for liberation, there is an apparent recovery of innocence through polarisation (locating evil in your oppressor). That neither exchanging roles nor changing the system abolishes original sin, each generation must learn for itself. The real world is a very ambiguous place. The profit motive may be regrettable, but without it there is soon nothing left to 'redistribute'. 'Free enterprise' leads to inequity, but government intervention distorts the economy and multiplies bureaucratic inefficiency. A sinful world needs a delicate balance of carrot and stick to keep the economy functioning at an optimum level (not maximum, for whatever politicians promise, continuing 'economic growth' in a finite world means inflation).

Aleksandre Solzhenitsyn rightly calls for 'repentance and self-limitation in the life of nations:'[7] 'We are always anxiously on the lookout for ways of curbing the inordinate greed of the *other man,* but no one is heard renouncing his *own* inordinate greed. History knows of several occasions on which the greed of a minority was curbed, with much bloodshed, but who is to curb the inflamed greed of the *majority,* and how? That is something it can only do for itself.'

But only the mature discipline themselves, or exert themselves voluntarily on behalf of strangers. Human nature is not regenerated by government action, which is presumably why our Lord declined the Tempter's offer of the kingdoms of the world. The only way to real improvement in society is the slow, patient way of personal discipleship. And that is the business of the Church. Really to serve others (and not inadvertently reinforce their errors), we must ourselves be not conformed to this world, but transformed by the renewing of our minds, so that we may prove what *is* the will of God. In this way we may so pass through things temporal that we finally lose not the things eternal.

REFERENCES:
[1] The best popular introduction is Jung's own beautifully illustrated *Man and His Symbols*; also his autobiographical *Memories, Dreams, Reflections* and Laurens van der Post's *Jung and His Times* (Hogarth Press and Pantheon, 1975).
[2] Hodder & Stoughton, 1969.
[3] Reprinted in 1973 by Mowbrays in *A Matter of Eternity*.
[4] *The Survival of English* (Cambridge University Press, 1973), pp. 24, 65. His chapter on 'Religious English' is required reading for English speakers who care about God and the things of God.
[5] *Conjectures of a Guilty Bystander* (Burns & Oates, 1968), p. 73.
[6] *Bomb Culture* (Paladin, 1968), p. 242-4.
[7] See his essay of that title in *From Under the Rubble* (Fontana, 1976), p. 136.

GUIDE TO FURTHER READING:
Enough is Enough, John V. Taylor (SCM, 1975).
Depth Psychology and a New Ethic, Erich Neumann (Hodder & Stoughton, 1969).
The Survival of English, Ian Robinson (Cambridge University Press, 1973).
The Abolition of Man, C. S. Lewis (London & Glasgow: Collins, 1943).
Take Hold of Change, John Lawrence (London: SPCK, 1975).

2 - Some influences of technology on contemporary life and thought

Sinclair Goodlad

Technology may be thought of as the systematic extension of human faculties. Each technological system or device extends our power to move, see, hear, manipulate material, process information, or compress or extend thought or action in time. All societies have technology; indeed, whole civilisations have been named after their dominant forms of technology—the Stone Age, the Iron Age, the Bronze Age. The systematic quality of modern technology is, however, distinctive. Just as science, with which technology is often confused, uses systematic observation to achieve precise knowledge, so modern technology uses systematic measurement, comparison, and organisation to achieve precisely defined objectives. Science and technology are, of course, symbiotic; precise knowledge aids the development of new techniques and new techniques (of measurement, information processing, and so on) contribute to the accumulation of knowledge.

Jacques Ellul has reminded us (*The Technological Society*, Cape, London, 1965) that technology is more than hardware. Technology concerns technique. A machine is, as it were, pure technique; but technique is any complex of standardised means for attaining a pre-determined result. Air travel, for example, involves more than just aeroplanes; it requires a complex organisation of baggage handling, food preparation, transport to and from airports, ticket agents and seat booking, publicity, and telecommunications. Most forms of so-called 'high' or advanced technology require specialised forms of social arrangement to support them.

Technology is purposeful. New techniques are devised primarily to achieve economic objectives, and because economics are the stuff of politics, technology involves a multitude of political questions. These questions in turn may be resolved into fundamental questions about human values. Accordingly, this brief essay will examine a few ways in which contemporary life and thought is influenced by technology, concentrating on questions which may be of particular interest to Christians.

The images of technology purveyed by the mass media are instructive because they reflect our ambivalent attitudes to technology. On the one hand there is uncritical adulation of a wonder-world of gadgets; on the other a fear that the monster we have created may get out of control. In the first category are television programmes (mainly of American origin) showing law enforcement agents, backed by mountains of equipment (computers, helicopters, 'bionic' assistants, and what not) pursuing the workers of iniquity (as in 'Mission Impossible' or 'The Six Million Dollar Man') or voyaging through space (as in 'Star Trek') imposing the protestant ethic and the spirit of capitalism on whole galaxies. This drama of reassurance suggests that the effects of technology are benign, contributing to our security and peace of mind.

The image of technology conveyed in news bulletins is, however, frequently negative. Like the human body, technology becomes most noticeable when it goes wrong. Much is made of accidents and disasters—such as the widespread diffusion of strontium 90 following tests of atomic bombs; the death of 6,000 sheep in Utah from the misuse of a biological weapon; the gross pollution of Lake Erie; the explosion of a chemical works at Flixborough; the escape of a poisoned cloud at Seveso; the collision of two jumbo jets; the power failure in New York City. It is little comfort to be told that catastrophes are nothing new—that the Romans over-cultivated North Africa; that goats ruined much of the vegetation in the Mediterranean; that the unsinkable 'Titanic' sank; and so on.

The bewilderment of lay people is compounded when *cognoscenti* seem to disagree with each other. For example, Barry Commoner (*The Closing Circle,* Cape, London, 1972) gives a sense of impending doom, pointing to our reckless use of non-renewable resources and our destructive impact on the ecosphere. By contrast, John Maddox (*The Doomsday Syndrome,* Macmillan, London, 1972) suggests that matters are not nearly as serious as Commoner claims, and argues that human ingenuity will ensure our survival despite temporary shortages of commodities currently believed to be essential.

It is possible to do an elaborate felicific calculus, drawing up a balance sheet of the good and bad effects of technological innovations. What is more important, however, is to consider some of the *choices* we encounter with every extension of human faculties. To put it somewhat dramatically: if one was asked whether one would like one's feet to grow to ten times their normal size (or one's ears, or eyes, or hands . . .), one would have pause for thought. Yet ultimately this is what technological innovation offers us. We can start to grasp the significance of innovations only when we concentrate on the purposes which they are designed to serve and the extent to which a growth of our faculties will interfere with our neighbours. We will then not be distracted either by outward appearances (gadgets) or by malfunctions (disasters).

SOME SPECIFIC EXAMPLES

Developments in technology do not necessarily throw up fundamentally new moral and political problems; however, by increasing the range of choice open to us, they make some of the problems more difficult to handle.

In *Medicine,* for example, it is becoming increasingly difficult to distinguish between life and non-life. Elaborate techniques of intensive care can maintain some body functions when others which many people would regard as necessary to a fully human life have gone. Doctors have strict procedures for defining the moment of death. But our capacity for keeping 'living vegetables' alive becomes increasingly harrowing particularly for relatives.

Birth defects can now be detected sufficiently early in pregnancy to make abortion of deformed foetuses possible. The abortion issue does not thereby change radically; but it becomes considerably more complex.

Psychopharmacology has produced a wide range of drugs to control moods—such as tranquillisers, stimulants, and anti-depressants. It is not so much that we do not know when and how to use these drugs (for most uses produce obvious relief of distressing symptoms); rather, our increasing knowledge of physiology and the brain raises more acutely the old question—who am I? Similar questions are, of course raised by experimental work in genetics, though there is at present (as Gerald Leach has argued at length in *The Biocrats,* Cape, London, 1970) very little possibility of science-fiction style genetic engineering, so complex and intricate are the procedures involved.

The most pervasive questions, however, are those of policy in the allocation of resources to medicine. Should money be invested in complex and expensive forms of treatment (such as kidney dialysis or transplant surgery) or rather in relatively cheap preventive medicine (such as fluoridation of water to prevent teeth from decaying, cervical cancer screening, or campaigns to reduce cigarette-smoking or road accidents). These questions, of course, merge with the even more vexing political questions concerning the allocation of scarce resources to other things— housing, education, nutrition, and so on.

Telecommunications might, at first glance, appear an undiluted good. As Colin Cherry has argued (*World Communication: Threat or Promise?,* John Wiley, London, 1971) the primary significance of telecommunications is the power of organisation which they permit. New forms of social institution come into being and a multiplicity of human contacts is facilitated. Telephones have become almost indispensable to modern business. Most travel depends upon prior arrangements being made by telecommunication—and this is where slight doubt creeps in.

Louis Turner and John Ash have noted (*The Golden Hordes,* Constable, London, 1975) that six per cent of all world trade is now in tourism. Since Thomas Cook first arranged for 570 people to travel from Leicester to Loughborough to a temperance meeting, tourism has grown into a vast industry which, for several countries, represents a major earner of foreign investment. Tourism does, however, have many features which are cause for concern. Barry Commoner has commented on the 'Technology Cycle' by which unpleasant work and tourism feed on each other: Routine work and urban life create a need to be refreshed; transport is needed to places of refreshment; this in turn requires high technology at low cost—which requires people to live in cities and work at routine tasks. (Fred Hirsch has made a similar analysis in *The Social Limits to Growth,* Routledge & Kegan Paul, London, 1977.) Rather than concentrating as we should be on making work rewarding and cities pleasant to live in, we may be building a way of life which depends more and more on high technology.

Perhaps more insidiously, tourism makes culture a commodity. Traditional customs become a sideshow for the amusement of visitors. Countries which preserve their tourist 'sights' run the danger of letting the weight of the past suffocate the creativity of the present. Tourism also constitutes a form of rapid and unstable industrialisation which may divert energy and resources from more worthwhile forms of national investment.

Other forms of telecommunication, too, are not without drawbacks. Radio and television have revealed enormous potentialities for education, and millions of people now enjoy serious music and drama who would otherwise be denied them. However, it is not without interest that in many 'Western' countries, television-watching has become the single greatest consumer of leisure time. Children may spend as many hours watching television as attending school. Despite research efforts to determine the effects of specific content (e.g. political broadcasts and violent drama), relatively little is known about the long-term effects of the massive public involvement with television.

Manufacturing industry makes extensive use of advanced technology and produces an abundance of systems and devices which improve the ease of living. However, several aspects of industry based on advanced technology are currently giving cause for concern.

First, industry is becoming increasingly complex. Huge industries may come to depend upon the output of a single plant, with serious lay-offs if the product of that plant is cut off by accident or industrial action (for example, in the motor industry). In similar manner, very large sectors of the population may be heavily dependent on services (such as electricity supply or transport); relatively small groups of people may exercise considerable power through the threat to disrupt these.

A different sort of political power is exercised by those organisations or countries which are already rich. Scientific and technological knowledge is a considerable source of industrial power. However, only those organisations which are already powerful have the ability to acquire the relevant knowledge—through expensive research and development. In this way, science and technology tend to increase the power of those who are already powerful.

Another objection to high technology industry is that it consumes huge quantities of energy (mainly from fossil fuels) and of non-renewable resources (such as metals). Each workplace may cost several thousands of pounds to establish, so that each worker can produce the greatest possible quantity of goods. However, this concept of 'efficiency' may neglect the social value of work to the individual. To make technology more appropriate to the social needs of workers, and to the needs of developing countries (which cannot afford an extravagant use of energy and metals, and which do not have the capital to invest in machinery), E. F. Schumacher advocates the use of 'Intermediate Technology' (see *Small is Beautiful,* Blond & Briggs, London, 1973).

More radical critics of high technology favour 'Alternative Technology'. For example, David Dickson (in *Alternative Technology,* Fontana, Glasgow, 1974), quoting Robin Clarke, contrasts a 'hard' or high technology society with a 'soft' or alternative technology society in, among others, these ways: large energy input/small energy input; high pollution rate/low or no pollution rate; non-reversible use of materials and energy sources/reversible materials and energy sources only; mass production/craft industry; high specialisation/low specialisation; city emphasis/village emphasis; destructive of local culture/compatible with local culture; innovation regulated by profit and war/innovation regulated by need; growth-oriented economy/steady-state economy; capital intensive/labour intensive; centralist/decentralist; technological accidents frequent and serious/technological accidents few and unimportant; work undertaken primarily for income/work undertaken primarily for satisfaction; science and technology performed by specialist elites/science and technology performed by all; strong work-leisure distinction/weak or non-existent work-leisure distinction.

Criticism such as this does a valuable service in pointing to areas of choice in setting goals for manufacturing technology.

Information processing techniques, notably the use of computers, are spreading rapidly. Operations research specialists and systems analysts point to the value of their techniques (of which computers are only part) in improving planning—for example in choosing the optimum location of hospitals or fire-stations or in stock-control. Also, so-called 'databanks' based on computers can give rapid access to files of information about motor-car licences, criminal justice records, educational achievement, credit-worthiness and so on. Some people are beginning to object to this because of the power it gives to planners and controllers.

SOME GENERAL INFLUENCES OF TECHNOLOGY

Examples could be multiplied *ad infinitum* of the ways in which specific technologies influence life and thought. There are, however, some general influences of technology which merit the particular interest of Christians. These are primarily values, commonly linked with high technology, which Christians might wish to challenge.

1. *Organisation.* High technology brings about or requires complex organisation which often generates a feeling of powerlessness and of the meaninglessness of individual effort. It is sometimes assumed that large organisations are automatically to be desired (so-called 'economy of scale' is often quoted). Two questions arise: Are large organisations in fact necessary? If they are, how do Christians engage with them?

2. *Law.* Technology involves explicitness. Objectives must be stated precisely and minutely detailed procedures must be followed if success is to be ensured. Special rules and regulations often govern technical systems—for example concerning the movement of traffic on the roads, or concerning standards in food processing. There is a related tendency to expect many other forms of human relationship to be governed by law. Legislation becomes increasingly the answer to all social dis-ease. How well does this accord with Pauline Christianity?

3. *Professionalism.* Many commentators (for example, Theodore Roszak in *The Making of a Counter Culture,* Faber & Faber, London, 1970) have commented on the proliferation of experts in all fields of activity. The precise and detailed knowledge required in some technologies soon leads to the expectation that only professionals or experts are competent. Property rights are established in one field of knowledge after the other. 'Closed shops' proliferate so that increasingly one needs a professional licence to help another person. Is this a necessary or desirable concomitant of technology?

4. *Specialist education* is increasingly seen as the necessary preparation for professionalism. Experts in all fields are seen to be needed. The danger here is of treating individuals only as technical 'functions' and thereby of neglecting the education of their complete personalities. If, however, one wishes to resist this tendency, one must face the question: What do we have in common? What are the ideas and values which constitute a satisfactory general education—regardless of what specialism the individual may wish to follow?

61

5. *Economism.* It is a small step from systematically studying a technique to seeking the simplest measure of that technique's effectiveness. Commonly this involves numerical measurement (rather than qualitative evaluation) with the result that economic efficiency comes to be sought—regardless of whether this is an appropriate objective.

6. *Technique.* A similar, and related, tendency is to value technique for its own sake, regardless of the purpose the technique is designed to serve. Bigger, better, faster, more. One can even interpret certain modern 'rituals' as the apotheosis of technique—for example Wimbledon tennis.

7. *Compulsion.* There is yet another related tendency which is difficult to describe simply. Technology as adventure? Technology to satisfy curiosity? It is more readily recognisable as the tendency to feel that because something *can* be done it *should* be done. The moon shot, the building of Concorde, heart-transplant surgery, are examples of complex technology which excite us because of their challenge—but might better not have been undertaken. We take it for granted that satisfying curiosity is automatically a good thing. If this seems self-indulgent, we talk of 'technological spin-off' and point to all the socially useful ideas which were discovered on the way to the self-indulgent objective. But might there not be equally impressive 'spin-off' from more humanely directed endeavours—such as trying to ensure that everyone in the world is fed, housed, and educated.

8. *Distance.* Because technological devices or systems are extensions of our faculties, they commonly have the effect of distancing us from direct experience, even of removing the agent from the effects of his actions. In this way, motorists who would not dream of pushing past as pedestrians on a pavement, behave with heedless brutality in their cars, and airmen can drop napalm or high explosive on people they cannot see. In a different way, bureaucracies (also based upon technique) can diffuse responsibility and cloud moral issues.

CHRISTIAN RESPONSE TO THE INFLUENCES OF
TECHNOLOGY ON LIFE AND THOUGHT

It is not part of my brief to develop at length a Christian response to the influences here adumbrated. However, three points bear mention in conclusion.

First, technology is purposeful. It is, therefore, highly appropriate and desirable that some form of technological criticism should be undertaken, judging each proposed new device, system, or administrative expedient much as literary criticism or artistic criticism evaluates work in those fields. Already Marxist criticism represents a powerful stream (of criticism directed at) of technology; but it is mainly limited to economic criticism, examining how particular forms of technology favour one or other economically-defined class. What would be a suitable form of Christian technological criticism? What would be the institutional vehicle for such criticism?

Secondly, much Christian teaching (and indeed social organisation in parishes) has emphasised private virtue and individual actions of neighbourliness and goodwill. However, if Christians are to influence the development of technology, they will need to become heavily involved in collective, political action. Individual Christians are, of course, already involved in many institutions concerned with technology. But can or should the Church exercise institutional influence to concentrate and focus Christian concern?

Thirdly, and this may seem paradoxical after the last paragraph, there may be a singular need to cultivate alongside political consciousness and activity a rich range of domestic virtues. Contemporary obsession with technique, with the means of achieving objectives, often distracts attention from ends. Ultimately, the purposes of technology are to facilitate human communication. The word 'communication' means 'sharing'—and has the same root as 'communion'.

Perhaps the antidote to the restlessness of much technological activity is the quiet rhythm of the Christian year with its festivals of Advent, Christmas, Epiphany, Easter, and Whitsun. Likewise, the antidote to the anxiety generated by, for example, the distribution of medical resources may be an acceptance of life and death enriched by Christian rites of passage. Interestingly, as contemporary civilisation becomes less aware of inner virtues it becomes increasingly obsessed with exteriorised virtue; pollution of the physical environment becomes an analogue of sin—the pollution of the soul. As technology extends our faculties, we must simultaneously be aware of the effects we may have on others (and take appropriate political action) and be mindful of the fundamental purposes for which we seek the new techniques.

GUIDE TO FURTHER READING:
The Social Limits of Growth, Fred Hirsch (London: Routledge & Kegan Paul, 1977).
The Biocrats, Gerald Leach (London: Jonathan Cape, 1970).
Small is Beautiful, E. F. Schumacher (London: Blond & Briggs, 1973, and London: Abacus edition, Sphere Books, 1974).

3 - Traditional cultures and technology

Kosuke Koyama

By traditional cultures I understand the great number of diversified cultures of man which continued relatively unchanged until they came under the decisive impact of modernisation, to be exact, of science-based technology. C. E. Black speaks of the three great transformations in the history of mankind; firstly, the very emergence of the human being with ability to create human culture about a million years ago; secondly the transition from primitive to civilised societies about 7000 years ago in the valleys of the Tigris, the Nile and the Indus, and thirdly, the universal change taking place in our time under the impact of the scientific revolution. 'What is distinctive about the modern era is the phenomenal growth of knowledge since the scientific revolution and the unprecedented effort at adaptation to this knowledge that has come to be demanded of the whole of mankind.' (*The Dynamics of Modernisation*, pp. 1-4.) In this grand scheme, the traditional culture is said to be about 7000 years old.

Thomas Newcomen invented the first successful steam engine in 1712. This thermodynamic event opened the door to the coming of science-based technology. Hand-operated machines gave way to the indefatigable steam engines which have undergone constant improvement since then. One of the significant dates in science-based technology is October 21st, 1879, when Thomas Edison succeeded in demonstrating the electric light. This event is significant because it is to do with one of the most basic of human experiences and religious symbolism: light. Traditional cultures had the sun, the moon and candles. But since about 100 years ago, modern cultures have the sun, the moon and the science-based light! Modern technology has made most impressive innovations in the areas of communication, transportation, education, medicine and the material condition of life. There is a qualitative difference between experience-based technology (traditional) and science-based technology (modern) when we measure their respective impact upon our life. This does not mean that we live today completely in the world of science-based technology. Experience-based technology is very much around us. But it has been integrated into the general scheme of efficiency dictated by science-based technology.

The traditional cultures express themselves in abundant varieties.

But they are one in their experience of facing the modernisation impact. What follows is a sketch of interactions between traditional cultures and technology (both traditional and modern) mainly taken from the cultural context of South East Asia where I had the privilege of working as a theological educator for more than a decade. This paper has two sections: in the first section I wish to raise the issues, and in the second I would like to make some brief theological observations.

(I) ISSUES

Traditional cultures are at home with traditional technology. They have grown together. On the same reasoning the science-based cultures would feel at home with science-based technology. Science-based cultures are emerging today. I say this on the basis of the astounding impact of science-based technology upon our physical and mental life. I do not think, however, that such emergence of new powerful cultures will take place independently from the historical reality of the traditional cultures of experience-based technology. We are today living at the critical moment of co-existence of the traditional cultures and modernised cultures. I prefer the word *co-existence* rather than transition. Human cultures are a living reality of great complexity. They do not simply move from one stage to another as we would like to see happen. It is important for us to know that we have more historical experience with the traditional cultures than with the emerging modernised cultures. We experience then the emerging cultures from the viewpoint of the traditional cultures. The human culture of 7000 years will not go away so easily by the power of the emerging science-based cultures. One of the major tasks confronting humanity today is to integrate creatively the traditional cultural values with the emerging ones. How to bring these two great historic values of tremendous human investment into a blessed unity for the benefit of mankind?

I would like to describe three characteristics of the traditional cultures seen from the view of technology.

(1) *Personalised space:* Traditional cultures are acquainted with the image of 'inefficient posture' that personalises space. (efficiency and meaning).

Traditional cultures breathe in space personally created. It is a space of myths, symbols and religions. It is that of experienced-based technology. Tane-mahuta, the god and father of forest in the Maori myth of New Zealand, is a hero who gave his people the personalised living space. In the beginning Rangi (the father heaven) and Papa (the mother earth) were clung together with no space between them for their children to grow and enjoy the freedom of movement. There was no light either. After a series of failures in attempting to separate the parents by the children, it is said that Tane-Mahuta was one who was able to rend apart Rangi and Papa. ' . . . he paused; firmly he planted his head on his mother Papa, the earth, and his feet he raised up against his father Rangi, the sky; he strained his back and his limbs in a mighty effort. Now were rent apart Rangi and Papa . . .'. The posture ('heading' instead of 'footing'!) with which this hero accomplished his mission is mytho-technological. Space is gained painfully at the strain to his back and limbs. Viewed from today's technological sensitivity, may I question if the upside-down posture in which the god engaged in his work is not technologically awkward, inferior and inefficient? Are not footing and posture important in any technological engagement of man with nature? In fact, is it not true that the presence of technology is most distinctively felt in its elimination of awkward and unpleasant postures from our everyday life? Not only physically but also psychologically? And perhaps even spiritually? Is not technology an expression of human spirit in the form of efficient administration of nature? Is not efficiency the fundamental mark of technology? Whenever man thinks of efficiency, is he not thinking about technology of one kind or another?

Compare a three-mile-an-hour oxcart with a powerful motorcycle! The motorcycle can run without indicating any fatigue and 'straining'. The power generated in the tiny engine is explosively efficient. How emancipated the posture of the young rider on the motorcycle! How streamlined, pleasant, efficient and free from 'strain in one's back and limbs'! Oxcart and motorcycle! Symbols of inefficiency *and* of efficiency!

History of technology is a history of elimination of physical strains. Aesthetically executed streamlining is an outward expression of the technological philosophy of the elimination of strains. Elimination of physical strains must be positively evaluated. It emancipates man from unnecessary hard labour. It is good to see remote villages electrified, water electrically pumped, necessity of life being transported by faster motor trucks than by slow oxcart. But the value of technology must be determined by the human and cultural context in which it is placed. The village people would not need a neurosurgeon (a highly invested, skilled man of science-based technology) with a set of medical machines of enormous price. They would need someone who can take care of basic medical troubles. In certain contexts a bicycle is an appropriate technology and even a motorcycle would be understood as inappropriate. Technology which is appropriate to the social reality of traditional cultures can make a decisive contribution to the life of the people. The benefit the community harvests from having appropriate technology will stimulate the community to become gradually more ready to make use of 'stronger appropriate' technology. In such case—a healthy balanced growth of culture and technology—the positive value of technology will become obvious. Here technology has been well contextualised. My

66

observation is, however, that unfortunately this happens only rarely. One often witnesses that the super-technology invades the milieu of the traditional cultures and paralyses the social fabrics of the cherished traditional values. Such technological invasion destroys the personalised space of the traditional cultures. With this brief observation on the importance of appropriate technology, we must return to that discussion on the contrast between oxcart and motorcycle. What does that contrast imply?

Strangely, the relationship between technology (efficiency) and humanity (meaningfulness) is ambiguous. Efficiency does not necessarily enhance the human meaningfulness or fulfilment. The glory of the traditional cultures is found in its insight that some form of 'inefficient posture' (strains) must be retained in the community in order to safeguard the sense of human value in the community. Traditional cultures are suspicious of 'streamlined efficient posture'. Indeed they may welcome it. But all the same they remain suspicious. They know the high human value of 'symbolism of inefficiency'. Therefore they are keenly interested in the possibility of obtaining the appropriate technology. Appropriate technology means the technology which contains a contextually meaningful symbol of inefficiency.

Granted that the traditional technology is primitive, inefficient and 'straining' must we not give a serious thought as to whether some *other* arrangement than the one of 'strain in one's back and limbs' is capable of creating a meaningful community for man? Can we have science-based technology fully at work *and yet* maintain a community in which human meaningfulness is safeguarded and fostered? How to retain the symbolism of inefficiency in the cultures dedicated to the value of efficiency?

(2) *Dialogue with the cosmos*: Traditional cultures are cosmos-oriented, and therefore they are enchantment-cultures. (monologue and symbols).

'In the paddyfield is rice, in the water fish'—this is the saying which is in the heart of the people of Thailand. It expresses their gratitude to nature's abundance. Abundant sunshine, rain and black fertile soil benevolently surround the people. The season circles: hot season, rainy season, cool season, hot season. . . . The regular cyclical beat of nature is the fundamental rhythm of the human cultures in South East Asia. The benevolence of nature is most eloquently symbolised by the regular coming of the life-giving monsoon. Without the monsoon, how can we cultivate our fields? Without the monsoon what is the use of expensive machines called tractors? Is not the monsoon primary and technology secondary? Here is a secret of the traditional cultures being enchantment-cultures. The feeling of the primacy of monsoon arouses an 'enchantment emotion' with the cosmos.

The pulse of cyclical nature is comforting to the people. They live with the image of the cosmos. The cosmos is orderly in contrast to chaos which is disorderly. Up-there, down-here, underneath-here, east and west, north and south . . . there the sun and the moon make their regular movements, there wind blows, water flows and there they find their nation and community. The cosmos gives man his basic orientation as it embraces him. Cosmic orderliness refreshingly visits the people every year with the monsoon it sends. A shipful of chemical fertiliser arriving from Japan is something different from the warm embrace of the living cosmos. Financial help from the World Bank after a series of hectic negotiations—though appreciated indeed! —is somehow external to the image of the cosmos with which and in which people live. The image of the cosmos is the image of life. It is the image of wisdom. To be alive is to be conformed to this image.

In Thailand there are two cosmos-oriented institutions: Buddhism (religion) and monarchy (politics). Thai Buddhism is a monastic Theravada Buddhism. It is a Buddhism of the monks—'religious virtuosi' (Max Weber)—subscribing themselves to the 227 traditional monastic rules to enter into the *summum bonum, the nirvana,* the bliss of absolute tranquillity and detachment. The impression which this virtuoso religion makes upon the people is profound. By supporting these specialists for the *nirvana* the people gain their religiously valuable merits. By making such merits they find their place in the Buddha's cosmos. These virtuosi become the silent centre of the enchanting *nirvanic* cosmos! The king is the supreme head of the religion. He is able to make a vast amount of merits. He stands at the centre of Buddha's cosmos. But this religious centre is at once interpreted as the cosmological centre. He is a cosmic tree and Mt. Meru in person. His authority is located in being at the centre of the monsoon cosmos *and* the Buddha's cosmos. The king is an extremely enchanting personage. He is a living mythological person. He is a symbol of the unity between religious centre and cosmological centre. The beauty of his wife, the queen, is both cosmological and religious.

I find the traditional cultures are cosmos-oriented. The cosmos consists of the three worlds: the upper, the middle and the under. Intricate and active interaction among the three worlds within one cosmos creates the universal framework of the human meaning. This division and interaction is the backbone of the traditional sociology, psychology, language and religion—cultures. This is a great living tradition. There will be no rice in the paddy fields, no fish in the water if these three worlds do not interact. The doctrine and practices of Buddhism are cast into the concrete image of the three worlds. Such division and interaction are enchanting. They arouse in man a warm feeling towards the making of the symbols. The cosmos inspires man to symbolism.

68

The culture of the cosmos-orientation and the personalised space created by the 'strain in one's back and limbs' are consonant. In the cosmos-oriented cultures the symbols of the cosmos prosper. When cosmos is personally touched (in awkward posture) the symbols of cosmos appear. There is a human emotion behind such cosmic symbols. Emotion and symbols come with stories. In the traditional cultures man is not lonely. He is surrounded by the symbolic stories, mainly the stories of self-identification though symbols. Such a world is enchanting. Man is personally engaged in a dialogue with the cosmos in the traditional cultures.

Technology has given man powerful tools to exact efficiently from the cosmos specific benefits for man. Technology is an administrative relationship of man to the cosmos. It does not make a dialogical symbolic relationship between man and the cosmos. Modernity represents an intensified scientific understanding of the cosmos. It intends, without hesitation, to apply *science* to the cosmos. Traditional cultures are built upon human *experience* of the cosmos. Scientifically appropriated cosmos tends to become one of disenchantment. That to which something is *applied* suffers the loss of enchanting dimensions. Enchantment is dialogical. Symbols are the crystallisation of the attentive spiritual dialogue. Today, all of us live in the two worlds simultaneously: the world of traditional enchantment and the world of revolutional disenchantment. None of us have the choice to live outside this tension. It is the time of 'cosmic' change. Personality of man is changing because of the impact of the science-based technology that engages in *application* rather than in *dialogue.*

Technology can give man a great possibility. But technology tends to disenchant the world (eliminate the traditional symbols and the structure of meaning). How can we have technological abundance *and yet* keep an enchanting world? How can we continue *dialogue* in the world of *application?*

(3) *Liturgical style of life:* Traditional cultures are liturgy-oriented cultures. They are acquainted with the holy. (control and the holy).

Traditional cultures have a long experience of the holy. They know how to approach the holy. Shwedagon Pagoda stands on Rangoon's Singuttara Hill. All visitors are required to remove their shoes and socks at the foot of the hill. The barefoot approach to the top of the hill prepares man to come into the presence of the holy. Every step is a liturgical step. The time spent as one walks up the hill is a liturgical time. Sweat you feel on your forehead under the hot afternoon sun of Rangoon is liturgical sweat. The holy must be approached slowly, carefully, humbly and even painfully, that is, liturgically. Traditional cultures abound with holy places: holy temple, holy shrine, holy icons, holy men (monks, *saddhus*), holy day, holy tree, holy cave and so on. In all these places the holy is liturgically approached. It is respected. For the Balinese people the news that the American astronauts rocketed to the moon and walked on the face of the moon is unpleasant since the moon, the holy heavenly deity, must not be approached technologically. (But . . . how can we approach 'barefoot'—without technology —to the distant object beyond space?)

Traditional cultures live with the presence of the holy and have a feeling for it. In this sense they are 'religious cultures'. Technology consists of power and control of power. Uncontrolled power cannot be called technology. The trains which perform a controlled run belong to technology. The trains that run in an uncontrolled manner would not be of technology. Controlling is an essential part of a technological system. Technology is then control-minded. Technology (technological man) has an inner drive to control and systematise. Here is a point of conflict between technology and the holy. The holy contains an element which refuses to be controlled by man. This refusal of the holy is the authority of the holy. This element is observable all the way from a holy tree in an Indonesian village to Rudolf Otto's description of the *numinous*. The holy demands man to approach slowly, carefully, humbly and even painfully. That which is controlled cannot be called the holy. Does not then technology by its very function foster secularisation? When one looks down on the famed Temple of the Sacred Tooth of the Buddha in Kandy, Sri Lanka, from the comfortable window seat of a huge jet plane, the holiness of the Sacred Tooth is seen at least from a completely new perspective, the perspective of technological mobility and altitude. There the holiness is 'viewed from above', at the speed of 600 miles an hour, 'diminished' and thus 'controlled'. Does not one perceive a similar uncanny feeling when one sees from the air the great National Mosque in Djakarta? To be technological means to be mobile. Technological mobility, which is beginning to be one of the fundamental characteristics of our civilisation, suggests the primacy of motion over station. It tends to disdain the stationary concept of the holy. At least it provides a technological perspective to experience the presence of the holy. Technological control and mobility, then, pose a direct challenge to the entire cultural framework of the traditional liturgical lifestyle.

Can the mobile technological man be liturgical? Is not technology forcing us to re-experience the holy? Can the holy be experienced non-liturgically? From the air? Or is the immense ability of technology in its control and mobility abolishing the sense of the holy among us? That cannot be! How can we enjoy the fruits of science-based technology *yet* retain the meaningful experience of the holy?

(II) THEOLOGICAL OBSERVATION

Within the limitation of the given space, I would like to make the following theological comments:

(1) *On 'efficiency and meaning'*
The biblical image of the covenant of God does not suggest an 'efficient technological posture'. He rather assumes an 'inefficient' and 'awkward' posture in his dealing with man. This posture is the posture of love. Love is not 'efficient'. It is not 'streamlined'. It is 'inefficient'. Love and suffering go together as it is expressed in the Chinese language: 'God pain-loves man'. The symbol of the cross is the maximum expression of inefficient *therefore* intense love. There can be no 'streamlined love'. The crucified Christ is the man without any fraction of mobility. Yet he is the symbol of meaning to all forms of meaning including technological one. In him is the paradox that the most inefficient is the most efficient. 'For the foolishness of God is wiser than men, and the weakness of God is stronger than men.' (I Cor. 1:25.) Where do we see the 'symbols of inefficiency' in our community? Where do we see 'the foolishness of God which is wiser than men'? The paradox!

(2) *On 'monologue and symbolism'*
The biblical world is not a lonely world. It presents an enchanting world. The basis for this enchantment is that God is portrayed as a God who engages in dialogue with man. He does so within the context of the creation, the cosmos. Man is surrounded then by the image (*eikon*) of the cosmos and the word (*logos*) of God. How can man be lonely when he is surrounded by the image and the word, the dynamic materials with which he can engage in meaningful dialogue with God and man? In the combination of the image of the cosmos and the word of God man finds his health. 'And she did not know that it was I who gave her the grain, the wine, and the oil, and who lavished upon her silver and gold which they used for Baal.' (Hosea 2:8.) The biblical God complains when man rejects the word and takes (exploits) the cosmos. Technology can do a great deal in increasing 'the grain, the wine and the oil'. But if one who uses the technology does 'not know that it was I. . . .' then man will eventually suffer. Ecological crisis will set in. Man will become lonely. Man will lose a dialogical relationship with the cosmos and the Creator. The world will then become not enchanting! When the image of the cosmos and the word of God are kept in unity we may find a possibility to continue *dialogue* in the world of *application*.

(3) *On 'control and the holy'*
The relationship between science-based technology and human value is ambiguous. It is very possible that technology itself will help us to see that *man* (human dignity) cannot be approached technologically. It can do so by the *irritation* it causes as it 'handles' man technologically. There

71

is something in man which refuses to be systematised and controlled. 'The wind blows where it wills, and you hear the sound of it, but you do not know whence it comes or whither it goes; so it is with everyone who is born of the Spirit'. (John 3: 8.) How to keep this dignity of man alive so that we can retain the meaningful experience of the holy in the technological age? And how is the holiness of the crucified Lord ('controlled Lord') related to this discussion?

4 - Changing ethical values: a Christian assessment

J. S. Keith Ward

The greatest change in ethical values in the modern world is that 'morality' itself is in question. We are not asking, 'What moral claims should we respond to in our age?' but, 'How should we live, if there are no such things as moral values at all?' We no longer ask, 'What ought I to do?' but, 'What am I likely to get most long-term satisfaction from doing?' Those who first divorced morality from religion thought that we could continue to speak of the 'moral ought' in the absence of that unduly anthropomorphic being, God. Their successors see more clearly that we cannot. Without a law-giver, the ontological status of the moral law evaporates. There is no talking of a 'natural law' if there is no creator who has planted that law in our hearts, and implanted a norm of human nature in the world.

Once the absoluteness of the moral demand goes, we are left with either an existentialist, criterionless choice of a way of life: anything goes; or the calculation of what will be most pleasant to us or others. This in the long run is a view which ends in rational egoism at best. I regard this prospect as disastrous; without self-transcending idealism, vision and a commanding ideal, the secular world will fall into moral bankruptcy; and will no doubt be overtaken by the creed which still does have a vision, Marxist-Leninism. There are dangers in moral absolutism too, of course; it can lead to an unsympathetic rule-worship; to intolerance and repression. Much of the modern revulsion against morality can be seen as a reaction to these dangers. The Christian faith itself is fundamentally opposed to moralism, to the view that human fulfilment is to be found by successful moral effort or conformity; if that were true, redemption would be unnecessary. But the Christian faith is also founded on the fact that God is holy; he makes inescapable moral demands upon us, and gives us, in Christ, an absolute moral ideal. In a world in which the very existence of morality is itself in question, the Christian vision of a creator who does make absolute demands on his creatures, and gives them freedom to meet or refuse them, may be the only support of morality. For a Christian, ethical values cannot be reduced

73

to matters of personal preference or long-term satisfaction; they are the absolute demands of a holy creator; there can be no compromise with any philosophy which rates them lower than that. In a sense then, Christianity stands against the world in many of its views of ethics. Yet does that mean it preserves unchanging moral rules, whatever the situation to which they are applied, or the consequences of their application? Of course not. The relation between change and permanence in Christian ethics must be explored further.

It seems that morality is precariously voyaging between Scylla and Charybdis, between a loss of vision and idealism and an intolerant and repressive rule-worship. Within the Christian tradition, these are the extremes of antinomianism and legalism; and both are clearly condemned in the New Testament. I suggest that a purely secular culture will always find itself swinging between these extremes; the pendulum will swing from permissive to repressive and back again; and changes in ethical values will reflect that swing. In addition to the economic, social and technological changes which will affect morality, this more basic change must be clearly seen and exposed. What has the Church to say about it? I believe that there is a tradition of Anglican Moral Theology which offers clear guidance; it is a tradition which might well be called 'Christian personalism'. It is securely based on the doctrine of creation, and on the insight that creation is a personal, imaginative and constantly developing process; that creativeness is one of the essential aspects of personality; and that its development in men is a growth into the fulness of personal life which exists in the Blessed Trinity, and was expressed in Jesus Christ. The basic clue to Christian morality is the nature of God himself, as revealed in Christ; a God who is creative, loving, knowing and possessed of supreme beatitude. In creation, God makes beings who can reflect these properties in themselves, and finally come to share in his being. So the world is purposive, and the purpose is that rational creatures should grow towards fulfilment, in creativity, happiness and love, fulfilling the personal being which God has given.

If we have a firm grasp of this view, and of the goodness of God's creation and the invincible purpose he has for his world, antinomianism is clearly excluded. For morality is founded on a vision, a vision of a fulfilled, happy and creative community, expressing in the world an image of the essential Trinity of God himself. And this vision is absolutely commanding; we are called to it, and promised its fruition. Legalism is also excluded; for the discovery of what makes for creativity, happiness and love in particular cases cannot be laid down in unchanging rules. The guidelines are clear; but, since creativity and insight are an essential part of the moral life, morality cannot be a matter of applying rules automatically. It must be a matter of sensitivity to the particular; of seeking to find what, in this situation, will most clearly express the nature of God in the world, the fulness of humanity that was in Christ. This is not, however, 'situation-ethics', as it is called. For it does not reduce all ethical values to one; certain acts are, as such, wrong if they impair fulness of life; and what that is can be spelled out in general rules enjoining the pursuit of education, leisure, minimum rights and freedom of co-operation. It is more closely allied to the natural law view, that acts which impede the purposes of God in creation are wrong, and acts which sustain and extend them are right. The difference from many traditional expositions of natural law is that the purpose of God is taken to be the creation of fulfilled human lives; it is not simply the biological function of procreation. The natural law is not a wall built around certain parts of nature, saying 'Keep out; do not interfere'; it is a signpost pointing to the ways in which we can constructively adapt nature to extend the Creator's purpose of producing rational sentient life, and of bringing it to its proper fulfilment.

I will briefly now consider three main areas of ethical change, and show how the view I have described applies to them. First, in the area of *personal relations,* economic changes in the position of women, the provision of child-care facilities; technological changes in the security of contraception; and social changes in freedom of travel, work-patterns and greater understanding of the psychology of sexuality, all work to modify the pattern of monogamous marriage, with the man as dominant partner. The Christian criterion here must be that of creativity, happiness and love in personal growth; though the Christian will also have a special regard for the marriage relationship as an expression or imitation of the relation of trust, faithfulness and loyalty between God and his people, between Christ and his Church. Christian marriage is a sacrament in this sense, that it is a visible sign of that utterly faithful love, whatever happens, which God has for his people. And, insofar as such a marriage is rooted in common prayer and devotion to God, it will be an effective means of grace to those who learn, in living together, what it means to be wholly committed in love. Here is the demand and ideal; the Christian can never say that 'anything goes' in personal relations. He will prize most deeply those life-long commitments which show a deep aspect of love not expressible in any other way. On the other hand, the Christian must be more aware of the great variety and complexity of personal relationships; marriage is not the only form of life-long commitment; and many people will not marry, or will marry disastrously, making a commitment which becomes impossible to fulfil, except on a totally superficial, even hypocritical, level. The Church has been legalistic on these issues, and has thus, I believe, betrayed her Lord on the most profound level, in making his words of demanding forgiveness into rules of hypocritical legislation. Jesus forbids divorce, as He forbids lust, anger and deception; but he forgives all our failures, and enables us to start

75

again, relying on grace alone, not complete obedience. The Church, however, has insisted on the letter of obedience with regard to divorce, while herself expressing intolerance and anger in many of her most solemn pronouncements. The ethics of Christian personalism is clear: the values to be pursued are those which reflect the nature of God: trust, loyalty, truthfulness and sympathy. Where rules for human institutions impede such pursuit, they are to be modified or even abandoned. There must be rules; but changes in social life of the sort experienced in recent years require modification of old rules, so as to represent and safeguard more clearly the old values.

Secondly, in the area of *responsibility for life,* there have been technological changes which make abortion safer, prolongation of life easier, and offer the possibility of genetic engineering, in various degrees. Here again, one must keep firmly in mind that it is not survival as such which is most important, but the growth in personal love, action and appreciation. The Christian should, I think, welcome any technological development which enables man to control his own destiny better, and to positively further personal potentialities. He cannot say, 'Nature is in order as it is; we must not interfere'. Rather, he must say, 'We have the responsibility as free creative agents to shape the creation positively in certain ways; we must ensure that those ways lead to that growth in love, peace and joy which Christianity proposes as the goal for all men'. What he cannot say is that men are merely macro-molecular structures, to be treated as objects for experiment, without freedom or moral capability. But two factors have become more apparent in recent times: one is the extent to which man has the capacity for technological change, which does transform the quality of human life, both for better and worse. We can take nature into our own hands, as long as we proceed with caution. The other is a greater awareness of man's continuity with nature. He is not a soul miraculously inserted into a mechanism; he is living flesh, part of a continuous chain of life, albeit with some distinctive features. This realisation should both affect our attitude to animal life, towards which Christians have sometimes been callous; and towards early embryonic or comatose human life, where there is often uncertainty about the beginning and ending of human life. Acceptance of the continuity of all life would suggest that there is no precise line to be drawn anywhere; that grey boundary areas really are grey, and cannot be made more defined by verbal legislation; so that they are significantly different from definite cases, ethically. What this, in turn, suggests is, not that there are no clear moral rules—there are; murder is still wrong—but that there are indefinite areas, where no clear answers can be expected to exist. The right thing to do in such situations, is surely to err on the side of caution, first of all, and then to consider in detail each specific case, in all its complexity.

76

Thirdly, the growth of Marxism and Socialism in many societies has transformed *the political situation* of the world. We have moved, or are moving, out of a patriarchal and hierarchical society, into a world which is much more interdependent, where industry has given rise to new power groups, and where nationalism is both increasingly popular and increasingly impossible—at least in the sense of economic independence. Christian attitudes to politics have varied enormously, from primitive communes to complete abstention from political life and to the justification of the State as the 'left hand' or secular arm of God, curbing immorality and heresy. The most vital issue is to get Christians to clarify their attitude to Marxism, a philosophy which is idealistic in appealing to human freedom and creativity; which does concern itself with the poor and oppressed; and which has helped to make it clear that many personal moral problems can only be solved at a social level. At the same time, however, it regards theism as an obsolete and reactionary superstition; officially regards all moral codes as purely relative and economically conditioned; and is prepared to encourage violence as a means of overthrowing unjust societies, and to encourage tyranny as a means of preventing counter-revolutions. Here again, the Christian faith has positive things to say. The unique value of every individual, symbolised in the parable of the lost sheep, and the doctrine of the sinfulness of mankind both exclude a theory of continual revolution—for one exhorts us to preserve human life, and the other warns us that a perfect society can hardly be expected as long as we are in it. Moreover, freedom must be a central value for Christians, who regard the whole world as a sphere of free decision for or against God. And some moral standards are affirmed to be absolute, especially that of concern for the well-being of all, even one's enemies. It does not appear, then, that Marxist-Leninism is an option for a Christian. But what he must learn from the Marxist is that practical, political concern for the poor which has been obscured by the Church's out-dated form of purely personal philanthropy. A Christian's political philosophy should always be decided by what it might do for the very poorest classes, and the extent to which it would preserve a personal liberty compatible with the greatest possible liberty of others. Especially in the West, the Church in practice supports the rich; Anglican bishops are often to be heard at Public Schools and City dinners. They are less often found campaigning for improvement in the toughest Comprehensives or at Trade Union Congresses. That in itself is a political judgment on the Church. Even in a relatively just society, the Church should in practice still be on the side of the poor, the relatively deprived. Until it actually is, it will have nothing of interest to say in politics, except to support the *status quo*; and arguments by the privileged on their own behalf never carry much weight. In short, I am suggesting that the political stance of Christians should be for an ideal liberal democracy; though circumstances may naturally require many modifications to that ideal. But, even within such a democracy, the Church, as an institution, should be found wherever the underprivileged are found. Marxism succeeds because it is precisely at this point that the Church is seen to fail almost completely.

As I see it, then, some traditional Christian moral teaching must change. But that is not because of conformity to the norms of the secular world. It is because the Church has been legalistic on many issues of personal relationships; it has misperceived the relation between human and non-human creation; it has identified itself with the legitimation of existing social privilege. Social, technological and political changes in fairly recent years have enabled us to realise that this is so, though it became so in the first place for perfectly understandable reasons. But, though particular teaching must change, the Church still has a distinctive ethical teaching, which, at its core, remains unchanged. For the Christian faith is that the world is God's creation; that it will embody his purpose, which we can share in bringing about; that we are challenged by a Divine objective claim upon us, and sustained by a Divine promise that all will not be in vain. What has changed is our particular understanding of this purpose, and how it may be worked out. What cannot change is that there is such a purpose, which cannot fail and which cannot be evaded. The greatest ethical changes of all in our world are those which rest on the denial of these truths; and those changes must be opposed and resisted. The Church must insist that there are moral demands made upon men; and she can best do this by proclaiming the call of Christ to give up all and follow him. But the Church must resist the temptation to be a moral legislator—a thing Jesus never was, or he could have written a book, after all—her job is to proclaim good news, not moral rules for all society. She can take a lead in outlining the sort of human life and society which will most adequately fulfil the Divine purpose, as shown in Christ. But, above all, she must show that if, as I have suggested, true morality depends upon a true view of God and his purpose for creation, then the community which claims to have the self-revelation of God must show in its life the love which is the proper response to that gracious gift. That sets limits beyond which ethical change cannot go; but it also ensures that ethical values must continually change, as they adjust to new insights and perceptions into the nature of God's world, and the development of new possibilities of action within it.

GUIDE TO FURTHER READING:
The Divine Image, Keith Ward (SPCK, 1976).
A Christian Method of Moral Judgment, Philip Wogaman (SCM, 1976).
A Survey of Christian Ethics, LeRoy Long (OUP, 1967).

5 - Christianity in a context of other faiths

C. L. Wickremesinghe

INTRODUCTION

This topic has assumed fresh importance because Christians have begun
to assimilate the significance of radical changes in their midst. Though
it is gathering momentum elsewhere, this process is most evident in Asia.
It is primarily in terms of Asian experience therefore, that this article is
written.

Christian enterprise was undertaken in the context of imperial
expansion within stagnant societies and moribund cultures. It was
accompanied by an urban life-style, a plantation capitalist economy, a
liberal democratic polity, an individualist ethic, and the outlook of a
sophisticated and racially conscious Western civilisation. It led to the
growth of local Churches, the fostering of Christian family traditions
along with the anglicising of manners, the translation of the Bible into
the vernacular languages, the opening of social service institutions for
the sick and the destitute, and the transmission of values, knowledge and
skills required for living in a modernised society. The world was viewed
as a stage prepared by Providence for Church expansion and the spread
of civilising influences, in which the agents of change were mainly
Christians.[1]

The radical changes which have gathered momentum in Asia signify
the reversal of this situation. There has been a resurgence of ancient
societies under the impact of imperial expansion and missionary enterprise.
Indigenous leaders of other religions have replaced Christians as agents
of change in refashioning their societies to revitalise their co-religionists
and to establish a sense of national self-identity. The rural masses with
their educated but unemployed children have been affected by these
changes and have begun to seek ways to emancipate themselves. The
ancient religions have re-emerged in the wake of modernisation to offer
both religious vision and social ideology as a basis for personal fulfilment,
cultural renaissance and social reconstruction. They also make the claim
that they alone have the resources to cure the ills of modern man and to
resolve the conflicts between nations.

This changed situation led to fresh insights emerging among Asian
Christians. Like the exilic prophets they sat astonied, reflected with

penitence and received a wider vision of God's activity in the world and their own role within it.

First, they realised the cultural particularity of the Christianity that had been transmitted to them in the era of Western dominance. Christians had been isolated from their cultural inheritance, which they viewed in fresh perspective.

Secondly, new attitudes emerged among them, regarding the status of other religions in relation to Christianity. They were totally committed to Jesus Christ, but they also appreciated the positive elements in other religions for their own worth; and they saw how these could enrich historical Christianity.

NEW RESPONSES BY CHRISTIANS

The responses made by Christians to the new situation can be described in three stages.

First, there was the process of *adaptation*. This could be likened to the transplantation of a potted plant brought from abroad. Transplantation exposes it to the local environment and begins the process of rooting it in the local soil. Likewise, Christians began to adapt features from local temple architecture in building their churches, elements from local arts and crafts, painting and sculpture to adorn them, styles of music and types of devotional practice associated with the offering of flowers and lights, dance and drums, to enrich the liturgy and other rites.[2] Ashram buildings with their ceremonies and styles of dress, are other examples.

Secondly, there was the process of *naturalisation*. This is akin to the shoot of a traditional local plant being grafted on to the pruned stalk of the transplanted foreign plant. Similarly, Christians began to relate the insights and values of other religions to their Christ-centred vision. This has been done quite often in consultation with persons of other faiths with expertise. Some examples are these: The creative use of words with technical meaning in the traditional culture to convey the meaning of the person and work of Christ in the new version of the Sinhala New Testament; murals in churches which make creative use of traditional and contemporary artistic imagery to communicate the meaning of the crucifixion of Jesus;[3] the use of lections from other Scriptures on particular occasions followed by Christian lections in the liturgy and daily office.

Thirdly, there is the process described as *dialogue*. Though last in point of time, it is the most mature response made by Christians. The kind of adaptation and naturalisation arising from dialogue has greater depth than previous attempts.

Dialogue describes the response of sharing and co-operating with persons of other faiths in a spirit of love, openness, and the desire for mutual enrichment. A person's faith is engaged by the faith of others. This safeguards against both fanaticism and also indifference to basic convictions; it also enables persons and groups to discover their specific identity in a community with a plurality of religions.[4]

At the intellectual level, dialogue enables a participant to view his basic convictions through the thought-forms of other religionists, reconceive them with fresh insight and communicate them to others with better understanding.[5] However, there are those who ask whether assimilating insights from other religions to enrich the apprehension of Truth based on one's own religion is sufficient. They desire also the discussion of the Truth and validity of each other's religions as part of the dialogue.[6]

At the experimental level, participants learn to incorporate the spiritual experiences and vision of other religionists into their own religious vision and experience. The creative incorporation of Yoga and Zen into Christian contemplative experience is an obvious example.[7]

At the level of working together to achieve justice, peace and development in society on the basis of common human values, more progress has been made. In Sri Lanka, there has been fruitful collaboration in producing suitable syllabuses for religious instruction. In the Sarvodaya movement, there is acceptance of common values, shared work and joint meditation over a wide range of rural development ventures. Churches have also released finance and personnel to inter-religious groups managing joint ventures.

A further development of such collaboration is found in inter-religious groups working for the liberation of the oppressed. They manifest a more secularised and interiorised spirituality, directed to social struggle. Liberation ideology unites them, while they also acknowledge religion as an important dimension in their common life. Their devotional acts symbolise their common values and shared activities as seen in a transcendental perspective. In one such commune, there is a para-liturgy in which acts of thanksgiving, confession and commitment are shared in the context of chanted readings from various Scriptures and radical writings. It takes place after shared labour or discussion, and is followed by a symbolic partaking of ordinary food and drink.[8]

Dialogue, whether intellectual, experiential or social activist, is limited at present to small groups, as only a minority in Asian societies share in this concern for pro-existence. In practice also, collaboration is effective in a society only where there is prior acceptance of one's respective majority and minority status among the participants. However, in the midst of the tensions and potential divisions of pluralist societies, they bear witness to a more excellent way.

Dialogue must be understood in its proper perspective; it need not undermine the communication of the full gospel message. In the past, the discerning Emperor Dharmasoka of India prompted what was best in other faiths, and encouraged mutual understanding and respect among diverse religionists.[9] He also combined this with missionary endeavours on behalf of Buddhism all over Asia. In the present, dialogue has yielded greater reciprocity and enrichment than was possible then. To the discerning Christian, it is a decisive way of receiving and communicating divine revelation at its appropriate levels.

BASIC PERSPECTIVES

There is a basic attitude underlying the dialogic process as understood by Christians. It represents a tradition of thought within the historical Church from Iraeneus,[10] through Cardinal de Lugo to Baron von Hügel.[11] But contemporary Asian experience has given it new directions.

It is an attitude of Christ-centred reciprocity towards other religions and their adherents. It yields insights which guide Christians in appreciating and assessing the value and efficiency of other faiths, within God's creating, saving and transfiguring purpose. Initial insights reflect experience of the Christian verities arising from initial dialogue both with the experience of other religionists and also with the experience testified to authoritatively in Scripture. They provide an 'interpretive model' which has to be tested further in the face of new insights emerging from the ongoing dialogue. Interpretation and the evidence of experience have to be continuously correlated.[12]

Present insights can be summarised in this way. God's prevenient love operates everywhere, at all times, in each person and group, but uniquely in biblical history centred in Jesus Christ. He is unique not merely because in the Nazarene, God is expressed from within a human nature realised to moral perfection, but also because the Son of God was embodied in Him to the fullest extent possible to the receptive capacity of human nature. His work is unique not only because it is fully effective to secure salvation for us personally, but also because God has set Him in the world and among men, as the inescapable saving Presence before whom all persons and situations are accountable. The Scriptures which testify to Him are unique because they record the normative, though not sole, interpretation of God's dealings with mankind. The Church which derives from Him is unique because it is the appointed, though not sole, sphere which expresses and makes effectual the kingdom of God.

In other words, the particular salvation history centred in Jesus Christ provides the unique model. The other salvation histories are analogues, but with their own range of effectiveness and antonomous contribution to the salvation history of mankind. Their saviours and saints are worthy of recognition and honour; their Scriptures and their community life have insights, values and spiritual authenticity available for enriching the thought and life of the visible Church. Though not the appointed sacrament, other religions are effective sacramentals, made available in the providence of God.

For example, in Christianity there is a covenant relationship between God and His people mediated through Jesus Christ. In other world religions there is a Transphenomenal Beyond (Yahweh, Allah, Brahma, Nirvana), and the manward relationship (love of neighbour, brotherhood, ahimsa, metta) mediated through saviours; and these are analogical ways of expressing this covenant relationship. In Christianity, the covenant people are a community of disciples who share in the experience of the covenant relationship, and who celebrate events and persons representing various aspects of it, through liturgy and calendar. Likewise, other religionists are communities of adherents who share in their experience of this dual relationship, and who give socio-cultural embodiment to it, through celebration of its various aspects (Passover, Ramazan, Maha Sivarthi, Wesak). In Christianity, the covenant people are conscious of a covenant history initiated by God and leading to a goal in which they and their Scriptures have a decisive role to play. In like fashion, communities of other religionists have in varying degree, an analogous kind of consciousness (Kingdom of God/Torah/Jewry; Kingdom of God/Koran/Islam; Brahman-Atman/Sruti-Smriti/'Sampradaya'; Nirvana/Tripitaka/Sangha).[13]

In what ways are Christians to testify to the ultimacy of Christ while appreciating other religions? Should a Christian offer flowers before the Buddha statue if occasion requires—is it an act of veneration or an act of worship? Should Christians managing institutions catering to all religionists permit them separate places of worship in the premises for their use, or should they permit only acts of worship as occasion requires? Does the former policy imitate the uniqueness of Jesus in His self-effacing humility for the good of others, or reveal an indifference to the basic Christian affirmation that Jesus alone is worthy of worship? Does the latter policy testify to this affirmation or reveal a crude and petty way of asserting His uniqueness?

Furthermore, what are the specific tasks of the Church in the context of dialogue? Other religions have their relative autonomy; in the providence of God they are not meant to be absorbed simply into the visible Church. At the end-time, they will bring their special gifts into the kingdom of God. On the other hand, the Church is required to draw others into its unifying membership from all religio-cultures, as a foretaste of and a testimony before all nations, to the kingdom of God.[14] What then is the mission of the Church?

First, it commits Christians to live alongside religionists, and to share life with them both in their search for salvation, and in their resistance to God seeking to save them. This is the way of Jesus.

Secondly, it obliges Christians to commend the values and insights of

83

the kingdom of God revealed in Jesus Christ, for other religions to absorb and manifest. For example, Christians have been able to transmit in Asia commitment to a historical purpose, social service and community reconstruction to religions pre-occupied with an other-worldly orientation, for incorporation into their total vision of life.

Thirdly, it involves helping persons of other faiths to accept Christlike values as Zacchaeus did. These values stem from Jesus but those who absorb them can remain in their own faith with a higher quality of life. It is a form of conversion. People are attracted to and altered by a challenging life-style, as many testimonies have indicated.

Lastly, there is the obligation to evangelistic witness. It makes a Christian present to others the claims of Jesus as Him alone who can save us from ourselves and lead us in love to the Father and to our fellow human beings. It may be testimony to the hidden meanings of a particular religious inheritance, as Paul did with the Athenians; or evoking deep within the personal longing for deliverance, as Jesus did with the woman of Samaria. It is essential evangelism in the context of dialogue with persons in their situations.

Christ-centred reciprocity with other religionists means relating to them as persons at different levels. In deciding how particular aspects of the gospel message are to be affirmed or commended in particular situations, Christians will differ in emphasis. The modernist and the fundamentalist, the proclaimer and the evoker of hidden depths are ever with us and perhaps within us. In any particular situation, the mind of Christ who indwells us, remains incognito in other religionists and interprets Scripture, will have to be discerned in the response of personal faith.[15]

SCRIPTURAL TESTIMONY AND CONTEMPORARY TESTIMONY

During the period of Western missionary enterprise, and even now, many Christians have understood the testimony of Scripture regarding the relationship of Christianity to other religions in this way: other nations and their religious cultures or histories serve as a preparatory background for the establishment of the kingdom of Christ through the expansion of His Church.[16] Adherents of other religions were reckoned as those living under the wrath of God and as stiflers of the truth they perceived, under the influence of the Prince of Darkness.[17] The duty of the Christian was to preach the gospel message of salvation to them all so as to seek their conversion to Christ as their Saviour and Lord.[18]

But there are other strands of scriptural testimony whose weight needs to be recognised. Other nations with their religious cultures are viewed as guided by God, and in the end they share in the inheritance of His kingdom without the intervention of Israel or the Christian church.[19] Adherents of other religions are seen as illumined by God who indwells

84

them within their religious commitment.[20] There are also those who finally find a share in His kingdom even though not members of the visible church.[21]

Jesus reveals diverse ways of ministering to others, especially in the synoptic gospels. Sometimes the emphasis is on the values or super-normal powers of the kingdom; sometimes it is on Himself. He heals and forgives a paralytic without indicating who He was, or asking him to become a disciple; as a Rabbi, He changed radically the values of Zacchaeus and left him in his situation; He exorcises the Gerasene demoniac as the 'Son of the Most High God' and asks him to witness among his own people to this God and His mercy; He reveals Himself as the 'Son of Man' to the man born blind who worshipped Him, but does not ask him to become a disciple; yet He calls others to join His company of disciples and trains them to recognise who He is. He remains incognito or reveals Himself with a sensitive appreciation of the occasion. From this it can be seen that scriptural testimony has other strands which provide a proper basis for the new attitudes emerging among Asian Christians. We must appreciate the diversity of emphasis in scriptural testimony for its own worth.

Asian Christians accept scriptural testimony as authoritative because of its divine inspiration. This is attested in the Scriptures, confirmed in the variegated tradition of the Church, and authenticated in their own experience. But this testimony must be seen in its proper perspective, especially in regard to the relation of Christianity to other religions.

The testimony in the New Testament records the realised experience of Christians in that era, arising from their many-sided engagement with surrounding cultures, under the guidance of the Spirit. For example, the Church realised the cultural partiality of some of its Jewish practices, such as circumcision, when it spread among the Gentiles. These were no longer imposed on them after the Council of Jerusalem. The term 'Messiah' with its Jewish associations was replaced by the term *'Logos'* borrowed from Greek thought, and by the word *'Christos'* associated with cult titles and saviours of the Graeco-Roman world.[22] The early Christians received fresh perspectives as they encountered other religions, which enriched their understanding of their own faith and helped them to present the gospel message more effectively.

The new perspectives emerging among Asian Christians record their realised experience as they have been engaged with other religions, seeking the guidance of the Spirit. Contemporary testimony is revealed in their specific insights. This testimony has to be scrutinised in relation to scriptural testimony, being the testimony of those placed uniquely in regard to the events concerning Jesus Christ. Such testing needs to take place in each era as the church journeys to the end awaiting the full manifestation of the kingdom of Christ. The authority of scriptural testimony is exercised through the guidance it provides in the face of new developments, in the ongoing history of the Church.

In other words, a dialogue takes place between contemporary testimony and scriptural testimony, until the Spirit provides a discernment for faith in the present situation.[23] When contemporary testimony is discerned as the development or re-discovery of scriptural insight for new contests, it is affirmed as arising from the inspiration of the Spirit[24]; as a result, what is culturally conditioned in scriptural testimony is also recognised. Where contemporary testimony is discerned as clearly undermining scriptural insights, it is not affirmed as inspired by the Spirit and its cultural conditioning is thereby discerned. At the present time for example, this dialogue is taking place with regard to such issues as the ordination of women, the relation of Christianity to other religions, the interpretation of the person and work of Jesus Christ in Asiatic cultures, in secularised societies, and in the face of liberation movements.[25] Recognised discernments of the Spirit have yet to be received in faith by the universal Church.

Such discernment is facilitated when dialogue takes place between particular regions and branches of the universal church. It is in such mutual openness that the universal elements or permanent insights belonging to Christianity will be discerned. It is church leaders who must make this possible as in the early Church.[26]

CONCLUSION

While the universal Church searches for the 'tradition' that should be handed down to the next era, the mission of the regional churches must continue. Local churches have their relative significance and autonomy.[27] Their task is to lay hold in obedient faith on those insights that will help renew the Church, and also communicate the gospel with effectiveness to others in their contemporary setting. Jesus Christ to whom we give our final allegiance, comes to us not only through Scripture and tradition, but also as the Living One who is saving and renewing life in our midst. It is as we are centred on Him with fresh vision, that we shall discover our unity in diversity.

REFERENCES :
[1] This summary makes no reflection on heroic missionary endeavour.
[2] Some ventures in the Diocese of Kurunegala.
[3] *Christian Art in Asia,* Masao Takenaka (Kyoto, 1975).
[4] *The Understanding and Goal of Dialogue, in Dialogue,* Lynn de Silva (New Series), Vol. IV, Nos.: 1-2; Jan.-Aug. 1977, pp. 3-8.
[5] *Why Believe in God,* Lynn de Silva (Colombo, 1967).
The Problem of the Self in Buddhism and Christianity, Lynn de Silva (Colombo, 1975).
[6] *Buddhist Critique of the Christian Concept of God,* Dr. G. Dharmasiri (Colombo, 1974), pp. ix-xi.

[7] *Prayer,* Abhishitkananda (Delhi, 1967); *Saccidananda,* Abhishitkananda (Delhi, 1974).

[8] *New World Liturgy,* Devasarana Collective Farm (Ibbagamuva, 1976).

[9] Rock Edict 12.

[10] *Adversus omnes Haereses,* Iraeneus, Book 3, Ch. 11, 8; and Book 4, Ch. 28, 2.

[11] *The Christian Attitude to Other Religions,* E. C. Dewick (Cambridge, 1953), pp. 120-125.

[12] *Science and Secularity,* Ian G. Barbour (New York, 1970), pp. 11-32.

[13] *The Church, the Kingdom and the Other Religions, in Dialogue,* Aloysius Pieris S.J., Old Series, No. 22, October 1970, pp. 3-7.

N.B. Maoism is a secular faith to be faced in the Asian context. It can also be likened, as can the religious faith, to an 'analogue'; i.e. 'Phenomenal Beyond' = universal love for humanity; 'manward relationship' = love and service for the people in the present order; 'celebrations' of events like the Long March or Chinese Revolution; the 'End' = classless society; 'Scriptures' = Marxist-Leninist-Mao's Thought/Writings; 'covenant people' = Communist Party/Cadres.

[14] Matthew 24 : 14; Galatians 3 : 27-28; with I Corinthians 10 : 32.

[15] *The Acknowledged Christ of the Indian Renaissance,* M. M. Thomas (Madras, 1970), pp. 246-288; Acts 16 : 6-10.

[16] Acts 17 : 22-30; Matthew 28 : 19-20.

[17] Romans 1 : 18; II Corinthians 4 : 4; Ephesians 2 : 2; II Timothy 2 : 26; John 3 : 19-20.

[18] Mark 16 : 15-16; I Corinthians 9 : 16; Romans 10 : 1.

[19] Amos 9 : 7; Isaiah 19 : 19-25; Revelation 21 : 22-26.

[20] Mark 12 : 28-34; Matthew 8 : 5-10; John 1 : 47-51; Acts 10 : 30-35; Acts 18 : 24-28; John 3 : 21.

[21] Luke 13 : 29; Romans 2 : 13-16.

[22] *Christianity in World Perspective,* Kenneth Cragg (London, 1969), pp. 55-62.

[23] *Revolutionary Theology Comes of Age,* J. M. Bonino (London, 1975), pp. 96-104.

[24] John 16 : 12-14.

[25] *Jesus the Buddha,* Kosuke Koyama (Cyclostyled manuscript); *Jesus Christ and Human Liberation,* Tissa Balasuriya O.M.I. (Colombo, 1976); *The Myth of God Incarnate,* Ed.: John Hick (London: SCM Press, 1977).

[26] *The Birth of the New Testament,* C. F. D. Moule (London, 1966), pp. 174-177.

[27] Acts 11 : 19-30.

6 - Nationalism and internationalism

Hugh W. Montefiore

Today there is 'only one earth'. We are aware, as never before, that we are all world citizens of 'space-ship earth'. Modern technology, and the complexities of world trade, make the nations of the world more and more interdependent. Increasing specialisation makes each country less and less self-sufficient. Nuclear proliferation raises the question whether the species *homo sapiens* could survive another world war. Escalating use of non-renewable resources brings all countries closer to the threshold of world shortages. Pollution does not recognise national boundaries. The United Nations Organisation, in a succession of world conferences, has focused attention on global issues such as the environment, food, water supplies, man's habitat, human rights, the status of women, a new economic order. Primary producing countries can form a more united front against industrialised nations. As wealthy countries get richer (and poor countries comparatively poorer), the mass media enable people to hear and see what is happening in distant parts of the world, sometimes as these things actually happen. There never was a time when the peoples of the world were more in need of the spirit and the practice of internationalism in the name of peace and justice, and for the relief of poverty, distress and starvation.

What, however, is actually happening? Between 1900 and 1970, 86 new nations have come into being. 'Twenty years after the founding of the League of Nations, the ferociously developed nationalisms of Europe and Asia produced the most destructive war in history. Twenty-five years after the foundation of the United Nations, the world is divided by national frontiers as never before'.[1] And this produces a perilous situation. 'A dangerous gap remains. In this day of advanced communication, when the nations of the world are closer together than ever before, virtually every important influence in the lives of men is international. Yet man's loyalty remains with the national state. The more closely people become interdependent, the more they react by turning to their national traditions'.[2]

Nationalism has been variously described. According to C. M. Woodhouse[3] 'Nationalism was invented in Europe less than two hundred years ago, and has since spread over the world. . . . Originally and

88

essentially it is the doctrine that mankind is naturally divided into nations and that these constitute natural units of political sovereignty. . . . Nature has decreed, so it is believed, that nations and states should be co-terminous'. A nation is usually thought of as an ethnic group, normally distinguished by language, culture and religion. But these distinctions do not always hold. The United States of America, to a great extent, embraces her citizens within 'the American way of life', but they consist of emigrants from many different cultures, and adhere to many and varying faiths. In South Africa, in one state there are two separate nations and the white minority consists of two main ethnic groups. The USSR and the People's Republic of China are empires comprising peoples of many cultures and languages. As for the United Kingdom, there are, as well as English, Irish, Scots and Welsh, immigrant Jews, West Indians and Pakistanis, to name but a few. In all lands, people may feel a strong love of their country, despite their ethnic origins. Balkanisation has not been without attendant problems, for where races are intermixed, no country however small is likely to be without minorities. While 'small is beautiful', moderate is usually more manageable, and the small countries, which result from Balkanisation, are often not large enough to make their way in the twentieth century world.

'No man is an island'. People find their identity not only in themselves, but in the larger units to which they belong. Family, kinship, neighbourhood, county, region, country . . . each forms its legitimate ties and loyalties. Within the larger groups, there are differences of language, literature, art, music and style of life.[4] Each nation has its distinctive flavour—or used to have before twentieth century technological society threatened to dissolve all into a grey modern way of life. If such dissolution is what internationalism means, then surely we would all condemn it.

But of course it does not. Internationalism implies a spirit of co-operation between nations. It involves the acceptance by nations of a rule of law which transcends each State. It requires the acceptance by each country that the good of the world as a whole has precedence over national self-regard. It presupposes a form of utilitarianism—the greatest good of the greatest number, measured not in terms of national satisfaction, but of global happiness. Internationalism thus requires co-operation among the nations for the relief of poverty and distress, for the planning of the use of future resources, for greater justice, equity and for the avoidance of future conflict. Internationalism may be structural, in some form of world federalism. But it may equally well be the result of co-operation, consultation and self-restraint among sovereign States.

If internationalism be prerequisite for the solution of the world's problems from the twentieth century onwards, the question arises: In what way or ways may nationalism frustrate the spirit of international co-operation and in what ways may it prosper it? Nationalism, defined as a spirit of loyalty and commitment to one's nation, has had many defendants. There were those like Hegel who so subordinated the individual to the State that he could say: 'All the worth that the human soul possesses, he possesses through the State'. But liberal thinkers, too, could approve of nationalism. Mazzini[5] wrote: 'Each nationality has its special mission of humanity. The mission constitutes a nationality. Nationality is sacred'.

Others have been more discriminating. They have seen limited good in nationalism. 'It is the sword and the shield of those who are achieving independence', wrote R. Emerson,[6] 'from being "natives", they rise to the honourable title of nationals. Through national self-assertion they achieve the spiritual satisfaction of demonstrating that they can make their own the forms on which the superior imperial powers pride themselves'. Snyder[7] echoes the same thought when he writes: 'Because nationalism is a sentiment, it has psychological overtones. . . . For people who have known the despair of frustration, nationalism provides a feeling of compensation. . . . The inferiority complex began to dissolve in the solvent of a new national consciousness'.

Baroness Jackson (published under her commoner's name, Barbara Ward) takes a wider view.[8] 'An astonishing release of energy, determination and mental vigour was needed to transform the whole of the economic system of mankind from static farming to our own modern dynamic technological system. This could not have been mobilised without this enormously potent propulsion of nationalism'. She goes on to add: 'Without the new sense of a *national* community, we might not have achieved the successful breakthrough towards the popular vote, towards the admission of every citizen to equal political rights'.

The good that lies in nationalism lies at a deeper level than this. Just as an individual must have sufficient self-esteem if he is to engage in fruitful personal relationships with others, if he is to fulfil his potential and release to the full his inherent dynamic powers, so a corporate entity such as a nation must have sufficient self-esteem if it is to play its proper part in world affairs. A nation must believe in itself, must believe in its own worth and values and goals, must believe that these are worthwhile contributing to the common good. It must treasure its culture and its way of life, it must be united by ties of loyalty and affection to the symbols of its past, it must not only cherish its own spiritual inheritance but also the beauties and loveliness of its physical inheritance. A country that does not hold the affection and loyalty of its citizens will have little to contribute to the well-being of the world. Patriotism, in the genuine sense of self-love, is as fundamental a good for the well-being of a nation as is self-esteem for the well-being of an individual.

90

We hardly need to be reminded that self-esteem in the individual can become self-assertion. The egotist accepts no restraint on his own satisfaction, he accepts no moral principle other than self-interest, and, rather than the enjoyment of genuine personal relationships with others, he prefers to dominate and to disparage. So too with nations. 'A stark contrast exists between the ever-present egotism of the nation as a whole, and the self-sacrifice which it demands of the individuals within it'.[9] Reinhold Niebuhr has pointed out that while patriotism may be a high form of altruism compared with most parochial loyalties, from a different point of view it can become another form of selfishness, and he notes that it has been used as a device for delegating the vices of individuals to larger and larger communities. In any case, nationalism in itself is not enough. As Lady Jackson[10] remarks: 'It gives no answer to the problems of human solidarity. It fails in all three areas of human need—kinship, cohesion and economic function'. She goes on to point out that nationalism can claim exclusive loyalty and authority. 'It has not yet shown that it can be the active principle of a new social order wide enough in political institutions, human loyalties and economic co-ordination to match a world made scientifically and technologically one'[11].

It is the appalling potentialities of nationalism for evil that have led some to condemn it roundly. Communists we would expect to vilify it, for in their view the revolution of the proletariat should lead to the appearance of a classless society which is genuinely international—not that there are many signs of its appearance. H. Laski called it 'a disease of the body politic'[12]. Bertrand Russell, however, condemned it for other reasons. 'Nationalism in our day is the chief enemy to the extension of social cohesion beyond national boundaries'[13].

The psychologist E. Fromm has described nationalism as 'our incest, idolatry, insanity'. He goes on to explain: 'The incestuous relationship not only poisons the relationship of the individual to the stranger but to the members of his own clan and to himself. The person who has not forced himself from the ties of blood and soil is not yet fully born as a human being: he does not experience himself nor his fellow men in their—and his own—human reality'[14]. This is too extreme. Man does not have to deny his ties to blood and soil in order to promote an international order any more than he has to abandon self-love to be free to love others. Whatever being born (or reborn) as a human being may mean, man must not turn his back on the natural world: the sovereign nation-state remains the basic politico-economic and military unit of world society. Supranationalism is still a dream.

Christians, in thinking through this pressing matter, will naturally wish to consider not only the attitudes which have been prevalent in the Church, but also those portrayed in the Bible. So far as the Scriptures are concerned, a distinction must be made between the two Testaments. The earlier books of the Old Testament naturally portray the attitudes of the ages in which they were composed. At a time when people did not think of themselves as individuals, but members of a racial group, it is hardly surprising to find them fiercely nationalistic. After all, it was not until the days of Ezekiel that the principle of individual responsibility was finally upheld. The nation was the object of God's call. He made a covenant with Israel and in this special relationship the Promised Land played a vital part. Israel was one nation among many: its uniqueness lay in God's choice of Israel to be his chosen people, a vocation not to power and privilege but to costly service and indeed to suffering, as events have proved.

Within this inheritance, Jesus was born. His ministry was to Jews; although prepared to minister to non-Jews, he did not go out of his way to do so. He appointed twelve apostles, to correspond to the tribes of Israel. Yet Jesus, patriot as he was, did not adopt an uncritically nationalist stance. Although he spoke of the End in terms of 'judging the twelve tribes of Israel', he declared that many would come from the East and the West, and the sons of the Kingdom would be cast out. He wept over Jerusalem, foreseeing the coming tragedy of revolt. Including pro-Roman tax-collectors and a fanatically nationalist Zealot among his followers, he refused to sanction violence against Rome and would not deny its right to levy taxes. His teaching, while addressed to Jews, burst through national barriers. Man must be as generous as God: he must love his neighbour as himself, and his neighbour is anyone who confronts him in need, even if it be his enemy. Jesus seems even to have preferred not to use of himself the title Messiah, probably because in popular parlance it had a narrowly nationalistic meaning. Pilate condemned him to death for fear of a charge of disloyalty to Caesar, but the real cause was that people felt too threatened by the radical thrust of his message.

When, after his death and resurrection the Spirit was later poured out on men, the Christian Gospel could not be contained within the Jewish race. Although at first links were close with the Mother Church at Jerusalem, after the city fell in AD 70, the Christian Churches became a truly international fellowship.

Centuries later, when Constantine embraced the faith, the Church entered into a new partnership with the State which made it harder to be independent. Later still, the Dark Ages descended, but in the mediaeval papacy and Holy Roman Empire there emerged some concept of Christendom, imperfect indeed but pointing towards a society transcending national loyalties. Meanwhile the Eastern Church seceded and the resultant Orthodox Churches became in each centre a focus of national sentiment. At the Reformation, the principle *cujus regio, ejus religio* prevailed, so that a national Church came under the protection of its 'Godly Prince'. Finally, in the last century, the Church spread to every part of the globe and in this sense is truly international; and this at a time when nationalism grows stronger, and the world is likely to collapse unless there appears an international spirit of genuine co-operation.

Such is our situation today. God has created all men in his image. God has placed us in families, neighbourhoods, regions and nations. Good in themselves, they can become occasions of sin, if wrongly regarded. All selfishness is sin, whether individual or corporate. Nations as much as individuals are called to love their neighbours as themselves. And this they do not.

What can the Church do to foster a right attitude to the nation? It has not always been successful. Lord Hugh Cecil, trying in vain to find a home for 50,000 Assyrian Christians from Iraq, once exclaimed: 'Christianity is a far feebler motive than nationalism; and in particular, there is lacking among Christians, in vivid contrast to their professed theological beliefs, a sense of corporate binding them to other Christians.'[15]

Theologically speaking, in Christ there is neither Jew nor Greek; differences of race, as of class and sex, are transcended within our unity in Christ. This means that a Church must never be identified with a nation, or it betrays its nature. (Not for nothing did the Confessing Church separate itself from the State Church in Germany under National Socialism). Since Anglican Churches are usually national bodies, it is particularly important that they emphasise their world-wide ecumenicity, and their membership of the Anglican Communion. Care must be taken in national celebrations that no hint is given of a nationalist cultus or idolatrous worship. National Churches have the duty of keeping a nation's conscience. However costly it may be (and there have been martyrs), they must speak out against abuse of nationalism. But condemnation is not enough. They must foster a real sense of international co-operation. They must encourage national self-restraint and international peace and co-operation. Their influence is sometimes greater than they know.

Encouragement is not only given by example and counsel. International co-operation is always more likely to be practised when it is seen as a policy of enlightened self-interest. If the nations are to survive, let alone flourish, in a world which is already one in terms of technology and information, then internationalism is essential. To this message of commonsense, religion adds a categorical imperative. The unity of God demands the unity of his world and the Christian faith transcends even this with its ultimate vision of all men spiritually united in Christ.

This vision of the future should inspire us to refashion the present, so that mankind expresses its true unity beyond the confines of separate sovereign states.

REFERENCES:
1 *Twentieth Century Nationalism*, G. St. J. Barclay (London, 1971), p. 197.
2 *The New Nationalism*, L. L. Snyder (Cornell University Press, 1968), p. 369.
3 *The New Concert of Nations* (London, 1964), p. 20.
4 *Nationalism*, cf. F. Catherwood, The Christian Graduate (Dec. 1973), p. 98.
5 *Life and Writings of J. Mazzini* (London, 1891), iii, 33.
6 *From Empire to Nation* (Harvard U.P., 1960), p. 380.
7 L. L. Snyder, *Op. cit.,* p. 41.
8 *Nationalism and Ideology*, Barbara Ward (London, Hamish Hamilton, 1967), p.54f.
9 R. Emerson, *Op. cit.,* p. 384.
10 Barbara Ward, *Op. cit.,* p. 55.
11 Barbara Ward, *Op. cit.,* p. 124.
12 *Nature and Future of Civilisation* (London, 1932), p. 42.
13 *New Hopes for a Changing World* (London, 1951), p. 69.
14 *The Sane Society* (New York, 1955), p. 58.
15 *Nationalism*, R. Inst. Internat. Affairs (O.U.P., 1939), p. 308.

SECTION III

Concerning the Church Context

The essays in this Section are about the Church at large, not the Anglican Communion only.

For a treatment of *'Authority in the Church'* readers are referred to the Agreed Statement with that title, issued in 1976 by the Anglican-Roman Catholic International Commission.

1 - Directions in Church growth

Tom Tuma

NUMERICAL GROWTH

Church growth, to most people means the winning of converts; the planting of more and more churches. This understanding makes it possible for one to determine statistically which Churches are growing and which ones are not growing. However, many people are critical of the practice of determining church growth only on the basis of statistics. This method, the critics claim, is rather narrow. Other critics are suspicious of the use of numbers or figures in determining church growth because, in their view, numbers mean nothing; they further argue that the main concern of the Church should be, to be obedient, proclaim the gospel and bear witness regardless of the results, which are in God's hands. However, for one to get some idea of what is happening in the Church, it is inevitable that one has to use some statistics. Statistics become even more reliable and meaningful when they are used in the context of a concrete background, as in this article, in which they are used mainly in relation to historical events and developments. In this sense statistics are reliable, and acting as a thermometer, they enable us to identify both the 'hot' and 'cold' areas in the Church(es). Considerable use has been made of statistics under preparation by the Rev. Dr. David Barrett, editor of *The World Christian Handbook,* who has kindly made them available.

Figures for membership reveal four major trends in the Anglican Communion. First, membership is falling in several of its 25 autonomous Churches.[1] This numerical decline is being experienced in Australia, England, Ireland, Scotland, United States of America and Wales. It will be recognised that these churches are the so-called 'Older Churches' from the Western World which have long been actively involved in the evangelisation of non-Christian peoples, particularly in Africa and Asia. Secondly, some of the Newer Churches (established in the so-called Third World) have experienced little growth since 1965. The percentage of professing Anglicans has remained virtually unchanged in the years from 1968 to 1978 in China (Hong Kong), Brazil, Japan, and South America. In these countries the Church is small, static, and probably numerically insignificant.

Thirdly, and in marked contrast, the rest of the Newer Churches are gaining converts. There is continuing rapid growth today in Central Africa, Kenya, Papua/New Guinea, Sudan, Tanzania and Uganda.

Fourthly, a majority of the people baptised into the Anglican Communion annually are infants; baptised because their parents are Christians. It is interesting to note that only the churches in Kenya and Uganda baptised more adults than infants in 1977. How do we explain these developments?

THE OLDER CHURCHES

Most church leaders in the Older Churches will readily admit that they are losing members through death, emigration and even defection, but they are quick to add that losing church members is a normal process which should not excite undue concern. Church leaders take this position mainly because of two reasons.

First, every year the Older Churches accept a substantial number of infants into the Church. Although church leaders are keen to keep count of those coming thus into the Church, they rarely make serious efforts to keep an accurate record of people lost particularly through emigration and defection to other confessions. In other words many of the Older Churches do not know how many of their members are lost every year. They remain under the illusion that all is well when in fact, the number of their flock is steadily declining. Secondly, some of these declining churches claim that the loss of some of their members is a blessing in disguise because it serves to separate the tares from the wheat. If this is true, it may well help to explain why the Charismatic Movement has gained momentum in Europe and America in the recent past.

It is also possible that what the Older Churches are experiencing is a normal development; one of the characteristics of Christian expansion, advances followed by recessions.[2] It seems, however, that the main reason for the loss of members in the Older Churches is the failure of those churches to respond effectively to a situation in which secularization is predominant and secularism is rapidly gaining ground. The Older Churches in Europe and America have reacted by stressing the need to perfect their own life; whether that is the best weapon against a vigorous process of secularization remains debatable. It should be remarked here that this tendency to stress caring for what is available makes it that much harder for the Church to carry out the great commission of Christ, to make disciples of all nations.

THE NEWER CHURCHES

In areas in which they are in competition with other major religions, the Newer Churches have remained static, but considerable growth has been experienced in other areas notably in Africa. In the early 1950s, just before the wave of political independence swept across Africa, there was a general climate of great anticipation, as nobody knew how or even whether the Anglican Churches, which had been so closely identified with colonialism, would survive in the new and independent Africa. These fears and anxieties have turned out to be unjustified, because since Independence, as already claimed, the Anglican Churches have been growing rapidly. This is because, first, the process of secularization has not yet become predominant in the Third World countries. Secondly, the rapid population growth in these countries has provided a major stimulus to Church growth. Thirdly, there is, in Africa, a large non-Christian population, still following African traditional religion, which can be converted to Christianity. Fourthly, and more important, is that the post-independence situation in Africa has encouraged church growth, not only among the Anglican Churches but among all other Christian Churches on the continent, including the so-called Independent Churches. By and large, post-independence Africa has been mainly characterised by rapid changes, growing political instability and repression, lawlessness and human suffering. In this fluid and insecure situation, many people in Africa (and in South America where a similar situation prevails) have found both comfort and security in the Church. In fact, periods of civil strife and persecution have been followed by rapid church growth. This has been particularly the case in Nigeria, the Sudan and Uganda; people coming forward to satisfy their spiritual quest and demonstrate their solidarity with the suffering people or Church.

Although the situation has been so conducive to conversion and church growth, the Newer Churches do not seem to have used the available opportunities in the interests of discipling the nations. This is so because these Churches have not been equipped to undertake such a task. It should be recalled that almost all church leaders in Africa today are products of the period which is often described in missionary history as the period of consolidation. After the pioneer period in which discipline was emphasised, the foreign missionaries tended to settle down and consolidate the Christian Communities they had just founded. It was during this period that institutions, including theological colleges were built. It is likely that training in theological colleges was geared towards equipping students with skills to perfect what had been gathered rather than breaking fresh ground.

Secondly, the Newer Churches have realised that so much is happening so rapidly that the Church must participate fully in all these developments to provide spiritual guidance; to search for new political, economic and social structures; to help to create the new man and community in the Third World. As a result of this understanding, the Church in Africa, has tended to be used as means for achieving justice, brotherhood, decency and a just society. It is little wonder that the Church has played

98

such important roles in bringing peace to the Sudan, involved in development projects and fought inhumanity incessantly. At the same time, however, the Church has been involved in the difficult exercise of putting its own house in order; searching, for example, for African liturgical forms and methods of artistic expression and their use in communicating the gospel.

It is clear that the Church in Africa has attempted both to discipline and perfect its own flock. But as the well-known church growth analyst D. A. McGavran once commented, discipling and perfecting are so intertwined that when both are going on in the same population, it is impossible to determine where one ends and the other begins.[3] The Church in Africa has, in spite of the great opportunity for 'discipling', tended to put more emphasis on 'perfecting'.

There are three important conclusions we can draw from all this. First the discussion above has helped to reveal that the Biblical command, to make disciples of all nations, has both a quantitative and a qualitative imperative. The Church both in Europe and the Third World recognises this. For example at the Second Assembly of the All African Conference of Churches (A.A.C.C.), the member churches declared,

'The Lord of the Church commissions us to "go into all the World" and free His people, to reject and combat injustices and to reconcile ALL to Him and to their fellow men. He also calls each of us today to be the new man in the fullness of Jesus Christ within the framework of our heritage.'[4]

The responsibility of seeking to grow continuously is acknowledged as well as that of liberating man, the whole man from physical and spiritual forces. Where the emphasis is put is determined by the prevailing situation in the countries concerned. It must be pointed out, however, that when a Church steadily loses more members than it recruits, as is happening in Europe and North America, its discipling machinery has gone wrong and should be re-examined.

Secondly, although the Church in Africa is growing steadily, this growth has been both encouraged and facilitated more by the prevailing situation than by a developed and systematic policy of discipling which the Church does not have the machinery to sustain. It may well be advisable to start developing a systematic policy of discipling before Islam, which is gradually increasing its influence in Africa, becomes a major threat to the Churches there.

Thirdly, it is common for one to hear people (especially young people) claim that they do not have any obligation towards this or that Church because they were baptised when they were infants and therefore not of their own free will. The number of people who reject the Church as a protest against their baptism during infancy seems to be increasing and with increasing secularization this number is likely to escalate, maybe spectacularly. As infant baptism is the main channel through which a majority of all new members of the Anglican Communion are recruited, this increase in people rejecting the Church as a protest against infant baptism may well be of significance to the future of the Anglican Communion.

ORGANISATIONAL GROWTH

There is a rapid growth in the number of dioceses in the various provinces of the Anglican Communion. One of the general observations worth noting is that those Churches which are rapidly growing numerically are also experiencing organisational growth, while those which are waning have scarcely reduced or streamlined their machinery over the last ten years. Some that are waning have even increased their organisational complexity. For example, the Episcopal Church in the United States of America has been losing members yet the number of its dioceses has risen in the last ten years from 103 to 113, of which only about half are in the parts of that Church which lie in the Third World countries outside the United States of America. One reason for this action is that smaller dioceses with fewer churches enable bishops to become closer to their flocks.

One of the problems of church growth is the maintaining of adequate Church nurture in an expanding Christian population. The growing Churches have responded to the challenge of expansion by sub-dividing existing dioceses to create new ones. Whereas this may be advisable in the new provinces in which existing dioceses can be very extensive, there is a danger that if it is over-done the vast number of bishops may make the administration of the province increasingly cumbersome. The practice of sub-dividing dioceses has generated a similar sub-division among smaller ecclesiastical units. In the diocese of Ruwenzori (Western Uganda), for example, there has been a rapid growth of parishes.[5]

In 1960 there were 10 parishes in the diocese but by 1976 that number had risen to 23. The creation of more parishes, and dioceses for that matter, in Ruwenzori has had the advantage of increasing the number of baptisms as more and more people have been confronted with the demand of the gospel. Secondly, the development has helped to bring more Christians within easy reach of the ordained clergy. However, as the parishes, and indeed the dioceses, have to be self-supporting, the creation of a new parish has often laid a heavy financial burden on the parishioners. Moreover people with inadequate training, have had to be employed to man the new parishes. In respect of the Churches in Europe and North America, it is worth remarking that if the numerical decline in these persists, the logical action worth taking may well be to merge some of the dioceses as is being done already in Ireland and Australia. This action

100

may be unpopular but it may be the only reasonable move open to these Churches.

It is impossible to mention all the various important aspects of church growth but it is important that in an article of this nature a few of them should be listed.

Spiritual growth

During the last two decades there has been spiritual growth in scattered Anglican communities. The Older Churches often claim, as already alluded to, that their declining membership is compensated by a growing Christian spiritual depth in those communities. Although claims of spiritual growth can only be empirically verified with difficulty, there are indications which help to reveal that in fact some of those communities have indeed experienced spiritual growth recently. The growth of the Charismatic Movement already mentioned; the growth of the Balokole (Saved Ones) movement in Eastern Africa; the growing number of Christians, especially lay Christians, who volunteer to work in and for the Church; the determination of Christians to continue confessing Christ publicly in areas where Christian persecution is rife are some of the indicators of spiritual growth in the Anglican Communion.

Anglican Participation in Ecumenical Bodies and Service Agencies

During the last decade Anglican Churches have supported, and even strengthened existing ecumenical bodies. Anglican Churches are, for example, members of the 81 National Christian Councils in the world; they also enjoy membership of the 10 continental or global councils (World Council of Churches, All Africa Conference of Churches, etc.). The Anglican Churches further participate in the activities of the Christian Service Agencies, for example, World Association for Christian Communication, Christian Organizations Research and Advisory Trust, United Bible Societies. Involvement in these ecumenical bodies and activities probably reflects a growing Anglican commitment to the spirit of co-operation and Christian brotherhood.

Anglican Publishing Houses

One of the interesting developments in East Africa in the recent past has been the establishment of Anglican publishing houses, Uzima Press (Kenya), Central Tanganyika Press (Tanzania), Centenary Publishing House (Uganda). Each of these publishing houses claims that its sales are rising and that it sells well over 100,000 books in either English or the local languages every year. The importance of this growing mass of Christian literature, especially vernacular literature, is that it may well help to solve some of the perennial problems of Christian nurture which are common, especially in those Churches experiencing Christian expansion.

CONCLUSION

Writing in the International Review of Mission in 1970, David Barrett observed that a situation was developing in which the centre of Christianity was shifting from Europe and North America to Africa and South America.[6] This article confirms that this trend has persisted. Statistics clearly reflect that this pattern is even more drastically the case for the Anglican Communities and there is no indication yet that the trend will either be halted or reversed in the foreseeable future. In other words, it seems the Third World has no choice but to assume the leadership role in the Anglican Communion. But are the Older Churches prepared to show their maturity by allowing Newer Churches to provide this leadership? Are the Newer Churches both prepared and equipped to assume that leadership role? These are but a few of the questions which must be raised now although we may not yet be in a position to answer them satisfactorily.

REFERENCES:
[1] In this article Church(es) refers to the 25 autonomous Churches of the Anglican Communion.
[2] D. A. McGavran (ed.) *Church Growth and Christian Mission*, p. 174.
[3] D. A. McGavran, *How Churches Grow*, p. 98.
[4] *Engagement, Abidjan 69*, p. 71.
[5] The information on Ruwenzori diocese is derived from B. T. Kisembo, *Baptism in the Church of Uganda in Toro*, M.A. Thesis submitted to Makerere University 1976, pp. 136-142.
[6] D. B. Barrett, 'A.D. 2000; 350 million Christians in Africa' in *International Review of Mission*, Vol. LIX, pp. 49-50.

GUIDE TO FURTHER READING:

D. A. McGavran (ed.), *Church Growth and Christian Mission* (New York: Harper and Row, 1965).
D. A. McGavran, *How Churches Grow* (New York: Friendship Press, 1959).
A. Hastings, *African Christianity* (London: Geoffrey Chapman, 1976).

2 - Ecumenism

Ian M. Fraser

Lord God,
whose son was content to die
to bring men life,
have mercy on your church
which will do anything you ask,
anything at all:
except die
and be reborn.
Lord Christ,
forbid us unity
which leaves us where we are
and as we are:
welded into one company
but extracted from the battle;
engaged to be yours
but not found at your side.
Holy Spirit of God —
reach deeper than our inertia and fears:
release us into the freedom of children of God.

History is cut loose in our time. It is there for the making. We must use the word 'new' with great frequency. The world is on the turn and the Church is on the turn. One can discern the Advocate at work, exposing our real state of affairs, pointing where sin, righteousness and judgment lie, bringing under question old patterns of living, accepted stances and relationships.

What is the ecumenical movement in this time but the whole inhabited earth rising with fresh determination to combat the chaos which continually threatens it in ever-new forms, and reaching out to a larger destiny; the whole inhabited earth lifting up its head, daring to have new hopes and aspirations; exposed, through them, to fresh sufferings.

In essence, the situation demands of the Church two things: that it join the human race in its search for a more ample future, and that it point to the one from whom the hope and the promise come — living out the solid character of that hope and promise by being itself the first-fruits of a great harvest. If the Church is to accept the challenge of this time, it must be prepared for a modest role alongside all types and conditions of human beings; and it must live its testimony to the Trinity convincingly.

In a short paper, there is time to probe only one main question. The one I propose is: How is the Church to handle a movement of this kind? All its instincts encourage it to reduce the problem to fit into compassable frames of reference with which it is familiar. The Church's reaction at this point of history is crucial. In the light of its own conviction that the mystery at the heart of the universe *affirms* humanity, it has a quite peculiar responsibility for distinguishing, in and through the flux of events, signs of 'kingdom stirrings'; and for pointing to their source and substance in Jesus Christ. The Church's instinctive reaction is to make kingdom things Church things, and then reduce them further to clergy things. When this happens, the understanding of the ecumenical movement suffers a sea-change. It becomes the *Churches* moving together in common enterprise and in new relationship. These common enterprises and the establishing of the new relationship occupy the centre of the stage. The groaning and travailing of the world towards rebirth takes second place. Commissions and committees are set up to fulfil these more limited purposes. They are dominated, virtually monopolised by ourselves, the ordained. We then smuggle in, as if they were matters of substantial importance to humanity, our peculiar concerns, and reduce still further the horizons of faith.

This process is understandable, even if damnable. Every kingdom thing threatens the Church as it is. The ecumenical movement is at one and the same time the greatest hope which has appeared in the life of the Church for centuries, and the biggest menace to its existing life:

*This kingdom movement, by its very nature, splits the Church on things which matter rather than promotes its unity on a lower plane. It forces the Church to decide whether it is going, in the last resort, to affirm the kingdom or to affirm itself. All over the world today, you will find one part of the church holding tight and trying to stay where it is, or seeking merely interchurch unity; while another part is intent on seeking God's kingdom and his justice and letting the unity follow which flows from that. It is the business of the ecumenical movement to split the Church, instead of leaving it settled in old conformities. The great promise of these times is where the Church becomes a kingdom, a sign of a new world order in justice and peace.

*The movement draws people out of denominational allegiances into new companies of venturing, and encourages them to invest time, money, thought, commitment in kingdom rather than Church enterprises. So it is a hazard to the institutional Church's very survival. Only a Church which is prepared to lose its life to find it will welcome this withdrawal and redirection of its resources.

*It exposes the biblical text to the understanding of 'wise' and 'foolish'. The cultural, class and other assumption — present but unacknowledged in traditional scriptural exposition — are being recognised. The basic hermaneutical principle is being re-established: access to true teaching is through *doing the*

104

will of God. For this, careful scholarship is a valuable aid. But it is auxiliary not determinative. Marvellously fresh understandings of scripture are now being produced by peasants, industrial labourers, illiterates.

*It rejects the old skins and fashions new wineskins for the new wine. Forms of the Church which have obtained for centuries no longer serve. That strong, centralised professional control exercised through hierarchy and bureaucracy, which Lenin also favoured for his own Church, only cracks and splits when it tries to contain the ferment.

*It brings under question not only forms of the Church as they have been, but its authority structures, ways of worship, styles and shapes of ministry.

*It produces crisis — it throws so many things most surely believed into the melting pot.

This is a bewildering situation for the Church to cope with. As an institution, the Church has a proper concern for continuity and respect for stability. These are real gifts, and are among the most important contributions that institutions can offer society. But this particular institution is meant to be a sign of God's transforming purpose, available to Him for participation in his mission, open to the changes He seeks to bring about — and, in consequence, itself open to change and reshaping. The Bishops' Synod in Rome, 1974, saw the need to '. . . render to the world a much broader common witness to Christ, while at the same time working to obtain full union in the Lord'. The Joint Working Group Report, 1975, stated that as the Church sees the '. . . possibilities of common witness, their search for unity will in turn advance. In the perspective of witness many of the problems which still divide them will appear in a new light'. As the Church digs up the talent hidden in the earth and risks it in mission, joining God in his determination to bring his whole beloved world to its liberation and complete fulfilment, it will be clear what stumbling blocks of history and relationship, that are barriers to the little ones, have to be cleared out of the way. Not otherwise.

Whether the Church will be prepared to engage in the ecumenical movement in its full range with full seriousness or seek to domesticate it, may be illustrated and tested by the way in which it does its work of theology, worship and ministry. (If one of these is given more attention than the others, that is only because common features obtain, and do not need to be repeated.)

THEOLOGY

For most of its history, the Church has treated theology as a reflection on its own life done for it by specialists. Now a larger task beckons — understanding the whole process of history under God, and redefining the responsibilities particularly committed to it. For this different work, it should be clear that scholars, specialists, professional theologians, are, by their discipline, training and inclination, also theological cripples. Partly this is inevitable and partly it is reprehensible. Certain work of scholarship quite properly withdraws one from the points of pressure which the majority have to reckon with. If the limitation is appreciated, the task can be given its true proportion. The problem is where professional theologians still try to do the Church's thinking for it. Two forms of theological withdrawal are reprehensible — from interaction with other disciplines, and from association with the people of God.

A substantial proportion of the Church, at least in certain parts of the world, has the education to enable it to cope with all but the specialist theological assignments. But that is not the main point. It is this. Only a whole body, variously gifted, distributed through the societies of the world, coming under different terms of pressure and opportunity, serving one Lord, can seek together to discern what God is doing in his world and to join him wherever opportunity offers. Theology in the end is a work of *perception*, into which all the other work of selection, investigation, research, evaluation is gathered. The Christian community, enlivened by faith, can draw upon the multiple resources and situations of its membership and contribute, through its hearing and seeing, to mankind's perception of life's significance and its open possibilities. That is the major work of theology. Only the theological community can undertake it. Relevant specialisms and technical knowledge can offer contributions which test and deepen insights. Should theology be thus understood, the following will ensue:

1. *Humanity will begin to be reinherited*
    For theology will no longer present itself as a sectional interest, pursued by specialists, requiring a language course as an entry qualification. It will encourage all kinds of companies of human beings, seeking to reckon with life as it presents itself, to drive their questions deep into the mystery at the heart of the universe. Knowledge of God will no longer be the preserve of sacred circles. It can become the bedrock of meaning for all that exists. Not only will atheists be compelled to rethink their theology (atheists are inescapably theologians and they must make clear what kind of God or gods they reject). They are already doing so. The Spanish and Italian Communist parties, finding Marxist Christians at least as deeply and perceptively engaged in the struggle for a new society as others, are now arguing that the atheism of Marxism may be a peripheral matter, or may be a mistaken path — at any rate, it is not an essential part of dynamic Marxism. (Nuestra Bandera. Nueva epoca — No. 85.)

2. *The Church will find itself reinherited*
    Class, cultural, racial, sexist assumptions which have been smuggled into the theological statements presented as objective, will be identified and shown in their true colours. Peoples who have been disinherited by the power-drive and status impact of western theology will come into their own — as they are, indeed, coming into their own. Theology will become the

work of the world Christian family. Many new styles and approaches will need to be respected and received by those who had traditionally called the theological tune. Women, young people and children, industrial workers and peasants, literate and illiterate will play a real, instead of a token or marginal, part. They will prophesy, as Joel promised. Cultures and languages will bring their different illuminations. All this is just at its beginning — but what a tough and exciting prospect lies before us!

3. *The commanding theological questions will get adequate attention*

Secondary matters, such as the validity of orders, will be recognised as in-church concerns which must not be allowed to divert from kingdom imperatives (false trails such as are laid by *The Myth of God Incarnate* also continually divert from these imperatives). The gospel will recover wholeness.

It is not haphazard that we are brought to birth — our contribution in the kingdom is defined and delimited by the particular terms of life we are presented with. In our day, we placard theology as betrayal if it does not deal with ways in which (a) the image of God in human beings is being defaced (b) principalities and powers manoeuvre to get life to run their way, heedless of God's future for mankind.

When we do thorough work of research and biblical discernment on matters such as: the ownership and use of land, of minerals and oil, of the means of production (especially concentrating today on transnational corporations); trade and investment policies; nationalism; the spread of military regimes and the spectacular growth of the armaments business; forms of personal and social alienation; the deep-seated basis of class, race, sex discrimination; the proliferation of hidden persuaders; medical technology and genetic manipulation; the creative responses met at all levels of life, which illustrate how human beings can live beyond themselves — we get into the fights God is engaged in and thus discover, together, his ways, his mind, his provision. Then, with the aid of scholars, we can contrast and compare notes in the communion of saints.

In some places where at least a part of the Church experiences the furnace of suffering, those things which many of us have separated, are fused in the heat. Gospel wholeness is regained. In the Philippines, Senator Salonga, professor of law and defender of the poor, stressed to me the *evangelical* necessity of research into multinational corporations, lest the world get into a powerful *grip which is other than God's*. Mrs. Trinidad Herrera of that same country, the squatters' choice as chairman of ZOTO — aware of the political and economic factors which her people had to deal with and their need to organise to claim a stake in life — answered my questions regarding the terrible torture she underwent. She spoke of the presence of God in a nightmare world of pain, his sustaining, and her determination to continue to do his will, whatever the consequences.

4. *Engage in kingdom enterprise — then you get kingdom insights*

Instruments must be forged which help Christian people to get purchase on life at these points, give them confidence for the work they have to do and train them in skills to play their part. People together will find some of the tools they need. But there must also be a conscious investment of resources to re-tool the Church for world mission, for participation in this drive to a new world. We are just making a beginning of this at Selly Oak.

WORSHIP

One of the Fathers (was it Gregory of Nyssa?) said: 'If you are a theologian, you will pray; and if you pray, you are a theologian.' Prayer and worship demand deep probing reflection upon experience in light of the testimony of scripture. So those who pray and worship in sincerity and truth are building up theological resources (whether they would be classed as educated or uneducated).

The reality of worship and prayer is not found in abstraction from life but in engagement with the kingdoms of this world, in light of the promise that they will become the kingdom. It is the whole world which is to be brought in and spread out before God when the people assemble, as Hezekiah spread out his letter before him. It is sin in all the dimensions in which it thwarts God's loving purpose, small-scale and large-scale, which is to be confessed. It is the whole field of the world which is to be irrigated by forgiveness, offered up with hope and expectation, entered into by a company prepared to present their bodies 'a living sacrifice'.

Where worship is done for people, or where they are offered only stage-managed forms of participation; where the concerns of the people are not expressed in their language and made the substance of prayer and praise — then what happens is, in the end, alienating. The great difficulty of the traditional leadership is really to believe that worship is the work of the people, the gifted people of God; that their endowments of the Spirit and many ministries demand outlet in prayer and praise as well as in service and prophecy. There is no need for fear. The moments of worship must have a blood-relationship to the rhythms of life, because they are universally recognised. The Faith and Order conference at Montreal distinguished seven moments of eucharistic worship which could be accepted by all the Churches that were present. Lay people, given freedom to develop acts of worship at Scottish Churches' House, Dunblane, might stand the accepted pattern on its head, plunge straight into intercession, and finish with confession, forgiveness and adoration. But the confession and absolution would have richness and depth denied it when it is so quickly disposed of at a beginning of a service; and all the moments would be there — a feel for them is in the blood.

Again, skills need to be learned for handing back to people what has been taken from them. In a country like the U.K. one of the gifts of black-led

108

Churches is a spontaneity and participation of the members which can instruct Churches that have become wooden.

Worship in the ecumenical movement draws upon the involvement, sacrifice, imagination of all who are engaged where God is transforming life, in family, neighbourhood, national, international environments; and through them lifts up a groaning and travailing creation.

MINISTRY

Acts of prayer and forms of worship disclose unwittingly the extent to which they are genuinely ecumenical or church-domestic. Where ecclesiastical dignitaries are first prayed for, then the categories of the ordained, then the ordinary people, a tale is told. It is arguable that very many Churches in the world, including those which would totally reject the Roman Catholic model, act as if they believed in a category of ordained ministry or priesthood which is separately constituted, has its own internal validation, and acts in a top-down way. Not only is this nonsense in light of the ecumenical movement — which calls for resources which are much more the province of laity than ordained. It is nonsense in terms of almost every statement now being made about the Church, whose direct participation in the ministry of Jesus Christ, whose furnishing with gifts of the Spirit, whose manifold servant availability is being recognised in word. It is implementation which has to catch up with profession. Time and time again, statements which seek to do more justice to the ministry of the whole people of God experience a slide, and bed down on the preoccupations of the ordained. What else can be expected when the trade union of the ordained is in full control of statements issued?

The laity are there to be cared for and cajoled out of apathy, for heads to be shaken over their stubborn refusal to pick up prescribed initiatives. If people do not come alive, could it be that we clergy are just too thick on the ground for the people to have space to exercise their ministry; could it be that we are too fearful of breakdown to trust the Spirit? We must ask most seriously where have we become stumbling-blocks, put in the way of the little ones, inhibiting them in their exercise of ministry in the world?

The call for more vocations to ordained service can be simply one for the provision of further stumbling-blocks. Only in light of the exercise of the many ministries can it be asked whether professional, ordained forms are required or not, and where and for what purpose they are needed. They must always be clearly auxiliary to the main ministry of the whole people.

When it comes to their deployment, the African indaba model, in which everyone participates and builds up decisions to a point where either one person or a group express the mind developed through the whole process, must now prevail instead of the top-down pyramidical model. But many forms of ministry are emerging in the World Church today under the pressure of the Spirit, and are there for our instruction. They have developed, not from past patterns — though they relate to signs in the church's past history — but from participation in the ecumenical movement of the whole household of mankind towards a fulfilment whose substance they discern in the biblical promise of a new heaven and earth.

THE CHALLENGE

We are called and empowered to live resurrection. We can face the reality of this world as believers (fatalists will say 'any system you substitute will be as bad as the one you have got'). We can live in the confidence that Easter brought and brings:

> The Lion of Judah
> flames out
> on the desolate band
> from his ambush of joy —
> Ravished,
> slain to life,
>   sing:
> 'Nothing, nothing,
> nothing, nothing, nothing
> now can destroy.'

So we must and can give up our practical atheism. In many ways we are like old-style Communists, scared of shaping communities of freedom which will participate in the ecumenical movement of humanity in ways which will be difficult to contain or control. It takes a Garaudy to affirm: 'Marxism is . . . an awareness of the underlying movement that governs our history' [1]; a Tito and a Carillo to make it clear that the Marxist-Leninist Church also has to learn to cope with the strains of ecumenism. Christians, like Marxists, need to be delivered from practical atheism and live a trinitarian faith.

To believe in God the Father is to believe that someone is in charge who sees the whole game. This should provide enough confidence to allow us church people to be prepared to see developments go out of our hands — without that meaning they get unfruitful or bring chaos. The insistence on having a controlling agent, like a Communist Party or a Curia or a bureaucracy, is a sign of unfaith (in processes of history, or in a Father of all). *Episcope*, the need at many levels to keep an eye on developments, test and relate them, is a different matter. Means to exercise it must never degenerate into instruments of control.

To believe in Jesus Christ is to be confident that, from a position stripped of power and privilege, we can successfully (though it may be, in the end, over our dead bodies) confront the massive and commanding powers of the world and help to make them serve the purposes for which God brought them into being. Neither Marxism nor Christianity has been very successful in stripping itself of unwarranted power and privilege.

110

To believe in the Holy Spirit is to believe that people can find resources in themselves beyond all expectation, sprout capacities to handle life, surprise themselves and others by what they can accomplish, and thus 'bring the house down', gaining the applause of the Universe (Romans 8). Neither Communism nor Christianity has shown the willingness or the skill to trust the people and believe in their giftedness under God.

REFERENCE
[1] *Marxism in the 20th Century,* Roger Garaudy (London and Glasgow: Collins, 1970). See the Introduction.

3 - Evangelisation

David E. Jenkins

What we do or should do about evangelism clearly depends on what we understand about the 'evangel'. The only proper motives for evangelisation and the only valid shapes which can be given to any process called evangelisation must come from and be consistent with the gospel. What is there, therefore, about the gospel which should set us busy about 'gospelising', and what would be properly involved in 'gospelisation'? Playing with words in this way may be a useful way of inviting members of an international and inter-cultural assembly to reflect realistically and relevantly about what is involved today in sharing the good news which Christians claim to have heard and to be hearing. For people of differing cultures and therefore of differing languages and habits of thought ought to be particularly able to help one another to get at the human and spiritual experiences and possibilities *behind* words. We may have to conduct our common business through the medium of English but we have no need to be trapped in any tiredness or stereotyping which has overcome the language among those whose only medium of expression and communication it is. Mutual stimulation and realistic reflection of this sort might help in planning more effective oversight in, among and for Christian people whose existence as Christians has no authenticity and no future if the gospel does not give meaning and direction to their lives, both for themselves and with regard to their neighbours.

For words become slogans and slogans trigger off patterns of behaviour which are then gone through because of their inevitability for, and familarity to, the group of people concerned. The words, actions and attitudes which make up the behaviour have very little to do with the powerful experiences which originally caused the now slogan-words to be used. (Consider words like 'freedom', 'democracy', and 'equality' in politics.) Further, the group and its behaviour associated with the slogan-words are very little affected by the realities of the people and the society around them as people outside the group understand and experience them. This is in fact the case even when the words and activities are explicitly undertaken as an exercise in addressing the people and society 'outside'. In fact, what slogan-words trigger off is a ritual required by the internal dynamics and beliefs of the group, not an open response to the wider realities from which the group claims to live and to which the group claims to be addressing itself.

'Evangelisation' is clearly one of these slogan-words. Firstly, it and other similar derivations from the Greek *evangelion* (gospel) tend to be party words and tend also to refer to one particular set of activities undertaken by or commended to Christians, especially as they are undertaken and commended by one set or type of Christians. It tends to be forgotten how shocking and distorting this is. To be called an 'evangelical' is to be called a 'gospel-ical' or, perhaps, an 'according-to-the-gospel'. For this to be an accepted and acceptable term for *some* Christians as distinct from others reveals a situation which is as awkward, contradictory and disturbing as that in first-century Corinth when some said 'I am of Apollos' and others 'I am of Paul' or even 'I am of Christ'. The drift of the argument in Paul's first letter to the Corinthians does not suggest that the 'I am of Christ' party were, by the mere use of that name, any more Christian than the rest. Presumably there is or can easily be the same problem if 'evangelicals' claim to be particularly in accordance with the gospel.

Secondly, this query about evangelical words as tending to be sectarian and slogan-like is reinforced by the actual separateness of 'campaigns' of evangelisation and by the development of separate and distinct organisations. For example, the British Council of Churches or, at least, a group of those most active in promoting the Council's affairs, recently invested a great deal of time and energy in developing a programme under the title 'Britain, Today and Tomorrow'. While this was still developing, however, much of the directing energy was switched to 'a national initiative in evangelism', sponsored by a group of people who were largely (although not entirely) different from those concerned with the first initiative and who certainly represented very different styles of Christian commitment and engagement. What sort of *evangel* is this that requires an initiative to — do what? — 'preach the gospel' (we shall return to this) — which is separate from an initiative to get to grips with 'Britain, today and tomorrow'. Perhaps 'God was in Christ reconciling the world to himself' really is an evangelical slogan which can be proclaimed apart from any need to be fully engaged with the realities which shape and colour people in the ordinariness of their daily lives, that is to say in the ordinariness, for me, of Britain today and tomorrow. However, the question suggested is at least a troubling one.

Unease is further stirred up by, for example, the existence and role within the structures of the World Council of Churches of a Department of 'World Mission and Evangelism'. It might not be so disquieting if the personnel and programmes of this department were clearly directed to emphasis, and to particular concerns among the other programmes and departments. But by and large this is not so. The Department has its own programmes and is concerned with its own 'constituency'. (A word which plays a large part in the planning and decision-taking of ecumenical departmental bodies). Now what sort of *evangel* is it which requires or authorises an evangel-ism separated from attempts in the name of Christ to, say, combat racism or promote involvement in health care, aid or development? Perhaps it is some sort of message which can be apprehended and experienced both as to its meaning and as to its effects quite apart from the experiences, sufferings and problems which shape the capacity of most people for hope or despair, for anguish or for celebration. But if so, one wonders what are the grounds for supposing the message to be biblical. Although the word *evangelion* emerged from the Bible there is a case for inquiring how far it and its derivatives have become, in current use, slogans for promoting or justifying stereotyped and departmentalised activities.

A third reason for pursuing the implications of this disquiet lies in the observed behaviour of at least some congregations planning campaigns. If a congregation has a tradition of a certain churchmanship and if its pastor(s) have been trained at certain centres then an 'evangelistic campaign', led by a person or a team from outside, occurs sooner or later with almost fatalistic inevitability. The plans do not arise from a heart-felt growth of feeling and insight in the congregation as a whole or a substantial part of it. They are proposed by some of the leaders, whose consultations with the rank and file often are in effect only the sharing of information and the dealing with objections or hesitations. Acquiescence in the proposed plans is not necessarily insincere, although it is less than whole-hearted. For many Christians are convinced about the need to be convinced. Is not conviction part of being strong in the faith? It is assumed to be evidence of conviction that you make direct attempts to share it and it is assumed that an evangelistic campaign is a way *par excellence* of sharing. Further, people desire to be obedient to obedience. And is there not a command associated with the risen Jesus to 'go and make disciples of all nations' (Matthew 28, 19) and to 'go into all the world and preach the gospel' (Mark 16, 15)? It is assumed that it is this command which is distinctive above all of the obedience laid on Christians and it is further assumed that evangelistic campaigns are, once again, the way *par excellence* of responding to this command. So the plans are accepted and collaboration, up to a point, forthcoming. But a considerable part of the campaign has to be directed towards persuading local participation and training local church members for it. Further, the planned events are led by people from outside (often specialists) and they are addressed to the 'religious' problems which people are supposed to have. Campaigns do not arise out of a long and careful involvement in the local problems as they are locally, naturally and humanely experienced. What sort of *evangel* is it, then, which makes of activities such as these an 'evangel-istic' campaign? And why this as an evangelistic campaign *par excellence*? Surely we need to spell out and take a careful look at the picture, understanding and reality of 'gospel' which is implied by such a procedure.

This is where we can usefully come back to basic questions of language and to the opportunities for mutual correction, instruction and enlargement which are offered us by the sharing of different cultures, languages and environments. First, the basic question of language. 'Evangelise' is simply a transliteration into English of the Greek word which added a verbal ending to the word we translate as gospel. The noun for gospel is turned into a verb. That is to say that 'evangelise' simply means to be active about or do something about the gospel. The fact that one of the things that Christian people (including New Testament people) have 'done about the gospel' is to 'preach' or 'proclaim' it is not necessarily either helpful or decisive for us today. For 'preaching' and 'proclaiming' are to do with presenting something, drawing people's attention to it, helping to put them in touch with it. And if preaching ceases to put people on to things because of changes in culture, or of changes in the way people perceive the realities of the world and themselves or because of ways in which preachers historically have been used by those in power or by those of an invading culture then *preaching* the gospel can become a most unevangelical and unbiblical thing to 'do about the gospel'. If people are alienated from preaching because it is contrary to their style of making sense and of appreciating truth, or because they have no reason to trust those preaching for their humanity, sympathy and realism, or because they have historical, cultural or social reasons for being separated from the institutions of those who preach, then their alienation from preaching has nothing to do with the scandal of the gospel. It is the result of a lack of humanity, sensitivity and sympathy in the preachers who are more concerned to be obedient to their ideas of obedience than to be open to the contemporary realities of God and man.

This brings me to the heart of an urgent concern about evangelisation, about being active about the gospel, which I wish to share through this article. I do not see how what are still received as the normal methods of evangelisation and preaching the gospel can possibly bring a hearing of the gospel to the masses of men and women who live in and are shaped by our present urbanised, industrialised and secularised culture. It is not a question of enabling the acceptance of the gospel. This men cannot do. Nor is it a question of making the gospel acceptable by conforming its expression to contemporary wants and ideals. The salvation of God is about judgment, redemption and fulfilment which changes all so that all can contribute to this fulfilment. It is not about solutions to current problems as currently conceived nor about the provision of a heavenly top-dressing to fashionable utopias or fantasies. Finally, I do not accept some absolutised sociological judgment that sooner rather than later we are all bound to be 'secularised' and that no-one will ever again be able to believe in God, experience transcendence or entertain the notion of a power, a help and an energy which comes 'from outside'. I cannot accept the thesis of a creeping monochrome modern culture nor do I believe in historical inevitability, still less in the capacity of some theory to indicate infallibly which way that 'inevitability' will go.

I am simply drawing attention to the conditions of living, thinking, feeling, experiencing and reacting which constitute the ordinariness of so many of us, perhaps especially in the West, but in many urban areas and in many cultural enclaves right across the world. We cannot expect to be part of 'converting' people to a conscious share in the reality of God and of his love unless we show that we are consciously aware of, and reckoning with, the realities which shape their daily lives and which they are obliged to take for granted.

In order to be slightly more precise about the problem which is troubling me let me give an impressionistic list of the sort of pressures which shape our ordinary sense of ordinary and taken-for-granted realities, especially with regard to people who come along 'from outside' with a religious message (a gospel). Thus:

Science is clearing the world of superstition and that goes for religion. (You do not need God to explain or operate the world. Moreover religion has maintained a lot of silly explanations and interfered with a lot of sensible operations. If you want to get to grips with reality you observe, test and get the relevant experts to check up.)

Technology has shown that you deal with human problems, insofar as you can, by planning, organisation and the development of resources. (You do not wait around for salvation. Moreover, see next point, this waiting around looks suspiciously like dodging the issue on the part of those who do not want change because they are doing very well as it is — at other people's expense.)

Marxism has shown that while religion was perhaps an inevitable anaesthetic when most men could do nothing about their sufferings and oppression now that they can it is clear that religion is a confidence trick. Moreover, you do not have to be a Marxist to recognise this nor to recognise how the institutions of society, the economic structures, the powers-that-be in industry, commerce and banking, the professions and so on determine what we do, receive and think. Authority is exercised for self-interest. Therefore one needs to be very suspicious of people who claim some external authority on religious or any other grounds.

Psychologists have shown that our ideas and attitudes about such matters as guilt, dependence, omnipotence, punishment and what is right and wrong, have aspects and explanations which call in question much that has been taken for granted or demanded in religion. Similarly, passionate and open investigation of public and private morality has revealed that religion is often related to much dogmatism, tyranny and insensitivity, especially in the field of sex and human relations.

Finally, the revival of non-Western cultures and a renewed sensitivity to the values of what have been called primitive cultures has shown

116

that Christian 'missionary' religion has been prone to trample on human experience and be the tool of a dominant culture.

This list is not inserted here to give a catalogue of philosophical issues to be discussed in highly sophisticated ways but to draw attention to what has percolated into a 'climate of opinion'; to point to pressures which influence everyone's sense of reality at levels other than the intellectual and in ways quite beyond what most people could or would want to articulate. Moreover they reflect real and widespread human experiences of life in the world and in society. As such they contain a great deal of truth which it would be unrealistic and faithless to ignore. It is pressures, ideas and experiences like these which shape the way in which we are bound to ask and answer questions like 'What do we know?'; 'What do we do?'; 'What do we suffer and why?'; 'What can we hope for?'. If we cannot show that we face up to and reckon with the powers, authorities and values which dominate daily life then we can scarcely expect to gain a hearing for some detached proclamation about 'Jesus is Lord'.

The situation could be even worse. It might be that by sticking to certain patterns and stereotypes of 'preaching the gospel' we shall pre-select who will hear. For instance we may, in effect, be addressing ourselves only to those who are suffering from a particular sense of individualistic guilt, a particular need for dependence, and a particular readiness to turn aside from the difficulties of their lives into a warm and womb-like fellowship which tidies up the raggedness of the real world with a set of authoritative pictures and myths. We may even be colluding in 'converting' people to a cult rather than sharing with them in the mystery, openness and energy of the living God.

Certainly one way of making sense of the patterns of 'evangel-ism' to which I have earlier drawn attention is to suppose that people believe themselves to be responding to a limited God who has a limited imagination, for he can visualise only certain ways of understanding reality or developing history, and a limited psychological range, for he can cope with only a certain range of human relationships and responses. This God is apparently 'carving out a Kingdom' for himself to be occupied by and shared with people who are like-minded to himself.

Many people may be convinced that this is an unfair travesty. But it does bring out sharply the intimate connection between procedures of evangelisation and the *evangel* which is spelt out, not by the words employed but by the patterns of behaviour and belief which are implied. Further, the issue is so urgent that it warrants the risk of offensiveness. For how is the gospel to be shared with or at least put before contemporary men and women whatever their culture, class or country? I would suggest that it cannot be done, except in a way which is so highly selective and narrow that it threatens to be contradictory to the gospel itself, as long as the gospel is

117

primarily thought of as a message which has to be got over in certain set forms or with a fixed verbal content.

In his letter to the Galatians, Paul speaks of the good pleasure of God 'to reveal his son in me' (Gal. 1, 16). Paul attempted to share the impact of this revelation through many messages and metaphors. He tried also to 'become everything in turn to men of every sort, so that in one way or another I may save some' (I Cor. 9, 22). To become engaged with men for an effective sharing of the gospel we have to be engaged with God through Jesus and engaged with the realities which now make us 'men of every sort.' The gospel is not some story or set of stories about God. It is Emmanuel, God with us as a power, a presence and an energy to overcome whatever separates us from one another and from him. (God was in Christ reconciling the world to himself — II Cor. 5, 19). The messages, presentations and sharings of the gospel will be as various and as pluralistic as the circumstances which shape us in our diverse humanity and the experiences which enable us to apprehend God as a contemporary presence and promise. Unless we can give new and much broader life to our understandings and practices concerning evangelisation and evangelism we shall continue to do violence to what we can know of God and to what we can experience as human beings.

This is why the coming together of people with responsibility in the church from a variety of cultures and languages is such an 'evangelical' opportunity. Experiences, insights and problems can be brought together from a variety of cultural, political and 'gospel-ising' contexts. The experiences can correct and enlarge one another as well as providing clarity about questions which have still to be pursued, insights which have to be developed much further and differences which have to be creatively lived with.

To organise all this so that it can help to inform the oversight which should be exercised in the Church with regard to its evangelical responsibilities and opportunities it may be helpful to share mutual information and responsibility concerning the following three sets of questions:

1. How do we perceive and experience the impact of the 'gospel' and how do we translate it to ourselves? (i.e. How do we give an account of our end and not the scriptural end of 'hearing the gospel?')

2. Where does this apprehended reality of the gospel have an impact on the ordinary human realities that we share with our neighbours, and in what way? Where it does not, who is being more realistic, ourselves or our unbelieving neighbours? Where it does, is the impact itself consistent with the gospel?

3. How then to set about sharing both the realities and the unrealities with our neighbours so that God may be discovered, and may discover himself to all of us?

GUIDE TO FURTHER READING:

International Review of Mission Vol. LXVI No. 263, July 1977. (Articles on Human Rights and Mission).

What Asian Christians are Thinking — ed. D. J. Elwood (New Day Publishers of the Christian Literature Society of the Philippines, Quezen City 3058, Philippines, 1976).

The Contradiction of Christianity, David E. Jenkins (S.C.M. Press, London 1976).

4 - Liberation and social change

José Míguez Bonino

There is scarcely any need for an extensive argument in order to show the close relationship that obtains in our time between social change and human liberation. Even those who would understand this latter expression in predominantly inward and individual terms would admit that such a development of the human spirit remains a foreclosed possibility for the vast majority of the masses of population — whose numbers reach almost two thirds of the human race — who have no access to conditions which we would consider 'human'. Consider, for instance, this description of starvation reported in *Time* (11 Nov., 1974, p. 68):

> The victim of starvation burns his own body fats, muscles and tissues for fuel. His body quite literally consumes itself and deteriorates rapidly. The kidneys, liver and endocrine system soon cease to function properly. A shortage of carbohydrates, which play a vital role in brain chemistry, affects the mind. Lassitude and confusion set in, so that starvation victims often seem unaware of their plight. The body's defenses drop; disease kills most famine victims before they have time to starve to death . . .

Five hundred million people on our planet live — if this is the proper term — on this borderline. When Gustavo Gutiérrez defines 'poverty', very simply as 'the lack of economic goods necessary for *a human life worthy of the name*',[1] one should pay attention to the last words. There is a condition in which human life, in any meaningful sense of the word, ceases to exist. What is the meaning of being 'father' when you have no protection to offer, no food to provide, no wisdom to transmit because your brain and your heart are damaged, and your eyes look without light or tears at the newborn baby lying on the floor? How can a man be a shepherd without a flock, or a peasant without land, or a husband confined in the compounds of Johannesburg — three or four hundred miles away from his wife, his people, his gods?

We know today that such poverty is neither an accident nor a mystery. It is not a disconnected fact, but the inevitable and quite normal result of a total situation determined by the laws, goals and structures of the economic system that we have developed — now at world scale — for

120

the production and distribution of goods, and consequently for regulating work, human relations, man's use of nature, the goals and values of human life. The poverty of nearly two billion people on this earth's landscape is not a foreign body that has suddenly landed on this planet: it is part and parcel of the way in which we have ourselves 'cultivated this garden'. If this situation is to be redressed — and I can hardly think of any Christian (or any decent person for that matter) who would deny the urgency of solving these problems — it would seem that some form of social change (i.e. a modification of the structures and conditions that create, perpetuate and even aggravate these conditions) is imperative. However one may want to define the nature and forms of 'liberation', it would seem that there is a bottom stratum of humanity for whom the attaining of 'social change' becomes a necessary precondition.

Once the question of social change has been raised, though, we are faced with a number of problems: what type of change? which priorities? what model for change? by what methods? what is the cost of change? who should take the responsibility? and many others. Christian theology and Christian ethics have to face these questions on the basis of the Christian understanding of human life and the world. Is the Christian Church responsible for social change? If so, from what perspective and with which criteria? In what follows I shall presuppose certain fundamental theological insights which seem to be already a part of our common ecumenical heritage, and I shall try briefly to explore some ethical 'middle ground' for a consideration of social change.[2]

THE BASIC OPTION

One might wonder why, if the need for social change is so obvious, so many Christians and Churches have been and are known to be less than enthusiastic about it. For, with some exceptions, one can say that, while the need of the poor has never been outside the bounds of Christian concern, it has usually been met on an individualistic basis, by the exercise of charity, and seldom by the advocacy of deep-going social changes. It would seem that the basic question that the Churches have attempted to answer has been: Given the existing circumstances, how is it possible to alleviate the condition of those who suffer? The premise has hardly been challenged until rather recently. Why?

A couple of quotations from St. Augustine may help us to see the question in perspective. On the occasion of discussing the punishments inflicted on the Donatists, he mentions several times the question of property rights. His point of departure is the common conviction of the Church: 'everything belongs to God'. Ultimately, he is the only legitimate owner of all that exists. But men are entitled to call some goods their own when they possess them 'justly' (*iuste*). On the contrary 'anything which is possessed badly cannot be called one's own, and that is possessed badly

121

which is badly used' (*male autem possidet, qui male utitur*). On that basis, many who possess much could be justly dispossessed (*Epistle* 153/26, to Macedonius). Side by side with this 'divine right' in virtue of which men possess rightly those things which they have justly acquired and which they use properly, there is, as a matter of fact 'a human right which is at the mercy of the rulers of the earth' (*Epistle* 93/50, to the Rogatist Bishop Vincent). Certainly the two 'rights' do not coincide. Augustine's answer is typical and worth quoting:

> Meanwhile, the wickedness of the bad possessors is tolerated (*toleratur iniquitas male habentium*) and certain rights called civil (*iura civilia*) are instituted among them, not because one might in that way make them into good possessors (*bene utentes*) but in order that, even using badly these possessions (*ut male utentes*) they may be less bothersome (*minus molesti sint*). (*Epistle* 153/26).

The true balance, the proper restitution will only take place when we arrive at 'that city wherein lies our eternal heritage'.

The immediate occasion of these reflections is here the question of the property of heretics, and Augustine is advocating a certain leniency. But the drift of the argument is clear and reappears elsewhere. Many things are badly ordered in the 'earthly city'. Those who are entitled to enjoy certain things do not have them and vice versa; some are unjustly treated; sometimes innocents are tortured as criminals. Whenever such injustices can be mitigated without endangering order and peace, it should be done. But if any redress threatens to become unruly, it should be avoided.[3]

The basis of Augustine's position in these cases appears quite clearly: peace, understood as order. The suppression of conflict or tumult is the chief purpose of the organisation of society. Changes or the respect for personal freedom might endanger such order. Whenever an alternative emerges, therefore, the Christian ought to work for the best possible solution, the most just and generous one, *short of endangering the existing order*. We need not discuss here the anthropological and historical pessimism that underlies this position: since mankind is *massa perditionis*, since the *civitas terrena* is 'wholly other' than the *civitas dei*, the former can, at best, only offer an external framework of order within which God elects and perfects his saints. History is no more than a necessary detour: it has nothing to do with the true meaning and nature of God's salvation. It would also be interesting to pursue the concept of 'peace' which Augustine uses, and which roots back in the Roman tradition rather than in the biblical *shalom*.[4] But it seems that these theological facts are related to a socio-political one: the Church has accepted the role of supporting, sustaining and guiding the State. In that sense, Christianity has become a political religion and develops a political theology. It is true that it is different from the 'political theology' of the classic Roman tradition but, within the eschatological limitations already mentioned, it fulfils a similar function: it sacralises the existing order. The Church takes responsibility for this order. It tries to humanise it, to curb its abuses, to Christianise it. But it will not challenge it. Social change appears as the threatening onslaught of chaos and has to be resisted.

There is, nevertheless, also a different tradition, which roots back in the prophetic theology of the Old and New Testaments. In this tradition, peace is a function of justice, and justice itself is measured by the condition of the poor and defenceless. The classic expression of this view is found, for instance, in Jeremiah's implicit definition of a good government — using Josiah as example:

Did not your father (i.e. Josiah) eat and drink and do justice and righteousness? Then it was well with him.

He judged the cause of the poor and the needy; Then it was well. (Jer. 22 : 15-16a).

This 'fundamental right of the poor', as some of the fathers would call it, becomes the basic criterion for an orientation of Christian ethics. For Jesus himself, it seemed to be the touchstone for discerning the presence of God's Kingdom and for establishing the legitimacy of his own ministry in relation to it.[5] In the early Church the 'privilege of the poor' seems undisputed (at least in theory!). He has the *right* to receive what he needs. Obviously, the apostolic and post-apostolic Church did not set out to advocate or to enforce changes in society. For several reasons, the problem of socio-political power was outside its ethical perspective. It affirms the right of the poor *unconditionally* and it tries to devise ways to make it operative within its own community life and order. Most of the early fathers (particularly in the East) seem quite unanimous and are quite outspoken in this regard.[6]

The story of the change that took place in the third and fourth centuries has been told many times . . . with different and conflicting interpretations. We are not called to sit in judgment on our fathers. But an understanding of the relation between the different conditions and relations is indispensable for a correct consideration of our subject. The early Church takes up the prophetic-dominical tradition of the right of the poor. In the situation of disestablishment and lack of power in which it finds itself, the assertion of this right takes predominantly the form of ethical teaching and internal discipline and different forms of service. The Constantinian--Theodosian Church has entered the sphere of power. This places upon it a fundamental duty: the preservation of public order. The right of the poor (which it continues to defend) is now placed within these new co-ordinates. The basic question within such perspective is: What degree of change in the conditions in which the poor live is compatible with the preservation of the existing order? It is, in its due place, a legitimate question. But it is important to recognise that it is radically different from the prophetic-dominical tradition.

It is my contention that we are placed today in still a different situation in most areas of the world. Most of our Churches are not any more 'established' in a Constantinian-Theodosian sense. They do not exercise any direct (or even indirect, in the traditional Catholic sense of the word) authority (*potestas*) in society. But they have not returned to the form of 'disestablishment' of the early Church. They are still within the sphere of power. In virtue of their history, of their number and recognition, they have a responsibility for the structuring of social conditions which the apostolic Church could not exercise. They cannot, therefore return to the practice of that Church. Furthermore, the condition of 'the poor' has also changed. Both in the form of social groups or classes and in the form of poor countries or peoples, the 'poor' have become historical subjects in a new sense. They are able, within certain conditions, to claim their 'right'. This is certainly not true of all the 'poor'. There still exists the defenceless, the powerless. But their condition is now set within this new fact of the struggle of the poor.

The problem of liberation and social change seems to me to revolve around these facts: (1) that social change is a necessary precondition for a humanising of the conditions of existence of a great majority of the human race; (2) that the Christian basis for responding to this challenge is given in the prophetic-dominical tradition of 'the fundamental right of the poor'; (3) that the Christian Churches have an unavoidable responsibility for the structures of society — the question of power; (4) that the poor, in several forms have themselves become active subjects of social change. It is my conviction that, taking this into account, we have to turn around the thesis of the Constantinian Church. The true question is not 'What degree of justice (liberation of the poor) is compatible with the maintenance of the existing order?' but *'What order is compatible with the exercise of justice?'* (i.e. the fundamental right of the poor). It seems to me that we would find an adequate point of departure for our ecumenical discussion of the responsibility of the churches in relation to society if we could agree on some such formulation. The fixed point is 'the right of the poor': this is the theological premise from which we cannot depart. The variable which has to be explored is the conditions and possibilities of an order which can best bring to fulfilment that right. In such a perspective social change is taken for granted, not as a good in itself (not just because it is 'change') but because it is implied in the search for an order (which has to be new since the existing ones do not attain this aim) in which this right takes precedence.

124

The formulation indicated in the previous paragraph is only a point of departure. Two vast fields of reflection and research remain open: the search for criteria to evaluate alternative orderings of society and the question of strategies and tactics for social change. Much ecumenical thought has already been given to these questions, but there is still a long way to go before we arrive at operative agreements. In what follows — more as an exercise than with any claim of conclusiveness — I shall try to suggest briefly two possible approaches to the question of criteria. They are given as illustrations of my conviction that we must try to overcome the dichotomy between theological and socio-political criteria and have to struggle for a dynamic incorporation of the theological insights into socio-political categories. Naturally, certain theological positions which I cannot at this point explicate or argue are implicit in the formulation of these affirmations. Also, there are certain views on socio-political questions taken here as 'acquired', although I have endeavoured to keep these latter presuppositions at a minimum in order to hinder communication as little as possible, even risking a certain imprecision or vagueness.

The measure and direction of the social change that is imperative for the Christian at any given time is determined by the relation between the best possibilities of human fulfilment available at that time and the structural conditionings that may prevent the access of all human beings to them.

This very simple and almost self-evident formulation should be developed in several directions, which I simply try to indicate:

1. The use of the notion of 'human fulfilment' as a theological criterion implies at least a theological and an anthropological presupposition. On the one hand, creation itself must be understood as an open process which includes human praxis within itself. In other words, the creational possibilities for human existence are not a fixed datum but a developing gift (of God) available in the measure of man's responsible praxis in the world. Moreover, human identity itself is expanded and enriched in this process: human nature also is not a fixed datum. For this reason the conditions for human fulfilment cannot be objectively determined once for all but have to be historically re-defined in relation to the 'creational possibilities' historically actualised at a given time. At the same time, we are affirming that the quality of personal human life is the goal of God's creational and redemptive action, thus rejecting a purely evolutionary or processive view of history for which human persons would simply be 'means' for some collective or final fulfilment.

2. The possibility of concretion of a criterion such as the one suggested requires an inclusive understanding of human life — the dimensions in which 'human fulfilment' can be defined. A crippled anthropology lies

at the root of the economicist, or spiritualistic visions of human development and fulfilment which are so frequently offered as alternative and
exclusive options. In specific analysis the conditions for human life must
be related to the scientific-technological, economic, political, cultural and
'spiritual' possibilities available at a given time.[7] To speak of starvation
or of cultural deprivation in terms of the conditions of the XIth or the
XXth century is, obviously to deal with two radically different questions
(not only in material but . . . because of material differences — also in
ethical and theological terms). Nevertheless, so many approaches to the
problem continue to build on views of poverty or deprivation as 'fate',
'accidents' or 'brute facts'!

3. The use of the adjective in '*best* possibilities' raises also some
problems — although not as many as some would want us to believe! It
would seem that, in the present conditions of large sectors of mankind,
there is no need for involved theological, philosophical or sociological
arguments in order to show that 'better possibilities' are materially possible and ethically desirable for them. There is a bottom level, which
Paul VI has defined rather clearly: 'More human conditions: to raise
from misery to the possession of that which is necessary, the overcoming
of social calamities, the widening of knowledge, the acquisition of culture'.[8] We hardly need a theological congress to tell us that everybody
should be able to obtain a minimum of food, clothes, shelter, health and
education. Common sense seems enough to teach us that.

The Pope, nevertheless, moves in his definition to other areas: the
recognition of human dignity, co-operation in the common good, higher
values and faith. At this point quantitative criteria are not enough and
we have to search for the 'directions' in which human fulfilment is to be
pursued. But we are not left without orientation. The prophetic-dominical
tradition to which we have previously referred is not silent about the
'quality' of human life that God intends. When Jürgen Moltmann speaks
of the 'future of Jesus Christ' as 'the future of life', 'of justice' and of
'human freedom',[9] he is giving us a valid summary of that tradition. The
eschatological feast of the Kingdom: the shared bread and wine, the joy
of fellowship in God's presence, the fulfilment of love, point to a fulfilment, the partial 'sacraments' of which give meaning to human life in
history. When the objective conditions made available by science, technology, resources — forms of production, communications, etc. — open
new levels of material enjoyment of the world, personal realisation in
sociality, joy in shared recreation and enjoyment of nature and human
creativity, then these new conditions become a 'theological *locus*' and a
call to Christian obedience. The humanisation of these new possibilities
and the universalisation of their accessibility become a Christian duty,
because it means the responsible reception of God's gift.

126

4. I have chosen on purpose the negative formulation about structural conditionings that may prevent such fulfilment. We touch here the delicate but crucial question of the relation between personal fulfilment and structural conditions. I do not pretend to solve the long debated question of relative priorities and determinations. But it would seem possible to agree on the operational axiom that, while changed structural conditions do not by themselves ensure personal human fulfilment, the prolongation of inadequate structures does prevent such fulfilment.[10] We must see structural change, therefore, at least as an enabling process, as a function of life. In that sense we can understand the form of the basic question that was formulated earlier: 'What order is compatible with the fundamental right of the poor?' here translated as 'What structural changes are necessary in order to universalise the best possibilities made available by the present development of human resources, knowledge and creativity?'

In carrying out the necessary structural changes we meet a tension between the human cost of their realisation and the human cost of their postponement. The basic ethical criterion for change is the maximising of universal human possibilities and the minimising of the human cost.

I think we would all find it easy to offer numerous illustrations of the question alluded to in this statement. I shall only indicate some points which should be taken into account.

1. The argument of the social cost of structural change is frequently evoked as a deterrent of significant action. There is here a not so innocent fallacy which consists in not counting the human cost of the postponement of change. Revolutionary changes, it is said, sacrifice human lives. How many lives are sacrificed by the prolongation over one or two centuries of a form of production or distribution of goods which has ceased to serve adequately the needs of a people? 'Crash programs' sacrifice a generation, it is said. How many generations are sacrificed in the hope of gradual changes? I am not arguing in favour of revolution over development, of crash programs over gradual plans. I am only arguing against the 'verbal terrorism' of an ideologically inspired fallacy. The question of the social cost works both ways. Any sound Christian social ethics must be aware of this tension.

2. All change involves the question of power since social structures are recalcitrant to change in a greater or lesser degree. There is necessarily a power which has to be built in order to push changes and a power which has to be overcome because it is entrenched in the obsolete structures. Historically this has always meant different proportions of three constant terms: pressure for change, consent to change and conflict. The human cost of change is determined by the delicate balance of these

terms. When change, rather than order is the premise, the reduction of conflict depends on the intensification of the first two terms. It is in this area where a Church which really wants to fulfil its social function should find its mission. If it sincerely wants to reduce conflict, it should work for a maximum of consciousness of the need for change and of consent to change. This very obvious fact is, nevertheless, almost systematically ignored.

3. In order to avoid misunderstandings, the previous point must be immediately supplemented by a consideration of the historical feasibility of change at any given time and place. A responsible advocacy of change can only be undertaken on the basis of a realistic assessment of the viability of change which includes the evaluation of the objective and subjective conditions, including consciousness and praxis. The old tradition of balancing courage and prudence finds here a proper place in social ethics. A failure in this respect has led many times to a reactionary conservatism or to senseless and suicidal voluntaristic adventures. Structural change which is humanly significant must have the people as conscious agents. Change that is obtained for the people without the people is only a new form of human enslavement. On the other hand, only effective achievement generates enthusiasm and awakens people. In theological terms this means a Church which is both prophet and shepherd.

4. The practical fulfilment of this task requires the elaboration of 'projects' and 'strategies' and the development of mobilising ideas. Without them, we remain in the abstract. A Christian social ethic which does not want to shipwreck on the rocks of a sterile idealism has to risk this level where we meet the thorny questions of programs, models and ideologies. A sad experience has made us sensitive to the danger of setting up idols, of falling prey to ideologies, of sacralising human projects. Christian social commitment has to raise constantly the critical warning of transcendence. But transcendence must also be related positively to human achievement lest it become a deterrent to significant action. This means that this sign can be significant only when it is raised within a definite commitment.

★   ★   ★

We have tried to explore some of the ethical questions involved in the quest for social change. Some of them are complex and do not admit of unambiguous or totally satisfactory answers. The basic question for the Christian Church is, though, one of commitment. A Church which discerns its responsibility for the poor of the world will find its way for discharging that responsibility. But how can a Church which has for a long time sat at the table of the rich and powerful really cast its lot with the poor? How can the rich enter the Kingdom of God? 'With God nothing is impossible'. What God can do is not to smuggle a rich Church into the Kingdom, but to convert it to Him . . . and therefore also to those with whom He identified himself in the man Jesus Christ. The first question for the Church is not an ethical but a spiritual question: repentance and conversion.

REFERENCES:

1   Gustavo Gutiérrez, *Theology of Liberation*, p. 288.
2   Ecumenical thinking on questions of social ethics covers a wide range and offers excellent material which is not always used to best advantage. An excellent discussion of the main trends is to be found in Carl-Henric Grenholm, *Christian Social Ethics in a Revolutionary Age* (Uppsala, 1973).
3   On Augustine's concept of property see further B. Roland-Gosselin, *La morale de Saint Augustin,* pp. 168-218; O. Schilling, *Die Staats-und soziallehre des hl. Augustinus* (Freiburg, 1910).
4   Cf. Hans P. Schmidt, 'Schalom: Die hebräisch-christliche Provokation', in *Weltfrieden und Revolution* (ed. H-E. Bahr, 1968) pp. 185-235. On Augustine, see especially pp. 226 ff.
5   Particularly if the categories designated in such passages as Luke 4 : 18, Matthew 11 : 4-6; Matthew 25 are not to be seen as an enumeration of different types of people but as characterisations of one basic social group: the poor, 'the people of the earth'.
6   Among the many works on the patristic teaching in this respect see especially A. Hamman, *Riches et pauvres dans l'Englise ancienne* (Paris, 1962). M. Hengel, *Property and riches in the early Church* (Philadelphia, 1974), Carmelo Giaquinta, 'Todo es común. La función social de la propiedad según la doctrina de los Santos Padres', *Criterio,* 1728-30; 720-725, 24 Dec. 1975.
7   I find here very valuable and illuminating J. Moltmann's frequent reference to five 'vicious circles' (or demonic circles) in which the struggle for liberation must take place: poverty, violence, cultural alienation, the destruction of nature and spiritual meaninglessness. Cf. for instance his *The Crucified God,* chapter 8. Though I miss a more systematic discussion of the interrelationship of these circles and therefore of an integrated vision of the struggle for human liberation.
8   *Populorum Progressio,* par. 15.
9   *A Theology of Hope,* Section III, ch. 10-13.
10   While I think that this formulation is valid to the extent that is claimed in this argument, any deeper consideration of the question would have to correct it insofar as it might be interpreted as considering 'structures' as external to personal life, a mere external framework. Naturally, such a view would be very superficial and contradict what social psychology has clearly shown us. At the present point, though, we are simply interested in pointing out the conditioning effect of structural factors while rejecting any form of mechanistic determinism.

5 - Pentecost and the Church today

G. W. E. Ashby

Pentecost cannot be ignored. It should never have been ignored because it is a peak event in the gospel, not merely in the history of the gospel. It cannot now be ignored because of the sheer size of the impact of what is known as the Pentecostal and neo-Pentecostal movement in the world-wide Christian Church.

(a) The Baptism in the Spirit, the Infilling of the Spirit, the gifts of the Spirit, ecstatic utterances, healings, all have a firm place in the New Testament Church. This undeniable fact will be examined in the next section. Yet after the second century, the manifestations have been sporadic, whilst the insistence on the experience by the believer of the Spirit in a special way was gradually replaced at first by an insistence on instruction and baptism followed in some periods by some instruction in the faith and by a detached portion of baptism, known as confirmation, and in other periods followed by no instruction at all. Later still in the Protestant West an insistence on a personal conversion to the Lord Christ preceded and tended to overshadow baptism in water.

Thus, both in doctrine and in experience, what has been happening in the Church of this century has come as new, sometimes as shocking and repulsive, sometimes as thrilling and disturbing. Yet it is impossible honestly to deny it, even by theology that would relegate it all to New Testament times only, since what is happening now has happened before and at a time (that of the New Testament) which makes it impossible to ignore. But the sense of shock is still present, and with it a continuing need for appraisal.

It should be pointed out that the long period from the second century to the twentieth is not really a Pentecostal tunnel period. There have been outbreaks of obvious manifestations of the Spirit like those described in Acts and the Pauline epistles. Some were readily accepted by the Church of the time, such as those described at the martyrdom of Perpetua and Felicitas and in the 29th catechesis of Simeon the New Theologian [1] and in the experiences of many mystics such as St. John of the Cross and St. Seraphim of Sarov,[2] to name but two. Others were either denied or viewed with suspicion by the Church of the time. Sometimes this was because of the excesses that went with a lack of teaching, whereas sometimes this was because of sheer conservatism. Montanism, Messaliamism, the Quakers, the Camisards, the Irvingites and the early Wesleyans are all examples of groups which certainly manifested the gifts of the Spirit on the New Testament pattern and which were either rejected or at least not accepted by the Churches of their time. Many Christian people in every country and age have been receiving the baptism of the Spirit and manifesting His gifts either unnoticed by the church authorities, or in ways that were readily acceptable to them.

The difference between the foregoing and what has been happening in the twentieth century has been the blatancy of it all, the quick growth of it all, and, latterly, the invasion of the traditional Churches by it all.

(b) It would seem that present-day Pentecostalism grew from a number of sources. The National Camp Movement at the turn of the century in the United States saw a dramatic outbreak of glossolalia (speaking in tongues) and miracles of healing. Parham's ministry, then that of Aimeé McPherson (quite different from each other in their methods!) led in time to the Apostolic Faith Mission and the Four Square Gospel. In 1914 the Assemblies of God were formed. They became the largest Pentecostal denomination. Even in those days the movement drew people together from all races and all denominations. At that time rejection by the 'main-line' churches was the common experience. Sometimes this was a case of mutual rejection, for many enthusiastic Pentecostals found the cold radicalism that they experienced in the main-line churches hard to bear. In this respect it has been amazing to see the growth in relationship between the Pentecostals and the main-line churches in the last 20 years. This has been pioneered by certain outstanding leaders, such as David du Plessis, and has led to official ecumenical discussions taking place with a real depth of understanding and prayer. There are reckoned to be about 20 million Pentecostals in the world, mainly located in the Americas, in Africa, in Indonesia, and in Russia. The story of the growth of the Russian Pentecostals from the ministry of Voronaev (who died in Siberia under Stalin) in 1920 to its present proportions, is an incredible chronicle of rapid growth during a period of comparative freedom under Lenin, followed by mounting persecution and martyrdom and of rejection by the official Baptist (Evangelical) Church.[8]

(c) The pattern of rejection by the main-line churches was seriously upset by what is variously known as neo-Pentecostalism, the Charismatic movement, or the Renewal, in the main-line churches themselves. The manifestations associated with this 'movement' were not of course unknown in the main-line churches, but the present movement can be said to date from Dennis Bennett's experiences in California in 1960. While acknowledging his debt to the Pentecostals, and despite the opposition of Bishop Pike, Bennett knew himself called to remain firmly and obediently within the Episcopalian Church. The movement grew rapidly within the Anglican and other churches, at first in the States, then in other parts of the world,

131

and from 1967 it broke out in the Roman Catholic communion, where it received from the beginning the cautious blessing and encouragement of the hierarchy.[4] Since then there has been tremendous growth and open fellowship and discussion with the traditional Pentecostal Churches, leading to a series of World Congresses of Renewal in the Spirit attended by large numbers of Pentecostals and neo-Pentecostals.

(d) South Africa shares with Belgium the unusual phenomenon of Renewal starting 'at the top', with leading members of the hierarchy of the Anglican Church. Since then there has been deep fellowship with Pentecostals, particularly with 'Father' Nicholas Bhengu, and with some dominees of the Dutch Reformed Churches Both groups have had to face degrees of rejection from Christians of their own race and religion. It is perhaps significant that at a time of diminishing hope for peaceful development in South Africa the Renewal movement has reawakened hope and love in many unexpected places.

The right time for an open discussion of the New Testament evidence for Baptism and Infilling of the Spirit and of the effects of the Spirit, is *now* — before an entrenched systematic theology grows up on either side. It is quite impossible to do more than outline some of the areas in which study of the New Testament evidence is vital.

(a) The words derived from the Greek root *bapt-* are used in various ways, sometimes to refer literally to a dipping in liquids, sometimes to refer more metaphorically to a 'dipping in God'. What arises from this is that it is a mistake to narrow the entry of a person into Christ and into Christ's Church down to one particular sacramental act or emotional response. Becoming a Christian, putting on Christ, is a many splendoured event, involving the whole man. It involves 'a constellation normally including proclamation of the gospel, faith, repentance, baptism in water, the receiving of the Spirit'.[5] What is described in Acts 8 and 10 and in other places is a series of responses to Christ by the believer. These responses do not come in the same order in each case, but they involve the loving and willing submission of the whole person to the Holy Trinity. This involves the mind and emotions, the body and the Spirit and is seen in a conscious turning to Christ, in proclamation of this fact through baptism in water and in the actualising of it in changed behaviour and freedom in praising God in all sorts of ways. Even though 'baptism' [5] sometimes refers to dipping in water, sometimes to a special possession by the Holy Spirit, sometimes even to martyrdom, it is clear that if baptism means becoming a Christian, or initiation, as it does in our own time, then baptism in the New Testament is a constellation of events and responses which add up to a person becoming wholly 'in Christ', in Christ's Church.

(b) Jesus's own baptism, far from being peculiar to him, as the unique God man, is in fact the *ur*-baptism event from which all other baptisms derive. Again, the Jordan event is a many splendoured event. First Jesus

132

at Jordan knows who he is. This is pronounced over him, to him, and the emphasis is on Jesus hearing the words from the Father 'This is my beloved Son'. Secondly he is dipped in the water. He goes down like the other penitents; he is washed; he is identified with their repentance and new hope for the coming kingdom. Thirdly, the Holy Spirit descends upon him in bodily form as a dove — that is flying straight down (not fluttering) on its target. There are no immediate ecstatic manifestations except that he is impelled into the wilderness to fight with the evil one and to defeat him, which is surely a manifestation in itself of the Indwelling of the Spirit.[5]

The constellation of events which for other people in the New Testament takes place in stages, in Jesus happens all at once. He experiences himself as Christ, knows himself for what he is (this is the nearest equivalent in him to what would be conversion in us), he is baptised in water, and he is filled with the Spirit — all at once. That Jesus's own baptism is little referred to outside the gospels does not indicate that the early Church ignored it. It is more likely to suggest that they took it for granted that being baptised into Christ meant being baptised into his own baptism in its entirety.

(c) According to the New Testament picture we cannot equate the Infilling or the Baptism of the Spirit with water baptism or with conversion. In several instances (including the 12 themselves) people had already been converted long before they were filled with the Spirit: in one instance (Cornelius and his companions in Acts 10) baptism in water followed the 'coming upon' of the Spirit. This is not to say that conversion and/or baptism in water is *not* the work of the Holy Spirit: it is to say that there is a special descent of the Spirit, bringing with him manifestations of joy and praise, including tongues, which rightly belongs to people who come to the Lord. On this score and on the evidence of the New Testament the witness in our own time of Pentecostals and neo-Pentecostals should not be seen as an attempt to exclude from the Church those who have not had certain experiences. Rather it must be seen as a clear proclamation of the richness and depth of what is promised by the Lord to those who surrender to his Son. What they are saying is in fact — 'All this is yours in baptism into Christ in the name of the Trinity and for the Church — claim it.'

So far the Pentecostal movement has produced no *summa* and no Church dogmatics. Nevertheless:

(a) The reality of the World of the Spirit as the reality for man and for the world is no platitude. It means that both the Holy Spirit and the evil one are taken seriously and that radical criticism is viewed with suspicion, not because it is radical but because it tends to deprecate or ignore as non-material the world of the Spirit.[6]

(b) Although there have been Unitarian Pentecostal groups in the United States, Pentecostals and neo-Pentecostals are strongly Trinitarian. This goes with a Holy Spirit theology of an intensity that has been lacking in the Western Church. The sad history of the *filioque* clause, in which the Western Church not only introduced the clause without adequate theological thought, but refused to take Eastern arguments seriously after introducing it, shows that the Eastern Church and the Pentecostals belong together in their concern for a theology of the Spirit placed firmly within the theology of the Trinity.

(c) Again, the Holy Spirit is seen as Christ-forming: there can be no room for a theology of the Spirit that does not bring men to Christ and cause them to grow in Christ. Hence mission has been seen among Pentecostals as the bringing of people to Christ, not the encouragement of the gifts of the Spirit on their own. This has also led the Pentecostals (and to a much lesser extent the neo-Pentecostals) to take the Second Coming of Christ seriously. This has sprung from taking Christ seriously. The sadness in this area lies in a polarisation — the Second Coming as a forlorn early Christian hope, on one side, and a literal millenarianism on the other.

In mission, Pentecostals have brought with them two very strong emphases which they again trace to the New Testament.

(a) The Spirit brings Christians into community. This is the work of the Spirit: it is Christians, not uncommitted people with whom he works in this way: and he brings them into a close, loving community which should be the wonder of the world around such as no other community can emulate. It is the body of Christ indeed.

(b) Experience of Christ is not to be confused with Christian instruction. There is a strong emphasis on basic teaching for all Christians in the Pentecostal Churches and this is growing among neo-Pentecostals. Yet 'whenever Christian identification resulted from instruction *without* personal experience, the church has departed from apostolic patterns'.[7]

Pentecostals find themselves driven by the experience of unity in the Spirit into the ecumenical search. This has been especially true since the growth of neo-Pentecostalism within the 'main-line' Churches. Especially remarkable has been the ease with which the ancient barrier between Rome and the Protestants has been breached.

Despite this it would be as well to list the most obvious areas of disunity and discovery.

(a) In 'Spirituality' or to use a more Pentecostal and biblical term 'the life in the Spirit', there has been real growth and learning on all sides. Broadly, non-Pentecostals have found the experiences in the Spirit both challenging and revealing. Pentecostals have found the liturgical and mystical traditions of the main-line Churches both as deserving more thought and as enriching for the individual and for the community.

(b) Infant baptism cannot be seen but as an obstacle to Pentecostals, just as rebaptism is to others. At this point dialogue involving both biblical and historical insights must be valuable.

134

(c) In the area of morals and family life the work of Larry Christianson and others deserves much more attention. Here again Pentecostals tend to be more rigid and react against what seems to them to be permissive and worldly.

(d) Pentecostals — and those involved in the Renewal Movement find it difficult to accept the radical dismissal of evil or of the evil one. They see this on biblical grounds and on grounds of personal experience as downright dangerous, and they would include all forms of spiritualism, freemasonry, etc., amongst the potential, if not actual works of the Devil.

(e) Sacraments unaccompanied by faith tend to be abhorrent to Pentecostals, as does any form of folk religion whereby people are treated as Christians when they give no sign of any commitment to Christ.

(f) Radical biblical criticism leaves Pentecostals either puzzled or angry. This does not mean that all are fundamentalists insisting that Jonah was swallowed by a whale. It does mean that any version of Jesus's Resurrection that does not proclaim him as literally risen on the third day is not likely to win much approval.

(g) It has often been said of the Renewal that it dilutes social and political witness in those who have experienced it. It is certainly true that the sort of social gospel thinking that finds a cause, takes it up with enthusiasm and acclaims it as Christian is completely repugnant to people who have found themselves and each other in the Spirit and in Christ *first*. It is also true that many Pentecostals and neo-Pentecostals opt out (and have always opted out) of social involvement. Yet as a whole there is a massive and very strong conviction, particularly in South Africa, that the Spirit has been poured upon Christians of different strata and race, so that they may find each other as Christians and together witness to their nation.

(h) Reactions to traditional church dogmas (e.g. Mariology, Purgatory, etc.) do not in fact spring from the nature of Pentecostalism at all, but from Protestant and Catholic origins. These are often more open to solution than other issues.

(i) Möller[8] characterises the emotional reaction from each side as 'the fear of spiritless ecclesiasticism from the ecumenical movement' on the one side and on the other 'the spirit of heresy-hunting' from some Pentecostals in whom 'the first fierce rapture of the baptism in the Holy Spirit begins to decline'.

(j) In all this perhaps there is to be found the voice of the Spirit calling Christians to a new ecumenism in which the Renewal Movement, drawing as it does so much of its membership from loyal members of the traditional Churches, has a significant part to play.

Little can be said about the healing ministry. This is, of course, not tied to the Pentecostal or neo-Pentecostal movement. Nevertheless the extent and depth at which God's healing power has been proclaimed by many Pentecostals and by such neo-Pentecostals as Francis MacNutt, shows that the gifts of the Spirit are not to be limited to forms of ecstasy. He sees the Spirit poured to heal at depth people who had been suffering without hope, often as committed Christians, for years.

At a local level, given on all sides that there are those who seek the kingdom, who are committed to the Holy Trinity and loyal to their Churches, there can be a real sharing of all sorts of ministries and the bringing of life to frozen Christian communities.

At the level of the world-wide Church there is so much to be discovered, recovered and uncovered that the Church in her witness to the world needs desperately to act on Karl's Barth's comment, 'only where the Holy Spirit is sighed, cried and prayed for does he become present and newly active'.[9]

REFERENCES
[1]   Louis Bouyer in 'One in Christ' Vol. 10, p. 155 (Kildare 1974).
[2]   Vinson Synan in 'One Christ' Vol. 10, p. 193 ff.
[3]   For further study see Steve Durasoff 'Bright Wind of the Spirit'.
[4]   Final report of the dialogue between the Secretariat for promoting Christian Unity of the Roman Catholic Church and leaders of some Pentecostal Churches and participants in the charismatic movement within Protestant and Anglican Churches, 1976 p. 7.
[5]   See Donatien Mollat in 'One in Christ' Vol. 10, p. 130.
[6]   A book which has received much praise in this respect is 'Encounter with God' by Morton Kelsey.
[7]   Womack, quoted by David du Plessis in 'One Christ' Vol. 10, p. 176.
[8]   'Die Diskussie our die Charismata soos wat dit in die Pinksterbeweging geleer en beoefen word'. F. P. Möller (Johannesburg 1975).
[9]   'Evangelical Theology', quoted by Möller, op. cit.

GUIDE TO FURTHER READING:
Nine o'clock in the Morning, Dennis Bennett (Logos International, 1970).
Gifts and Graces, Arnold Bittlinger (Eerdmans, 1968).
Bright Wind of the Spirit, Steve Durasoff (Hodder & Stoughton, 1972).
Baptism in the Holy Spirit, James Dunn (S.C.M. Press, 1970).
Encounter with God, Morton Kelsey (Hodder & Stoughton, 1972).
Healing, Francis McNutt (Ave Maria Press, 1974).

6 - Theology under re-appraisal: an Indian view

S. Amirtham

'Indian Christian Theology has arrived! It is far from negligible in volume, it is marked by a lively concern to grapple with the problems of witnessing to the gospel in the Indian cultural environment, and it represents a wide variety of traditions and viewpoints.' So concludes Robin Boyd in a survey of the different theological attempts in the past and present in India.[1] At the same time, he feels the need to explain why no Indian *Summa* had yet appeared. The early church, after all, he remarks, also took a long time to produce a *summa*, for their concern was more forging single doctrines in controversial situations. This is defended by M. M. Thomas in the foreword to this book when he writes, 'But living theology, which arises as tools for confessing the faith and fulfilling the mission in specific situations, is often fragmentary and partial in character. It is the raw material for systematic theology. Systematisation may have been an important aspect of theological development; and in the past such systematisation was deemed necessary to build up and carry forward a tradition of theological teaching. Today we have realised the deadening effect of total systems of thought on human creativity in any field of life, and we are justly suspicious of premature systematisation and synthesis.'[2] These statements make two points clear. Indian theology is missiological in its intention; it is fragmentary in form. It may be added, that it is not only fragmentary, but that it has often to be sought in other places than books on theology. The lyrics and liturgies used in worship, the sermons and dialogues in the church, the occasional bulletins and reports are also the source books for much of Indian Christian theology.

In Asia, one speaks of 'living theology'. It is living theology, because it is produced in a living missiological situation, because it is concerned with the living issues of today and not just the concerns of the past. It is living also because it is 'theology for living' in a wider sense, releasing the power of the gospel for meaningful living in society, enabling participation of the Church in the struggles and sufferings, aspirations and expectations of the people in Asia. Living theology is done in the context of the real world, and not just learnt in the context of an academic world.

An EACC consultation at Kandy enumerated four principles of living theology:

(i) 'A living theology must speak to the actual questions men in Asia are asking in the midst of their dilemmas . . . It must also speak in relation to the answers that are being given by Asian religions and philosophies both in their classical form and in new forms created by the impact on them of western thought, secularism and science.'

(ii) 'A living theology discerns what God in Christ is doing in the situation . . . The belief that the dialogue between God and man in Christ through the Holy Spirit is previous to the presence and words of the Christian are basic to the theological participation . . .'

(iii) 'The stuff of living theology is the life and witness of the laity in daily life and fellowship of the church's congregation responding in Christ to save the secular neighbourhood.'

(iv) 'Any theology developed in the frontier between Christian Faith and the cultural and social revolution of our time will contain not only inadequacies but even blindness to some aspects of Christian truth.' [8]

Living theology in any context is missiological for it is concerned with God's purpose for the world as revealed in Jesus Christ and its function is to mobilise the Church for participation in God's mission. This means that in relation to the gospel it has a witnessing role ; in relation to the Christian Faith, it has an interpretative role; in relation to Christian living, it has an activating role; in relation to society, it has a transformative role, serving the realisation of God's intention for His world.

Let us for the purposes of this article limit our attention to two aspects of the theological task in India. First, witnessing to the Christian gospel and interpreting the Christian Faith in relation to the religious and cultural heritage of India. This has been the main concern of many Indian Christian theologians from Brahmabandhab Upadyaya to Raymond Panikkar. In this process, the pre-understanding of the Indian mind, the categories of Indian thought, the religious experience of the Indian soul, are all factors to be taken seriously. In the New Testament itself we have different christological affirmations depending upon the pre-understanding of the groups for whom they were intended, whether they be Palestinian Jewish Christians, Jewish Christians of the diaspora or the Hellenistic Christians. The affirmations about Christ in India are therefore bound to be different from those made for example in Europe. The Indian pre-understanding or in religious terms, the Hindu pre-understanding would demand that Jesus Christ is affirmed in Hindu categories, and that Hindu reasons are offered to consider His claims. But then, in this process the concepts and categories themselves may need transformation to contain the import of the confession of Jesus Christ as Lord and Saviour. The inadequacy of categories will continue to pose a problem, offering no final answers. Tentative solutions will have to be tried and then changed to more adequate ones. Sankara, Ramanuja and others would become the philosophical counterparts to Plato and Aristotle in

138

this process. Brahmabandhab's attempts to interpret the Christian concept of God through the Advaitic concept of *Saccidananda Brahman* (Sat — being, Chit — Consciousness, Anada — bliss), Chenchiah's attempt to interpret the raw fact of Christ as the birth of a new order in creation, as emergence of life not bound by *karma* (the chain of sin, death and rebirth), Chakkarai's exposition as Jesus Christ the *avatar* (the incarnate one), Mark Sunder Rao's description of the believer's relationship with Christ in terms of *Ananyatva* (non-alterity) are known sufficiently well not to need any discussion at length here.

Raymond Panikkar tries to relate Christ to the Hindu tradition, by interpreting the Hindu sacred texts themselves in the light of Christ. For example his commentary on Brahma Sutra 1 : 1.2 reads 'That from which all things proceed and to which all things return and by which all things are (sustained in their own being) that 'that' is God, but *primo et per se* not a silent Godhead, not a kind of inaccessible *Brahman*, not God the Father and source of the whole Divinity, but the true *Isvara,* God the son, the *Logos,* the Christ.' [4] Thus he argues that there is a hidden presence of Christ in Hinduism which is fully revealed in Christianity. The loving task of the Christian is to unveil this Christ.

It was P. D. Devanandan who through his theological writings prepared the Church for open dialogue with Hindus. He realised a new phenomenon in the Hindu religious scene. Modern India is concerned with such matters as changing society, secularism, value of person as individual, meaning of history etc. There are also conscious attempts to relate the old and the new, the traditional and the modern. Here Devanandan sees great potential for Christian theology. 'The real problem in Hindu India is to effect a synthesis between traditional world view and contemporary secularism. Thoughtful Hindu leaders are wrestling with this problem and it is in relation to this concern that the good news of God incarnate in Jesus Christ will have to be spelled out.' [5] He also believes that in sharing of experience in the common cultural and community life, and in seeking together, we may arrive at some firm theological basis to understand and interpret the movement towards God's new creation. M. M. Thomas takes us beyond this position. The possibility of dialogue according to him lies not in classical theology, but in modern anthropology, because of the new humanity revealed in Jesus Christ. He perceives the significance of the quest for new humanity in other religions and sees not only possibilities for dialogue, but also for a 'Christ-centred secular ecumenism' or 'a secular fellowship in Christ'.[6] He writes, 'In other words, the final test of faith acknowledgement of the death and resurrection of Jesus Christ is seen in men's participation in the work of the Holy Spirit in building tissues of genuine "human" community within and between the communal groupings of men in history, as signs of the ultimate kingdom to come. The eucharistic community and the wider communion in the Messiah are sacramental signs of it; but they are really credible only in so far as they express their eschatological hope in action, in *praxis,* by mediating the spiritual dynamic of the New Humanity in Christ through their concern for human community.' [7]

The second aspect of the theological task is the interpretation of the gospel to bring out its implications in relation to the socio-economic realities of the Indian society. Here the concept of contextualisation popularised by the Theological Education Fund through its discussions and publications, is of great significance. Till recently indigenisation has been the subject of discussion. While indigenisation promoted the need for gospel taking roots in the Indian soil outgrowing its stuntedness as a pot plant in Western soil, the Indian soil was primarily understood as the cultural and religious tradition of the past. Indigenisation thus had a tendency to look backward, to glorify the past, and so to become static. Contextualisation emphasises 'the capacity to respond to the context'. And context includes both the cultural religious heritage and the socio-economic reality. The problems related to people's development, social revolution, economic justice, self-reliance of the people, participation and self-determination, secularisation, industrialisation, technology etc., become now vital issues for theology.

Contextualisation does not mean that theology adapts the gospel to the context. It means it is in the mutual impact of the gospel and the context that the gospel can be truly understood and interpreted. Contextualisation involves 'a double wrestle', as a report on theological education from Indonesia puts it. It says, 'The rethinking of theology must produce a theology that is relevant, that is to say, theological thinking which is systematically based on the word of God, which reflects the double wrestling of the Church. This double wrestle is, on the one hand, the wrestling of the Church with its Lord in the sense of incarnating the truth and grace of God in Jesus Christ and on the other hand, and at the same time, it is a struggle with the culture and society in the midst of which the Church lives.'[8] This understanding of the role of theology implies that participation in the struggles of the people, involvement in their present conflicts and ambiguities, is a condition for doing theology. A workshop on Theology-in-Action raised this issue and asked: 'can responsible theology be "done" anywhere but in the midst of a concrete involvement in the sufferings, conflicts and struggles of the poor and oppressed?' and in very picturesque words said, 'weak involvement produces weak theology, cool involvement produces cool theology, hot involvement produces hot theology'.[9]

Theology involves critical and reflective processes, and contextual theology demands the use of adequate tools for analysis of society, in which theology is done and the forces that condition the experience and understanding of God in that society. As Father Kappan in a talk to the Senate of Serampore [10] elaborated, theology should lay bare the layers of conditioning in which we find ourselves and their relationships to the dimension of meaning that we grasp. We meet God not in a vacuum, but in a historical situation. The class relations, for example of reproduction (man and woman), of production (owner and labourer), of power (makers of decision and victims of decision) are all decisive for grasp of ultimate reality. It is, for example, important for theology to show that class position makes one's religious perception selective, refusing and refuting those elements which are a threat to one's own interests, and supporting the status quo as if it were the will of God. The selective bias in reading and interpreting the Bible must be exposed, to discover the total message of the Bible and the bias in the Bible itself, if any.

It is the task of theology in India, not only to expose the class interests within the country but also international class interests, for hidden exploitive gigantic forces today are international. In dialogue with theologies from the developed nations, people everywhere must be sensitised to the fact of international interdependence and need for a more just international economic order. Until this is done, the task will remain far from being complete.

What we have said so far, has direct implication for theological education, which in India is integrally related to training for the Church's ministry. Three questions arise here: (i) How does one enable the student to theologise contextually? (ii) How does one enable the student to translate his theological insights into adequate forms of ministry? (iii) How does one enable a person to continue to grow in Christ, while at the seminary and in the parish and what is the type of spirituality we need to foster?

(i) There are welcome attempts in some theological institutions in India to discover a more adequate method of 'doing theology'. On the one hand there is a great emphasis on the study of the Bible and biblical theology, and on the other hand there is a great emphasis on involvement of the seminary in society. 'Doing theology through involvement' is becoming an acceptable model. There are groups of students living in the slums or villages, identifying themselves with the people there, studying their problems, conscientising them to the contradictions in society and organising them for action for justice. Some seminaries have programmes for students to live off campus and for periods of internship away from the seminary letting them have society's impact on them, and also enabling them to be self-reliant. In some places, seminary students are encouraged to participate in concrete political action with the risks involved. Regular joint student-teacher reflective sessions help them to digest such experiences theologically, and use them as data for theological reflection. There are programmes which bring students in meaningful contact with the religious life of the people, and problems of modern secular and industrial society, meeting them in the temple or festivals, factories or homes. Opportunities are thus created and structures provided whereby an action-reflection model or a praxis-oriented style of theological education is developed.

(ii) A theological student in India is normally preparing himself to be a future minister in the Church. Very often there is a tension between the theological understanding he gains in a seminary and the theological understanding prevalent in the Church; between the theology of the seminary and the theology of the Church. This can be sometimes creative, and desirable. A consultation on theological education held in Bangalore in 1968 said, 'The theological colleges must understand that they are not merely training institutions, but are directly involved as servants of the Church's mission. In the field of theological thinking, the college must stimulate the Church, must be with the Church and ahead of the Church.' The problem, of course is to know *how much* to be ahead of the Church! But this means that the pastor has an important ministry, as a teacher, raising the level of theological awareness of the parish through systematic teaching on the Bible and on social issues. Some seminaries in India are also directly involved in programmes for lay theological education, like the Theological Education for Christian Commitment and Action of the Tamil Nadu Theological Seminary. But more important than having direct lay education programmes is the fact that the theological students are trained to take this teaching aspect as vital to their ministry. At the seminary, students gain professional skills in preaching, conduct of worship, counselling, sick visiting etc. There is always a danger that this church-oriented ministry is taken as the main task of the Christian minister. This is not true. These acquisitions become meaningful, only inasmuch as they are exercised with the perspective of concern for justice in society.

Further, the Christian ministry is not primarily what the minister does in his church, or for that matter, what he does in society, but it is essentially what the Church does in, for and with the society. The minister's role is that of an enabler, enabling the members of his parish, challenging them to serve society by getting involved in it and turning them to be agents of change with others. The various involvement opportunities in a seminary, one hopes, will sensitise students to help their parish and church to identify areas of need and effectively meet the situation. In India, service to the under-privileged will have to be expressed in both forms, in institutions of charity and in programmes of conscientisation by catering to the needs of victims of injustice in society, and also through programmes of action with the people to remove the cause for such injustices.

The Andhra Christian Theological College, Secundarabad, has done special study in new patterns of ministry. A full-time paid ministry is not perhaps the most relevant pattern for India. It is financially non-viable, sociologically undesirable and theologically unsound. The college has suggested a pattern of four-fold ministry. This includes the ministry of the lay people in the context of secular vocation, a ministry of development by qualified people with the expertise needed, a sacramental-pastoral ministry which is largely voluntary and has ministerial training, and a ministry of teaching by theologically well-trained persons, who may be paid and whose number will be small. They will be the theological enablers for other ministries. Such a ministry also will provide opportunities for team ministries in each situation. This is being experimented with in the Andhra Church and one hopes that the results will be rewarding.

(iii) In all these the spiritual growth of the student and minister is important. Our relationship to God in Christ is not something that is static but something that needs growth towards the maturity of the stature of Christ Himself. Training in worship, corporate and private, promotes the sense of dependence on God, and the knowledge of availability of His grace and power, forgiveness and justification in the ministry. Christian ministry must come out of a life rooted in Christ. This rootedness in Christ must be related to the fellowship of the Church and the community around us. It is a total commitment to Christ which means a total availability for all. What we need is a spirituality that helps us to get involved in the struggles of people and does not yield to the temptations of withdrawal. Only such a spirituality will be adequate to the demands of the Christian ministry. Some seminaries are consciously attempting to foster such a spirituality in their community life.

This spirituality calls for a genuine sharing in the sufferings of the people. The Christian minister needs an emphatic heart. A spirituality of involvement fosters this sharing, which in a sense, is also participation in the Cross of Christ. C. S. Song observes, 'Aching of heart is the beginning of theology, for God's heart aches.' [11] Such spirituality is also fertile breeding ground for living theology and loving action.

REFERENCES
[1] Robin Boyd, *An Introduction to Indian Christian Theology* (C.L.S., Madras, 1969), p. 254.
[2] *ibid.*, p. vi.
[3] M. M. Thomas, *The Acknowledged Christ of the Indian Renaissance* (C.L.S., Madras, 1970), pp. 315 ff.
[4] Raymond Panikkar, *The Unknown Christ of Hinduism* (London, 1964), p. 126.
[5] P. D. Devanadan, *Preparation for Dialogue* (C.I.S.R.S., Bangalore, 1964), p. 38.
[6] M. M. Thomas, *Man and the Universe of Faiths* (C.L.S., 1975), p. 141.
[7] *ibid.*, p. 139.
[8] Cyclostyled manuscript available to me.
[9] *Theology in Action* (E.A.C.C., 1972), p. 25.
[10] A paper presented for private circulation.
[11] C. S. Song, *Doing Theology Today* (C.L.S., Madras, 1976), p. 47.

7 - Theology under re-appraisal: a Latin American view

J. Andrew Kirk

INTRODUCTION

Approximately 150 years after Latin America gained its political independence from Spain and Portugal (1810-1824), the Church on the continent has begun to question very seriously its theological dependence upon the structures and method of theological thinking being carried out in the United States and Europe. This article will attempt to explore the extent to which certain trends in modern theological reflection in Latin America demonstrate a radical shift of emphasis in comparison with the method, content and purpose of classical theology and a resolute bid for theological independence.

Our survey will cover two theological movements as such and a third movement which, although it cannot claim to have given rise to any systematic theological reflection, nevertheless does possess profound theological, as well as practical, implications for the mission and ministry of the entire Church.

The first movement, the *Theology of Liberation,* is by now the most famous. It has become a centre of discussion and controversy across the world: to traditional theology undoubtedly a thorn in the flesh, but to many Christians in the Third World the hope of a fresh approach to theological thought. The Theology of Liberation is probably the first attempt to do theology systematically outside the context of European civilisation since the very earliest centuries of the Christian Church.

The second movement I have elsewhere called *The New Evangelical Theology of Mission.*[1] Slightly later on the scene than the Theology of Liberation, it is intimately connected with the rise of the Latin American Theological Fraternity (1969). In the last eight years it has begun to create a new theological consciousness amongst many leaders in the Protestant Churches, a consciousness of the need to replace imported theological categories of thought for those which may arise from a creative interplay between the biblical message of total salvation in Jesus Christ and the distinctive Latin American context of the Church's mission.[2]

The third movement, originating in Guatemala in 1962, has become known round the world as *Theological Education by Extension*. Although its main purpose is to apply new insights in educational methodology to the preparation of Christian leaders, nevertheless the logic of its perspective demands a reconsideration of many traditional assumptions concerning the style and purpose of the theological task.

As we outline the critical contribution of each movement we hope that the extent to which each one in a different, but often complementary, way represents a very fundamental re-appraisal of contemporary theology will become evident.

THE THEOLOGY OF LIBERATION

In general terms the Theology of Liberation is a 'political theology',[3] for it springs from and relates to the particular political situation of Latin American countries today. As Gutierrez says, 'it is a critical reflection on a particular set of issues'[4]: those pertaining to the global reality of Latin America and, by transference, to the rest of the Third World whose economic position is analogous. As critical reflection it fulfils a prophetic function, that of contributing to the understanding of historical events in order that the Christian's commitment within them may be more radical and clearer.

However, as a political theology it offers, within what one might loosely call the modern debate on social ethics, a highly distinctive stance. It is no coincidence, for example, that the latest book by Juan-Luis Segundo of Uruguay should be called *Liberation of Theology*,[5] for in principle this movement is as much concerned with liberating theology from its present cultural and ideological captivity as it is in proposing a wholly new agenda for theology: 'the theology of liberation offers us not so much a new theme for reflection as a *new way* to do theology'.[6]

By looking at this theology's distinctive aspects we should receive a clearer vision of its real concerns and its unique approach.

It begins from the premise that no theological reflection is neutral. Theological thought has always been conditioned by the historical context in which it has been done. This fact is not necessarily negative; it is inevitable. It becomes detrimental to theology in two particular instances: firstly, when the conditioning is not recognised and theologians believe that the method they are using is unbiased and universal; secondly, when the particular historical conditioning (the 'spirit of the age'), which is unconsciously absorbed into the reflection, runs counter to the Christian message of complete liberation in Christ.

The first task for theology, therefore, is to become aware of both the past and present socio-cultural factors which have helped to shape its method and content. This process of 'conscientisation'[7] is a kind of 'proto-theology', an indispensable first step before theology proper can begin its task. An adequate awareness of historical influences is only possible through

145

the use of those auxiliary sciences which have been developed and refined in order to interpret and transform modern humanity's global context (sociology, psychology, economics and anthropology).

Of these social sciences the most relevant is the socio-economic analysis of Marxism. The reason for adopting the Marxist analysis of economic imperialism is the failure of the 'functionalist' approach to contemporary Latin American society to account for and change the persistent situation of grinding poverty for the majority, and indescribable opulence for a tiny minority still capable of controlling the levers of power in their own interests.[8] Theology must be aware, therefore, that contemporary society points in the direction of the class struggle and the total socialisation of the means of production as the only possible solution to the growing phenomenon of under-development.[9]

Both the proven fact of conditioning and theology's own consciousness that the God of whom it speaks is the Lord of the whole created order indicate that theology can only be undertaken within the context of a 'hermeneutical circle'. Segundo [10] gives an initial definition of this method as: 'the continuous change in our interpretation of the Bible in relation to the continuous changes in our present reality, both individual and social.' In effect, the unavoidable reality of the hermeneutical circle means that theology is incapable of carrying out its task without constant reference to the context in which it is being done. Theology is not an autonomous discipline; the only way its sources, especially the Bible, can be really available to us today is through a constant coming and going between the past and the present.

Because of the particular stance from which it is forced by historical circumstances to view the Church's mission, theology may be permitted to select those biblical themes which most clearly tune into the Church's particular context in any moment of crisis. Just as the German Confessing Church stressed in its Barmen Declaration (1933) the absolute Lordship of Jesus Christ over all 'lords' and powers, a theme which led to Bonhoeffer's celebrated distinction between the 'ultimate' and the 'penultimate', so theology in Latin America must give pride of place to Liberation, as prefigured in the Exodus and completed in the Passover mystery of Christ's death and resurrection.[11] Liberation, at the deepest level, means liberation from sin 'which is the ultimate root of all disruption of friendship and of all injustice and oppression.[12] Sin is manifested in many different processes: today, particularly in economic and social oppression and political impotency. Sin is everything which destroys and disfigures a solitary human existence. Its opposite is the Kingdom, the transformation of bodily life by the elimination of corruptibility and weakness.[13]

Finally, the aim of theology is not just to give a more adequate explanation of a concrete reality; it is an intellectual and pastoral discipline put very definitely at the service of a cause. Throbbing through all the writings of the liberation theologians is the burning conviction that the *raison d'être* of theology is negated as and when it becomes a mere academic discipline removed, for the sake of a pretended objectivity, from personal and community commitment to a transforming mission in history. Fundamentally, Liberation Theology is a liberation of theology in order that it may become a liberating instrument within a society characterised by conflicts, struggles and injustices: 'it is a theology which is open — in the protest against trampled human dignity, in the struggle against the plunder of the vast majority of people, in liberating love, and in the building of a new, just and fraternal society — to the gift of the kingdom of God'.[14]

A NEW EVANGELICAL THEOLOGY OF MISSION

Whereas the Theology of Liberation originated amongst Roman Catholics and, even today, has found few whole-hearted supporters amongst non-catholics, this second movement represents in broad terms the *avant garde* of the Evangelical Churches.[15] Some of the theological concerns are similar, though tackled from a distinctive viewpoint, whilst others, as one might expect, are quite different.

Evangelical theologians, principally through the forum created by the Latin American Theological Fraternity (LATF), have begun to search for a genuinely Latin American expression of the Christian faith (contextualisation). This undertaking springs from a basic conviction that the Churches of which they are members to a large degree understand and propagate a gospel incrusted with foreign cultural elements. The concern for contextualisation shows a growing theological maturity and independence, for all evangelistic and ecclesiastical formulae are submitted to the rigorous tests of their cultural identification and their biblical authenticity.

If it is true that Liberation Theology sprang on to the world scene at the 1966 W.C.C. Geneva Conference on Church and Society, this new evangelical theology did the same at the 1974 Lausanne Congress on World Evangelisation.[16] There, René Padilla in his main address startled the evangelical world by referring to its missionary work, in so far as it has confused gospel and culture and promoted the latter as if it were equivalent to the former, as 'worldly': ' "culture Christianity" . . . is the "religious product" of a civilisation in which *nothing*, not even man himself, escapes technology . . . This is another form of worldliness. The manipulation of the gospel to achieve successful results inevitably leads to slavery to the world and its powers'.[17]

In the polemic against culture-Christianity and in the desire to create a new evangelical school of thought on the continent these theological thinkers stress particularly the following issues:

The gospel committed to the Church to proclaim 'throughout the earth as a testimony to all nations' (Matt. 24 : 14) is the gospel of the Kingdom. Amongst many other things,[18] the Kingdom theology being developed by members of the LATF involves a radical commitment to the values of the new age which God is creating among his people and the concomitant refusal to support strategies and programmes which involve the use of any means that do not conform to these values.[19]

The ethical qualities demanded by the Kingdom must touch social as well as personal life. Samuel Escobar in his Lausanne paper speaks of those Christians who 'condemn all the sins that well-behaved middle-class people condemn but say nothing about exploitation, intrigue, and dirty political manœuvring done by the great multinational corporations round the world'.[20] It is inconceivable that the authentic biblical gospel can be preached without a call to repentance not only of individual sins but also of social sin, because evangelism involves the prophetic preaching of God's wholly new order in Christ: 'the call to repentance . . . is a change of attitude that becomes concrete in history . . . The change involved imposes a new life-style'.[21]

Behind many evangelicals' indifference to Christian social and political involvement lies the age-old dichotomy between spirit and matter. Non-involvement has many different rationales, among them the concept of the two kingdoms, dispensationalism and the dualism which accompanies the hyper-spirituality of part of the charismatic renewal movement. This stance is widely diffused within Latin American evangelical Christianity and promotes the great theological and political error of believing that the gospel is apolitical, only concerned with the soul and the future. In fact, much evangelical Christianity, because of its deep political commitment (by default) to maintaining the fatalism of the *status quo,* has become, in the words of a Swiss sociologist, 'the haven of the Masses'.[22]

A holistic approach to Christian mission [23] implies the communication by verbal and non-verbal means of the whole biblical message of grace, liberation and the call to costly Christian discipleship. This approach has led our evangelical thinkers to adopt for theology the same kind of 'hermeneutical circle' as that proposed by Liberation Theology, although they would give the Scriptures a more definitive place within the circle. In particular, they emphasise the reality of the Christian Church as a hermeneutical community, out of whose combined study, experience and action alone can come greater faithfulness to Christ today [24] and theological reflection as an interdisciplinary task in which serious dialogue with all non-theological disciplines becomes the *sine qua non* of any theology wholly committed to mission.[25]

THEOLOGICAL EDUCATION BY EXTENSION (TEE)

Though formally independent of the two previous movements we have described, and though not representing any systematic theological reflection, the methods and interests of TEE reinforce the growing conviction in Latin America that a new age is dawning in the Church for the theological task.

Extension education simply means that continuous theological training is now available, in principle, to the whole Church. No-one need be excluded any more from access to a learning process because of a lack of previous academic attainment nor because other commitments do not allow full-time dedication to study.[26]

Some of the implications of TEE for the theological task are already evident and have been proved highly significant in practice. Amongst others we would mention the following:

Theology in a real sense is becoming the concern of the whole *ekklesia*. There is ample evidence that many ordinary Christians are involved in a creative interaction between the problems of secular life and the principal sources of the Christian faith. The resulting theological reflection is more integrated and less specialist than the normal 'academic' variety, which, though it may achieve a high level of detailed precision and rational proficiency, often either ignores or side-steps the real issues which Christians face in the path of daily obedience. The seminar sessions of TEE become miniature theological workshops in which systematic theological thinking is constantly being related to the concrete demands of the Church's mission. The theological learning process from the beginning is carried out within the sphere of the hermeneutical circle, in touch with the living situation of the Christian community and the drama of the wider human society. The aim of TEE is to produce 'thinkers' who are capable of reflecting theologically out of their daily experience not 'academics' whose training has largely consisted in amassing theoretical knowledge.

Meaningful theological thought depends upon a conscious understanding of the personality, context and role of the thinker: his unconscious presuppositions and his cultural, racial and class backgrounds. The reason for this new insight is that, through TEE, theory has to be tested against the reality of live situations, the participants in courses are also protagonists in these situations. Their study of God's revelation confronts them with a word of discernment, command or encouragement which uncovers hidden assumptions and motivations. In the midst of complex situations the learner cannot abstract himself artificially from the daily challenge to test what he is understanding by seeking to hide behind the unreal ideal of pure objectivity and disinterestedness. Once one appreciates that those doing theology, both educators and learners, are real human beings inserted in ambiguous cultural situations, then complete objectivity is exposed as a chimera.

Theological learning is a continuing process. The horizons of understanding are continually being pushed outwards, as knowledge is linked to discernment, decisions and actions in changing situations. This fact tends to diminish the arbitrary distinction between 'experts' and 'ordinary people', for the learning process involves the contribution of a variety of people, all of whom possess different abilities, personalities, knowledge and experience.

Theological thinking thus becomes both a permanent enterprise and a community responsibility in which all involved are, in differing degrees, both teachers and learners. The community is not measured principally by the yardstick of high academic excellence, nor by its ability for abstract theoretical thought, but by its willingness to share what it 'knows' (in the Hebrew sense), continuing its theological study as a conscious service to the needs of each of its members.

CONCLUSION

Those who have never experienced the inferiority complex born out of a permanent state of cultural, intellectual and economic dependence may be tempted to dismiss the new Latin American theological movements as the primary result of psychological defence mechanisms.

Without doubt extreme positions have been taken.[27] Nevertheless, sensitivity to extreme situations of deprivation and repression hardly allow for carefully balanced theological statements which try to defend the legitimate interests of every faction in society.

If these theologies appear to be strongly polemical, even overtly hostile, it is because they spring from the conviction that pretended neutrality is just another way by which much Western theology refuses to acknowledge its own subservience to a particular political and economic order which maintains the world dangerously divided into the possessors and the dispossessed.[28]

In point of fact, the theological stirrings here reflected are very far from being counteractionary and negative. My own personal impression after ten years of being immersed in each one of these rather distinct, but in some ways complementary, debates is that they represent the beginning of an exciting renewal of contemporary theology. It is true that what has appeared up to now may lack sophistication if measured by the requirements of academic excellence set by Western universities. Nevertheless, in so far as theology has to do with life — God's free offer of a new life in Jesus Christ and the normal unregenerate life of the multitudes who do not yet know from whence comes their hope of salvation — then these new movements are reverberating with the reality of life, both in its immense possibilities because Jesus died, came to life and lives for evermore, and in its sordid perversion and alienation. As Bishop McGrath of Panama once said, theology in Latin America is, of necessity, 'market-place theology'. Now, this does not imply a lack of seriousness nor a rejection of profound dialogue with theology being done in other places. On the other hand, it does mean, and this is stated with the utmost vigour, the end of all compartmentalisation of theology.

The challenge to theology from Latin America is contained in two simple, but very basic, questions: 'In what historical (and geographical) context is theology being done, and how is it interacting within this context?'

and 'What are the basic aims it is setting itself?' Upon the answers to these questions depends, to a large extent, its faithfulness or its irrelevance.

REFERENCES

[1] Cf. J. A. Kirk, 'Ferment and Challenge in the New Latin American Theologies' (The Kingsman, No. 18, 1975-76), pp. 30-42.

[2] Cf. S. Escobar, 'Una teología evangélica para Iberoamérica' in *El Debate contemporaneo sobre la Biblia* (ed. P. Savage), (Barcelona: Ediciones Evangelicas Europeas, 1972).

[3] Cf. Alistair Kee (ed.), *A Reader in Political Theology* (London: S.C.M. Press, 1974).

[4] See Gutierrez *A Theology of Liberation* (London: S.C.M. Press, 1974), pp. 6-15.

[5] *Liberación de la Teología* (Buenos Aires: Lohlé, 1975).

[6] Gutierrez, *op. cit.,* p. 15.

[7] A term first used by the Brazilian educator, Paolo Freire. Cf. *Pedagogy of the Oppressed* (New York: Herder and Herder, 1970). Its meaning, with no direct equivalent in English, is the apprehension of the demand for change inherent in a particular situation.

[8] Cf. H. Bernstein (ed.), *Underdevelopment and Development: the Third World Today* (Harmondsworth: Penguin, 1973).

[9] Whereas W. W. Rostow speaks of *stages of development* for the Third World, cf. *The Stages of Economic Growth: a Non-Communist Manifesto* (Cambridge: Harvard Univ. Press, 1961), the economic philosophy behind John Kennedy's Alliance for Progress', Cunder Frank speaks of 'The Development of Underdevelopment' cf. 'El desarrollo del subdesarrollo llogotá' as the inevitable result of the application of Rostow's economic views.

[10] *Op. cit.,* p. 12. This concept is being used in a different sense from that of Bultmann or the so-called 'New Hermeneutic'. There is no space here to develop the differences, but cf. my article, 'The Bible in Latin American Liberation Theology: a review essay' in *The Bible and Liberation: Political and Social Hermeneutics. A Radical Religion Reader* (Berkeley, July 1976).

[11] Cf., for example, J. S. Croatto, *Liberación y libertad: pautas hermenéuticas* (Buenos Aires: Mundo Nuevo, 1973).

[12] Gutierrez, *op. cit.,* p. 37.

[13] Cf. J. Miguez, *Doing Theology in a Revolutionary Situation* (Philadelphia: Fortress Press, 1975), chapter 7: Kingdom of God, Utopia and Historical Engagement.

[14] Gutierrez, *op. cit.,* p. 15.

[15] Evangelical is the adjective applied to all non-Catholic Churches. The term Protestant is largely unused, except in the context of Church history.

[16] The full report, plus all the papers presented, are contained in J. D. Douglas (ed.), *Let the Earth hear His Voice* (Minneapolis: World Wide Publications, 1975).

[17] *Ibid.,* pp. 125-127. Much of his criticism is directed against the modern 'Church Growth' school of missiology which has grown up around the figure of Donald McGavran.

[18] The L.A.T.F. dedicated its 1972 continental conference to the biblical/ theological theme of the Kingdom. The papers are collected in R. Padilla (ed.), *El Reino de Dios y Latinoamerica hoy* (El Paso: Casa bautista, 1975). An important distinction should be drawn between the theologians of liberation and the L.A.T.F. with regard to the use of Kingdom theology: the first accept a much greater degree of continuity between present history and the fulness of

the Kingdom than the second. At the same time the second stress more the continuity between the present visibility of the Kingdom and God's special redeemed people. The distinctions are derived, so it seems to me, from the relative importance given, in each case, to man's freedom and God's participation in the bringing in of the Kingdom.

[19] Perhaps, the key concept being developed by the L.A.T.F. in its new theological method is that of discernment. This method is only possible where there is full commitment to the complete reliability of the entire Scriptures and to a global mission for the Church in the modern world of Latin America. Cf. 'Evangelism and the World', the reply of Dr. Padilla to the criticisms of his Lausanne paper in Let the Earth . . . op. cit., pp. 134-146. From outside the continent the major theological influence has been the rediscovery of the tradition springing from the radical Reformation in the theological reflection of J. H. Yoder, cf. especially, The Politics of Jesus (Grand Rapids: Eerdmans, 1972).

[20] 'Evangelism and Man's Search for Freedom, Justice and Fulfilment,' ibid., p. 304.

[21] Cf. Padilla, op. cit., pp. 129-132.

[22] Cf. Lalive d'Epinay, Haven of the Masses: a study of the Pentecostal Movement in Chile (London: Lutterworth Press, 1969).

[23] For the meaning of 'holistic' in connection with mission, cf. Orlando Costas, The Church and its Mission: a shattering critique from the Third World (Wheaton: Tyndale House, 1974), pp. 59-83, 310-311.

[24] Cf. P. Savage, 'The Church and Evangelism' in R. Padilla (ed.), The New Face of Evangelicalism: an International Symposium on the Lausanne Covenant (London: Hodder and Stoughton, 1976).

[25] In 1976 Kairos, a Community for biblical-theological formation, was started in Buenos Aires by seven members of the L.A.T.F. Its principal purpose is to encourage creative, interdisciplinary, Christian thinking and action amongst Christians who are graduates in non-theological disciplines.

[26] A thorough account of T.E.E. is given in Ralph Winter (ed.), Theological Education by Extension (South Pasadena: William Carey Library, 1969). T.E.E. is also having a profound effect on the understanding and structures of the Churches' ministry, though it is beyond the scope of this essay to elaborate upon the changes which are taking place, cf. Howard A. Snyder, The Problem of Wineskins: Church Structures in a Technological Age (Downers Grove: I.V.P., 1975). It is true that not all that is said in this section applies exclusively to T.E.E. However, there is a specific challenge to revise theological methodology inherent in T.E.E., because the nature of the situation has proved traditional methodology to be inadequate.

[27] Particularly by H. Assmann who has tended to reduce theology to sociology. Cf., Practical Theology of Liberation (London: Search Press, 1975).

[28] Amongst many analyses of the captivity of Western theology we could mention: José Miranda, Marx and the Bible: a critique of the Philosophy of Oppression (New York: Orbis Books, 1974).

8 - Theology under re-appraisal: black theology

Warner R. Traynham

During the 1960s much of the attention of the world was riveted on the United States. The social upheaval that occurred during that decade, known as the Civil Rights Movement, fascinated and involved millions. Americans abroad were stopped and grilled about the unseemly events occurring in the 'cradle of liberty' or dined out on their ability to apply the perspective of a native toward what was going on across the water. The Civil Rights Movement was not a national but a world event and Martin Luther King, Jr., the symbol of that movement, became an international figure.

In one sense Dr. King was the 'provocateur' of the phenomenon known as Black Theology. He galvanised the masses in a religio-political movement. He interpreted in evangelical concepts and language the political and social struggle. More than anyone King was responsible for increasing the racial consciousness and pride of blacks so that they might become a militant force for the achievement of their liberation. King objected to the term 'black power' though he did the most to create the reality behind it.

If one takes the long view of course, Black Theology is as old as the black community's sojourn in America. For blacks came here a religious people, a people soon to encounter in one fashion or another the Christian faith to which they were ultimately largely to subscribe. Black Theology etymologically at least, describes the black religious communities' reflection upon its experience in the light of its faith, whether that faith be traditional African religion, a syncretistic mix of African and Christian elements or Christianity itself. Black Theology's most ample corpus for an orally oriented people can be found in its folklore and its music, especially the Negro spirituals.

But if Black Theology is more narrowly defined as the systematic and orderly reflection upon the gospel in the light of human experience, then Black Theology, while it may be found essayed in the works of a Henry Highland Garnet or an Alexander Crummel has had to wait for this century and for the civil rights movement just mentioned to come into being. Joseph Washington, in his controversial book *Black Religion* published in the '60s asserted that blacks had contributed nothing original to the theological tradition of Christianity. When he wrote those words they had the ring of truth. There were virtually no black theologians. What theology had been written by black people previously was occasional, written in response to some particular circumstances or event. Washington's book has been cited by some as the provocation that elicited Black Theology. Certainly those theologians who subsequently entered the field had at least one eye on Washington's assertion.

I believe, however, that King must be credited with providing the agenda for Black Theology if not for beginning the movement itself. For Black Theology is a distinctive phenomenon. Some of you will be quite conscious of the movements in Africa and Asia to indigenise Christian theology. To express the faith once delivered to the saints in terms native to the place in which it is proclaimed. Some, especially in Latin America, will be conscious of another movement, to find in the gospel a brief for, and a call to, social and political liberation. One can encounter there a quest for empowerment of the oppressed through the faith of Christ, to rise and throw off the bonds that shackle them and deny to them that abundant life which he promised.

The one is ethnic, the other is liberation theology. The one is cultural, the other is a class phenomenon. Black Theology is peculiar in that it claims to be both an ethnic and a liberation theology. In most of the world, there is no necessary connection between these two realities or concerns. But in America where oppression has so largely been a racial matter, race and oppression, symbolically, if not literally, fuse.

Now the problem is that there is among black theologians some confusion and some ambivalence of purpose in this area. Is the issue to evolve an ethnic theology or liberation theology? For while for black Americans these categories largely overlap, there are those who would argue that there is more to blackness than the experience of oppression and so more to Black Theology than a concern for liberation. Others argue, nevertheless, that the core of the gospel and the besetting preoccupation historically of the black Church and the black community is the quest for liberation. Clearly there is also an issue of focus, for ethnic or indigenous theology is of interest primarily to the ethnic group or community into whose thought forms, etc., the faith is translated, and only secondarily is it of interest to the larger Christian community. Liberation theology, on the other hand, is addressed at least as much to the oppressor if he or she claims to be Christian, as it is to the oppressed. To the latter it is a word of hope, to the former a word of judgment.

Before examining the context of Black Theology, let's look at its legitimacy or lack of it. We are talking of a racial perspective, a racial theology. One may ask if that is not initially precluded by a faith in which there is neither 'Jew nor Greek, male nor female, bond nor free'.

The argument of the black theologians is that all theologies are con-

154

ditioned by the race or class or social condition of those who write them. The gospel preached to the slaves in the course of their evangelisation during the first half of the 19th century, is a clear case of theology edited by one class for the consumption of another. It is an extreme example. Black theologians assert along with the sociologists of knowledge that everyone speaks from a perspective and that those perspectives are not only individual but socially conditioned. Unless one is content to commend the intellectually dishonest idea of viewing the faith through someone else's eyes, different groups are bound to reflect on the same gospel and to do so differently. That variety of viewpoints enriches the prospect of all the others and in theological terms makes sense of the Johannine vision of the New Jerusalem into which the nations bring their treasures.

There is no plain theology then, the black theologians say there is only Black Theology or white theology or European theology or Oriental or African theology, etc.

Beyond this relatively uncontroversial statement the black theologians make another less obvious assertion. To whit, that the situation of the oppressed is the situation to which God as revealed in the Old and New Testament comes most directly, and is the situation that is most congenial to apprehending Him and His promises. Further they assert that the core of the biblical message is the liberation of the oppressed. Theology therefore done from the perspective of the oppressed and to motivate their liberation is more truly Christian theology than that done from the position or perspective of the oppressor, which overtly or covertly almost inevitably sanctions the oppression God comes to destroy.

In short, conditional theology is inevitable whether conditioned by class or race or culture. Secondly not all conditioned theologies are equal. Those done from the perspectives of the poor and disadvantaged, in so far as they are done from that perspective, are more consonant with the gospel than those done from other or opposite perspectives.

It is because of these convictions and because in America blackness and oppression, a racial and class phenomenon, are so closely identified that a black theologian can make the claim that in America the only Christian theology is Black Theology and not be peremptorily dismissed as hopelessly chauvinistic and racist.

One final note by way of preface. While from outside, the black community may appear to be a unified whole, internally it does not appear so. Blacks in America are unified in their quest for liberation. But on the matter of its attainment, they hold a variety of views. It is impossible, therefore, to state comprehensively the perspective of Black Theology. What one must do is present individual or party views within the area and the rationale for them.

With this proviso let us turn to a brief review of four major themes that have emerged or are emerging in Black Theology.

155

One distinctive factor about Black Theology is that except for one singular exception, those who do it are Christian. It sees itself as not only a Christian phenomenon but also an evangelical Christian phenomenon reflecting the black communities major religious commitment to the Baptist and Methodist Churches. This is not strange for American blacks for the last century have either been Christians or in reaction to the Christian gospel primarily represented by the Baptist and Methodist traditions. The reaction to that faith commitment has taken two forms in this century, secularisation, a falling away from organised religion and religious practice, and the generation of variant religious cults and sects. The period from the first World War to the present has seen the rise of Daddy's Grace's; United House of Prayer for all People; Father Divine's 'Peace Mission'; a collection of black Jewish sects and Moorish or Islamic groups culminating in the Black Muslims, etc. Religiously then, blacks are not all evangelical Christians although they are predominantly so. And certainly blacks as a community are not all religious in the formal sense or even predominantly so.

Black Theology is essentially a church response to the call for black power. It asserts that there is no fundamental contradiction between black evangelical Christianity and the goals or the attainment of black power. One of Black Theology's first and central tasks is to rationalise that relationship. It may be said to have two tasks, this rationalisation, and the provision of the theological motive power to black Christians to attain the substance of liberation through black power.

In so far as black power is a community concern and the black community is neither universally religious nor religiously Christian, some black theologians are calling for an ecumenical theology — one encompassing the various faiths of the community, or for a community rather than for a church theology. This kind of question arises precisely because of Black Theology's relationship to black power.

It will be interesting to see if such a concern can move beyond theory, if an 'ecumenical' theological referent can be found from which basis a theology can be built, or if any community consensus will be forthcoming which will justify the use of the term 'theology' black or otherwise. I confess that I am sceptical of both possibilities. I think that even the reactions to the Christian Church and the Christian faith in the black community have characteristically Christian underpinnings. I am convinced that the only *real* faith substratum available to be tapped generally in the black community, for the present at least, is Christian and that Black Theology will for the most part remain Christian for some time to come.

In any case, for the black Christian certain key questions must be addressed in doing Black Theology. One of these is the question of evil.

156

How does one account for the experience of blacks in America in the face of the Christian doctrines of the nature of God and of providence? Various answers to this question have been advanced. In the early 19th century the most common response was that God permitted slavery so that blacks might be exposed to the gospel and then return to 'redeem' Africa. Currently, one black theologian has held that blacks have been chosen by God as suffering servants to bear witness in a fallen world to the brotherhood of man as Israel was chosen to bear witness to the oneness and the fatherhood of God. Another, James Cone, the most prominent of the black theologians, holds that blacks are indeed chosen by God, not to suffer but to be championed by him because he is the deliverer of the oppressed. For Cone, black oppression is no mystery, it is white power and racism operating in the area of human freedom. Both these views have been challenged from the humanist perspective: the first because there is no evidence to support the claim; the second because Cone does not say why God would allow so much racially conditioned suffering in the first place. William Jones, the author of this critique, believes that 'ethnic suffering' as he calls it, is conclusive evidence against either the omnipotence or the benevolence of God and that either God is limited, a view contrary to Christian doctrine, non-existent or a white racist.

Practically I think Black Theology as all theology, must suspend judgment on the problem of 'ethnic suffering' as well as any other kind of suffering. Beyond that, two things must be said. Ultimately, because God is the creator, he is responsible for evil as well as for good because he is responsible for the arena and the rules by which the game of life is and must be played. If the game comes out right his gamble will be vindicated. The real issue is not therefore why this has been allowed to happen, but what we can do about it and what he, God, is prepared to do about it. Black Theology asserts the oppressed must be active in their own liberation and that God stands with them and against oppression in the contest. It further claims that the thrust of both the Old and New Testaments must be understood in this way. God is encountered by Israel as a community first, as Saviour of that community and then as creator of a people and only later as creator and saviour of a world. This is, say the black theologians, the key event of the Old Testament. Jesus' 'humiliation', becoming not only man, but a special man — an oppressed Jew and one of the people of the land — is the key event of the New Testament. He came to the despised, not just to men, with the promise and the reality of deliverance, from socio-economic and political oppression as well as from individual and spiritual sin and death. God, say the black theologians, is encountered in both covenants as related to the community and to socio-political events first as the reality and paradigm of his relationship to individuals. American religion with its strong admixture of evangelical pietism tends to see sin and evil almost

157

exclusively in individual terms, the black revolution and Black Theology insist that first it must be seen in community terms for it is in a community context that people are oppressed. People in America are not encountered first as individuals but as representations of social and racial groups and that perception qualifies all subsequent perceptions. Scripture addresses this reality in the context of oppressor and oppressed and chooses sides. Its end is to liberate both, but to liberate both it must equalise the unequal relationship — this is perceived by the oppressed as liberation and by the oppressors as judgment and revolution.

Black Theology asserts that the Christian gospel is itself the answer to the question of ethnic suffering, in that it commands a response. It is in this context that James Cone sees the imperative of Christian theology to be what Marx believed to be the imperative of reflective thought 'not simply to understand the world, but to change it'. This is a key focus of Black Theology.

If the answer of Black Theology to the problem of evil is to respond by correcting the situation, how is that correction to occur? At this point theology has moved into the arena of ethics.

CHRISTIAN ETHICS AND BLACK THEOLOGY

How are the demands of black liberation on the socio-economic level to be harmonised or reconciled with the demands of the gospel? Once again the real question in ethical guise is, is black power compatible with the gospel? The black theologians answer yes, but to do so they must recapitulate their understanding of the ethical demands. The key ethical command of the gospel is love, love commanded and therefore distinctive from either erotic love or affection. Like parental love *agape* is and can be commanded because it is more akin to respect than to passion, it is an act of will. We might I think appropriately describe *agape* as willing the fulfilment of the other and working to that end. Other definitions are versions of the same idea. Christian love then is an act of will motivated by our response to God's care and Christ's sacrifice for us.

When one tries to apply Christian love to the relations of the oppressed and the oppressor, we discover that the implementation differs for each group because a radical inequality exists. Oppression is the very opposite of love. It is the use of people as means only. Oppression restricts and distorts the realisation of the potential of both parties — oppressor and oppressed. So the first requirement of Christian love is to limit the power of the oppressor and increase that of the oppressed. It is as I have said, to equalise the relationship. Christian love in such a context therefore is necessarily revolutionary — it moves to turn the situation upside down, to set it right. So in America where whites are identified with oppression and blacks are identified generally with the oppressed, whites can show Christian love to blacks only by joining the struggle for liberation and coming out from the

158

community and advantages that shelter them and identifying with the oppressed. Blacks can show Christian love to whites only by asserting their integrity in the face of its denial and struggling against them insofar as they support or are supported by the structures of oppression. The first stage or precondition for Christian love then, is justice. Any other relationship of love in such a context which leaves that context unaffected is a sick, distorted and un-Christian love.

'Revolution' in this sense black theologians would agree, is mandated by the gospel's command to love one another.

When one tries to act on this understanding in the realm of history and in the context of social and political realities one encounters the tool of oppression, power. Then the question becomes, how does love alter the distribution of power? Martin Luther King, Jr. answered by an appeal to conscience and the application of non-violent pressure. King's methods worked, up to a point. Beyond that point inevitably the question of the Christian's access to violence as an ethical tool, was bound to arise. Even King's method had intrinsic to it, the willingness to engender violence on the other side through the application of pressure. Resistance cannot ultimately be non-violent, it takes two to tango. The same ambivalence which infects pacifism in the face of responsibility for others is magnified by non-violent action that actively seeks encounters, where pacifism is passively seeking to avoid them.

From the perspective of black theologians the question is not — is violence ethically permissible to the Christian in the context of the liberation struggle? The question is rather — is the violence of liberation permissible in the face of the on-going violence imbedded in the system of oppression? Webster's dictionary defines violence as 'an exertion of physical force so as to injure or abuse', and secondly 'injury by or as if by distortion, infringement, or profanation'. In short, violence is doing injury to the integrity of a person, relationship or thing. The oppression of blacks in America qualifies under both definitions. The question is whether the first can be adopted by the oppressed to address both on the part of the oppressor.

Black theologians split on this issue, some holding that the gospel precludes violence or a response in kind, no matter what the provocation. They tend to cite Christ's obedience to the cross. Others hold that nothing in the gospel requires the rejection of violence as a last resort. They may cite Jesus' expulsion of the money changers from the temple. In any case, they insist that the determination must be made responsibly by the oppressed in the face of tactical issues since the moral question is not clear. At this point the lines tend to be drawn on the basis of whether the speaker is a normative ethicist or a contextual ethicist. It is a question that has received much attention, especially since the black church tends toward pietism and is quite conscious of scriptural limits on such activity. At the same time it feels the internal pressure and is often aware of the apparent need for such action.

Black Theology focuses on the gospel imperative in the socio-political arena and has yet to work through its insights in that area as they modify the black church's traditional understanding of individual ethics. That is one of the tasks that remain.

LIBERATION, RECONCILIATION AND BLACK THEOLOGY

When one begins to talk about the means of obtaining liberation, one must speak of the nature of that goal and its relationship to reconciliation.

Liberation for black theologians generally means at least three things. It refers in the first instance to elimination of effective racism and the establishment of a more equitable distribution of the power and goods of American society. It is real, tangible and historically verifiable.

As there is bondage without, however, there is also a bondage within. So liberation also means psychological freedom; freedom from the sense of inferiority bred into blacks by 350 years of slavery and discrimination and freedom from the sense of superiority bred into whites by the same phenomenon. It is the liberation of the whole person from the sinful past for the risk of trust in God and a new future.

Finally, liberation is the conquest of sin and death, in which man and God are active in combating the specific and historical manifestations of these realities.

Liberation then has a socio-political face and a psychological and spiritual one.

Beyond this, liberation is not simply an objective state but the struggle itself, it is the active discovery that your struggle is God's. The struggle liberates, restoring the self image that oppression defaced, and affirming the increasing capacity of the individual and the group to shape their destiny. As James Cone puts it, in a fallen world, the only true freedom is that which the oppressed experience in the fight for liberation, for in an oppressive society all are victims but only the oppressed know it. Because this is so, the struggle of the oppressed is a service they render to all, even the oppressors. 'Liberation', says Cone, 'is not a status but an action one undertakes.' Because the struggle is God's struggle, liberation has an eschatological reference. It is the inbreaking of the kingdom which is the success of the enterprise. Because of the conviction of ultimate success Cone can say the goal is the struggle, not winning. Here other black theologians however, notably J. Deotis Roberts and Major Jones, part company. At least in terms of the first two expressions of liberation, they believe blacks certainly are interested in winning, in actualising that liberation quite concretely. If one adopts the latter view, then tactics become very important and this brings us to a discussion of reconciliation.

160

For some who profess a concern with winning, the use of violence for instance as a tactic, however one resolves the moral issue, is precluded because they believe violence will make reconciliation between blacks and whites impossible. Indeed some black theologians believe it would provoke genocide.

At this point a division among black theologians appears. Some place a major focus on reconciliation as the goal of the gospel and the context of true liberation, others refuse to discuss reconciliation insisting that when the two are mentioned, even though liberation is described as the precondition for reconciliation, whites are constitutionally incapable of hearing that distinction. They want to move immediately to reconciliation leaving the circumstances unchanged. They want cheap grace.

This analysis of this tendency is, I believe, a true one. But I also believe that reconciliation cannot be ignored because it is the premise and the goal of the gospel.

Clearly liberation must precede reconciliation, otherwise the latter is merely a mask for oppression. If liberation is undertaken to free the oppressed and the oppressor, insofar as liberation is achieved, just so far would reconciliation be achieved for free persons. That is true in the sense of being free of the need to oppress or the experience of being oppressed, since they would have nothing to keep them unreconciled. The truly free must be reconciled since nothing divides them. This is true not only at some ultimate level where we would escape the bondage of ancient hatreds or desire for revenge, but also on the more immediate level. For the degree that external restraints on the oppressed are removed and the objective powers of the oppressor restricted, and the former disavows vengeance and the latter believes the disavowal and adjusts to the new state of things, just so far are they reconciled already. Historically reconciliation is the other side of liberation. They cannot be separated.

One should certainly be agnostic about the details of ultimate reconciliation. Scripture lapses wisely into symbol at that point. We are well advised to do the same. But an historical hope is not misplaced.

Beyond the description of liberation already given one may say the hope of the faith, as Black Theology understands it, is to produce a people sensitive to the needs of the oppressed whatever the form of that oppression, even if their own experience of oppression should be modified or cease — a people conscious of the call to preach release to the captive and recovery of sight to the blind.

Aspects of liberation will co-exist with aspects of reconciliation as they should. The end is to proclaim the acceptable year of the Lord and to behave so that acts of liberation and reconciliation occur to the end that each year may be acceptable.

GUIDE TO FURTHER READING:

God of the Oppressed, James H. Cone (New York: Seabury Press, 1975).

This is the most recent and the most careful statement of Dr. Cone's theological position to date. In its use of folk material, etc. it emphasizes the ethnic. In its argument it focuses on liberation and therefore on the universal.

A Black Political Theology, J. Deotis Roberts, Sr. (Philadelphia: Westminster Press, 1974).

Dr. Roberts' racial perspective was formed largely during the era of civil rights rather than that of black power as Dr. Cone's was. His perspective tends therefore to be less rhetorical and more conservative though he must deal with the same issues Cone deals with.

Christian Faith in Black and White, Warner R. Traynham (Wakefield, Mass.: Parameter Press, 1973).

This is both an introduction to black theology aimed at the uninitiated clerical or lay as well as an attempt to further the discussion by raising issues unaddressed at the time.

SECTION IV

The Church as People

The essays in this section are about the Church at large, not the Anglican
Communion only.

1 - Christian ministry and the people of God

Robert M. Grant

When we think of the ministry and the people of God (whether one topic or two) we who are members of the most tradition-minded of all Churches tend to consider the question historically, as if 'whatever was, is right'. Even in the reign of Queen Victoria this approach had drawbacks. We tended to prepare our clergy to serve the churches of the past, and we did an excellent job. Now, however, it is impossible to continue walking backwards into the future. This is so for two reasons. First, the enormous increase in the world's population means that even apart from any doctrine of one man/one vote, communities that live by nostalgia do not have much chance for survival. We have to make or earn our way in a new and competitive situation. T. S. Eliot liked to think he had the backing of the dead. But there are more people alive now than all his backers put together. Second, the modern development of the media of communication means that our sensibilities have been mechanised, made cruder, perhaps, but in any case enhanced. We can journey world-wide instantaneously via TV; we can do so by plane in a few hours. The cultural gifts and limitations of our local parishes have so shrunk as to be nearly insignificant. In a city like my own (Chicago), the importance of the Church in most areas of life steadily declines. In America all Churches are sects, but under the new conditions they tend to become nothing but not-very-interesting clubs of like-minded folk with a faintly spiritual aura.

This situation resembles almost nothing in the Christian past and it presents tremendous difficulties, psychological and otherwise, to those who insist on attending church or participating in worship. The social rationale of parish life is slipping away, and no alternative seems open. Under these circumstances it is tempting to quote New Testament texts, especially those texts directed against Sadducees and Pharisees (obviously prototypes of Christians other than ourselves).

In recent times, critics of the clergy have used New Testament texts. One of their favourites is Mark 12 : 24, where Jesus says to the Sadducees as a group, 'You know neither the scriptures nor the power of God.' Don't the clergy spend too much time on the problems of our age and their parishioners, not enough on scripture study and prayer? Or there are words to Pharisees (Mark 7 : 8): 'You leave the commandment of God and hold fast the tradition of men.' Any stick will do to beat clerics. In the third century, Origen, when a cleric himself, used texts like these against bishops, presbyters, and deacons. Some things do not change.

But are the clergy really that important? Shouldn't the texts be applied to Christians generally, not just to ministers or priests? Today, the clerical world is not as significant as it was in Trollope's time. The population of the city ward I live in is about seventy thousand, and it cannot be the case that divine revelation and the whole history of Christian experience finds its culmination in our ministers or rabbis or in us happy few who attend assemblies. In a sense, we are both Sadducees and Pharisees and scripture is addressed to us all. We should rethink Church and ministry, move away from a restricted understanding of both, and, hopefully, come to some measure of consensus as to what the ministry and Churches ought to be and do.

Indeed, all along the line, we need clearer understanding of Church life in relation to the wider world. There is no need to look for secular man somewhere else. If we are honest, we ourselves must admit that we are secular almost all the time. We would do well to think clearly about this instead of retreating into what the novelist John Cheever calls, 'habit, superstition and sentimentality'. One way to look at our world is through church history, especially contemporary church history. Church historians (ancient or modern) often ignore the secular world. They usually neglect the obvious social or even sociological components in the history of the Church. It became obvious to me years ago when a fascinating pair of articles in *The New Yorker* (August 1 and 8, 1964) gave details about the Church of St. Matthew and St. Timothy in Manhattan and explained how, in the 19th century, Episcopal Churches followed the frantic migrations of Society with a capital S. This is why in lower Manhattan there are so many Episcopal churches without vitality commensurate with their endowments. What was the meaning of ministry during their heyday? What, more recently? What, now? Can one give a prescription, or must one simply hope, while giving support to creative flexibility?

But is a sociological understanding enough? This brings me to the second point. Something rather novel has been happening in the Episcopal Church. A recent article says that for the past decade we have lost one Episcopalian every five minutes. That's an arresting figure — but it may require a bit of background. There was a post-war religious boom in America, sometimes ascribed to President Eisenhower and the mood of his terms of office, but, in fact, simply post-war. From 1944 to 1959, the membership of the Episcopal church rose to $3\frac{1}{2}$ million and one net member was added every six-and-a-half minutes. Then came a decade of stagnation.

The population kept growing; Church membership did not. Then, in 1969, the membership began to slip. From 1969 to about 1974 — call it five years — there was a net loss of half a million, and a net loss of one member every five minutes. Such a loss could obliterate an ordinary American congregation within two days.

Bad enough? There is more. At the end of the period of growth, the number of clergy started to rise sharply. In the four years from 1955 to 1959 (remember that 1959 marks the peak), the number rose from 7,500 to 8,700 — not quite proportionate to the number of laymen. It was after 1959, in the decade of stagnation, that the number of clergy kept rising. The worst comparison I can make is between the year 1972 and 1957; fifteen years apart. The number of Church members was almost exactly the same; however, the number of clergy increased by 47 per cent. Small wonder that sensible people speak of clergy surpluses and note that there are now nearly two clergy (1·8, actually) for each church position in the Episcopal Church.

Should we blame our local clergy for this situation? Are our local ministers too outgoing or too introverted; too socially-minded or too modern? Even in 1966, it was clear that on the south bank of the Thames these charges would not hold water. An article in *Harper's Magazine* (N. Stacey, 'The Decline of the Church in England', March, 1966) showed that, in Woolwich, super-modern parishes and super-antiquarian parishes suffered attendance declines at about the same rate as middle of the road congregations.

One of the most radical solutions to the problem renews the radical Reformation's cries against Churches and is in favour of sects or small spiritual groups. There are plenty of such groups around, often quite successful, that people want Churches to emulate. However, it is hard to recover the imagined spiritual atmosphere of the primitive Church. Also, there is no reason to suppose that human life is best conducted under pure confrontational democracy. At the same time, we should not suppose that any of the old institutional arrangements, including ministerial, mean exactly what they meant a millennium or even a decade ago. Times and modes change, and while the ship of the Church should not put about with every gust of wind, we continually adjust both sails and rudder. Anyone who does not pay attention to the needs of the times in parish, diocese, or beyond, should not be out sailing.

Yet we need ministers, not just laymen, since the life of the Church does not just happen. Life needs spirit. Certainly, spirit is not imprisoned but given substance and strength when related to mind and body. When the apostle Paul tried to restore or create administrative order in the Corinthian community, he was not obliterating freedom but trying to prevent anarchy. This is why his words seem to have some permanent validity — though of

166

course not in every detail; I would not require veils for the majority of our congregation.

What kind of ministers do we need today? Given the over-supply of mill-run candidates, we can boldly lay down a guideline or two. First, they ought to believe in God — and contagiously. We presuppose a decent self-esteem; we add to it love of neighbour as self, at least in intention. Love of God comes first and without it the rest is valueless in this context. Love, in general, depends on the constant effort to understand. Our ministers can be liberation theologians because they must constantly free their picture of God from the outmoded or the trendy, and from their picture of themselves. Second, candidates for our ministry must believe in the Church — also contagiously. This does not mean swallowing every dictate or tradition or current authority, nor populism. It means constantly and devotedly caring for the community as the representation of Christ's body in the world. 'Love of the brothers' and sisters is the Johannine interpretation. Though the Church has a world mission, the place where we can express it and discover it is here and now. Just as diseases can spread from pinpricks, so health can begin with a local inoculation.

Above all, we must stop thinking of the ministry as that of the clergy alone. We who are laymen or think as laymen must think of our own ministry as brought into existence by God. It is a ministry for mission. What if yearly, in some five-minute period, a few of us could bring a new member to this church? Not that we ourselves would bring about this happy event, but that the power of God would make use of us.

We were all called to ministry. But what is it?

CHANGE AND RECONCILIATION

When the Christian Churches first developed out of sectarian groups within Judaism and entered into the wider Graeco-Roman world, they inevitably lost some of the functions they once exercised. Graeco-Roman law provided the context for Christian morality; Graeco-Roman society itself provided the context for Christian social life. With the continuing changes in historical circumstances, the functions of the Churches change, too. Sometimes functions were added, as in the case of Byzantine and mediaeval hospitals and charities. Sometimes they were dropped, as in the case of modern income maintenance, medical care, and insurance. Churches, to be sure, continue to maintain schools, colleges, and hospitals, but in the western world most of these functions have been taken over by the State.

Sometimes we yearn for golden days when all such activities were the province of the Church. These golden days did not exist. Instead, the Church performed one function after another. Except for the initial change from apocalyptic intensity to life in the world, loss of one activity has usually been accompanied by the gain of another. The Church when alive has constantly adapted its activities to the needs of the times.

167

Is there any constant in the midst of this change? If we search for a constant firmly rooted in human nature, presumably it is to be found in what an early papyrus calls 'the gospel of reconciliation' (2 Cor. 5 : 19). The ancient stories of the Book of Genesis tell us of mankind, sinful and disobedient, at war with God and with one another and in need of reconciliation with God and neighbour. The Genesis situation has not changed much, as far as our human situation is concerned. The apostle Paul tells us of a cosmic alteration that took place with the crucifixion of Christ. 'While we were enemies we were reconciled to God by the death of his Son', and 'now that we are reconciled, we shall be saved by his life' (Rom. 5 : 10 RSV). Since, according to tradition received by Paul, 'Christ died for our sins in accordance with the scriptures' (1 Cor. 15 : 3) he can say that 'in Christ God was reconciling the world to himself, not counting their trespasses against them' (2 Cor. 5 : 19).

The reconciliation of human beings to God is obviously of supreme importance, but it is not all there is. Something has to happen in human relations as well. When Paul speaks of reconciliation on the human level, he talks about two of the most important areas of human achievement and failure. First, he speaks of marriage, sexuality, and separation in 1 Corinthians 7. He urges a separated wife to be reconciled to her husband and implies that a separated husband should be reconciled to his wife (1 Cor. 7 : 11). This is an area of personal relations. Without reconciliation with God and in personal relations, it is pointless to discuss world affairs or the need for reconciliation in cities and nations. Charity, in the sense of love and reconciliation, begins at home.

The second example, to which Paul devotes more attention in his letters, is the broader sphere of group relations. Paul is concerned with 'the ministry of reconciliation' which God gave him (2 Cor. 5 : 18), for which he is an 'ambassador for Christ' (5 : 20). In his experience it has much to do with Jewish-Christian relations. We should look at what he says. As a Jew he is tormented by the failure of the Christian mission to the Jewish people, and he expresses his anguish in Romans 9-11. He suggests that in the mystery of the divine election, non-Christian Jews were 'hardened' until 'the full number of the gentiles come in, and so all Israel will be saved' (11 : 25-26). This process has meant 'the reconciliation of the world', and when completed it will be 'life from the dead' (11 : 15). In Ephesians 3 : 14-16, then, we read that

> He is our peace, who has made us both one, and has broken down the dividing wall of hostility, by abolishing in his flesh the law of commandments and ordinances, that he might create in himself one new man in place of the two, so making peace, and might reconcile us both to God in one body through the cross, thus bringing the hostility to an end.

The literal meaning of these passages is that Christian conversionism, slander, ignorance, and lack of fellow-feeling in regard to Jews is directly opposed to the apostolic mission. This means not only Jews in Russia or in Israel but also, precisely, where we live.

To go beyond the letter of Paul's words, we should note his reliance upon the double commandment of love of God and of neighbour. These commands come from Hebrew tradition. The first is in Deuteronomy 6 : 4, the second in Leviticus 19 : 18. Paul quotes the second in two of his most important letters (Gal. 5 :14; Rom. 13 : 9). This is important because of the word 'neighbour'. It is easy enough to think about loving distant peoples. It is much harder to love one's neighbour, whether next door or down the street or at work, or even at church.

Now we should think about groups. The first translation of reconciliation is called for in nearly every nation and city of the world. The two groups needing reconciliation are black and white. This is not the place for an analysis of means. It is simply the occasion for recalling that the goal is a Christian one and closely related to the goal for Jews and gentiles. Equally close at hand is the call to the reconciliation of rich with poor, nations with individuals, and men with women, not just in relation to marriage. We cannot get lost in generalities about groups and classes, however. We need reconciliation within groups, not just among groups. Churches with their rival claims need attention too.

All of this may seem either obvious or unnecessary. Even in the area of reconciliation parts of the Church's task i.e., the task of all Christians, are being taken away by governments and social agencies. There are federal and state mediation officers. Psychiatrists and social workers are often doing work Churches could do, and the Church seems to oscillate between retreat and ill-considered pronouncements. Still, given the nature of human existence, there is enough reconciling for everyone. Not all of the Sermon on the Mount can be taken literally, but one thing seems clear. In personal relations Jesus had little concern for righteousness or self-righteousness. 'Make friends quickly with your accuser', he said, 'while you are going with him to court.' If you do not, you will end up losing 'the last penny', whatever the merits of your case may be (Matt. 5 : 25-26). In other words, failure to reach reconciliation is likely to have disastrous practical consequences. This obviously extends to groups. As we read the papers or watch TV, we are tempted to suppose that only the modern world cracks up. This tendency is universal. Matthew quotes, 'Every kingdom divided against itself is laid waste, and no city or house divided against itself will stand' (12 : 25). As individuals, and often when together, we cannot do much about the affairs of nations. We act in our own social groups, and each of us belongs to many. These groups are where we are called upon as Christians to take up our own ministries of reconciliation. We are called to do unto others as God has done unto us.

If the ministry of the people of God is a ministry of reconciliation, why do we need an organised Church and organised services of worship? Must

169

not we move on to desacralise our old ways of doing things? Does not God himself, according to Amos 5 : 21, hate and despise festivals and take no delight in solemn assemblies? In the first place, to take isolated expressions, even biblical, as giving instant access to God's will is a bad exegetical method. Second, the theological goal of reconciliation needs to be dealt with practically. When people stay apart there is no chance for reconciliation in its final stages. When people come together for services of worship and other church meetings, hostility and other difficulties often arise, but so does the possibility of renewing some relationships. Again, the most practical expression of reconciliation is often found through and in compromise. Of course, we cannot compromise the truth. However, if we boldly and honestly look at our own motives, and those of others as well, we may be able to keep from identifying the truth either with ourselves or with them.

Beyond this, we have all been taught that to draw near to God is to draw near to one another. This seems to be true whether we are considering theological definitions or actually participating in cultic worship. Cultic worship, in and outside of the eucharist, necessarily brings participants out of the isolation they experience as individuals. The experience of worship can provide a setting for reconciliation. To be sure, it does not always emerge. It comes neither automatically nor magically but as a gift of grace. Our part is to offer ourselves in services of worship to God in the hope of finding and expressing the peace that is the consequence of reconciliation to God and neighbour.

In our emphasis on the duty and goal of reconciliation we have obviously neglected the virtues and necessity of diversity and the tangible benefits produced by competition. Perhaps these do not need stressing in our 'pluralistic' age. Though we have to admit that Churches have grown and grown strong in the midst of bitter controversies (the 4th century; the 15th; the 19th), we must recall two statements about origins and goals expressed in the New Testament. In Acts 17 : 26-27 the primal unity of all mankind is emphasised as well as the human quest for God. In John 11 : 51-52 we find that the death of Jesus was for the nation Israel, 'but not for the nation only, but to gather into one the scattered children of God'. Looking at the context suggests that both texts were written in times when unity was less than universal. The study of Church history, too, casts doubt on the existence of a primitive golden age. What remains unquestionable is that the drive towards unity through reconciliation is central to Christian gospel.

2 - Christian ministry and synodical government

D. M. Kennedy

This article is a contribution to this particular discussion from a united — and uniting — Church in 'a developing' country, the Church of North India, a Church which seeks to combine and harmonise, according to a recipe going back to the Faith & Order Conference held at Lausanne in 1927, three types of Church Government or 'Policy' — Episcopal, Presbyterial (Presbyterian) and Congregational.

In the statement on the *Polity of the Church* (Plan of Church Union in North India and Pakistan, IV Edition, 1965, Part I, Chapter X, page 21) we read: 'The Church of North India affirms that the Lord Jesus Christ is the only Lord and Head of the Church.'

At first sight this statement might appear to be one of those lovely, ecclesiastical or homiletical phrases which lack definite content because they lack practical methods of implementation.

If, however, we examine the North India Plan and Constitution more closely, we see that the Founding Fathers of the CNI *did* have a definite idea as to how the laudable theological concept of the Lordship and Head-ship of Christ in his Church could be implemented. For the immediate succeeding clause in the section on Polity goes on to say: 'The CNI accepts the Episcopal, Presbyterial and Congregational elements in Church Order, as the means through which the Lordship of Christ in his Church may be realised.'

This basic affirmation is supplemented by four more definite detailed statements:

1. Three traditional elements of Church Order are to be combined in such a *harmony*, which is to be shown in *episcope* (oversight). Though the word is not used, the underlying idea is very much that of our Eastern Orthodox Brethren, the idea of *sobornost,* the members of an orchestra keeping harmony with the conductor and with each other;

2. Over-all oversight (*episcope*) in the Church becomes effective through the legislative, administrative, liturgical and pastoral functions assigned to the Synod, Diocesan Council and *'other organs of the Church's Life'*. It is

perhaps to be regretted that the vital role of the local Church and its infra-structure is thus dismissed in the rather off-hand phrase 'other organs of the Church's Life';

3. *The personal oversight* of a diocesan bishop must go hand in hand with a *corporate responsibility,* shared by bishops, presbyters, deacons and lay people acting together.

4. The CNI also speaks of 'the corporate responsibility' of the episcopate of the Church as a whole. The CNI Synod does not have a separate House of Bishops; but, usually once a year, the bishops of the Church, now nearly two dozen in number, gather from all over Northern, Western and Eastern India for mutual counsel and discussion.

Problem: How are such 'Bishops' Meetings' to be co-related with the formal structures of Synodical Government?

The theological sections in the Plan, and in the Constitution, on polity, are followed by definitions (a) of the diocese, (b) of the congregation and (c) of the synod in the structure of the Church. These are designed to implement the Headship of the Lord Jesus Christ over the Church at grass-roots, regional and All India levels.

Significantly, the sequence is not congregation, diocese, synod — or even, 'synod, diocese, congregation'. Rather, *the diocese,* often covering an area as large or larger than a European country, is recognised as the key to any realistic implementation of the theological affirmations outlined above. (Both in Synodical-Diocesan relationships and in Diocesan-Congregational (local church), relationships, the CNI has its centralisers and decentralisers. No doubt it is not unique among the Churches of Christendom at present in experiencing a certain creative tension here.)

We shall therefore proceed as follows: We shall discuss Christian Ministry and Synodical Government first at the diocesan or regional level, then at the local level, and finally at the national level.

CHRISTIAN MINISTRY AND SYNODICAL GOVERNMENT IN A DIOCESE

In all our discussions it is to be remembered that, right across the Indian sub-continent, and, indeed, wherever the missionary journeys of John R. Mott made their impact or left their mark, the consummation of organic Church Union was preceded by a period of 'missionary co-operation and comity'. The practical effect of this has been that the various Anglican, Presbyterian and Congregationalist missions were spread out unevenly over the sub-continent. The result being a high concentration of Anglicans in some areas, of Presbyterians in another, and so on. In some predominantly 'ex-Anglican' dioceses, the regional embodiment of the CNI in the Diocesan Council was originally strongly bishop-centred, not to say Lordship-centred! In strongly Presbyterian areas, on the other hand, the Diocesan Councils,

172

at least in some places, have presented an image of a non-episcopal Church 'taking episcopacy into its system', after the pattern which Archbishop Fisher's famous Cambridge sermon desired to see established in non-Anglican Churches in the British Isles.

This basic contrast should not be exaggerated however. It has already been modified by various factors — especially the fascination which forms of *political democracy* exert in Church as well as State in developing countries at present. (If it be objected that there is something unspiritual about democracy, or that the Christian Church is basically not a democracy but a theocracy, the retort from the developing churches would understandably be, 'If democracy is unspiritual here, why has it been adopted in the West, not only in classical Presbyterianism, with its pyramid of "Church courts", but in the current Anglican taking of democracy into *its* system?')

At the diocesan level, the combination of Episcopal and Presbyterial systems is in effect a combination of monarchical Episcopacy and oligarchical Presbyterianism. The Presbyterian contribution has been seen in a vast expansion of Committees and sub-Committees, and it is sometimes the responsibility of the bishop to humanise some committee decisions, and even to baptise them in the insights of the gospel, by drawing attention to Christian traditions more universal than that of the majority denomination in particular regions, and by stressing the claims of *outreach*. A United Church should not simply become a static synthesis of old-fashioned English Anglicanism, Scottish Presbyterianism etc., but part of the ongoing People of God, with a sense of mission in later 20th century India. (It is both encouraging and disturbing to note that this sense of mission is at present more in evidence in 'para-church' evangelical organisations than in the main-line churches themselves. This was evident at the post-Lausanne Evangelisation Congress at Deolali, India, in January, 1977.)

In all this, the bishop has to avoid giving a goody-goody impression that he is the only 'charismatic' individual in an inter-locking system of Committees dominated by hard-faced realists, clerical or lay. The basic problem is to allow significant movements of church renewal actually to affect the style of work of the Church at every level, including the work of its Synod, super-synods and mini-synods.

THE LOCAL CHURCH

With this in mind, we turn to the question of Synodical Government at the grass-roots, in the context of the local church, to which, in both the CSI and the CNI, a rather uninspiring title 'Pastorate' has been given.

The local church or parish is, in a sense, a diocese in miniature; and, ideally, just as a bishop should work in collegiality with his fellow-Presbyters and duly authorised lay representatives, so the ordained Presbyter (ministerial priest) has to share his responsibilities of *episcope* with the local Pastorate Committee or Parish Council.

173

This in fact involves persuading them to see two things:

(i) The Pastorate Committee — a better name for it might be Parish Pastoral Council — is not just a Finance Committee or Committee of business management. Nostalgic Presbyterians sometimes feel that the problem would be solved if such a committee were exclusively composed of Life Elders, forming a Kirk Session more restricted in authority than a Regional Presbytery (Diocesan Council) or a nation-wide General Assembly, but similar to those higher bodies in its awareness that their work is basically spiritual and not just administrative. A closer look at Presbyterianism would however modify that nostalgia in two important aspects. First — even in Scotland — there has been increasing criticism of the idea of Life Elders, with a preference for the American Presbyterian system of Elder-ship for a term of years only. In Ireland, during the preliminary Tripartite Talks between the Anglican, Presbyterian and Methodist Churches, representatives of the Anglican Church of Ireland were emboldened to claim that their system of Elected Synod, men and women, was in fact more democratic than the Presbyterian one of Life Elders.

(ii) Secondly, and more generally, if we critically admit that no system of church government fully solves the problem of power, we would also have to admit that, if the built-in danger of Anglicanism is a monarchical style of episcopacy, the built-in danger of Presbyterianism, will be one of oligarchy, i.e. the danger of the domination of the local church by a particular social, racial, economic or linguistic background.

If we ask the question how far uniting churches have succeeded in conserving the good points of *Congregationalism*, the answer has not always been encouraging. Church meetings — i.e. meetings, annually or more frequently, of the whole body of the faithful in a local congregation — are not always well attended; and when they are, it may be for wrong motives. We can even expand our tabulation of the characteristic dangers of various types of Church policy as follows:

Episcopacy	....	....	....	Monarchy
Presbyterianism		....	....	Oligarchy
Congregationalism	....		....	Anarchy of Mob Rule

Protagonists of each of the three systems, who have known them at their best, may object that these defects are found only in *degenerate* Episcopacy, *perverted* Presbyterianism and *unrestricted* Congregationalism. Theological theorists may say that the lack of a quorum at an AGM is as shocking as an attendance of a mere handful at Holy Communion in Easter Sunday. But the basic difficulty remains; how to 'motivate' the ordinary church people, men or women, young or old, so that they do not apply to church affairs the cynical saying that 'Politics is a dirty game'.

Rather, with appropriate guidance and stimulus from the Regional Church (diocese) and the Nation-wide church (synod), the local congregation needs to think out the various spiritual gifts and talents in its membership, discovering ways of using all those talents in a total ministry of outreach, edification and nurture. Only so will the 'Christian Community' of which a local Parish or Pastorate is the embodiment, become part of a Christian *Movement*, travelling in the same direction as the Lord Jesus Christ.

In all this, the ordained Presbyter has his distinctive part to play. On the one hand, a type of Clericalism (Sacerdotalism!) allows an ordinary clergyman to take the place of the Lord Jesus Christ as Head of the Church, concentrating all conceivable ministries and functions in him as a kind of ecclesiastical Pooh Bah. On the other hand, a fashionable kind of anti-clericalism, found both among the highly educated laity and the not so highly educated, regards the ordained clergyman as a kind of full-time employee of a local Religious Club, or rather of the dominant majority on its Committee. To mix the metaphor slightly, he is then regarded as a Religious Petrol Pump attendant, dispensing Baptism, marriages and funerals at certain stated hours, and concentrating on other Religious 'Services' (the term is perhaps significant) demanded by the local church-going community. The only real way, at local as well as diocesan level, to avoid these two extremes is to develop a really healthy collegiality, with the ordinary presbyter as the President (overseer) of a body of pastoral councillors living and working in the world, but regarding themselves as partners with the presbyters — and with the local bishop — in the work of the Kingdom of God. In countries of increasing leisure, where some of these lay leaders have a real opportunity to make an in-depth study of theology, some of them could be given ordination, as Honorary Assistant Clergy. Experiments in developing, as well as developed countries, including the TAFTEE Movement, are quite significant in this respect.

SYNODICAL GOVERNMENT AT NATIONAL LEVEL

We turn finally, still from the perspective of a United Church in an Asian setting, to the question of nation-wide structures for a style of synodical government, which will combine personal and corporate *episcope*. Churches formed on the model of the CSI do not have Archbishops, but Moderators (presiding bishops), elected for three years in the first place, with a possibility of re-election. But the position of Moderator is inevitably a more shaky one than that of an Archbishop, or even than that of a bishop in his diocese, or a presbyter in his pastorate. In these complex times, a nation-wide church will certainly need — and benefit from — a secretariat, and the Moderator or Presiding bishop will depend on the day-to-day guidance of the General Secretary or Chief Executive Officer of the synod, who will be in constant touch with the diocese, and, hopefully, with concrete local situations also.

A 'charismatic' leader very prominent on the present Indian political scene, Mr. Jayaprakash Narayan, has always stood for 'partyless democracy'

175

or 'non-political politics'. Perhaps if he had read Reinhold Niebuhr, Mr. Narayan might have developed as a more realistic political thinker! There are those in church administration also who look wistfully for 'non-church-party politics', for synods run on purely charismatic lines. But it would be more realistic for churches developing synodical government to balance their charismatic enthusiasm with realistic awareness of the fact of original sin. In that context, the Headship of the Lord Jesus Christ over the Church will in fact be reflected in the organisational Church structure by a system of checks and balances, of the type so eloquently expounded in the 18th century by the Princeton-educated American statesman James Madison.

We close by raising a question which has not always been faced: 'What are the geographical limits of synodical government?' The fairly recently formed General Synod of the Church of England brings together in one synodical body, representatives of two ecclesiastical provinces, those of Canterbury and York. But, significantly, it has not, I think, been suggested that the Church in Wales, the Church of Ireland, or the Episcopal Church in Scotland should merge themselves organisationally with the new English synod! Nor — to take a parallel case — would it be at all acceptable to the Presbyterian Churches of Ireland or Wales, or to the United Reformed Church in England, if it were suggested that they should simply become provincial Synods of the Church of Scotland. Even in a shrinking world, direct rule from Canterbury or Edinburgh (or Geneva) would not be acceptable to the Anglican Churches in Britain, or to the Reformed Churches in Europe.

On the North American continent, the situation is otherwise. While organised Churches in Europe cover relatively small nations, the denominational churches in the United States and Canada are highly centralised in their administration. (The American Episcopal 'Provinces' and the 'Conferences' of the United Church of Canada would appear to be rather shadowy parts of their respective ecclesiastical machinery.)

This whole matter has importance for the growth of synodical government in developing countries *and* in developed countries. Already there are plans in India for a merger between the CSI, CNI and Mar Thoma Churches, and there are concurrent talks between the CSI and the Lutheran Churches in South India. To offset the horrors, real or imaginary, of an over-centralised computerised bureaucratic machinery, Regional Synods, intermediate between the diocese and any proposed All India Synod, have already been suggested. But these are details of administration. The main problem facing any uniting church is how to combine the three traditional elements in Church polity in such a way that, in fact, the spiritual and not the demonic predominates. In other words, the right combination of different polities can allow Jesus Christ to be Lord. But a wrong mixture or injudicious synthesis might result in the *de facto* rule of His Satanic Majesty!

If Synodical Government is not to be a stumbling block but a means of grace, considerable thought and experiment will be needed. Perhaps this is also true of Churches not yet united!

GUIDE TO FURTHER READING:
On the whole matter of 'democracy' in Church Government, see Rajaiah D. Paul's too little known book *Ecumenism in Action* (C.L.S., Madras, 1972; available from Lutterworth Press, London), particularly pages 212-218.

3 - Women and the ministry

Barry Valentine

'Why', sang, or rather said, Rex Harrison, 'can't a woman be like . . . me?' Shaw's main point in *Pygmalion* is not perhaps quite clear; it is still less certain that *My Fair Lady* expresses it. It is abundantly clear, though, that the famous song catches something of the complexity of the male mind — a curious amalgam of puzzlement and anger, of delight and dismay, of selfishness and ultimately perhaps fear. It is equally certain that Eliza's famous comment, though offered in a different context, substantially conveys the response of many women — 'not bloody likely'.

The membership of the Lambeth Conference is, one might suppose, dramatically inappropriate to express the 'female view' — or even the feminine view — about anything. In any society, where the female view' were considered, or even declared to be, inferior or non-existent, or sinful or insignificant, no further comment or action would be expected. It would seem naturally, and indeed supernaturally, right that men should arrange the affairs of the Church — notwithstanding that half of both society and Church were not men. It would not seem strange, much less inadequate or deficient, that the discipline, order, government, theology and style of the Church should be male in assumption. It might even be possible that faith and scriptures could be so built and interpreted as to give a dubiously divine sanction to a thoroughly human shape.

In our times, though, and in many areas of the world, the 'maleness assumption' is at least open to the beginnings of questioning; and as soon as the fundamental assumption is brought into question, much of the argument, much of the conclusion and even much of the procedure from one to the other, is brought into question too. These are indeed, titanic (in the sense of size, nót outcome) questions in human society; they have us glancing uneasily at everything from ancient myths and legends to modern psychology. They are also very painful questions, forcing us to confront realities and possibilities which we would really not see 'Why can't a woman be like me?' is far more than an outburst of exasperation; it is a tacit acknowledgement — however reluctant and angry — that she isn't. 'Not bloody likely' — admittedly out of context — is a simple statement that she doesn't want to be and perhaps ought not to be required to be.

In such circumstances, the Church can neither expect nor pretend to be immune, existing somehow in isolation from the world around her. This does not mean of course that what the world does is always or even sometimes right. Neither does it imply that the world dictates to the Church — it is facile biblicism of the worst kind to suggest that this is to be 'conformed to the world'. What it does mean though, is that what is happening in and to the world, is, and must be, on the agenda of the Church — it is, indeed, determinative for the ministry of the Church.

In particular, what is happening to the role and status of women in society must, in appropriate measure, be determinative for the ministry of the Church to and among women. As relationships and responsibilities change, as stereotypes and assumptions are modified, so the shapes of the Church's ministry must also change, if it is to remain significant in its perceptions and pertinent in its support and guidance. No doubt the underlying goals and principles of ministry do not change; but it is quite clear that the forms of ministry that emerge in Trollope and the Brontës might not be entirely appropriate now — whether or not they were then.

But if this is true of the Church's ministry to and among women, how much more complicated are the questions as we confront the reality that the Church's ministry is also exercised *by* women. Of course it always has been; whether it is one of the great spiritual leaders like Teresa or Clare or a faithful unknown who tends the altar or delivers the parish magazine or works in the Mothers' Union, or visits the sick and elderly, large segments of the Church's functioning have, since biblical times, been performed by women; that is not the issue. The new questions include such matters as, how do new self-understandings in women's roles correlate with traditional opportunities for ministry by women in the Church; how far is the whole concept of ministry — including woman's part in it — a 'masculine assumption'; above all, perhaps, what has the historical emergence of a full-time professional ministry done to the concept of the ministry of the whole people of God; how far is elitism in the ordained ministry and clericalism in the Church, somehow bound up with 'masculine' images and systems; how far was and is the exclusion of women from ordained ministry a genuinely theological reality and how far an outcome of, and reinforcement for, male supremacy?

The tentative agenda for Lambeth underlines that, in a variety of manifestations, the subject of ministry dominates the contemporary church. The nature of ministry as both nurture of the Body and mission to the world, the organisation of ministry in systems and forms of government, the authority for ministry and its accountabilities, the relation between lay and ordained ministry, between amateur and professional ministry, between personal and sacramental ministry — all these and others are to be found precisely because the demands of the world for ministry have thrust them into the foreground.

The very nature of the Church as serving, forces upon her a constant re-examination of her servant-hood. In a sense, which must be carefully defined, the Church is essentially derivative — she takes her very being from her Lord whose Body she is, and her function from serving Him and the creation for which He gave Himself. The vocabulary of her activity, then, will comprise words such as listen, respond, accept, forgive rather than, for instance, dictate, demand, reject and judge. She must inevitably expect, in this matter, to renew, again and again, the struggle between continuing loyalty to her historical reality on the one hand, and present accountability to her immediate situation on the other. Far from finding such a struggle as somehow inconsonant with her peace, she will see it rather as the indwelling of her Lord who is her peace.

'Women and ministry', curiously, both forms a simple segment of the wide-ranging subject of ministry, and also underlies, and even to some extent exemplifies, the subject as a whole.

Before, though, pursuing particular significances of ministry to or by women, one further contextual element may be adduced through exploring the 'femininity' of ministry. Certainly much confusion can be caused by too easy an indentification between male and masculinity and between female and femininity. Equally certainly, some of the worst examples of male and female chauvinism occur when this confusion is perpetuated. It may not be easy, especially for a male clerical order, to examine with genuine openness, such a topic as the femininity of ministry — there are too many fears and memories, too many images and experiences.

Yet many of the words and concepts which spring to mind about ministry and ministering occur also — no matter how wary we are of sexual stereotyping — in any attempt to give word-shapes to perceptions about femininity. Words such as caring, gentle, nurturing, reconciling, loving, protecting do not convey the whole of femininity, nor are they the exclusive properties of femininity; and yet — with still a wary eye on accusations of male chauvinism — they are the kinds of words which are seen as affirming a feminine principle within the complementary relationship between feminine and masculine.

Equally, of course, such words do not express all the fullness of ministry; and yet, images about lay and clerical ministers, loved and revered in our history or experience, would be affirmed in very similar words. At the very least, it would seem, attributes often thought of as feminine, are essential contributions in the fullness of ministry; it might be averred that they are and ought to be the major elements; some might even suggest that they are the only authentic qualities. It is, no doubt, intriguing rather than significant that the Church, which exists only to serve God and His people and which is ultimately characterised as ministering, is — whether by linguistic accident or elemental sign — normatively discerned as feminine. The mind, in the end, perhaps, dares not explore too far the images of the Church as at once the Bride of Christ and the Body of Christ.

The ARCIC Statement on Ministry [1] well illustrates and summarises such perceptions about ministry; e.g. para. 3, 'the communion of men (*sic*) with God (and with each other) requires their reconciliation . . . while the Church is still in process of sanctification, its mission is nevertheless to be the instrument by which this reconciliation in Christ is proclaimed, his love manifested, and the means of salvation offered to men.' Again in para. 4, 'Within the whole history of mankind the Church is to be the community of reconciliation'; and again in para. 7, 'The Christian community exists to give glory to God through the fulfilment of the Father's purpose. All Christians are called to serve this purpose by their life of prayer and surrender to divine grace, and by their careful attention to the needs of all human beings. They should witness to God's compassion for all mankind and his concern for justice in the affairs of men. They should offer themselves to God in praise and worship, and devote their energies to bringing men into the fellowship of Christ's people, and so under his rule of love.'

Even this tentative skirmish with femininity and ministry and its attendant risks of stereotyping, substantially exemplifies the particular necessity for a ministry by the Church at this time to women. It is precisely because so many women are involved, whether eagerly or reluctantly, with awareness or indirectly and ignorantly, in the contemporary process of role-restatement, that the Church must be present with illumination and support. In this as in many issues, the Church will not lightly make assumptions; she will not automatically re-assert the social systems of the past nor yet, in some Pavlovian response, proclaim that all change is for the better. Neither, of course, will she fail to realise the complexity of changes which impinge on all the structures of family and society. The concern of this paper, though, is women and ministry and more immediately, for the ministering responsibility of the Church to women — women who today find themselves in various ways trapped and angry, or bewildered and uncertain, or, indeed, enthusiastic and welcoming, in the midst of, and because of, kaleidoscopic change.

It used to be said — not always entirely in jest — that the Church was 'for motherhood and against sin'. Some opponents of liberalism with slightly excessive zeal, assert that the contemporary Church has reversed that statement of policy. Without conceding to either position, it is surely true that the Church in many parts of the world must face the fact that 'woman-ness' itself, much less a sense of vocation and ministry, is no longer necessarily satisfied and fulfilled in a version of life as 'pregnant in the kitchen'. More significantly, there are various movements and organisations for justice and equality which are not only vigorous and vocal, but which have also discovered and publicised some startling and even frightening examples of discrimination, both in the customs of society and in the very law itself. The Church need not necessarily associate itself with any movement or organisation as such; but she cannot dissociate herself from any

181

persons or groups who are in some way victims of injustice or oppression or deprivation — and this, when some of the oratory is over, is the factual and legal position for many, even most, women in society.

Much more powerful, perhaps, because more subtle and insidious, are all the processes of feeling and attitude and custom, which, in effect, the formulated laws and regulations only reflect and codify. All too often — and perhaps much more often than is realised — women are victims of society, whether in such obvious forms as the plight of single parents and unwed mothers, and the inequality of pay and job opportunity, or in less obvious ways such as non-effective sharing in community decision-making.

Quite simply, a total ministry which cannot or will not grapple with these issues and move to the support and guidance of those involved in them, can scarcely be termed a ministry at all — or at least not in any Incarnational sense of that word. The fact that for centuries — despite modest ameliorations from time to time — the Church has done little about it, condoned it and even sanctified it, does not add to her glories — and possibly gives at least momentary pause to those whose theology of Church and ministry seems to rest primarily or solely on an appeal to the past and its tradition.

If this situation is expressed as the need of women in the modern world for a particular ministry of the Church, perhaps it is allowable also to speak, in terms of need, of the Church's contemporary requirement for the ministering gifts of women. Women, it was noted earlier, always have played a part in the ministering of the Church, even though it might not do to examine too closely the form and extent of it as permitted or encouraged by each contemporary social order; there were times, indeed, when the segment of ministry allowed to women did little more than reinforce images and structures of inferiority and servitude.

The issue of this particular time is fundamentally twofold: in the first place, it is at least arguable that in a world and a world society which hovers on the brink of extinction because of masculine, male-macho systems of organisation, goals and styles, the femininity of ministry has a classically Incarnational and saving role to play; and, while all women are not, in this sense, feminine, for the Church to ignore the reality that many women have substantial gifts of femininity is to ignore a huge and critically pertinent resource; and in the second place, it seems self-evident that in the ongoing process of enabling and illuminating women who find themselves in the midst of contemporary role-changes, women, who have themselves found strength and insight to deal with the problems, will be pre-eminently fitted to share in the Church's ministry to other women.

The need of the ministering Church for the peculiar gifts and styles which women can deploy is given additional emphasis by other concomitant explorations in the whole context of ministry. In particular, experiments in many parts of the Church with such schemes as team ministries, lay

182

ministries, 'eucharistisers', non-stipendiary or self-supporting clergy have begun to re-align some of the traditional pictures of professionalism and authority in the ministry of the Church.

Despite the very real ministries which have been exercised by the laity throughout the Church's history, the fact is that in the minds of the vast majority of people — in a sense, therefore, in the common mind of the Church — ministry has come substantially to be identified with and reposed in, the ordained ministry. It is by no means uncommon — at least in some parts of the Church — for candidates and parents and even clergy to talk about a student as 'going into the ministry'. Equally — although there are perhaps other questions involved — many clergy are known in a parish or community as 'the minister'. Beneath that simple nomenclature is unhappily concealed a whole network and structure of assumption and practice which not infrequently issues in the worst kinds of clericalism on the one hand and a debilitating erosion of lay responsibility and participation in the other. It is buttressed too, by concepts of professionalism, of training, of recruitment and of deployment which are not only dangerously inflexible but have the even more sinister quality of self-perpetuation.

The Conference, of course, will be dealing in other contexts, with many of these questions. In this context, it is, at the least, ironic that women who could by their very nature, as it were, redress some of the images of authority and professionalism, and who, in the present shapes of society — despite all the changes — constitute an immense untapped resource for non-stipendiary or part-time ordained ministry, are, in very large measure, rendered unavailable by decision of the ministering Church itself — or, as some might say, by a male-dominated power structure in the decision-making process of the Church.

It seems urgent and imperative that the subject of 'women and ministry' should be approached in a comprehensive sense and not narrowed artificially to the issue of the ordination of women to the presbyterate. Indeed, it would be a tragic loss of the opportunity to re-examine the whole matter of ministry, if the discussion were to be turned aside to the more particular issue of women and priesthood. Still further, it would be inexcusably shortsighted to accept without honest examination, a view of priesthood only as transmitted in the male image — or for that matter to construct images and expectations of presbyteral women out of simplistic imitations of the male. Equally certainly, though, no examination of ministry could be considered complete without reference to an ordained ministry within it. To quote again from the ARCIC document,[2] 'The goal of the ordained ministry is to serve this priesthood of all the faithful. Like any human community the Church requires a focus of leadership and unity, which the Holy Spirit provides in the ordained ministry. This ministry assumes various patterns to meet the varying needs of those whom the Church is seeking to serve, and it is the role of the minister to co-ordinate the activities of the

Church's fellowship and to provide what is necessary and useful for the Church's life and mission'; and again in para. 13, 'Christian ministers are members of this redeemed community. Not only do they share through baptism in the priesthood of the people of God, but they are — particularly in presiding at the eucharist — representative of the whole Church in the fulfilment of its priestly vocation of self-offering to God as a living sacrifice. Nevertheless their ministry is not an extension of the common Christian priesthood but belongs to another realm of the gifts of the Spirit. It exists to help the Church to be "a royal priesthood" . . .'

It will be obvious immediately that none of this constitutes a determining argument for the ordination of women to the presbyterate and it is not intended as such. But it seems to demonstrate an interesting series of continuities — the 'femininity of ministry' and the need for such ministry, the ministry to and by women, the re-examination of ministry and the relationship to it of ordination — which at least suggest that the ordination of women is a legitimate matter for serious discussion in the Church. Contrary to an assertion that is occasionally heard, the onus of proof seems, at first sight, to rest upon those who would deny the possibility.

Clearly, in such a compass as this, it was not intended that the arguments for and against the ordination of women to the presbyterate should be explored or even summarised.[3] They are anyway well-known and share the interesting characteristic of being totally convincing to those who hold them and abysmally inadequate to those who don't. Such threatening certitude is usually a sign of insecurity in the argument and it is probable that most churchmen find themselves with varying feelings of ambivalence.

It seems all the more important, therefore, to maintain a certain discipline in discussion, by attempting to observe certain categories of argument. One such category, for instance, would be the biblical, another the historical-traditional. Clearly there are several others; often they overlap each other or a line of demarcation is difficult to define — such areas as theological, sociological, psychological and one best described as organisational or institutional. Under each such heading it is possible to marshal arguments both for and against. The canon of discussion, though, must be that arguments in any one category should be countered only by argument from the same category — it is inconclusive and unproductively irritating to see a sound biblical argument met by a comment — however profound — on the sexuality of women. Ultimately the findings in the several categories must be weighed against each other as a final resolution is made, but the preceding process must be clear and precise.

One particular aspect of this problem of categories is, of course, that of competence in decision-making[4] — again a subject which is to be dealt with elsewhere in the Conference. Questions as to whether the Anglican Communion, or Provinces of it, or national churches within it, or synods or Houses of Bishops or the Lambeth Conference itself — are legitimately able

184

to decide about the ordination of women and to act in the decision taken, are clearly important because they concern the very unity of the Communion; but they must be seen as what they are and not as determining an issue which must surely be decided on other grounds.

Without thereby entering directly into the arguments, one factor in the present situation does seem especially worthy of remark and examination: it is an unprecedented and widespread phenomenon in parts of the Church that women have sensed themselves 'called' to the presbyterate. Every bishop — in whom the Church's responsibility of ordaining is personalised — is only too familiar with instances, piteous and sometimes tragic, where some sort of 'mystical experience' or 'divine intervention' is cited as a claim for ordination; it is usually not difficult to discover the weakness, even if it is sometimes hard to find a gentle and pastoring way of conveying the mind and will of the Church. But in this new experience, the clear vocation seems to spring, not from the fringes, but from the very heart of the worshipping and serving Church; it falls mainly, moreover — despite some unhappy aberrances — on those whose devotion to Our Lord is not only personal, but is manifested primarily through witnessing and obedient service within the Catholic Church. Often it seems to fall on those who are most humble in their reluctance to set foot on such a high path. It may well be that, even as the Church looks for guidance and direction in this matter so crucial to her life and ministry, the sign has already been given, by her Lord the Spirit, in the very call to presbyteral service. In such a serious matter, it would be inappropriate to turn again for authority or even support to Rex Harrison and Bernard Shaw; it is tempting, just the same, to remember the song about the rain in Spain that falls mainly in the plain — and the exultant obbligato by Colonel Pickering and Professor Higgins, 'I think she's got it; by jove, she's got it.'

REFERENCES
[1] Ministry and Ordination—A Statement on the Doctrine of the Ministry agreed by the Anglican-Roman Catholic International Commission, Canterbury 1973.
[2] *op. cit.* para 7.
[3] A clear, succinct and fair summary of the major arguments can be found in 'The Ordination of Women to the Priesthood, Pro and Con', by J. P. Peck. (Toronto: Anglican Book Centre, 1975).
A similar useful and more extensive document is the report to the General Synod of the Church of England, of the Advisory Council for the Church's Ministry, *On the Ordination of Women to the Priesthood,* 1972.
[4] 'Declaration on the Question of Women to the Ministerial Priesthood', issued by the Sacred Congregation for the Doctrine of the Faith is helpfully clear in its initial exposition and useful though tendentious in its patristic documentation; it will be thought by some — including its supporters — less convincing in its conclusions.

★For the Guide to Further Reading *see* page 203.

4 - Christian understanding of community

John S. Pobee

Let me first comment on the two major terms in the subject assigned to me, Christian and Community. Christian, like its cognate Christianity, represents the amalgam and confluence of several traditions: the teaching of Jesus, Semitic culture, Graeco-Roman culture, Western European and American cultures, East European cultures and now African and Asian cultures, not to mention the traditions of the Church itself down the centuries. Thus the Christian faith has in the past found and still does find expression in several cultures, moulding the way of life, be it in Europe, America, Asia or Africa. The term 'Christian' has cultural additives because the culture becomes impregnated with the gospel and becomes a vehicle of the gospel. Therefore, it becomes difficult to give precise meaning to 'Christian'. Furthermore, past affirmations have been bound up with world-views of bygone ages, past pictures, ideas, assumptions and statements, some of which are no longer live options. In full consciousness that the content of 'Christian' may include the ideas etc. of various and diverse ages and places, we shall endeavour here always to begin with the biblical notions, if for no other reason than the Bible, particularly the New Testament, constitutes the charter documents of the Christian Church, containing fundamental principles for the Church's action throughout history.

I also affirm with the late Dietrich Bonhoeffer that 'to be a Christian does not mean to be religious in a particular way, to make something of oneself (a sinner, a penitent or a saint) on the basis of some method or others, but to be a man'.[1] This is not to deny that Christians have an understanding of the world. To be a Christian is to be a man 'in the image and likeness of God', i.e. a man who shares in the creative work of God the Creator, a man with reason, prerogative dignity and the capacity to love. And justice is the removal of all contradictions of love. This means to be a 'man for others', living in a community, in relationship with others. And this brings us to the other important term 'Community'.

A community may be defined 'a concentrated settlement of people in a limited territorial area, within which they satisfy many of their daily needs through a system of interdependent relationships. A community is a self-

186

conscious social unit and a focus of group identification'.[2] A community, therefore, is a group of human beings, men and women living together as a group. They may be persons in one geographical area with specific hopes and fears. But they may also go beyond a geographical area to envelop more than one tribe, one country or even one continent. In this way one is modifying the definition adopted above, going beyond the territorial reference because it is too narrow. A community needs to be neither too small nor too large. Three persons standing and chatting in a street corner may not constitute a community. But three persons stranded on an island and forced by circumstances to relate to each other to their mutual benefit may constitute a community. In other words, neither numbers alone nor a common territorial base is by itself the determining criterion for a community: a smaller collectivity than the millions of New York City or London may be a community; on the other hand, a large collectivity, with several high-rise skyscrapers, each of which contains hundreds of human beings, may not have the sense of community, as indeed is the problem with the big cities of the developed world. To have a community, the society must go beyond numbers to 'a complex of human relationships, a system of interaction'.

'Interaction' at the minimum means to have dealings with another; at least two persons exchange actions. There are at least two types of interaction, a superficial or merely functional one and a deeper or personal one. An example of the superficial interaction is the situation in which a man may be driven every day for years by the same bus driver and yet there may be no personal relationship between them. Similarly, it is possible to buy groceries from the same shop and to be served by the same salesgirl for months or years without interacting on a personal level. In either case, the driver like the salesgirl is just another agent, This type of interaction is only an encounter without sustained relationship and the interaction vanishes as readily as it emerged.

The deeper interaction, in addition to exchange of actions, includes the possibility of forecasting how the other person will react. This argues for the existence of a common understanding. Both actors have a substratum of 'shared meaning'[3] and expectation giving rise to sustained relationship. This brings us to the idea of *sensus communis*.

Sensus communis, sense of community, is the awareness that whether we like it or not, other people's lives will influence ours for good or for ill and ours theirs. Our acts impoverish or enrich others as well as theirs do ours. Thus the bus driver's life *will* influence me for good or ill in the sense that he will get me to my destination or into the ditch. And we proceed to act on that awareness. In short, interaction involves interdependence which means an awareness that we need others to help us define ourselves and our problems, an awareness that we need partners not patrons, brothers not benefactors. And it implies some equality as men bearing the *imago dei*. It demands a recognition of the other person as another human being. And

187

as Hegel has put it, 'self-consciousness exists in itself and for itself in that and by the fact that it exists for another self-consciousness; that is to say, it is only by being acknowledged or recognised'.[4]

However, the *sensus communis* is not the same thing as the stratum of 'shared meanings'. The story of the bus driver implies an understanding of roles and their implications, so that even if his enemy comes along, he, the driver, cannot deny him a ticket or drive him into a ditch without having to answer for his action. He interacts with his passenger as a matter of duty and he is expected by the society to do it as a duty. But that is not the same as *sensus communis*.

Interaction, then, is common encounter for the survival of people. The difference between the deeper and the superficial inter-action is whether the common encounter is permanent or not.

With regard to the *sensus communis*, African culture and the biblical world-views coalesce. Whereas Descartes spoke Western man's epistemology and ontology in saying that *Cogito ergo sum* i.e. I am thinking, therefore I exist, *homo africanus* theory of existence is *Cognatus ergo sum* i.e. I am related by blood, therefore I have my being, *or* I exist because I belong to a family group, a community. Consequently, the family is the basic unit, consisting of the living, the dead and the yet unborn. Through the family the race continues and by it is found the proper integration of the growing child, the adolescent into the community. It also provides for the satisfaction of a man's emotional needs and his sense of belonging. The family is itself a unit in the clan whose main functions are: (i) the regulation of marriage, (ii) the upbringing of the child; (iii) supporting relatives in times of need; (iv) arrangement and supervision of funerals; (v) regulating succession, taking care and preserving of family property; (vi) performing custom. The clan 'acts as the second line of support to the members of the family and strengthens it, giving cohesion to the whole society'.[5] Thus the African *sensus communis* involves a sense of family brotherhood and sharing. A Luba proverb articulates it for us: *kwa mukulu kantu, kwa muakunyi kantu* i.e. for a brotherhood to be good, it is good and necessary for the younger brother to give something to the elder brother and vice versa. But above all, the *sensus communis* receives its strength from morality. Evil is my act, motivation or conduct which is directed against the *sensus communis*, the social harmony and the personal achievement sanctioned by the traditional code. Thus morality is the soul of the idea of the community.[6]

A community may be visualised as concentric circles: the family is a smaller unit in the bigger clan unit. The clan in turn is a smaller unit in the tribe, the tribe a smaller unit in the state; the state a smaller unit in the continent and the continent a smaller unit in the world. Actually there are at least three different models. A family model in which the community has three concentric circles — the nuclear family inside the extended family which itself stands in the still larger circle of a city comprising different

188

tribes, religious and social classes. The second model is the inhabitants of cities: (a) the whole populace (b) various church groups — denominations, fellowships, lodges, etc., and (c) tribal societies, professional associations. The third model will be the Christian model: (a) the laity and the clergy, the local assembly (b) Church universal — 'body of Christ' and (c) the Church universal together with the Church triumphant. A small community (or to use the fancy expression a micro-community) is in a larger community (or more fancifully a macro-community). Today we are more than ever before impressed by the larger community because as a result of the communications and other scientific revolutions, there is a breaking down of existing barriers and frontiers, geographical, political, social, etc. The world has been reduced to neighbourhood size, so that one breaks his fast in Accra and eats his lunch in London. But this means that the burdens of one corner of the globe become the concern of other parts, even though of different racial stock. This is the significance of world organisations like U.N.O., U.N.E.S.C.O., W.H.O., F.A.O., I.P.P.F., E.C.O.W.A.S., etc. It is precisely because of this sense of a larger community that Uganda under the Field Marshal, South Africa, Rhodesia, Middle East, etc., are the concern of many outside those areas. It is this sense of community which accounts for the concern of people in the U.S.A. and Africa for the fate of the dissidents in Russia and Czechoslovakia. M. M. Thomas has put it well: 'There is a growing sense of common humanity of human solidarity in the world which finds its expression in mutual concern, a sense of participation in the struggles of others for their fundamental rights, and a common endeavour in building structures of a world community and searching for an ethos to make them stable. This "secular ecumenical movement" may be only a beginning, but it is already a genuine movement of human solidarity which we must recognise as a new factor of no small significance in the world today.'[7]

In view of a tendency to glorify excessively the past, I wish to make a few comments about the African *sensus communis*. The *sensus communis* was not first evolved in Africa nor is it peculiar to Africa. European societies once had it until they were affected by the Industrial Revolution etc. It is a phase of African history and culture and unless a conscious effort is made to retain it, Africa will go the way of Europe if it has not already begun to go that way. The *sensus communis* is best suited to esentially small-scale society, small not only in terms of numbers but also in terms of the range of social contacts, functional divisions of labour, technological development etc. Thus given some patterns of institutions, the *sensus communis* is reinforced as an ideal. Therefore, let us be careful not to emphasise too much the ideal rather than what happened or happens in practice. Secondly, the ideal of the *sensus communis* had some terrible aspects: (a) it was the atmosphere for conflicts of individual interests. If lineage is a big un-differentiated group, it is also a very differentiating institution in which

189

conflicting interests often become subjects for intense rivalry. That is why there are allegations of witchcraft within the clan and why the most vigorous and aggressive claims and counter-claims take place within the lineage with regard to property and succession. (b) The *sensus communis* is restrictive in the sense that the ideal does not extend to the man defined as an outsider to the lineage and clan. Kinship entitles a man to membership of the group by giving him a status and unless he is adopted into the kinship system he remains a man to be preyed upon. This is the theory behind exogamy: you marry those that do not like you so that you can walk safely in a wider area. (c) In fact, even in the kinship groups there is evidence of fratricides and banishments, e.g. among the Zulu at the time of Shaka, partly for personal survival. The essential question then is how to retain the essentially good points of the *sensus communis* but eliminate the indisputably unfortunate aspects of it. This is where Christianity goes the extra mile because it goes beyond the kinship ties to mankind (*cf.* Gal. 3 v. 28).

I wish to suggest that what has been said so far about community is applicable to the Church and her understanding of community. The Church founded on the Christ event was a small community, a minority group within the society and the world. In the second century A.D. the Church was recognised as *tertium genus* [8] a third race, a new subculture, a micro-community, a smaller community in a big world. In many parts of the world today the Church lives in a minority and in a pluralistic society. History teaches us that when the Church has been in a minority, she has been a vigorous subculture [9] and that when she has been in the majority she has been 'neither hot nor cold' and arrogant as well as intolerant. And so, in my heart of hearts, I welcome the Church in the minority, though I also accept the dominical charge to go out and make disciples all over the world. (Matt. 28 vv. 19, 20.) The Church is aware of being a community which paradoxically is not supposed to cut herself from the rest of the people because she has a mission to them and yet by her mission and ritual reminds her members of what ideas she stands for, which set her apart from the rest of society.

The enduring result of Christ's life, death and resurrection is the emergency of a body (Greek: *soma*), that which ties men up with each other, rather than separates them as individuals. The body 'stands for man, in the solidarity of creation, as made for God'.[10] In an age when a man's home is his castle, self-contained and self-sufficient, the theology of the body needs emphasising if we are to have *sensus communis* which is the qualitative element of community. And the biblical faith affirms that the Church is the paradigm *soma*, of which one is a member through believing, acceptance of baptism and active participation through the Holy Spirit (I Cor. 12 vv. 13, 18). Here the N.T. goes beyond the secular and non-Christian conceptions outlined above. The Church is a community not because a few like-minds got together to establish a society but because it is the 'Body of

Christ' [11] (Eph. 4 v. 12). A Christian is related to others because of Jesus and therefore, the path to others is primarily through Jesus Christ. Jesus is the 'focus of group identification'. Paul's first letter to the Corinthians (12 vv. 11-26) gives the classic statement of the point that the 'unity in diversity . . . is as necessary to the Church as is the unity of the organs in an "organism" . . . It is not nature which makes us members of the organism, but grace . . . It is the Spirit communicated through baptism which binds the individual to this body'.[12] We as a Church have a *sensus communis* because we also have one allegiance to Christ: 'Christ is the head of the body, the Church' (Col. 1 v. 18). One would add here that we relate to others outside the Church because they too bear 'the image and likeness of God'.

The other relevant biblical idea is the Greek *koinonia*, fellowship [13] or participation, communion and contribution. At the heart of the biblical conception of *koinonia* stands the Incarnation as its foundation and expression (*cf.* Heb. 2 v. 14): God has shared in our common human nature. 'There is thus a *koinonia* of man and God in Christ which is the direct outcome of God's condescending and creative love.' [14] But that also has a horizontal reference, a man to man reference: 'The *koinonia* into which we are summoned is the "fellowship" of the redeemed in Christ but this *koinonia* is also "participation in" Christ i.e. it refers to the sharing of a common life of which Christ is the source' [15] (*cf.* I Cor. 1 v. 9; Eph. 3 v. 6). The Spirit is the source of the fellowship (II Cor. 13 v. 14; Phil. 2 v. 1). Christians participate in the Spirit when they enter into the *koinonia* of all believers whose supreme mark is love (I Cor. 13). And by participation we mean active interaction.

A bit more must be said about the Spirit. The Spirit is often characterised as holy (*hagion*). That description is a reminder that the Spirit has relations with the *hagioi*, the term which the early Church used of God's dedicated people. God's people are marked by God's dedicated Spirit. The Spirit stands in closest relation in the new corporate life, it is the harmonising vital power to integrate the limbs in the body. And here we sense the revolutionary ideas of the Christian Church. In Judaism holiness tended to be segregation and separation. But in Christianity holiness means separation for mission and therefore, segregation turns out to be our invitation to inclusion. As O. C. Quick epigrammatically put it, 'Only there (i.e. the Church) can exist the true *koinonia hagion* which is also the *hagiasmos koinon* which is the sanctifying of the common. But because it is in this respect that the Church is exclusive, the Church is seen to be potentially all inclusive too. For there is nothing in nature which cannot in the Church's fellowship be made into a holy and acceptable offering to God.' [16] I believe the Church should express and be the embodiment of the spirit of neighbourhood and personal acquaintance.[17] The Church should stand as brother and partner of others in God's world, not only locally but also in the entire world.

191

We suggest that the Church is a smaller community within the larger world. In practical terms two main manifestations have been possible. The first is the Constantinian position that the Church is co-terminous with the world. That position, perfected by Emperor Theodosius I, continues in some form with the establishment of the Church of England. Constantine even styled himself 'the bishop of those without'. Needless to say, this situation *inter alia* brought many unworthy elements into the Church and was a catalyst in lowering the standard of the fervour of the Church. As such it is not a satisfactory development.

The other line of development is *regnum Caesaris regnum diaboli* i.e. the kingdom of Caesar is the rule of Satan. The classic statement is by Tolstoy who maintained that any co-operative contact with secular civilisation was a betrayal of faith and a contamination of the faith. For this school, II Cor. 6 is a key support: 'Do not unite yourselves with unbelievers; they are no fit mates for you. What has righteousness to do with wickedness? Can light consort with darkness? Can Christ agree with Belial or a believer join hands with an unbeliever? . . . Therefore, come away and leave them, separate yourselves . . .' (vv. 14, 15, 17). This passage appears to deny any collaboration with unbelievers, the world outside the Church which symbolised anarchy and atheism, while the Church symbolised justice and religion. The world outside the Church is supposedly Belial, i.e. worthless and satanic (*cf.* James 4 v. 4, Jn. 5 v. 19).

One would submit that the passage cannot be taken literally. For one sees a lot that is good in the world outside the Church. I affirm with D. Bonhoeffer that for all the sinfulness of man, 'the world has come of age'. We earlier cited the world organisations which have been doing a lot of good things for the less fortunate. Besides, the apostle himself elsewhere writes 'I wrote to you . . . not to associate with immoral men; not at all meaning the immoral of this world, . . . since then you would need to go out of the world' (I Cor. 5 vv. 9-10). It is just impossible to have no contacts with the world outside the Church. In any case, Christians themselves are also sinners.

IN A NUTSHELL

And so, the Church should be a micro-community within a macro-community. This is not to deny that she is distinctive. She is in the world and yet not of the world. She is a *koinonia* of the Holy Spirit: a community called to a life of holiness and love in a pluralistic society, but cannot be a holy huddle. To be a living community she has to interact with the world outside for at least two reasons: first, it is only in relating to others that she can find herself and the meaning of her existence. Secondly, 'religion that is not embedded in the common life too soon degenerates into religiosity and an inward looking Church is a dying Church'.[18] And so, the Church as a micro-community is called to encounter the world, enter into dialogue with it, uphold the principle of tolerance i.e. realistically taking into account other existing institutions as they are, in their particularity and peculiarity. The Church may not treat the world outside as cases: rather she should face the world with a personal loving concern and interest and that, in practical ways. One of the ironies of our time is that the emergence of the Welfare State often goes with the loss of the human touch. The Church should teach the world that serious interaction goes beyond sending charity or a mere cheque; interaction involves a personal and loving concern and interest. It means also that the Church should stand as the conscious of society, standing as referee and linesman in the game between the warring factions of society. She should take seriously her ministry of reconciliation (II Cor. 5 v. 19f). That is where the Church should put her house in order. How can the Church exercise successfully her ministry of reconciliation when she herself is hopelessly divided? To me Church union is not a theory or a game; rather it is a matter of the credibility and integrity of the Church as a community set in the world to reconcile all things to God. Her worship is not only an attempt to commune with God but also to remind her members of what she stands for so as to bring deviants back into line and better equip them to do the extensive mission.

'The Church's supernatural life is in itself a holy communion; its sacrament is a holy act which is also a sharing in common. And, therefore, its relation to the world is expressed by the similar paradox of its title "holy" and "catholic", separate and yet all-inclusive. The Church can be in truth both holy and catholic, because it is also apostolic, sent from God into the world with the gospel of the world's redemption. In this world holy fellowship exists for the sake of those who are still outside it." [19]

REFERENCES

[1] D. Bonhoeffer, *Letters and Papers from Prison* (London: S.C.M., 1967), p. 118. 'Religious' is for Bonhoeffer 'churchiness'.
[2] G. A. Theodorson and A. G. Theodorson, *Modern Dictionary of Sociology* (New York: Thomas Y. Crowell Co., 1969); Apollo Edition (1970), p. 63.
The phrase, 'focus of group identification' is itself a difficult concept. But it is similar to Durkheim's idea of solidarity which is characterised by willy-nilly involvement and participation of all inhabitants. It involves institutional networks. Inherent to the solidarity are rules of social behaviour, the three elements of which are legitimacy, authority and sanction. For example, a chief or the Queen of England is the focus of identification because he/she is the custodian of what is deemed proper. The focus of Christian group identification will be Jesus Christ and the message of the Cross. In short, 'the focus of group identification' is what gives the 'we-feeling', as W. I. Thomas would put it. See also:
E. Durkheim, *Division of Labour in Society* (Glencoe, Illinois: The Free Press, 1949), especially chapters 2-7.
E. Durkheim, *Elementary Form of Religious Life* (London: Allen and Unwin, 1926).
F. Tonnies, *Community and Association* (Gemeinschaft and Gesellschaft). Translation by Charles Loomis (London: Routledge & Kegan Paul, 1955).

[3]   Cf. W. I. Thomas, *Social Behaviour and Personality: Contributions to Theory and Social Personality,* (ed.) Edmund H. Volkart (New York: Social Sciences Research Council, 1951).
To some extent this is true of the merely functional interaction. But there is a difference of degree (See p. 6 below.)
[4]   G. W. F, Hegel, *The Phenomenology of Mind* (Translation by J. B. Baillie), 2nd Revised Edition (London: Allen and Unwin, 1949), p. 230.
[5]   Susan de Graft Johnson (Mrs.), 'Family Institutions and Development' in *Religion, Morality and Population Dynamics,* (ed.) J. S. Pobee (Legon: University of Ghana, Population Dynamics Programme, 1977). Chapter xi.
K. A. Busia, *Africa in Search of Democracy* (London: Routledge and Kegan Paul, 1967), p. 20.
[6]   Prof. E. Laing, a Botanist of the University of Ghana, who consents to be one of my lay reactors, has raised the problem of 'How one can practically make an effective community out of groups with different interests or emphasis e.g. different races'. One would still say that the answer to that problem is a strict moral standard such as is reflected in Gal. 3 v. 28 and Col. 3 v. 11, a denial of any preoccupation with one's own race and focusing on the common humanity and the *imago dei.*
[7]   M. M. Thomas, 'The World in which We Preach Christ' in *Witness in Six Continents* (London: 1964), p. 15.
[8]   Third because the Church stood 'as a new thing over and against Jews and Greeks'. See P. Richardson, *Israel in the Apostolic Church* (Cambridge: C.U.P., 1969), pp. 22-25.
[9]   David Barrett, 'A.D. 2000; 350 Million Christians in Africa, in *International Review of Missions,* Geneva, Vol. LIX No. 233 (January 1970), p. 47. One is not particularly enamoured of this rejoicing in numbers. One is more interested in their keenness.
[10]   J. A. T. Robinson, *The Body* (London: S.C.M., 1952), p. 31.
[11]   The identification of the Church as *the* body of Christ needs a lot of qualification because more often than not it is a body (i.e. an organised society) *belonging to* Christ.
[12]   J. Herring, *The First Epistle of Saint Paul to the Corinthians* (London: Epworth, 1962), pp. 129-130.
[13]   *Koinonia* does not mean 'fellowship' in the concrete sense; it is an abstract noun. By joint participation in Christ or in the Spirit it *becomes* 'a fellowship', but that is not what *koinonia primarily* means. Cf. H. Seesemann, *Der Begriff koinonia* in N.T. (1933), F. Hauck, *koinos* in T.D.N.T. III, pp. 789-809.
[14]   J. G. Davies, *Members One of Another: Aspects of Koinonia* (Oxford: A. & R. Mowbray, 1958), p. 7.
[15]   *Ibid.,* p. 8.
[16]   O. C. Quick, *Doctrines of the Creed* (London: Nisbet, 1949), p. 311.
[17]   Cf. G. D. H. Cole, *Essays in Social Theory* (London: Macmillan, 1950), p. 95.
[18]   F. R. Barry, *Christian Ethics and Secular Society* (London: Hodder and Stoughton, 1966), p. 117.
[19]   O. C. Quick, *op. cit.,* p. 311.

5 - The Church and the use of its resources

Martin Conway

> Peter said 'I have no silver or gold; but what I have I give you:
> in the name of Jesus Christ of Nazareth, walk.' (Acts 3.6, NEB)

In this article I hope to set out a possible framework within which Christians whether bishops or lay people, can think through the many questions that constantly come up about the management of the resources of the Church.

THREE PRELIMINARY POINTS

(1) I lay no claim to be an expert in these matters, and cannot pretend to have first-hand experience of the kind of burdens carried by almost any Anglican bishop. But in nearly twenty years of working in 'church administration' (in a broad sense) I have constantly been struck by how difficult it is to bring together in a satisfying way what we say about Christ's Church in our theology or policy discussions with what we are accustomed to doing with the available manpower, money or buildings. Behind the ideas in this article lie many conversations and experiments; I should particularly like to acknowledge my indebtedness to a memorandum from the Rev. Denys Whitehead of the Anglican Church of Zambia, which has helped me stretch my ideas and sympathies beyond the conditions of the churches in Europe with which I am most familiar.

(2) I lay no claim, equally, to provide 'answers' for any of the immediate puzzles which any bishop readers, let alone others, will be facing. There are no answers in theory, only those that are made in practice. What follows is bound to seem annoyingly generalised, even abstract, to those who are wrestling daily with intractable situations. Yet I have dared to accept the invitation to write out of conviction that our inadequacies in handling the Church's resources are due not so much to any 'wrong answers' to each successive dilemma as to an inadequate framework of judgment within which we choose one answer rather than another, a framework in which all too often the dead hand of 'what has always been done before' outweighs any imaginative spark that could lead to a fresh and true grasp of a new possibility.

(3) Questions of administration and management may seem prosaic and shallow compared to some of the other great themes tackled in this book. But they should not be downgraded on that account. The Church is after all a human institution, in no way divinely protected from the administrative feelings and muddles that affect all institutions. Moreover any of us in leadership positions in the Church are constantly taking decisions about resources, and thus owe it to our fellow-Christians to take them as carefully and imaginatively as we can. Most important, it is an undeniable fact of history that time and time again it has been the insensitivity of Christians in their actual behaviour towards other people, the inadequacy of what the Church has actually done with its resources, rather than any personal evaluation of the teachings and achievement of Jesus Christ, that has kept people outside our fellowship. Success in the mission Christ has entrusted to his Church, as a corporate body, depends far more than we usually acknowledge on the way we order the Church's life and activities. The Church can only be an effective sign and instrument of the Kingdom Christ announced if its institutional habits and attitudes strike other people as exemplary and promising.

AIMS AND DEFINITIONS

Next, a working definition of the Church: that community, within the total community of men and women, which confesses Jesus Christ as Lord and Saviour and therefore seeks to serve, in all that it and its members are and do and say, the loving purpose of God the Father to bring all things to the fulfilment he intends in his Kingdom.

Other articles in this book will no doubt round that out. But for our present purposes it immediately points in three crucial directions:

(a) The Church exists in order to serve God's Kingdom, that culmination for which he created the entire natural order. His purposes are always wider and longer than ours, and it is those we are to serve, not our own. This puts a standing question mark over any striving for a 'bigger and better Church'. The results we are after are not primarily in the Church but in the world. All our decisions about the use of Church resources deserve to be tested by their effectiveness in showing forth some first-fruits of the Kingdom.

(b) By the same token, the first duty of the Church is mission. William Temple's famous saying that the Church is the only human institution devoted to those who are not its members deserves to be recalled at least once in every meeting of a parish church council or a diocesan synod. In particular this must help us to counter the otherwise irresistible tendency in a pluralist and consumer-conscious society for the Church to be seen, by its members as much as anyone else, as designed 'for those who like that sort of thing'.

196

(c) The Kingdom of reconciliation over which the one God and Father reigns can only properly be heralded by a united Church. There is no such thing in the will of Christ as an Anglican Church (or a Roman Catholic, or a Lutheran, etc.). All that we say about 'the Church' must be applied to and by 'us-and-all-those-whom-Christ-gives-us-as-partners' as the Church in each place. The way we use our resources, in particular, will be a constant test of whether or not we are really serving and leading '*the* Church' or '*our* Church'. It is one of the notable tragedies of contemporary Anglican churches that while we are almost everywhere engaged in negotiations towards church unity we almost as seldom do our planning and administering together with those partner churches. Our self-concerned actions daily contradict our ecumenical words.

PEOPLE COME FIRST

Which 'resources' are we talking about? Not, in this essay, the most important: the Holy Spirit and the spiritual resources which he makes mysteriously available to his Church. I must leave consideration of these to other writers. The resources I am to talk of, while not totally separate from those, are the more tangible ones of money (whether it comes from direct giving or from inherited endowments), of buildings, of tools of communication (whether books or filmstrips, bicycles or buses) and of people.

But that is precisely the wrong order. People should come first. This is indeed the chief thrust of this essay. The Church is for people, consists of people, has its main resources in people and should only bother with money, buildings, or whatever else in so far as they can genuinely serve and release people towards the fulness of life God intends for us all.

No one will disagree in theory — but in practice? Let's test it out on the question whether or not to build a new church building in a new housing area. The first idea of many church leaders will be to put up a building in order to show that 'the Church' is concerned for the new area, even before there can be any idea of what sort of Christian community will spring up there or whether they would ever be able to repay the expense. Would it not be a much more effective sign of concern to send a person or a family to live there and make contact with the new settlers, let alone cheaper? But even on the question of a building, if we ask 'what do the people there need?' and ask it for the total community not just for the Christians, then almost always — at least in temperate climates where activities have to take place indoors — the answer will be in terms of a wide open community centre in which all sorts of different things can go on, from baby-sitting to table tennis, from a public library to a family planning advice centre, rather than purely a place for worship. From there it is an obvious step to look to Christians working with the local political authority to ensure that such a community centre is provided, with one room suitable for worship on Sundays, rather than trying to build something separate of their own. In

197

warmer climates, where people naturally gather in the open, is it not anyway appropriate to hold a service of worship or a bible study where the curious or the not yet convinced can listen in without having to take the decisive step across the church threshold? Either way, to give first consideration to people, and to the people outside the fellowship of the Church, leads to cheaper and more creative missionary provision than to an inevitably expensive and inflexible building. Any reader with time to wander in England would do well, for instance, to compare what has been done in Blackbird Leys, on the edge of Oxford, and in Danesholme, on the edge of Corby.

The Church is for people and the resources it administers are for the sake of people, of what God intends for them. That suggests immediately that it really doesn't matter much whether there are many material resources or not. People can love and serve one another, as they can love and serve God, whether or no they have much by way of money, possessions, education and so forth. Is it not the clear thrust of Jesus' teaching — e.g. the instruction to the twelve in Luke 9.3, the lesson from the widow's gift in Luke 21.1-4, the parable of Dives and Lazarus in Luke 16 — that it is those who are comparatively well off who need to look to their spiritual danger? The Church has certainly no mandate to increase its store of material resources (contrast Matthew 6.19!). That some churches do have a certain amount is entirely a matter of the contingencies of history and society, of no eternal significance. Those concerned must beware of becoming dominated by their possessions, just as those without should beware of any form of envy! Any material resources we happen to have are to be at the service of people.

But which people? Because of the largely uninterrupted continuity of the Church of England with a medieval Christendom, Anglicans have all too often a basic mental framework of three concentric circles: in the inner ring the clergy, surrounding them the lay members of the Church and surrounding them in turn 'the world'. This tends to determine the priorities of bishops and synods: first and most important the salaries and training of the clergy, followed closely by what it takes for them to do their work (buildings, prayer books, etc.); only then — if anything is left — some particular provision for the training of laity (conference centres, study courses, etc.); and as good as nowhere any specific resources for mission in the surrounding world (whether for an ecumenical youth club or for first-rate programmes on radio and TV). Here again the Church needs to turn itself inside out and take those concentric circles in precisely the reverse order of priorities: first the world in general, its opportunities and needs as seen in the light of God's intentions; within that active and committed Christians equipped as far as may be for the service and witness to which they are called; and within and for the sake of the laity a much smaller number of the ordained, trained and where appropriate freed from other

198

work in order to give the back-up services that the total missionary demand on the laity may require.

Test that out, in turn, on the questions: who do we know and how do we make the most of each other? It is horribly easy for church leaders to know few people beyond 'their own' clergy, and for clergy to spend almost all their time with 'their laity'. Whereas precisely those relationships will be strengthened the more the leaders and clergy are out and about in the world, sharing for Christ's sake in all the joys and sorrows and struggles that have to do with God's purposes for human living. Baptism, the entry into the fellowship of the Church, is an act of solidarity with sinful and needy humanity (Matthew 3.15) and thus also the gateway into a life-long adventure of growth into abundant life, of search for the fullness of truth, of reaching out into the depths, of opening ourselves into ever wider and richer love. None of this can be 'administered' but it is what the Church is all about; what does it say to our habits of mind and of decision-making?

One practical conclusion from this train of thought is that first priority in the use of resources must go to adequate, painstaking knowledge of the people with whom any particular cell of the Church is concerned, so that all decisions about buildings, money, clergy, and so forth can be clearly seen to depend on their specific needs and opportunities. The ways in which this knowledge can be gained and then made available will be many and various — from parish maps to an observer seat on town planning committees, from freeing a qualified person to visit new industries springing up to a careful monitoring of the newspapers. Then it must be shared from time to time with the Church as a whole — whether local congregation or national synod — so that all of us who bear Christ's Commission can know that we are taking our individual decisions within a coherent total framework.

A second step is then the no less adequate recording of the experience and skills of church members, so that all of us can draw as fully as possible on each other's resources when we are confronting major questions. The worship and teaching of too many churches pre-supposes a 'privatisation' of faith and church membership that positively prevents the layman from bringing his experiences in the secular world into active use in the church setting, and is thus a capitulation to the ruling powers of a fragmented and consumer-dominated world. Worship especially should be a moment when the knowledge and experience of lay people can be shared, re-ordered and recommitted to God's service. Card indexes, tables of secular involvement, eldership schemes by which each member of a parish council is responsible for being in contact with a certain part of the total constituency, etc. can all be useful; what matters here as always is not the particular forms chosen as most practicable but the intention and persevering care with which they are invested.

A third step will then be to make the most of the people whom God has given as fellow-workers, so that we can both seize hold of our present chances and train likely people for opportunities as yet untapped. Which of our congregations/dioceses/councils of churches have so ordered their lives that 'adult education' takes an equal place with worship? — the two should of course be complementary rather than in any way rivals. Living in Christ is always to be growing into the fullness of Christ (the constant theme Ephesians 2.21, 3.19, 4.15 etc.), and taking others with us. Thus publishing programmes and conference centres (and perhaps the transport to make them accessible) deserve a high place among 'material resources; in our personnel policies, the releasing of people with educational skills and experience by which others can grow.'

'People for people' is the basis of all deciding about the use of resources in the Church.

SPLENDID DIVERSITY IN A UNIVERSAL FELLOWSHIP

But people vary. This is the second main point that we need to make to one another. God has created us all different. As the WCC Nairobi Assembly report *Confessing Christ Today* so memorably put it in speaking of the effects of conversion: 'Jesus Christ does not make copies; he makes originals.' Decision-making in the Church as in any other human context, goes wrong when it results in forcing people to do something they cannot feel as appropriate. Resources are there to be used so that people may grow freely into being themselves in an ever truer and deeper way, which will by no means usually be the way of the next man or woman, let alone of the fellow-Christian in another culture or continent.

There is in fact a double point here: just as Jesus was a Jew, in all the particularity of his time and race, but lived and died for all mankind, so each of us and each cell of his body is to live out our highly particular, unique opportunities in time and culture while always being conscious of the universal fellowship and universal purpose in which we do so. Authenticity in the particular is not to be an excuse for any isolation or self-satisfaction. On the contrary, a care for the adequacy of the universal Church in all places must be a care for the adequacy of the local Church in each place, and precisely not the imposition of foreign models, as the Roman Catholic Church is so excitingly if painfully learning in our generation.

This double point applies in the case of resources just as much as in that, say, of doctrine. The essence of Christian mission lies in an imaginative grasp — with an imagination attuned to the promise of God's Kingdom — of the unique opportunities and needs of each community and of how to serve those in Christ's name. That service will suggest some specific pattern of the use of manpower or buildings. Full-time, professional clergy, for example, belong typically to urban living where everybody is characterised by his or her specialist work roles and where there is evident need for

200

persons free to build bridges between all the so easily isolated 'worlds'. Buildings in plain grey stone with high arches may have expressed the aspirations of medieval Europe but are seldom likely to be appropriate symbols — let alone functional in shape and acoustic — for warmer climates and more energetic, dancing cultures. The financing of a large part of clergy salaries from a substantial capital fund is one result of the inimitable history of the Church of England — many would say to her good fortune, others to her spiritual danger — but is certainly not appropriate as a model, let alone an ideal, in other areas. Only on the basis of free and original thought and prayer about ways in which the Christian community can appropriately serve the human community in each culture and place can one expect to come to adequate decisions about the manpower which that church should seek to employ (if any) and thus to corresponding decisions about the raising of the finance by which to pay them.

That is, admittedly, a mere dream inasmuch as none of us can ever expect to be totally free and original. We all inherit given situations and given patterns; we are all thoroughly conditioned by our heritage and our environment in ways that it is hard enough to become aware of, let alone to change. The possibilities realistically open to us may often seem but small steps in face of the ideal reshaping of the Church of which we can dream. But realism need never be the same as defeatism, let alone as worldly wisdom. The 'real' to which Christians are properly devoted is that for which God has created us all, always truer and deeper than the state in which we have landed ourselves; a way of living governed by the free Spirit of Christ, not by the predictable princes of this world. Is not one of the tangible effects of commitment to Christ, of the death to self and the rising to new life in him, a freedom to decide freshly and differently about one's personal priorities? No less so with Church leaders and the decisions entrusted to them. We never have to do things the way they have been done before. Indeed, in a rapidly changing world there will be a presumption that imitating the past is more likely to be damaging to effective mission than otherwise. A proper gratitude for one's heritage, whether of the past or from another country, is best incarnated in a fresh creativity geared to one's own immediate present and the future that God may be seeking to build out of that.

Another factor that calls for and encourages a fresh response is that of partnership with Christians of other heritages — confessional or cultural — in one's own place. In no country, and in very few localities, are Anglicans now without sister Churches: of various sorts, of course, some much more friendly and easy to get on with than others, some much more willing than others to contemplate a measure of sharing resources and common decision-making; but all given us by God as potential partners. Sometimes it will quite evidently be cheaper and more practicable to use resources jointly — e.g. in running expensive TV studios or in comity agreements in opening new work. But even where it is not, where ecumenical schemes seem all the more demanding in time and energy, it is a false and deceptive way to fall back on doing things separately. That can only harm a truly missionary stance, while the wrestling to find an appropriate way through the puzzles of differing attitudes and procedures can itself be a worthwhile contribution to witnessing to the Kingdom.

It is built into the essential structure of all Christian faith and obedience that they point to the whole: to the wholeness of God's single purpose for all creation. In terms of the use of resources this surely says something about how we decide to share them — with the surrounding community as a whole in mission, with our neighbouring fellow-Christians for the sake of the common mission, and with people further away for the sake of God's universal mission. It would be good to anchor in every decision-making body the principle that the first call on time and budget be assigned to that which we share with others; that which we allot purely to ourselves should come at best second. Mutuality belongs to the proper use of resources quite as much as to authority or intercession. All parts of the church, within their own autonomous deployment of the Spirit's gifts for their own missionary situation, have something to give; to pretend otherwise is to pauperise oneself in unfaith. No less, all parts of the church need and deserve companionship, strengthening and a critical eye from elsewhere; to pretend otherwise is naked pride.

Such sharing, again, is primarily a matter of people, and of lay people. Other forms of sharing — chiefly no doubt of money — have their uses, and much effort is rightly being invested in our time in ways by which that sharing can be freed from wrong forms of paternalism and outside control. But it is all in the context of a community of people, of people freeing and encouraging each other into contact with yet others in the name of a person, Jesus Christ. People vary. Thank God. It is because of our diversities that we can help one another to see fresh possibilities. We vary not least in the amount of resources we have or expect to have available. The richer among us may be able to share something with the poorer, as the world measures rich and poor. I suspect that in the present generation (speaking from among the richer) it is even more important that the poorer teach the richer how to do with less.

In conclusion let me simply stress again that the essential context for any decisions about what we Christians are to have and do is found in what God has done and is doing with our world as a whole. We must always look beyond our established priorities and patterns to what we can know of his, and of what he intends for our particular here and now. Never easy to fathom, but then we were not promised certainty and success; rather the adventure of pilgrimage and of an ever-risky self-surrender in the sure knowledge that in the end nothing can separate us from God's love.

202

GUIDE TO FURTHER READING:

The Church for Others, Ed: W. J. Hollenovegar. Two Reports of the Missionary Structure of the Congregation, A67, pp 135ff. (Geneva: World Council of Churches).

The Secular in the Sacred, Brian Frost, pp 45ff. (Great Yarmouth, Norfolk; Galliard Ltd., 1972).

Can Churches be Compared, Ed: Steven G. Mackie. Reflections on Fifteen study projects, pp 101ff. (Geneva: World Council of Churches and New York Friendship Press, 1970).

Article by Bishop Valentine (pp. 178-185).

GUIDE TO FURTHER READING:

Religion and Sexism, Rosemary Reuther, ed. (New York: Simon and Schuster, 1974).

Women in Christian Tradition, George H. Tavard (Univ. of Notre Dame Press, 1973).

Towards a New Theology of Ordination; essays on the ordination of women, Marianne Micks and Charles Price, eds. (Virginia Theological Seminary, 1976).

Women Priests, Yes or No, Emily Hewitt and Susan Hiatt (New York: Seabury Press, 1973).

SECTION V

Episcopal Ministry

PART A : Origins and Influences

PART B : The Bishop in Person

This Section was planned to conclude with an article from Asia on 'The Bishop and Life-style'. It is much regretted that illness has prevented the writer completing the essay.

1 - Episcopacy in the New Testament and early Church

Henry Chadwick

All Christian ministry is a gift of the Spirit, a charism. It is neither an end in itself, nor an entity independent of the community, but rather a service for the building up of the Church (Eph. 4 : 7-16). As a supernatural call, a charism belongs to the transcendent, divine order. As a service within the community, its action is seen in the visible historical order, in the society grounded in the discipleship of Jesus Christ and rooted in the continuing life of the Church. This society is ever vulnerable to temptations and to secularising pressures; the treasure may be contained in very earthen vessels. Nevertheless, if the revelation of God in Christ is rightly seen not only as a word of justifying grace in mercy to the ungodly, but also as a sanctifying power mediated in, with and under the means of grace in word and sacrament and shared worship, the role of an ordered ministry in relation to these means of grace is of essential importance to the maintenance of the Church in the truth of the gospel and the life of the Spirit. For in these words and acts, done in obedience to the Lord's command, the presiding minister is called to act in the name of Christ, the head of the body. He is not merely carrying out a function which the community delegates to him. Himself a man under obedience, he calls those whom he serves to a like obedience.

Charisms differ (I Cor. 12 : 4-13). The ordained ministry is one of the Spirit's gifts to the Church, by which ministers are specially appointed to an office and authorised both for the proclamation and guarding of the word and for the due administration of the sacraments. They are not to lord it over the community they serve (I Peter 5 : 3), but to protect the means of grace upon which the community as a whole depends for its life. Among the Spirit's gifts this ministry is called to ensure that the very diversity of charisms does not endanger the essential unity of the one fellowship of Christ's flock. Accordingly, the oversight given by the ordained ministry always has a dual role or relationship — on the one hand in service to the local Christian community; on the other hand, in relation to other churches in the federation of local communities bonded together in love and constituting the visible universal Church.

The New Testament does not show a precise form or single structure of ministry which can be seen to be there from the day of Pentecost and can in the simplest sense be claimed as a direct and express institution by Jesus. The primary ministry in the apostolic age is that of the apostles themselves; and we have to look partly beyond the first century documents to see what forms of ministry the Church developed as and after the apostles passed from the scene. In fact the later books of the New Testament provide a substantial body of historical evidence for the earlier stages of this development. One essential principle, however, remains constant from the start through all variations of form, namely that the pastoral ministry is not a human invention but a gift of God to his Church to enable it to be what he intends in mission, unity, and holiness.

The *Apostolate* was strictly no doubt neither a charism nor an office in so far as the latter concept would imply a more constitutionally structured society than the earliest Christians possessed. The apostles are witnesses to the resurrection of the Lord and from their glorified Master receive a commission to preach the gospel. But they are not an authority only in the sense of good historical testimony for the events of Christ's coming and triumph. In the communities which their mission founded they also become a source of contemporary jurisdiction. The power of the keys is a dominical commission to decide points in dispute as well as a discretion to give rulings concerning the position of erring individuals within the society of disciples.

In respect of their witness to Jesus Christ (both of his words and deeds 'in the days of his flesh' and as to the fact of God's triumph in his rising again) there is an obvious sense in which the apostles had and could have no successors. What they said and did in their generation no one else can say or do at a later time. The refusal of the Church to add to the canon of the New Testament (i.e. to admit later Christian writings to the lectionary) is a way of making this point, that in the apostolate certain essential functions are not transferable or transmissible, and that primary apostolic authority is permanently contained in the written records of apostolic literature. At the same time the historical continuity of the Church means that in another sense there are responsibilities and powers of the apostolate which have not died with them. Not only does the Church as a whole have an apostolic mission and character. The authenticity of the tradition about Jesus needs to be preserved in the process of transmission. The local families of Christians gathered in scattered communities need pastoral leadership for decisions on questions of right training and practice in obedience to the revealed will of God. As the early Church came to understand that history was not coming to an immediate end, they also came to see that some permanent structure of ministry was required.

In the earliest stage of pioneer missionaries, the ministers will often have been itinerant 'prophets' or teachers, not tied to any single congregation, but going about from place to place encouraging and correcting, and receiving hospitality (according to the Didache, up to a limit of three days). But the congregations will also require resident shepherds to guide and protect the flock. Accordingly there come to be those 'set over' the congregation whose position of authority (I Thess. 5 : 12f; Heb. 13 : 17) derives sanction and lifelong tenure from the sacred nature of their functions.

During the first century some diversity in structure between different regions and local churches seems to have been characteristic. In some churches spiritual leadership was in the hands of a group of elders or 'presbyters', as at Ephesus (Acts, 20 : 17), under the overall authority of the apostle. On the other hand, the mother church at Jerusalem had a single head in the person of James, the Lord's brother. This 'monarchical' and apparently earliest form of pastorate could easily be fused with a presbyteral council, in which it would be natural for one man to be held as first among equals if he possessed special charismatic powers or seniority in years and wisdom, or, like Stephanas at Corinth (I Cor. 16 : 15-16), was the first convert who then devoted himself to forming a community round him.

At Philippi Paul sends greetings to the 'bishops and deacons' (Phil. I : 1). This reference is the only Pauline allusion, outside the late Pastoral Epistles to Timothy and Titus, to permanent ministerial offices in a local church. In Paul's letters the overwhelming emphasis lies upon the Spirit as the creator of both vitality and order in the Church (as in I Cor. 12-14, order at Corinth being less evident than vitality); and the only controversy about 'office' revealed in the epistles concerns Paul's own standing as an apostle. The Gentile churches he has founded are themselves the living vindication of the Lord's call to him to be apostle to the Gentiles; and their membership and acceptance in the one universal Church, with its focus and touchstone of communion in the mother church of Jerusalem (Gal. 2 : 1-10), depend upon the authenticity of his apostolate (I Cor. 9 : 1-2). While Paul has much to say of the principles and nature of Christian authority, e.g. that its function is to set free, not to enslave (II Cor. 1 : 24; 10 : 8), he has nothing to say about the practical provision of a formal constitutional structure for his missionary churches, for whom he himself, through his letters and his helpers such as Titus, is the focus of loyalty under Christ. The reference in Philippians 1 : 1 shows that in time the general itinerant care exercised by Paul and his helpers is being supplemented by resident officers. Although one cannot be sure just what functions the Philippian bishops and deacons had, the subsequent development suggests that the deacons helped on the administrative side, while the spiritual leadership of the community would be in the hands of the 'bishops' with pastoral oversight, subject to Paul himself. The Didache (15) shows how there was a natural tendency for local churches at first to value their resident bishops and deacons much less than itinerant prophets and teachers, perhaps not only because they seemed less obviously charismatic, but also because of the limited and local character of their responsibilities.

The twofold designation of 'bishops and deacons' attested in Philippians 1 appears both in the early (probably first-century) church order, the Didache (chap. 15) which never mentions presbyters, and also in the epistle written by Clement in the name of the church of Rome to the church of Corinth about the end of the first century (I Clement 42). In the Rome of A.D. 100 the name 'bishop' may be applied to church leaders who are also called 'presbyters'. At least, therefore, the presbyterate is a function and office in which bishops also have a full share. A similar pattern of terminology appears in the Pastoral Epistles to Timothy and Titus, where presbyters are generally plural, the bishop is singular, suggesting the probable conclusion that already among the college of presbyters exercising *episkope,* or pastoral oversight, one is the commonly accepted president. Of the bishop the highest qualities are required, and they are not only spiritual or supernatural but include natural qualities of leadership and common sense (I Tim. 3 : 3-7; Titus 1 : 6-9). The likelihood is that in some local churches an initially single pastor subsequently became joined in authority by a council of presbyters, while in others the development went the opposite way; i.e. among a group of equal 'presbyter-bishops', one became distinct as presiding bishop without losing the sense of fully sharing a common pastorate and liturgical duty with his presbyteral colleagues, sitting with them in common council much like the 24 elders of the Revelation of John of Patmos (Rev. 4 : 4). In a relationship of primacy among equals, it is likely enough that in some places the primacy was more apparent than the parity, and elsewhere the other way round. In the first epistle of Peter addressed to the Gentile churches of Asia Minor the 'presbyters' are instructed to be shepherds after the pattern of Christ who is the Chief Shepherd, and are therefore to be living examples to their flock (I Peter 5 : 2-4). The author of the second and third Johannine epistles, 'John the Presbyter', exercised authority not only as a local teacher but as a shepherd of a region in which there were a number of churches. Like Timothy and Titus in the Pastoral Epistles, John the Presbyter probably had special responsibilities in ordinations of local clergy, since at ordinations the choice of local congregations would need to be guided and even in some measure controlled to maintain the fellowship of churches with each other. As the local churches grew in strength and independence, the authority of the ministry of local congregations became more securely recognised. It was then natural for the presiding minister in each local church to play a principal role in, and to bear ultimate responsibility for, ordinations of presbyters and deacons in his church, though always with the consent of the people. Likewise this presiding 'bishop' or 'presbyter' was responsible for correspondence with other churches, for hospitality to travellers, for going to represent his own people at the ordination of the ministers of neighbouring churches. He was therefore the person through whom the local church realised its links with others in the worldwide fellowship of churches.

Each local church is to be a self-sufficient fellowship, in which all the elements of the universal Church are present. Yet its independence is simultaneously limited by the mutual care that local churches have for each other or by the leadership given particularly by prominent churches looking back to an apostolic foundation (a feature exemplified in the epistle of Clement of Rome to Corinth). The synodical idea imposes a restriction on what any individual bishop or church may do. At the same time the second century Church found in churches of apostolic found-ation (in the West, in Rome as the city where St. Peter and St. Paul died) a touchstone of authentic communion. Accordingly, frequent contacts between churches act as a check upon private idiosyncrasies in teaching, at the same time as they help the realisation of catholicity. Through their fellowship with one another, at first expressed in informal ways and without formalised patterns of conciliarity, the presiding clergy of local churches are a living embodiment of the sacred tradition about Jesus Christ. This special ministerial responsibility for safeguarding what is taught in the churches goes back to an early stage. In Paul's discourse to the presbyters of Ephesus (who are called 'bishops': Acts 20 : 24-28) these leaders of the church are warned to be guardians of the true trad-ition against the false doctrine that threatens the very existence of the Church of Christ's redemption. (It is not thereby implied that laymen have no responsibility to interpret the faith.) This protective, guarding role comes to be especially carried out by synods, in which the bishop is the sacramental representative of his local community.

Of the manner of the making of clergy in the New Testament period, the Pastoral Epistles and Acts 13 : 3 mention the laying on of hands, the rite associated with the giving of the power of the Spirit in the sacrament of baptism: 'Do not neglect the spiritual endowment you possess, which was given you, under the guidance of prophecy, through the laying on of the hands of the elders as a body.' (I Tim. 4 : 14 N.E.B.) 'I now remind you to stir into flame the gift of God which is within you through the laying on of my hands' (II Tim. 1 : 6). Ordination is here understood to be a sacramental act conferring a charismatic gift of grace appropriate to the office. There is or should be no antithesis of office and charism, because the laying on of hands with prayer, in a solemn act by the council of 'presbyters', is at the same time a recognition of the prophetic call and a sign of the Spirit's gift. The gift can be nullified, or Timothy would not need to be warned to take good care to act according to the charism

210

bestowed (I Tim. 1 : 18-19; II Tim. 4 : 10). At the same time the gift and call in ordination are to be the ground of his confidence as a minister, and the commission of ordination is apparently accompanied by a most solemn charge to keep 'the good confession' (I Tim. 6 : 11-16). So also St. Paul tells the presbyters of Ephesus that their appointment to exercise episcopal oversight comes from the Holy Spirit (Acts 20 : 28). Hence the ancient Church's conviction that in ordination God's call is irrevocable; the shepherd of the flock is to represent the Chief Shepherd whose constancy is unfailing.

The ancient Church understands ordination as more than a local authorisation limited to the local community where the ordination has taken place. The orders of episcopate, presbyterate, and diaconate are universally extended orders; that is to say, a presbyter ordained at Corinth needs only a letter of recommendation by his own bishop to be accepted, without reordination, in, say, Rome or Ephesus, and allowed to officiate there with the agreement of the local bishop. The priesthood in which he shares belongs to the universal Church and at his ordination other presbyters join the bishop in the laying on of hands. A newly elected bishop, chosen by his flock, is duly entrusted with the charism of episcopal office by other bishops, who represent, therefore, this universal recognition. This is in line with the New Testament records in which all those commissioned to exercise pastoral oversight are appointed by those who themselves have previously received such a commission. Nevertheless, the ancient Church had a deep sense of the intimate bond between a bishop and his own flock. He is, or ought to feel himself, married to his church. Hence their censures of episcopal translations from a small see to a greater as a secularising concession to worldly ambition.

This bond was inevitably weakened by the success of the Christian mission, which so enlarged the size of local churches that at least in large cities it soon became impossible for the bishop to know each of his sheep personally. It then became common to assign suburban or rural parishes to one or, in Rome, two presbyters. This increase in the number of presbyters, and the growth during the fourth century of the notion of grades of ordained ministers constituting a ladder of honour, like a civil service, came to erect a barrier between the laity and the president of their diocesan family. By the fourth century the clergy came to play a more prominent part than the laity in the election of a new bishop. Even so the rule (expressed by Cyprian and enacted at Nicaea, 325) that each city may have only one bishop, continued in force.

The early Church learnt by experience that the diocesan family needs to have one man rather than a committee as the focus of unity both in the local church and in his fellowship with the college of bishops. Despite the strong language of Ignatius of Antioch, the 'monarchical' character

211

of the episcopate is not, as such, a matter of fundamental juridical or dogmatic principle, essential to the Church in the sense that if the episcopate were shared and not monarchical the Church would be amputated, but is a practical need for the expression of unity. Nevertheless, Ignatius is surely right in seeing the bishop's central authority as linked to his presidency at the eucharist, in which he stands in a sacramental relation to Christ. He is there a focus of 'harmony' (Ignatius does not say unison) in the family of God. Ignatius never alludes to a historic succession as the ground of episcopal authority. But he simply assumes that what orthodox bishops are teaching is what the apostles taught; he holds office in a society that is continuous with that of Peter and Paul.

Ignatius is the earliest writer to attest a three-fold ministry in which bishop, presbyters, and deacons are distinguished as separate grades, 'without which a community cannot be called a church' (*Trall.* 3). This three-tiered structure is well attested (and taken for granted) by later writers, and must quickly have become universal without trace of controversy. The three grades were seen to correspond to the three grades of Old Testament ministry, high priest, priest and levite. It cannot, however, be this correspondence which made it seem natural to use the Greek *hiereus* or the Latin *sacerdos* of the Christian minister (attested from the beginning of the third century in both East and West), since these words were already being traditionally used of the bishop rather than of the presbyter. The Old Testament hierarchical typology did not create the threefold Christian ministry, a structure which owes its origin to the second century Church's inheritance from the sub-apostolic generation in which an originally two-tiered local ministry, under general apostolic oversight, passed into a three-tiered ministry, with the presiding bishops representing apostolicity. The earliest deacons were needed primarily for administrative duties; male deacons gradually acquired limited liturgical functions, especially reading the gospel (power to celebrate the eucharist being expressly denied to them), but remained the bishop's personal staff. As the congregations grew in size and number, presbyters also acquired wider duties. From being a council, sharing the pastoral and teaching responsibility with the bishop, they began to look after suburban parish churches for which they performed all functions shared with the bishop other than ordination and (except in Egypt) confirmation; these the bishops kept in their own hands, ordinations being among their most solemn responsibilities, and confirmations being a direct link with the lay members of their flock. In the fourth century the extension of presbyteral duties was given a theological justification by the presbyter Jerome (letter 146) who argued from New Testament texts that bishops and presbyters belong to a single order of ministerial priesthood, sharply distinct from the diaconate. Jerome regretted the performance by deacons of certain liturgical functions as obscuring their distinction from the pastoral and priestly order of presbyters and bishops, and so encouraging mistaken pretensions.

In the conflict with gnostic dualism, perhaps the gravest crisis of the Church's history, the early Church found the centralising of authority in the bishop a necessary safeguard against centrifugal forces, whether heretical or schismatic. Formal institutions in the ministry, in the pattern of baptismal confessions of faith, and finally in a fixed canon of the New Testament were developed in the course of the second century. Clement of Rome sees the duly ordained ministry as the embodiment of the principle that God wills order in his Church, so that a local church like Corinth cannot simply get rid of its clergy without satisfying other churches in the universal fellowship that the deposed clergy have been unworthy of their holy office. This principle of order is linked for Clement with the idea of apostolic succession. The fact of a succession in ministerial commission is not asserted by Clement in controversy, but an agreed datum from which he argues for the security of tenure of worthy ministers. Against the Gnostics' claims that their bizarre theosophical speculations represent a secret tradition handed down from the apostles, the second century Church pointed to the publicly verifiable succession of bishops in the churches, especially in those of known apostolic foundation, and to the consensus of all the churches that authentic Christianity does not include these gnostic fantasies. The second century bishops stand in the apostolic succession not merely (or even mainly) because of those who laid hands on them, but because the churches over which they preside do so in universal communion with each other. There is no question in the early period of an authentic ministerial succession having a career apart from the one holy catholic and apostolic Church and being empowered independently to minister the word and sacraments according to the mind of the Spirit. The local churches together with their clergy are authentic because they stand in the true and universal succession, which is accordingly a transmission of faith together with that recognized order of ministry which serves it. So Irenaeus excludes from the apostolic succession heretics, schismatics, and orthodox bishops of evil life.

The Donatist schism in fourth century North Africa moved Augustine to find reasons to dissent from the general patristic view that outside the catholic Church there can be no authenticity; but his argument that if valid baptism can be received outside catholic unity, the same holds good for orders, was not generally accepted and acted on in the West until medieval times. The generous intention of Augustine's doctrine was to make reconciliation with the Donatists easier by allowing the unconditional validity of their orders. The form of his argument, however, had an obverse side. It unhappily encouraged men to think of ordination by a bishop in apostolic succession as if this were the exclusive and sole test of ministerial and ecclesial validity. The early Church did not think

213

in this way. When the Council of Nicaea in 325 decreed that a bishop should be consecrated by the metropolitan with, if possible, all the bishops of the province or, if not all, a minimum of three, the Council understood its minimal three to be representing the wider fellowship. The Nicene bishops would never have thought that a person consecrated by any three bishops in any circumstances whatever had claims to catholic recognition.

The recognition of the orders of separated ecclesial bodies is invaluable as one element in a total reconciliation but useless if taken in isolation. When it becomes treated as a technical way of 'foot-faulting' other communions, argument about ministerial validity quickly comes to look trivial and pedantic, and can carry more than a suggestion (which would be alien to the thought of the early Church about apostolic succession) that the transmission of sacramental grace through the apostolic ministry is mechanical. On the contrary, for the early Christians the participation of bishops of other local churches in the consecration of a bishop is a sign and instrument of the continuity of both the new bishop and his church with the apostolic communion extended through time and space; and this is the nerve-centre of the concept of apostolic succession. It is a positive doctrine which has also a negative side in that it presupposes the presence of some defect of order in a separated ministry which is 'self-made' or is dependent on the private enterprise of a particular congregation. Such an independent pastorate may indeed be blessed by God as an efficacious means of proclaiming the gospel; but if it rejects communion with the apostolic and catholic tradition, something is lacking; it may assume a radical disjoining of charism and office which is out of line with the New Testament and the early Church; its authority and recognition are restricted; and ultimately the comprehension of the faith becomes one-sided and partial. Accordingly, the defect is one of universality: that is, it is not a technical fault of pedigree, but an isolation from the organic spiritual life of the one holy catholic and apostolic Church, in which the pastoral ministry has received its commission in a succession of order that goes hand in hand with a succession in faith and life.

2 - Sociological factors that have shaped episcopacy

G. M. D. Howat

There lies in front of me, as I write, an old autograph book of the 1940s in which I collected the autographs of bishops and first-class cricketers. The great majority are cut off from letters and pasted in, not only because bishops and cricketers of antiquity were prize items but also because Scotland was not a natural area in which to find either genre in large supply.

A random selection of pages reveals George Cicestr, Henry, Bishop of New Guinea, Archibald the Arctic, A. J. Moravian (one for the connoisseur to work out), and — collector's piece — Cosmo Ebor with the Ebor crossed out and the Cantuar written underneath. The list continues — Frank Nyasaland, Harold Gibraltar, Thomas Zanzibar, Theodore St. Johns, Joseph M. Francis, Bishop of Indianapolis. Cheek by jowl are Len Hutton, Bill Bowes, Learie Constantine, A. L. Hassett, Jack Hobbs and — another collector's piece — C. Aubrey Smith, cricketer and actor.

It is not an incongruous collection. Church and cricket have been in social alliance over the centuries. The game has its origins in monastic sports in the Middle Ages. The Stuart kings — proud supporters of episcopacy — were in sympathy with recreations and (by implication) cricket as the Declaration of Sports in 1618 indicated. It was left to Oliver Cromwell to utter specific strictures against cricket in the 1650s — and he was no friend of episcopacy, either. The eighteenth century cleric, Lord Frederick Beauclerk, played cricket with distinction. In the nineteenth century the paternalism of the village parson found expression in using the game as a vehicle of social control. The twentieth century has seen a continuing association between clerics and cricket. There is the *Church Times* Cricket Cup in which bishops compete with agile young curates for a place in the teams. An Anglican diocesan of today has captained England — two entries in the autograph book?

One may take the argument further. The structure of church government and organisation through bishops assumes an hierarchical role besides expressing the need for certain acceptable conventions to meet particular generations. Cricket, too, has both an hierarchical structure and a code of convention which has had to be adapted to changing circumstances.

What of those autographs of a generation ago? The names have a certain mystique for the informed. There may be alliterative appeal or euphoric harmony. They bespeak the pioneers of the British Empire and the opening up of Africa. There is the great nation of America with its pecularity of a Christian name plus an initial. From the heritage of the Latin language preserved by some to the geography of the vast spaces of the frozen North come names and sees. These bishops are a fragment of the Anglican Communion. Their common tongue is English. Their allegiance — save for the historic ally of America — is to a British Sovereign.

An autograph hunter a century earlier would have had a slightly different experience. In the 1840s he would just have been able to collect the signature of an Anglican episcopate within the Empire as new sees were created in the Antipodes in that very decade while India could claim three dioceses by 1840 and Africa three by 1850. Such activity was a consequence of a long sequence of missionary endeavour pioneered by the great Societies. His eighteenth century predecessor would have been daunted by the frequent absenteeism from their dioceses of the Hanoverian episcopate in England, and by the obscurity of the tiny Scottish episcopate persecuted since the Revolution of 1688.

It is fanciful but not altogether unhistorical to imagine the activities of our autograph hunter in earlier centuries. Did he, with courage, seek out the imprisoned Laud and the non-juror Ken or — with equal convictions in a divided seventeenth century — spurn episcopacy and pursue the autographs of the Levellers. And did he, in the sixteenth century, smirk at the scurrilous Marprelate pamphlets — 'proud, presumptuous, profane, paltry, pestilent and pernicious prelates' — or admire the humble Latimer and scholarly Cranmer, victims of an England divided by the Reformation?

The Reformation whether in England or in Western Europe in the fifteenth and sixteenth centuries had profound effects on episcopacy. In the Reformed countries where episcopacy survived, bishops found themselves facing a new society in which the individualism of the Renaissance had triumphed. The historic role which bishops had played as politicians and statesmen was now to be shared with an educated laity. The prince-bishop met the secular anti-clerical. In England, Wolsey gave way to Thomas Cromwell; Elizabethan government was vested in the layman, William Cecil. French cardinals vied with lawyers and bankers to rule during regencies and minorities.

The conflicts which post-Reformation Europe experienced in one way or another — the French Wars of Religion, the Thirty Years War, the English Civil Wars — had complex origins and particular developments. They were variously related to the emergence of nation-state, social and economic divisions, and the nature of authority. Within England, the conflict

216

over authority found the Stuart kings dependent on an association with their bishops which gave to both groups an absolution their opponents found unattractive. Monarchy and episcopacy survived the seventeenth century but not without heads falling.

The monarchy which emerged from the Revolution of 1638 was limited and constitutional. Neither Dutch William nor the German Georges had any particular affinity with episcopacy. The bishops of the eighteenth-century Church in England were thus supporters of the Establishment — of King, Lords and Commons — rather than of monarchy in any divine sense. Moreover, they tended to be supporters of the political party which dominated public life for the larger part of the century — the Whigs. Preferment came at the hands of the Whig politicians. Men of other political thinking were unlikely to enjoy the richer plums of ecclesiastical patronage. The Whig bishop possessed emoluments, status and political associations which set him far apart from the country clergy whose political allegiance was different and whose social aspirations were humble. This is to give the conventional view which can be overstated, and must be qualified by recognition of the endeavours in the eighteenth century of bishops who chose not to be tied to political apron-strings.

In Scotland a totally different situation existed where the Episcopalian Church was a non-juring body whose bishops endured the penalties imposed by the Hanoverian government since presbyterianism was the established form of worship. Because the Scottish episcopate owed no formal allegiance to the Crown, it was able to consecrate Samuel Seabury as bishop of Connecticut in 1734. This was an event which, in a sense, gave birth to the Anglican Communion in the nineteenth century. As our brief look at those autographs showed, there grew in this new century a Church in Africa, Canada, the Antipodes, India and the West Indies with its own diocesan structure, while the Protestant Episcopal Church in America likewise prospered.

These branches of the Anglican church — with the exception of the United States — drew their bishops from the United Kingdom. Such men reflected collectively many of the qualities associated with the British nineteenth-century style of leadership. They were scholars and administrators. They shared the Victorian propensity for hard work. They were enthusiasts. Enthusiasm had been a quality rejected by their eighteenth-century predecessors. The nineteenth-century prelates revelled in it with all the confidence and optimism that graced so much of Victorian activity in those who provided leadership in church and state. To single out names is invidious but perhaps that of Samuel Wilberforce may serve to illustrate the dedicated Victorian bishop whose pastoral concern and administrative abilities were matched by his interests in education and social reform — as befitted the son of the famous humanitarian and slave-trade reformer. The century brought great movements associated with both the Tractarian and

Evangelical tradition: the working Victorian bishop gave the necessary leadership.

It was the view of Lord Macaulay, shared by many other leading Victorians, that Britain should send men of outstanding calibre to serve in the Empire. Civil Servants, engineers, doctors and teachers poured forth from the mother country to undertake pioneer work in undeveloped countries. With them went bishops, often young on appointment, to organise new or infant dioceses, grapple with problems of synodical government, smooth over conflicts between European and indigenous interests and justify a Christian incursion into lands of other faiths. It was a pattern of activity which continued until the Second World War. Thereafter the role of the colonial bishop changed.

Historians have seen both world wars as major factors in social change. The years between, the 1920s and '30s, were a time of disillusion, escapism, apathy, depression and idealism. In the growing concern in the western world that wars neither solved problems nor were over for ever, ecclesiastical leaders shared with their secular counterparts in examining the new social issues of the times. Bishops, such as William Temple and George Bell did so at the cost of being identified as political figures. Calumny might come their way whether they were *laissez-faire* or interventionists. Bishops on the whole were ready to face criticism for being involved in social and moral questions. Many of these questions intensified in the post-1945 period. Moral issues such as birth-control and divorce, became more openly discussed and bishops such as Robert Mortimer would go on record with controversial utterances.

More especially since 1960 immense social and economic changes have taken place affecting both Europe and America, and the Third World of underdeveloped countries. In the former, the western world, social change has diminished authority. Hierarchies and established status have been challenged while the medium of television has brought instant contact between well-known figures in public life and viewers numbered in their millions. In economic terms, a degree of levelling has been achieved through varying factors which include taxation, social welfare and wage-parity.

The bishops have not been untouched by these phenomena. Frequently bishops appear on television. Their dress has changed. Gaiters, which lingered longest among English diocesans within the Anglican Communion, have disappeared. Palaces have given way to houses which are manageable with little or no domestic help. Episcopal cars may well be 'minis'. The bishop's wife — a formidable Mrs Proudie in the previous century — may well be an S.R.N. or social worker who met her husband in their college days.

These are the outward expressions of a change in attitude which has brought episcopacy closer to ordinary people. That sense of contact, once limited for many to social functions following confirmations, is now widened

218

in shared membership of broad-based Synods. It may be argued that much more contact is still needed: bishops in huge dioceses still seem remote. So do headmasters of large comprehensive schools. 'Small is beautiful' has much to commend it as a philosophy.

One further point needs to be made: the English episcopate in the nineteenth and twentieth centuries has been largely the product of men educated at the independent public schools and the ancient universities of Oxford and Cambridge; a sort of ecclesiastical administrative civil service. Men went from public school headmasterships to bishoprics with little or no pastoral experience in a parish. Within the last few years this has changed. Those appointed to sees have sometimes come from different educational background. They may not necessarily be graduates and they might have had experience in business or the armed forces. Practical pastoral experience in a parish has been seen as essential. This has to a much greater extent always been true of episcopacy in Canada and the United States where structural educational and social patterns have been less evident.

In the post-war years the expatriate colonial bishop has gradually disappeared giving way to an indigenous episcopate more sensitive to local political issues in territories which have passed from colonial status to independence within the Commonwealth. Bishops in these churches of the Anglican Communion are no more conscious of a Lambeth 'model' which they ought to follow or be behoven to than their political colleagues are of a Westminster 'model'. The essential virtue of such an episcopate lies in its acceptance by politicians and people still resentful of colonial days, and of western-style capitalism.

One political factor has remained constant in England throughout the last four centuries. The Church of England, in the post-Reformation years, continues to have bishops taking their seat in the House of Lords. While no evidence for change seems apparent (as distinct from suggestions for reforming the House as a whole), two opposite points of view may be offered. On the one hand, the Anglican episcopate might be joined in the House of Lords by leading bishops within the Roman Church to whom life peerages might be given. On the other, the Anglicans might cease to sit in the upper House as a body, and merely take their chance, as public figures in their own right, of being given life peerages by the government of the day. So long as the House of Lords is defensible as a second chamber of independent judgment and talent, there is a case for the representation of bishops — whatever their obedience.

This article has had little to say upon the sociological factors which have shaped episcopacy so far as the Roman Church is concerned. Roman bishops have met the impact of many of the changes which have affected their Anglican counterparts. But some important distinctions must be made. They have been no part in the political life of England: indeed, the restored hierarchy dates only from the nineteenth century. Their personal background has been more widely based than that of the Anglican bishops. Despite the far-flung nature of English dioceses, they have been closer to their flocks.

The title of bishop was also retained in the post-Reformation era in certain Lutheran churches and in some non-Anglican branches of the Protestant churches in Africa and America. To examine the sociological role of such episcopates would need to be the subject of a separate article. Sufficient to say that the style and title of bishops, in its Greek origins, means one who oversees. Bishops wherever they may be, are overseers: leadership is embodied in their person. It is a vocation not without risk in a world in which the bishop of 1977 walks a tightrope far different from that of his predecessors. In his earnest intent to be seen as a humble man of God, especially by a society which will expect of him a humility compatible with the teaching of the New Testament, he must yet remain the man of standing whose administrative competence, business acumen and personal status allow him to move with ease in the ranks of men and women who lead and govern in secular walks of life. His autograph must be worth collecting.

GUIDE TO FURTHER READING:

Anglicanism in History and Today, J. W. C. Wand (Weidenfeld & Nicolson, 1961).
The Episcopal Church and its Work, P. M. Dawley (Connecticut, 1955).
Bishops and Societies, H. Chattingius (S.P.C.K., 1952).

3 - Religious and ecclesiastical factors that have shaped episcopacy

G. V. Bennett

Since the close of the patristic age episcopacy has exhibited an astonishing diversity of form. In the West bishops have varied in character from a simple Irish monk, living under the rule of his presbyter-abbot, to an Archbishop-Elector of the Holy Roman Empire, himself the ruler of a State. In the East the same office has been held by the pastor of a single, small Greek island and by a Russian metropolitan with a jurisdiction larger than many European countries. The Church has existed within many different cultures, and the office of chief pastor and teacher of a local community has often been of such importance that it has been easy to assimilate it to the hierarchies of civil authority and interpret it according to the categories of secular thought. Conversely, it has been one of the prime aims of ecclesiastical reformers to revive a theological understanding of episcopacy and restore to it a genuinely pastoral ministry. This article attempts to consider briefly some of the forms which this protean order has assumed and their impact on the life of the Christian community.

FEUDAL EPISCOPACY AND PAPAL SOVEREIGNTY

Between the Barbarian invasions of the seventh century and the Reformation of the sixteenth century the episcopacy known to Ambrose, Augustine and John Chrysostom was transformed into the prelacy which the Reformers so decisively rejected. With the spread of Christianity into Northern Europe there appeared the 'tribal' diocese, covering not just a city and its surrounding countryside but a minor kingdom. Its bishop was likely to be the educator and adviser of a warrior-king, for whom the clergy would provide a chancery and administration. By the twelfth century in virtually every part of Northern Europe bishops had become great landholders and an integral part of the feudal order; they possessed private armies, levied taxes, and dispensed justice. It seemed only natural to emperors and kings that they should appoint the holders of offices which were of such importance to the peace and good order of their realms. But it was a system which could, and did, produce a widespread secularisation of the personnel of the episcopate. Even in the age of Anselm and Lanfranc it was rare to find a scholar occupying one of the great sees of Western Europe. And the development was not confined to the West. In the Eastern Church episcopacy remained for the most part what it had been since the seventh century: bishops were drawn from the monastic clergy, dioceses were moderate in size, and the bishop retained his function as leader of the liturgy of his people. But as, by the tenth century, Orthodoxy expanded to the north and evangelised the Slav peoples so vast dioceses replaced the smaller ones of Greece or Asia Minor. By the twelfth century a Metropolitan of Novgorod was head of a large state. Already a pattern had emerged by which Christian bishops were magnates and royal servants rather than teachers or pastors.

It was this secularisation of the office which the Papacy attempted to remedy by developing a new theory of episcopal authority. For the Hildebrandine reformers the Church itself was a kingdom; it was a hierarchy with the Pope as its head and, below him, subordinate ranks of officers. As the Sovereign Pontiff derived his authority from Christ so the lesser orders derived theirs from papal commission. Bishops were thought of as 'servants' of the Pope, just as the diocesan clergy were the 'servants' of their bishop. The twelfth century saw an impressive growth in legal science, and the new Canon Law was studied side by side with the Roman Civil Law, and obtained many of its concepts of authority from the later Roman Empire. Thus Popes claimed not only to appoint bishops but to interfere in their pastoral office: to act within a diocese by ordinary jurisdiction and set aside local procedures. The patristic notion of the relationship of a bishop to his clergy and people was replaced by an all-pervading legalism. Thus just as the Papacy came to be thought of as a source of legislation and a judicial tribunal, so the diocesan bishop became not so much a Father-in-God as an ecclesiastical magistrate for the punishment of spiritual offences.

MEDIEVAL PRELACY

The pastoral result was disastrous. In the Empire there were no less than 120 prelates who were accounted independent princes, and three of the seven Imperial Electors were bishops. Such men were the scions of aristocratic families, often without priestly vocation, who spent their lives amid the business of secular rulers, Martin Luther's bishop, Albert of Brandenburg, had at the age of twenty-three accumulated the archbishoprics of Magdenberg and Mainz, the latter the primacy of Germany. In France and England bishops were immersed in secular affairs, acting as royal ministers and diplomats, and engaged in administering their estates. Even with the occasional assistance of auxiliary bishops close episcopal oversight of the flock was impossible. Some dioceses were of immense size. That of Lincoln stretched from the Humber to the Thames, and the whole province of York had only three sees. Inevitably diocesan administration was in the hands of legal officials, the archdeacons, the vicar-general, and the official-principal of the consistory court. Perhaps symptomatic of the bishop's pastoral eclipse was his loss of any important liturgical function. While Mass could be celebrated with special pontifical ceremonial, it was exceedingly rare for any bishop to visit his cathedral, which would usually be served by a community of monks or a college of secular priests. The mighty medieval cathedrals were built to the glory of God and His Church; they were practically never centres of an active episcopal ministry.

EPISCOPACY AND THE REFORMATION

It was not easy for the sixteenth-century Reformers to distinguish between episcopacy and this medieval prelacy. Luther, Zwingli and Calvin were each concerned that the Word of God should be given free course, and their preaching seemed on all sides to be opposed by prelates and the papal church. Luther, in particular, responded by setting out a view of the Christian ministry which contrasted sharply with medieval theory. For him the Church was simply the company of those to whom God had given justifying faith, and the true Christ existed wherever the Word was preached and the sacraments rightly administered. A Christian minister was defined not by his legal status but by his function in setting forth the gospel in word and sacrament. Luther was not without a reverence for traditional ways and he was prepared to accept a reformed episcopate (as he was ready to accept a modified papacy) as an expedient form of church-government. But he firmly denied that any particular form of ministry was necessary to the existence of the true Church. Lutheran bishops (where they existed) were superintendent-ministers without privileges or official property; for the most part, except in Sweden, they were not in the historic episcopal succession. With Calvin, however, there was a vigorous attempt to recover what the great Genevan reformer believed to be a scriptural and primitive pattern of episcopacy. His four orders of pastors, teachers, elders and deacons conjoined preaching, doctrine, discipline and pastoral care within the context of a city-community, and the whole found its focus in the eucharistic worship of the church. The powerful appeal of Calvinism was due not only to the dynamism of its doctrinal system but to its revival of the notion of an ordered but genuinely pastoral form of ministry.

ROYAL SUPREMACY AND THE ENGLISH EPISCOPATE

The Reformation in England was founded on a theology of kingship more than on any particular doctrine of Christian ministry. Over against the claims for a papal supremacy the English reformers appealed to those biblical texts which indicated the right and duty of a 'godly prince' to reform and order the affairs of the Church. Indeed the Elizabethan settlement was itself an affirmation of this Royal Supremacy in ecclesiastical causes. Even though the Act of Uniformity of 1559 was a compromise which emerged out of a parliamentary struggle between the queen and those who wished for a more radical reform, the new Anglican establishment was, from the beginning, dedicated to the maintenance of royal authority and the enforcement of royal policies. From the institutional point of view it was deeply conservative. The Elizabethan episcopate was Protestant in theology and shorn of its medieval trappings but it retained much of the character of medieval prelacy and most of its pastoral ineffectiveness. The great medieval dioceses, virtually unaltered, remained; cathedrals continued as collegiate bodies: and vicars-general, officials-principal and the other legal officers exercised their traditional jurisdiction. Bishops were still lords of Parliament and, though their temporal possessions were plundered by the Crown, they remained substantial.

The first Anglican apologists for episcopacy thus found themselves attacked on two fronts: by 'Papists' who accused the bishops of being merely royal officials, lacking any continuity with the medieval Catholic episcopate, and by 'Puritans' who demanded that there should be a parity of ministers, according to scripture and the usage of the 'best reformed churches abroad'. John Jewell (1522-71), Bishop of Salisbury, was the ablest defender of the bishops against the Roman attacks. He took his stand on a scholarly appeal to Christian antiquity and insisted on the essential identity of Anglican episcopacy with that of the Primitive Church. They had reverently preserved the order in its historic succession while purging it of accretions and errors. But at no time did Jewell assert that an episcopal ministry was essential to the Church: mere succession was profitless if bishops did not exhibit the characteristics of a true Church by preaching sound doctrine and rightly administering the sacraments. On the continent rulers and prelates had conspired to thwart the gospel and it had been necessary to abandon episcopacy in order that true religion might flourish. In similar vein Anglican writers set themselves to refute those, like Thomas Cartwright, who argued that the Genevan system was the only one prescribed in holy writ. Whitgift, Hooker and Bancroft sought rather to set out a doctrine of episcopacy in which the scriptural texts were interpreted in the light of usage and antiquity and the order was demonstrated in reason to be useful and godly.

Yet however skilled the scholarly case for episcopacy, in practice the English bishops were utterly bound up with, and dependent upon, the monarchy. It was inevitable that those who opposed the policies of Charles I should regard the bishops, and particularly William Laud (1573-1645), Archbishop of Canterbury, as agents of tyranny and religious oppression. Thus the defeat of the king was accompanied by the abolition of episcopacy, the sale of church lands, and the ending of the Church's legal jurisdiction. It is perhaps not remarkable that with the end of the monarchy the Anglican episcopate came near to extinction. A few bishops continued to ordain but most lived quietly in retirement, making no effort to organise an independent episcopalian Church or even to consecrate any successors to themselves. In 1660 only nine elderly men survived to continue the episcopal order. It was the unexpected restoration of Charles II which brought about the return of episcopacy; it was small thanks to the bishops themselves.

It was not easy to maintain any clear doctrine of Church or ministry in the 'age of reason and natural religion' which ensued after 1660. During the years of deprivation and disestablishment a formidable group of patristic scholars had developed a new apologia for episcopacy. John Bramhall, Henry Hammond and Herbert Thorndike demonstrated that the bishop was the key to understanding the system of church government known to the Fathers. If they were ready to admit a distinction between primitive episcopacy and later prelacy yet they insisted (in contradistinction to earlier Anglican divines) that episcopacy was the *sine qua non* of a true and valid Church. Their writings clearly influenced the framers of the Act of Uniformity of 1662 which, by insisting on episcopal ordination for all ministers in the re-established Church, drove into formal Dissent a considerable body of those who had served in the Cromwellian Church.

Such a definite theological position was difficult to hold in the era of Locke and Newton when any beliefs or practices which appealed to antiquity or tradition for their authority were widely discounted. And, after the Toleration Act of 1689, the Church of England found itself in an invidious position. It was now one religious denomination among many. It was legally established and amply endowed but it could no longer exercise any compulsion over the laity. Now, if at any time, a new pastoral strategy and a new understanding of its mission was needed. Some 'High Churchmen' continued to write about the apostolical authority of bishops but in an age when patristic scholarship was almost wholly laid aside this meant little to most churchmen. The bishops of Hanoverian England were often worthy and benevolent men but, lacking any clear theological understanding of Church or ministry, they too readily accepted a role which the secularist politicians allotted them: that of being the allies of aristocrats and gentlemen in assuring political quiescence and social subordination. Recent studies have emphasised that the eighteenth century was the time when the urban population and the industrial labourer were lost to the Church. It is easy to argue that the bishops were denied by their political masters an opportunity to reform an archaic pattern of parish and diocese so that they might meet the pastoral problems created by the industrial revolution. The truth is that, cultured and well-intentioned gentlemen that they were, they lacked the theological resources to insist on the Church's mission, and the influence of their office was often used to hamper those who tried to do the work.

THE OXFORD MOVEMENT AND APOSTOLICAL SUCCESSION

By the second decade of the nineteenth century the condition of the Church of England was causing alarm even to its friends, and it was apparent that there was danger of a root-and-branch reform imposed by Parliament. There was little in current theology which could prepare churchmen to resist an Erastian assault. The 'high and dry' school seemed to possess no basis for the order of the Church apart from its legal establishment and its long history, while the Evangelical school, with its emphasis on a personal experience of conversion and a cult of moral pietism, seemed to have no churchmanship at all beyond a general support for the establishment as providing a useful framework for their preaching and pastoral work. It fell, then, to a group of scholars at Oxford to renew the appeal to the Fathers and to recover the teaching of the seventeenth-century apologists for episcopacy. These 'Tractarians' attempted to give back to the Church its independence by appealing to the authority of 'Catholic tradition', a living continuity of doctrine and worship mysteriously and graciously preserved from the time of the apostles down to the present time. In particular they fastened on the idea of Apostolical Succession. Often they spoke of this as if it were an unbroken chain of consecration of bishops from the first age but it would perhaps be unjust to them to imagine that their argument stood or fell on the historical fact of an unbroken succession of consecration. The apostolical succession was only one manifestation, one guarantee, of a holy community living down the ages its distinctive life of faith and love. Nor was their teaching intended merely to defend early nineteenth-century prelacy. Indeed they longed to transform the office of a bishop by conforming it to the character of a 'Primitive Episcopacy' as it had been known in the early and undivided Church.

EPISCOPACY AND CHRISTIAN UNITY

The Tractarian claim for a ministry within the historic episcopal succession was widely accepted during the nineteenth century and did much to restore the confidence and sense of purpose of both clergy and laity. It tended, however, to be an exclusivist claim. 'We must', wrote J. H. Newman in the first of the *Tracts for the Times*, 'necessarily consider none to be *really* ordained who has not *thus* been ordained.' Such a view undoubtedly was to prove a major stumbling-block when Anglicans came to consider co-operation, especially in overseas missions, with those Churches which did not possess the historic episcopate, and it has continued to provide a major cause of dissension among Anglicans themselves. Indeed, research into the historical origins of episcopacy has proved a topic of perennial interest to English-speaking scholars. It is impossible adequately to summarise the debate. An over-simple description would be to say that it has been between those who believe with Cyprian that the validity of orders depends on the authorisation of the Church and those who believe with Augustine that the life of the Church depends upon the validity of the ministry. Recent proposals within the context of the Ecumenical Movement for an organic union of episcopal and non-episcopal ministries have caused great heart-

226

searchings among Anglicans and, in the cases of the Church of South India and Anglican-Methodist union, even threats of schism. On the whole Lambeth Conferences have adopted a cautious approach to the subject. In 1886, 1920 and 1930 they affirmed their adherence to the Historic Episcopate but they have been equally careful not to deny that other ministries have been blessed by God as effective channels of grace.

MODERN DEVELOPMENTS

To outside observers it sometimes seems that Churches which possess the historic episcopate are better at insisting upon it than defining its use. The Second Vatican Council set forth a theory of the 'collegiality' of the episcopate but it would appear that the Roman Catholic Church has yet to engage in hard theological study before it can clarify the relationship of its bishops to the Papacy, the diocesan clergy and the body of laity.

In one sense episcopacy among Anglicans has become more prominent in the life of the Church. As there has been a greater freedom from dependence on the civil power so bishops have assumed a more central role in government and ordinary mission. Even in 1867 only a minority of those attending the first Lambeth Conference came from established churches. Much of the great missionary expansion of the nineteenth century was founded on episcopal initiative and leadership, and bishops were seen once again as evangelists and pioneers. At home Samuel Wilberforce (1805-73), Bishop of Oxford and later Winchester, effected a revolution in the character of diocesan episcopacy. His example excited a new zeal for parish work, for Church schools and for mission preaching. Many bishops attempted to recover for themselves a central liturgical role by making their cathedrals places where an episcopal ministry was available to the whole diocese. Victorian bishops were often drawn from the ablest men of their generation, and they brought to the episcopate rich experience as scholars, teachers and writers, and in public office.

In another sense, however, bishops have become less sure of their role. In England, at least, as the number of practising Christians has decreased so the Church has become preoccupied with its domestic concerns and with a comprehensive reshaping of its government, finances and liturgy. Independence from state control has been achieved by establishing a complex system of 'synodical government'. At the centre and in the dioceses there has been a proliferation of councils, boards and committees; and much of a bishop's time may be consumed by elaborate procedures of consultation and consent. It may well be suspected that suitability for the episcopate is now measured by performance in the business of synod or diocesan administration rather than by gifts as a theologian, preacher or pastor of souls. Recently, however, there seems to have been a greater realisation that a reshaping of administrative structures and a rewriting of liturgies will not solve the Church's basic problems, and that more urgent priorities are a renewal of the gospel message and a deepening of spirituality. It may be that a prime theological task for today is to discover a genuinely apostolic role for bishops.

GUIDE TO FURTHER READING:

The Apostolic Ministry: Essays on the History and the Doctrine of Episcopacy, Kenneth E. Kirk (editor) (London: Hodder and Stoughton, 1946, reprinted with a new Foreword, 1957).

The Historic Episcopate in the Fullness of the Church, Kenneth M. Carey (ed.) (London: Dacre Press, 1954).

Old Priest and New Presbyter: The Anglican attitude to episcopacy, presbyterianism and papacy since the Reformation, Norman Sykes (Cambridge, 1956).

1 - The bishop and his relationship with God

Alan Ecclestone

Dear Bishop,

Re-reading the service of your consecration I am moved to write to you, not simply to wish you well, not just to inquire how you have fared since its words were spoken, and certainly not to offer you advice, but to think aloud with you as a fellow-Christian about one aspect of it, one that indeed underpins all the rest.

I do so simply as one of the many on whose behalf you yourself undertook your difficult job. It is, as all Christian life-commitments must be, a completely personal thing; that is to say, it is unintelligible apart from its relation to that communion-in-love which Christian belief regards as the foundation and quickening creativity of all that is, the Divine Nature itself. I write because I feel that we all should try to see and pray for you in your job as a matter of continuing personal concern, for it matters a great deal not only how you yourself see it but how each one of us does.

I am aware of the dangers that arise and always have arisen both for you and for the people of God from making too facile and too presumptuous distinctions about your office. The high dignity ascribed to it, the vicariousness suggested by it, can be insidious temptations. All too easily an impression can be given and allowed to take root amongst us that there is, for example, one standard of holiness for the clergy and another for those not thus set apart. The consequences can be disastrous. The peculiar function of *episcope*, the very thing for which you were distinguished in that act of consecration, may be submerged and lost to sight beneath a host of less worthy considerations.

It would be wrong to blame bishops only for faults and failures of this kind. They reflect so often what an unpraying Church expects and shapes. What people desire of us weighs heavily with us all, can even bend us, and there is good reason to think in the light of much of Church history hitherto that these expectations have not always been really helpful. What are they like today?

One must ask whether we as a Christian people take enough trouble to see this as a shared concern and try to keep clearly before our eyes the basic

229

matter of which I write — your relationship with God, His expectation rather than anyone else's about the job you were asked to do. Certainly your consecration service emphasised that, but we all grow forgetful of such things. The inspiration of the Holy Spirit then invoked for you can so easily be treated as if it could be taken in a passive way, a way which goes far to impede if not destroy personal relationship at all. Some of our troubles in Church history do appear to have stemmed from that and there is no reason to suppose that we are exempt from temptation of like kind today. There are, no doubt, special pressures to commit these old sins in the newest kind of way bearing heavily upon us now.

I am equally aware of those seemingly proper expectations with which men commonly approach you, desiring you to be an able administrator, a wise theologian, a conscientious pastor, a man of prayer, an apostle, teacher and prophet. The lineage of your task in history as well as immediate necessities make it almost inevitable that this be so. You will not be alone in lamenting your insufficiency for all these things, and in respect of so daunting an office it may seem almost inconsiderate of me to press the claims of one thing alone. Yet I do so now because I believe that all else turns on this.

I am speaking of your relationship with God. Clearly there is a sense in which yours differs nothing from that of any other child or servant of God. You stand with the rest of us in a perspective that makes nonsense of all human distinctions whatsoever and invests the least as well as the greatest with the one glory that is His.

But having first quite properly humbled our distinctions to the dust may we not then with like humility consider your setting-apart as a bishop an act of God? It gives you at once a distinctive character notified to us in a rite in much the same way as marriage presents us with a husband and a wife. Something new has been introduced into life. I cannot forget that the God with whom we have to do appears to take infinite delight in the diversity of His creatures, in the variety afforded to plants and men, to rocks and beasts, insects and birds. Episcopal purple may vie with finches' wings or the peacock's tail!

Nor can I ignore a much more important, indeed basic feature of Christian belief that may be described as the particularity principle. It says that God Himself has come amongst men as a particular man at a particular time in history and in a particular place in the world. 'Get me a body' the Divine Lover has been described as saying on that occasion as if nothing in time or space must impede the purpose He had in mind. In these days when we have grown familiar with cosmic implosions as well as explosions, I can think of nothing so implosive as that taking of manhood by God in that particular body born of that particular woman.

In that light your own particularity as a bishop may be seen to be both credible and important. Whether it be scaled down from divine to human

230

provision or scaled up from earth's concerns to heavenly ones, the truth remains that in being thus chosen and set apart you were given an authentic distinctive place in the Divine Economy. You are, if you will permit me to say so, one of the consequences of that implosion called the Incarnation.

We should lose no time moreover in taking seriously and pursuing our particularity principle further, or we shall be, as I suggested earlier, beguiled into fastening our own expectations too quickly upon you. It is with His expectation of you that we must be concerned. Is it possible to particularise on this?

Let me say at once that I believe it to be important in Christian practice to do so, whatever the difficulties it raises. Implosions cannot be tidily arranged for, and the Bible quite often, and rather specially in its presentation of the apostolic ministry of Paul, keeps the implosive aspect well to the front, difficult as this must prove to be for religious institutions. God's continual rethinking and refashioning of the world has at various times been expressed in the very singularity of the man sent by Him to effect it. The hour was matched by the man.

There is no fixed pattern then to make clear the relationship of a bishop to God. On the contrary it is held in the grip of that unpredictable thief-in-the-night syndrome of which the gospels warn us, and there is a particularity attaching to *episcope* from the Godward side which is a stark reminder to the Church in venturing to make men bishops that its true life depends at every turn upon revelation of a quickening relationship with God. Consecration does but begin a process by which a man is wedded to the service of God. Judgment, furthermore, in difficult times may not only begin with the household of God but with the bishops therein. It could well be, as the prophet Isaiah made clear, a searing experience. Events of the last few years in one continent after another have gone far to confirm that nearness to the fire!

But the particularity of bishops is not restricted to such singularity of men and occasions. I think that its true nature is more helpfully illustrated by the Neo-Platonic doctrine of 'signatures' which could regard every feather of a bird's wing, every leaf on a tree, in all its particularities as manifesting an identical form repeated generation after generation. As one modern writer has said, 'The holly leaf simply by being itself celebrates a spiritual order, just as, by an old compassionate doctrine, the simple man fulfilling his proper vocation, makes thereby an act of piety: *Qui laborat, orat.*' It is of the unchanged, unchanging *forma* of your episcopal vocation that I am compelled to think.

Since bishops down the ages have appeared in a multitude of styles it is not easy to do this. What is the *forma* and whence is it derived? One must go back to the biblical account of that creative-redemptive activity in which Man's salvation is wrought to discern its lineaments. Only here shall we find a sufficiently firm basis for our conception of it. The writer to the

Hebrews, late on in the process of reflection on it insisted that it was discernible in the sending of the Son into the world by the Father in the particularity of the flesh He took. The writer was at pains to make clear how different this *forma* was from those patterns of priesthood with which men were already familiar. The gospels are no less insistent that such sending was repeated by Him-who-was-sent in commissioning His apostles for like purpose and intention. The Book of Common Prayer service at the consecration of a bishop can find no more exact description of the character to be observed than by emphatic reiteration of such sending. The *forma* is 'One sent' and its entitlement no less than 'As my Father hath sent me, even so send I you'.

Everything turns then on the implications of this sending. What, in the first place, was it for? It was for the world's sake, this world that God so loves. Whether we see it as a rescue operation or as a piece of going-ahead, it suggests that apostolic *episcope* is the continuing re-assertion in human terms, age after age, of the Divine anxiety for a world beset by dangers and imperilled by temptations, an anxiety such as a parent would show for the welfare of children, extending quite naturally to the minutiae of the equipment of those sent. 'When I sent you forth, lacked ye anything?'

This is not a poetical fancy but the assertion of an experience of travail such as attends all birth. The business of the bishop so sent may well be defined in the general terms of Divine comparison such as Jesus used when sending out the Twelve but only the actual context into which they moved could reveal the kind of personal involvement required. It means, as a consequence, that we are to visualise the relationship with God as a process of coming up to Him at the places which He has appointed. We shall look for the bishop not among those who stand like the Twenty-four Elders about the throne but in some particular place to which he has been sent, in a see where he has sat down, quite often one poetically described in medieval romance as 'a siege perilous' and more laconically today as a 'hot seat'. His relationship with God is not attenuated by this — he is not in exile from the royal courts — but is in the Presence simply because it is with the Exodus God that he has to do.

To say this is not to lose sight of the fact that he may lose his way. The essence of a personal relationship is that it allows and indeed demands a freedom of will. Only in coming to that place may he know in the existential terms of biblical knowledge what is rightly to be done, but the place itself is never neutral. 'Come over to Macedonia' sounds fine but who knows what lurks there conspiring to seduce the one who comes? Would that the writer of the book of Jonah had told us what happened in Nineveh when the mission of Jonah got under way. What did it mean to Hosea to have to live with a faithless woman? In a witty passage on Bishop Creighton, Lytton Strachey wrote. 'The ironical fact was that those events happened to take place in a world where no clever and studious clergyman of the Church

232

of England had any business to be. Sobriety, as he himself said, was his aim; but what could sobriety do when faced with such figures as Savonarola, Cesare Borgia, Julius II, and Luther? It could only look somewhere else.'

Mr Strachey was wrong. It is the business of a bishop to be in all places whither God would send him however fearful, corrupting, appalling, they may be. It is his business if so required to look evil in the face and to withstand it, not to look somewhere else. In the very particularity of this or that fiery furnace the relationship with God that your consecration declared must take the strain. How that is to be done can only be revealed in that place. The New Testament insists that it is not a matter than can be prescribed for beforehand. We must count it as one of the gifts of God to our generation that we have been given some glimpses of that relationship dwelling amongst us in the experience of men like Bonhoeffer.

To this fact of place I would bring also the co-ordinate of time. A relationship with God the Eternal is not something impatient of the temporality of things but charged rather with a heightened awareness of their significance in the eternal order. *Episcope* means insight as well as oversight, and demands an attentiveness to the changing world that is not beguiled by appearances but is sensitive to the revelations of the finger of God at work. The 'clean heart' of the psalmist's prayer is something akin to an unclouded mirror in which the reality of God may be reflected and like those screens on which the tiniest particle of matter are traced. They simply cannot work if we crowd them with the presuppositions of yesterday's picture of reality. Your relationship with God demands a stripping off of accumulated impressions valid enough in their day but likely to prove a handicap in the new times in which you have to live. I spoke earlier of being exposed and I can think of few more clear examples of this than one which requires so drastic a letting-go of things in which we have hitherto trusted. Nevertheless I believe that the particularity of your sending into specific circumstances does entail what St Paul experienced as a condition of blindness, the effacement of those well-known images of reality, in order that the new vision may be seen. Martin Buber put it starkly enough: 'Meeting with God does not come to man in order that he may concern himself with God but in order that he may realise meaning in the world.' Where meaninglessness threatened to triumph (and it is a constant threat) it has been the job of a man sent by God to embody a new meaning, even if it be no more than a heightened degree of suffering or mourning for things cruelly destroyed.

I cannot therefore see you and your brother bishops at this time but as men whose relationship with God is not to be described in mechanical terms or of delegated or developed authority but always in that condition of openness to God that He may print in you that new revelation of Himself that is demanded by the new circumstances into which His children have come. 'New every morning is the love . . .' but it needs men to notice it, and

233

the nights which Jesus Christ spent in prayer made possible, I believe, His continuing discernment of the ever-new operations of that love. I have not so far even referred to your own prayers but what I have spoken of in terms of your job done, I hope, suggest what shapes and energises your praying. It is the very gesture of response that you make to being so sent. It is the necessary sifting or winnowing process through which you take a firmer hold on reality and make it apparent to other men.

That this is a particularity specially significant of your office as a bishop today I am quite convinced. Not for many centuries has there been such a situation throughout the world in which men have felt so much in need of help from those whose relationship with God is quickening and sustaining and capable of piercing the opacity of the world. It is the homelessness of modern man that sets the problem, the alienation from himself, from his handiwork, from his fellows, from nature, that lends its intolerable weight to a condition bereft of the theodicies which gave meaning to life in the past. That homelessness was once ascribed to the Son of Man as though to make clear His identification of Himself with men who 'at sundry times, and in divers ways' would find themselves overtaken by the darkness of a meaningless existence. For their sake He came, and to speak of Him as 'being without sin' is, amongst other things, an attempt to say that He retained one thing which defied separation, the fact that He had been sent. 'If there is meaning, it is unconditional meaning, and neither suffering nor dying can detract from it.'

May I conclude therefore with this final comment upon the nature of your relationship to God, to the God and Father of Our Lord Jesus Christ. It is a relationship most specifically described in terms of mission and of mission raised to the highest term of personal involvement. I am bound to see this, though it is grasped in different ways by the artist, the parent, the teacher, the cultivator of the soil and a hundred others, as being an acceptance of responsibility on your part of answering with your life to those expectations which just because they are both human and divine constitute the relationship itself. In one of those great moments of insight which characterise the apostle Paul who quite rightly never ceased to ruminate upon the strangeness of his own being summoned to such a task, he spoke of the emptying, the *kenosis*, of the Son's glory in His coming as Man. I can believe that he came to it not as a piece of theological speculation but as something to which his own experience pointed him. He knew what it was to be thus emptied, to have nothing left but the fulness of Him that filleth all, and to find that fulness in communion with Him who sent him. Of His fulness have we all received, and we have received it in passing from one to another the heavenly bread of such a relationship. Apostolicity meant that, and means it still today.

I remember reading in the Life of Mother Janet Stuart the words: 'I must never be bored, never be offended, never be busy. To be busy is to be

engaged in an occupation which makes it inconvenient to be disturbed.'
I am suggesting that your calling has its particularity in this commitment
to meeting God in conditions where all of us are tempted to take refuge in
boredom or business. I am not suggesting that you won't have moments of
transfigured living, but those are bonus points and not the stuff of your
calling.   Yours most sincerely,
                                                  Alan Eccleston.

GUIDE TO FURTHER READING
Essays and Addresses, 2nd series. Van Hugel:
    1. Official Authority and Living Religion.
    3. On the place and function, with Religion, of the Body, of History, and
       of Institutions.
Celebration of Awareness. I. Illich.
Religion, Art and Science. J. MacMurray.

2 - Bishop and Pastor

Francis H. Moncreiff

A few years ago when Lambeth Palace was used and so arranged that part of it could be used as a kind of club where bishops and others who had business in London could book a room and stay the night I found myself on one occasion staying there when the only other guest was the late Dr George Bell at that time Bishop of Chichester. He had known Lambeth well under four Archbishops, Randall Davidson the statesman, Cosmo Lang the priest, William Temple the philosopher, teacher and leader, and Geoffrey Fisher the administrator, four men so different in so many ways with so many and varied gifts yet each making a great contribution to the office of Archbishop of Canterbury. He became quite fascinating as he described how Lambeth Palace itself in its ordering and routine and even the furnishings seemed to reflect the character and personality of each of the four Archbishops.

Today it would have to be admitted that none of the four images, Statesman, Priest, Scholar or Administrator would be acceptable as the image of what a bishop should be. Now the demand is for pastoral bishops. Pastoral, pastoral, all is pastoral! Such is the image of the bishop that appeals today. This desire for pastoral bishops is good not only in itself but as being necessary in any attempt to commend episcopacy as exercised in the office of the bishop to those denominations who do not possess it. In all ecumenical relationships the pastoral image of the bishop is the one to appeal. About the time when Cardinal Mindszenty had been released from his long detention a rather moving photograph appeared in a paper of his welcome in Rome which showed the Pope clasping the cardinal in his arms. At an ecumenical meeting held at that time one of the members brought this photograph and put it up on the mantelpiece for all to see. 'There', he said, 'is what we mean by a bishop. You can't be clasped to the breast of a committee or even a synod or an assembly.' It made the point and I think the meeting was suitably impressed.

The bishop then today must be one who cares and who is seen to be exercising a caring ministry. In going about this, however, there would seem to be a danger of presenting the image of the bishop as pastor over against or even in opposition to the bishop in his office as teacher and priest and administrator. Rather the true conception of his pastoral office combines in a right proportion each and all of these. *Dominus regit me* could be translated equally as the Lord is my King, Ruler, Governor, Shepherd. For instance the writer in a book of essays in describing the office and work of an Orthodox bishop writes 'the power of administration in the Orthodox Church can best be described as "Pastoral Care".' Thus administration is seen as part of pastoral care and not something apart from it much less in opposition to it. The term 'pastoral care' presupposes that the bishop is exercising every element of his apostolate as Shepherd.

From the beginning the bishop has been regarded as having a special responsibility as a teacher of sound doctrine and in a special way as being a guardian of the faith. To drive away erroneous and false doctrine is part of his consecration pledge and is thus an important part of his pastoral office. Today the responsibility in this area is great and no less difficult than great. It will be remembered that Mr. Slope preaching at Bishop Proudie's enthronement encouraged him in the words of St. Paul to Timothy to show himself 'approved of God, a workman that needeth not to be ashamed rightly dividing the word of truth', and in drawing out the latter part of the text did so alarm and discompose Bishop Proudie that he was not able to give the blessing in a manner at all equal to that in which he had long been practising it in his study. For the phrase 'rightly dividing the word of truth' our modern translators have 'been straightforward in the proclamation of the truth'. Even so Faith in relation to modern knowledge highlights the responsibility of those instructed in the kingdom of heaven to bring out of their treasure things new as well as old, things old as well as new, to relate the one to the other, 'to bridge the gulf that is said to exist between the theologians and the pew'. Another essay will deal with the bishop as teacher and guardian of the faith.

No less do the priestly functions of the bishop belong to his pastoral office. Christ the great High Priest is also the great Shepherd of the Sheep. Priestly devotion and pastoral care are two great marks of the bishop. He is the President of the Eucharist in his diocese, the Sanctifier at confirmations, ordinations and consecrations, he sets men and things and places apart and commissions them and blesses them for particular functions and purposes. Thus no less than in his own devotional life and discipline he is equipping himself for, and exercising and fulfilling his pastoral office.

There is no doubt that in their desire for pastoral bishops people are expressing a desire for one who will care for them. The time is one of great perplexity about many things and not least about the Christian faith and standards of conduct and what the Church stands for, or what it should stand for. Without in any way denying the existence of evil or that there is much wickedness and that 'it is a shame to speak of the things that are done of them in secret' it is equally true that departure from traditional and Christian standards of behaviour and conduct is very often due to an honest perplexity about what does constitute a sin and what is consistent or is inconsistent with Christian conduct. So the pastoral office of the bishop today is to be exercised not only in times which are evil but in an age of quite honest perplexity.

This can be seen at more than one level. The bishop has a special relationship with the clergy of his diocese, and today it is said that there is a growing identity crisis in the priesthood as a result of which many priests are not clear about what their function is, or if they have a clear idea about it as to whether it is a worthwhile one. Would they not be better employed in some other way? There are those who give up the ministry and betake themselves to teaching or to the social services where they hope and expect to find a more 'meaningful ministry'. Many are perplexed about their life style. The old disciplines no longer hold. The 'traditional ascesis' is abandoned in order not to appear to be saying 'no' to life or to be thought to be world rejecting rather than world accepting. Adrian Hastings in his book *The Faces of God* gives this situation as one which demands the pastoral care of the bishop. He writes 'in the pressures of modern society, with the cassock and collar seldom seen, with Christian names everywhere . . . they do slip'. He is of course writing of the situation within his own Communion but what he writes is not irrelevant for others. If the old 'ascesis' is abandoned as being out of date and not for our time then it is not enough to leave it at that. Another must be found to take its place. To do this or rather to relate the old disciplines and standards to the new situation does and will demand helpful guidance and pastoral care on the part of the bishop. New insights may need to be matched by a recovery of an appreciation of some of the old values and vice versa, to the advantage of both. Again we are living in a time when new patterns of ministry are emerging. This is not unique to our generation. In the primitive church the number of Christians was small enough for them all to assemble each week at the Eucharist presided over by the bishop with the presbyters, assisted by the deacons and surrounded by the faithful, a true concelebration. In a measure this pattern can be realised today on certain diocesan occasions and well it is when it is so. The bishop is as much exercising his personal office when he presides thus at the liturgy as when he presides at a diocesan council or synod or similar occasion. In primitive times as the number of Christians grew so that the one Eucharist was no longer possible, a new pattern of ministry emerged by which the presbyters celebrated the Eucharist in different parts of the diocese and the Parish Eucharist grew up alongside what might be termed the Diocesan Eucharist. No doubt there were those who in those times did not care for the new ways. Today for other reasons new patterns of ministry are being developed. In many places the part-time or non-stipendiary ministry is being implemented. It will bring its own problems, the choice of candidates, their qualification and training, their relationship to the whole-time ministry, some of whom feel themselves threatened in certain ways, all of which will demand a good deal of pastoral care and wisdom and understanding on the part of the bishops. As much or even more so will these be required as regards the implementation or non-implementation of women ministers and their ordination to the priesthood.

Some months ago a study in the anatomy of religion in Britain was published. It contained an analysis of the situation in which a Christian makes his witness today. It shows how the Church's moral authority has been challenged and relaxed. Discipline has gone by the board, worship has been demystified, theological diversity and doubt are tolerated and often found acceptable and much that the Church of the past regarded as essential is in jeopardy. In addition there is perplexity in the moral sphere. Traditional attitudes towards divorce, abortion, birth control, homosexuality, euthanasia are challenged. Along with these there is the whole area of religious education, or the lack of it, today. Although all this is given as descriptive of Britain it is true also of many other parts of the world and of other Churches than the Anglican. All this points not only to the need for pastoral concern but to the areas in which it needs to be exercised. It should operate along the line of reconciliation and should be directed not only towards reconciliation between the churches, important as this is, but to maintaining the unity that already exists within the churches. There is a danger of fragmentation within existing churches over very divisive issues, some of which have already been mentioned. It must be a matter of pastoral concern that these matters be dealt with by way of dialogue rather than by 'the method of confrontation and walkouts'.

In the pluralist society of today the two divergent strands, the secular and the religious, make themselves felt not only in the Church but in the life of the individual. The secularisation of religion has gone a long way, affecting piety, devotion, worship, theology, ministry and priesthood. The rational may so take over that for many it would seem that the 'element of mystery has gone out of religion' and this needs to be recovered. To steer between the danger of making the gospel so acceptable to a secular society that it ceases to be the gospel or of 'retreating into religion' so as to deny the working of the Holy Spirit in the modern secular world has been described as one of the most difficult but one of the most pressing pastoral responsibilities of the Church today.

As Pope John XXIII said, 'The Faith is one thing. The way we present it is another'. So with the Pastoral Office of the bishop. The important thing is how it is exercised. Pastoral sentiment is not enough unless it is applied with pastoral expertise. Very relevant to the pastoral functioning of the bishop is the question of the size of a diocese. It would seem to be recognised now that there is no ideal size for a diocese (as to the number of clergy and parishes and geographical area) to which all should conform. The size will be bound to vary as between the vast industrial dioceses on the one hand and the large country areas on the other. There is no clear blueprint for all. For instance it would seem at one time to be thought that the ideal was to break up large dioceses into much smaller ones, each

239

independent. Now it would seem that the best plan is to keep the large diocese and for the bishop to have area bishops within the diocese with a much larger measure of responsibility each in his own area. In other situations smaller dioceses will be regarded as more appropriate. Obviously all such decisions will call for pastoral care and wisdom not least on the part of the bishops. In the past, no doubt on arriving at these and similar decisions, much depended upon the exercise and the decisions of authority which was understood and acceptable in the context of the time. Today it will depend more on dialogue. There must be those who are responsible for making decisions and taking action. Acceptance and respect will be much more readily given to the bishop who thus arrives at them.

It is becoming noticeable that there is a growing sense that the Church and the bishops should have a feeling of pastoral responsibility towards their separated brethren and even towards those outside the Church altogether. The presentation of the episcopal office is of course relevant to this. Like the faith as mentioned above much depends on the way it is done. On the one hand it can be done in such a way as to give the impression that it is something to be forced upon them rather than something to be offered and shared with them. It is probably true that this approach belongs rather to the past than to the present. On the other hand it may be presented in such a way as to make it appear of little importance so as to raise the question 'is it worth having?' or 'why bother about it?' It is to be observed that episcopacy is probably most attractive when presented in terms of pastoral care. It is important therefore that the pastoral office should be presented in its fullness and that the bishop should be seen as providing something more than a 'shoulder on which to weep' as I once heard it described.

I am aware that this essay has been written by one almost the whole of whose ministry has been exercised in the west in the Church in Britain. Yet in whatever part of the world our ministry is or has been exercised the fundamental conceptions of the Bishop's Office hold good. The wise Ruler, the sound Teacher, the faithful Priest, the caring Father, not in any one alone but in the coalescence of all is to be seen the image of the bishop as pastor. Discussing once with an African bishop the difference in the mission of the Church in Africa and in Britain, he said 'the problems may be different, the difficulties and the opportunities may be different but, brother, that doesn't matter. The thing is that we are all in it together.'

The Church as an 'event' is manifested in the diocese and as we are often reminded, in it the bishop represents the wider Church to the diocese and the diocese to the Church. It is part of his pastoral office so to do. In this context can be seen a meeting such as the Lambeth Conference.

The pastoral image of the bishop has traditionally been presented in terms of a Father in God, unpopular today in some quarters as being suggestive of paternalism. The office it endeavours to express is as necessary today as it has ever been and cannot be summed up better than in the

240

words of St. Augustine to his flock: '*For* you I am a bishop, but *with* you I am a Christian. The first an office conferred and accepted; the second a grace received . . . As then I am gladder to be redeemed with you than I am to be set over you I shall, as the Lord commanded, be more completely your servant.'

3 - The bishop and the ministry of mission

Lesslie Newbigin

The two key words of the title assigned to me — *ministry* and *mission* —
are both words which can be used in a wider and in a narrower sense.
Clarity required both that the two meanings be distinguished, and that they
be rightly related. 'Ministry' can refer both to the servanthood to which all
the followers of Jesus are called, and to that particular kind of service which
is entrusted to a person in ordination. If all the stress is laid on the narrower
meaning, we get a clericalism which reduces the rest of the Church to the
status of passengers, and 'lay activity' is regarded as a form of organised
back-seat driving. If all the stress is laid on the wider meaning the call to
servanthood loses its sharpness. The Church also needs ministries if it is to
be a ministering Church. The whole Church learns to be a servant Church
through the teaching and example of those who have been called and
ordained to be the servants of the servants of God.

So also with the word 'mission'. It can be used in a very broad sense
which covers everything for which the Church has been called into being.
'As the Father sent me, so I send you' defines the very being of the Church
as mission. In this sense everything that the Church is and does can be and
should be part of mission. At the present time this broad use of the word is
dominant. The danger here is that the word — and the idea — loses its
sharpness. 'When everything is mission, nothing is mission.' The contemporary need is to recover the narrower meaning of the word. The true
statement that the Church is itself mission becomes an empty slogan and an
escape from reality, unless there are specific activities which are missionary
in the narrower sense. The usual name for such activities is 'missions' —
activities undertaken with the specific intention of making Christ known as
Lord and Saviour in situations where he is not so known. To use the language of Vatican II, the Church cannot justify its definition of its own
being in terms of mission (*Lumen centium*) unless it is also ceaselessly
engaged in efforts specifically directed to those who do not belong to its
membership (*ad gentes*).

But it is equally true that 'missions' will fail of their true purpose if
they are not held within, and seen to be held within the wider mission

242

which is the being of the Church always and everywhere. Missions which do not arise from and lead back into life in communion with God and his people are ultimately sterile. Unchurchly missions are as much an anomaly as is an unmissionary Church.

I think that the bishop has a very important role in holding together these two meanings of mission within the life and activity of the Church, and I will try to spell out what that role is by means of four statements.

1. The promise 'You shall be my witnesses . . . to the ends of the earth' is made to the Church as a whole in its corporate being, and is linked to and depends upon the promise of the Spirit. It is the Spirit who is the essential witness. The Church is witness in that the Spirit inspires and leads the Church. The promise that this will be so is linked to the promise of tribulation. The Church is promised a share in the messianic tribulations — the suffering and conflict which occurs at the frontier where God's reign meets the usurped reign of the prince of this world. At this point, where the Church has no strength of its own but can only put its trust in God, the promise is given that the Spirit will bear his witness.

The same Spirit inspires a great variety of ministries — distinct and different from each other. The temptation is for these to fall apart. Absurdly the different organs of the body disown one another (I Cor. 12 : 15ff). The evangelist, the social revolutionary, the pastor and the administrator vie with one another in exalting the significance of their own offices and downgrading that of the others. When this happens, the activities of each become ends in themselves and cease to be occasions for the Spirit to bear witness to the totality of the new being in Christ. On the other hand, when these different ministries honour, support and sustain one another, being manifestly different expressions of the same new being, then they can become opportunities for the Spirit to convict the world and bring men and women to conversion. One could illustrate this statement from very many actual experiences.

The task of the bishop, as it seems to me, is very crucial at this point. It is his task to help those who are gifted in different ways to honour and accept one another's different ministries, to seek to ensure that all of them — whether widely praised or widely ignored — are honoured as gifts of the one Spirit and are seen to be part of the working of the one body.

In the contemporary situation there is, I think, one point where this general statement has to be particularly applied. The Church is everywhere threatened at the present time by a dichotomy which is deeper than the traditional differences between denominations. It is the split between those on the one hand who see mission in terms of winning individuals to conversion, baptism and church membership, and those on the other hand who see it in terms of action for the doing of God's justice in the life of the world. Each of these ways of looking at mission can claim solid support in Scripture.

243

Each of them can furnish devastating caricatures of the other — and frequently does so. In theory it is not difficult to stand above this division and to point out that a true understanding of the gospel does justice to both without denying either. The gospel in its most original and authentic form is the announcement that the reign of God has drawn near in Jesus. This announcement calls for a response which includes an inner personal conversion of the heart, commitment to the company of his chosen disciples and costly following along the way of the Cross in confronting all the powers of evil. It is easy to show — in theory — that all these things belong together in the New Testament.

But it is very much more difficult in practice to hold them together. In practice what seems to be happening is somewhat as follows. The Churches are seeking to express their commitment to social and political action for justice by means of programmes conducted either by diocesan and synodical boards and committees, or by inter-denominational agencies of a similar kind. Meanwhile the life of the ordinary congregation continues, little affected by these activities. The dichotomy between these two ways of thinking of the mission of the Church is reflected in a dichotomy between ordinary congregational life and the programmes conducted by supra-congregational boards and committees. But this is disastrous — for both sides of the divide. On the one hand the life of the congregation is not deeply changed by what is done in the name of the Church for the world. It is not seen — to put it sharply — that the Liturgy does not end with a benediction for the participants, but continues straight out from the communion of the Body and Blood of Christ into the street and the factory and the office where his righteousness and peace meet the powers of evil. It is not seen that one cannot be an authentic communicant without being committed to action in the world, that what is done in the sanctuary is not a private act for the benefit of the participants but the focus of a public action which is for the whole of society.

And on the other hand this dichotomy destroys the proper character of what is done in the name of justice and compassion by the supra-congregational agencies of the Church. It is not seen that these words and actions spring directly out of what is done in word and sacrament at the heart of the Church's congregational life. It is not seen that these words and actions are nothing in themselves except signs pointing to that greater reality which can never be fully grasped in a programme of social action. Cut off from their real root they become merely programmes alongside the programmes of other agencies. They become expressions of a bad conscience and a sense of moral indignation rather than an outflow of the gospel. They do not challenge the Churchman to recognise that he cannot be an authentic participant in the sacramental life of the Church unless he is committed to action for justice in the world. And they do not challenge the unbeliever to recognise

244

that there is a bread which does not perish with the eating, and a healing which brings wholeness even in the midst of continuing pain.

The bishop in an Anglican diocese is acknowledged as leader of his family in following Christ both in their congregational life of worship and celebration and in the organised activities which they carry on through diocesan boards and committees. If my understanding of the present situation is right, he has here a very special task which no one else can perform. It is to seek the healing of this dichotomy. At the simplest level this will mean devoting a great deal of time to helping those clergy who are in parochial work and those who are in extra-parochial work to understand and honour one another's ministries. It will mean using all his influence to seek the involvement of congregations in these extra-congregational tasks, and to seek to root the 'sector ministries' firmly in the liturgical, congregational life of the diocese. In so far as he is able to do this, the extra-parochial work of the diocese will recover its 'sign' value and will become the kind of activity which the Spirit can use in his work of converting men and women to Christ. At the same time the life of the local congregation will no longer appear to the outsider as that of a club dedicated to satisfying the supposed needs of religiously-minded people. It will begin to be credible as a place where the secret of healing for the world's wrongs is to be found.

2. I have said that the word 'Mission' loses its sharpness where 'everything is mission'. There must also be 'missions' — whether they are called by that name or not. That is, there must be activities of the Church which are directed to situations where Christ is not acknowledged, where there is no credible and effective witness to him as Lord and Saviour, with the specific intention of bringing such a witness into being. These will not happen of themselves. The Church is always inclined to settle down into a resigned acceptance of its existing situation, to nurse its own members, to forget that it exists only as God's commissioned advance-party for his kingdom, as the sign, instrument and first-fruit of his purpose of blessing for the whole community in which it is set. The temptation to become a comfortable, tolerated minority in society is enormously strong, and one can see it operating equally in an English parish and in the so-called 'mission fields'.

It is an essential part of a bishop's duty that he should be constantly remembering the true dimensions of his task. He is not called simply to be the bishop of those who are already believers; he is called to leadership in God's mission to the whole human community of his diocese. He must be constantly reminding his people that they are called not for themselves but for God's reign among all their neighbours. And he must make it his business to seek out areas and situations in his diocese where there are opportunities for Christian witness and where it is lacking. In some parts of the world this may mean — first of all — the simple business of studying maps and seeing what are the unevangelised areas or communities. In many

245

places, especially where the process of 'modernisation' is far advanced, it will mean sensitive awareness of new types of human situation, new sectors of public life, of culture, or the professions, which call for such a fresh witness. Usually the 'call' will take the form of some man or woman who is in that area or sector and whose life has been touched in some way by the Spirit. This 'touch' will lead to a longing that others in that area or sector of the community may share the knowledge of Christ, and at the same time to a recognition that they cannot come to that knowledge simply by being directed to one of the existing Christian congregations. What is needed is an alert and teachable readiness to support and strengthen what the Spirit has already begun, to nourish and encourage the early stages of a new style of Christian witness appropriate to the new situation, and at the same time to keep open the channels of communication so that old and new may mutually learn from and strengthen one another.

What I am saying here, to put it briefly, is that an essential part of a bishop's ministry in mission will be the encouragement in the area of his diocese (and — where appropriate — beyond it) of specific missions.

3. I would want to go beyond this, however, and to say that the bishop should do more than simply encourage such missions. If he is wise, he will himself be involved in them. Here I recognise that there are conflicting views. In reaction against clericalist views which made the bishop the director of everything in his diocese, the tendency in recent years has been to stress the bishop's role as a resource person, as an enabler, as one who serves in 'the equipment of God's people for their ministry' (Eph. 4 : 12). This is a most important emphasis and I would not wish to belittle it. But, taken by itself, it can lead to another kind of distortion. The bishop can be seen (like the Duke of Plaza Toro) as one who leads the army from behind. The New Testament hardly supports this view! If we are to be guided in our understanding of the apostolic ministry by St. Paul's acount of his own, we shall see it as a costly leadership in the way of the Cross. Paul speaks of what he has suffered in the work of a missionary as the proof of his apostleship. He can dare to say to his friends: Be imitators of me as I am of Christ. The bishop must certainly be an enabler of others, eager to discover and to foster the special gifts of each, but this means being ready when need arises to go out ahead and encourage the others to follow.

This means, I think, that the bishop should be ready himself to be engaged — as opportunity offers and calls — in direct evangelistic efforts or in pioneering movements of Christian action in the secular world. This will bring controversy. It will also bring the authentic experience of the frontier where the reign of God meets the powers of the world — and this is where the presence of the Spirit is promised. It will also help to bring the bishop into close contact with those who are newly converted to the faith, for whom the love of God has become a wonderful new experience. I do not think that one maintains the vigour and freshness of the life in Christ without some opportunities for such contact. A bishop whose life is confined to the sanctuary, the office and the committee room will find it hard to remain spiritually fit for leadership in the Christian warfare.

4. This leads directly to my last point, which is perhaps too obvious to be stated. In the long run the missionary effectiveness of a Church (be it parish or diocese) does not depend so much upon individual efforts and programmes as upon the extent to which the Church as a whole is living by the gospel. In listening to the stories of scores of men and women who have been converted to Christ I have been impressed by two things: one is the enormous variety of the means by which the Spirit draws people to Christ. No two people come by exactly the same road, and normally it is not one single experience but a long succession of experiences which brings a man or woman to the point of conversion. The strategy of God's mission is not in our hands but in his. This is one side of the matter which is of fundamental importance. The other is that the background of these experiences is always the reality of a believing, caring, loving community. Where that is absent, the work of evangelists, prophets, teachers and helpers does not bring conversion. The foundation is a Christian community living by the gospel.

We know how easily a Christian community — in parish, diocese or nation — can sink into conformity with the world, lose the glow of faith, settle for an existence which does not challenge the dominant powers. Perhaps the most important element in the bishop's ministry of mission is simply the faith and vigour with which he leads his people in their spiritual warfare. One thinks here of St. Paul's picture (I Corinthians 9) of his apostleship, in which he likens himself to an athlete who knows that he must keep in training if he is to win. The bishop's own spiritual life, his own hidden life of renunciation, of commitment, of continually renewed surrender to Christ in the circumstances of his daily ministry: perhaps nothing is more important than these in determining whether the church which he serves will be a truly missionary church.

GUIDE TO FURTHER READING:

The Pioneer Ministry, A. T. Hanson (SPCK, 1961).
A Time for Building. Report of the Joint Working Party on Pastoral Strategy (Catholic Information Services of the Bishops' Conference of England and Wales, 74 Gallows Hill Lane, Abbots Langley, Herts. WD5 0B2).
The Good Shepherd, Lesslie Newbigin (The Faith Press, 1977).
Beyond the Either-or Church, Alfred C. Krass (Published in the USA).

247

4 - The bishop and theologians

John Macquarrie

Ideally, the bishop and the theologian ought to be one and the same person. At least, this is what one is tempted to say. However, when we remember that, ideally, the bishop ought also to be a pastor, administrator, fund raiser, representative of the Church in public life, and so on . . . and when we remember further that this is not an ideal world, then perhaps we must accept that usually the bishop and the theologian will be different persons. Still, one would like to think that the bishop, if not a theologian in the sense of one who teaches or writes theology, would be at least a theologically minded person, and that among the many qualities demanded of a bishop, sound theological learning and the habit of thinking theologically would rate very high. For when we consider the decline in the Churches today, I think David Edwards is correct in saying that 'the basic problem confronting the churches is unbelief'.[1] or it may be that one should say 'lack of belief' rather than 'unbelief', by which I mean that there is ignorance and bewilderment concerning Christian belief as much as straight rejection of it. In any case, there is a crying need for theology, if that means elucidating Christian faith in terms that are understandable to the modern world and designed to make contact with its ways of thinking. It is for this reason that theology ought to get a much higher rating in the Church than it usually does, and it is for this reason too that any bishop who hopes to give leadership to his flock in these days must be theologically informed.

I was careful to say at the beginning of this essay that one is *tempted* to believe that the bishop and theologian ought to be one and the same person. But theology is so dialectical and dialogical in character that it is probably better that the bishop and the theologian should be different persons. Yet to say this is to assume that the bishop is theologically minded, the theologian is pastorally concerned, and that the two of them are in regular dialogue with each other. I doubt whether this is the case in many dioceses.

In earlier centuries, bishops often were themselves the leading theologians of the Church. Perhaps they were not so harassed with other matters in those days, though this is by no means certain. One thinks of men like Irenaeus, Athanasius, Augustine and many others. Admittedly,

248

the great episcopal theologians accounted for only a handful of all the bishops at any given time. But there was a clear recognition of the bishop's close concern with theology. His seat was still more the chair of a teacher than the throne of a ruler. His responsibility was to hand on the faith and to maintain Christian truth. Yet we need not suppose that this was conceived as something utterly static and unchanging. New questions were always arising and had to be settled. From the beginning, there was a twofold mode of succession — succession in the doctrine received from the apostles, and the personal succession of the bishops as the chief teachers of the Church. This twofold mode ensured both stability and development in the understanding of the Christian faith.

I mentioned that only a small number of bishops were great theologians even in the early centuries, and we must not imagine that there ever was a time when all bishops were also creative theological thinkers. From a very early time there were theologians who were not bishops and who were sometimes consulted by bishops. According to Eusebius, when Origen took up his residence in Caesarea about the year 217, 'he was requested by the bishops to expound the sacred scriptures publicly in the church, although he had not yet received the priesthood by the imposition of hands'. Some seem to have believed that 'this was never before either heard or done, that laymen should deliver discourses in the presence of the bishops'. But others claimed that there had been precedents.[2] A little further on in Eusebius we read that Firmilianus, bishop of the Cappadocian Caesarea, 'was so favourably disposed toward Origen that he then called him to the region in which he dwelt, to benefit the churches; at another time he went to visit him in Judea and passed some time with him there for the sake of improvement in things divine. Moreover, Alexander, bishop of Jerusalem, and Theoctistus, bishop of Caesarea, attending him the whole time nearly like pupils their master, allowed him alone to perform the duties of expounding the sacred scriptures and other matters that pertain to the doctrines of the Church'.[3] So there were precedents for bishops taking counsel of theologians long before the days of Vatican II and Lambeth X.

The position today, of course, is vastly different from what it was in the early centuries. It is truly remarkable, in view of all the pressures upon them, that some bishops and even archbishops have been able to keep abreast of theological developments and make their own contributions to the debate. Perhaps they do show that it is possible even for a twentieth-century bishop to arrange his priorities in such a way that theology is not crowded out or kept far down the list because of the demands of administration and the like. However, it is perhaps only in exceptional cases that the bishop can remain as a creative theologian, and more frequently his theological reflection will take place in dialogue with full-time theologians acting as advisers.

But here we strike on another difficulty. We hear much about the divorce nowadays between theology and the life of the Church. This is in part due to the fact that bishops and parish priests are so overwhelmed with a multitude of duties that they have little time left for theological reading and reflecion. But many of them would lay the blame on the theologians, and say that they are not dealing with questions that are germane to the life of the Church and that they are frankly unhelpful.

I do not believe we should talk of blame in these matters or try to apportion responsibility. The divorce does exist, but it is due in the main to changed social conditions. We have already noted how the bishop is under demands that keep him from theologising, but we have also to consider sympathetically the situation of the modern theologian. The theologian today is caught up in the academic life of the universities. Theology is often suspect in university circles. What place is there for theological studies in a secular society? Is not theology a survival from pre-Enlightenment times? The young theologian especially may be very much aware of the apparently marginal position of his subject, and he may feel that the pressure is on him to establish its intellectual respectability, so to speak. All young academics are under pressure to do research and to publish contributions to their subjects. The theologian may feel that to maintain his position in the academic community, he has to devote his inquiries to strictly academic questions, and to eschew issues that might seem to be 'apologetic' or even 'propagandist'. So, for instance, he may devote himself to some fairly narrow historical inquiry, and may in consequence seem to have little to say about the significance of Christian faith for the contemporary world.

Since he is an academic as well as a churchman, the theologian some-times experiences a tension. Even if he is a committed churchman, he is also jealous of academic freedom, and would be resistant to any attempt by the bishop or the church authorities to persuade him to produce theological reasons for pursuing a course of action that the church authorities con-sidered desirable. To give an example of what I have in mind; I have known of theologians being put under pressure to find good theological reasons for certain ecumenical policies, and I could give other examples. Such pressure is utterly destructive of theological integrity, and ought to be resisted. It is quite another matter to ask theologians to investigate with an open mind questions that are of special interest to the Church at any given time.

But just as I have suggested that bishops might order their priorities in such a way as to give a proper place to theological reflection, so I think it is not unfair to ask theologians, whatever the pressures upon them in the academic context, to hold themselves open and available as far as possible to the Church. Many of them do in fact serve on commissions and com-mittees, lecture at diocesan conferences or at institutes of theology for clergy and laity, and so on. When this occurs, I think the gap between theology and the life of the Church often turns out to be narrower than has been supposed. Churchmen cannot get along without theology, and theologians can scarcely be good interpreters of the Christian faith unless they have a living relation to the community of faith. The precise relation of the theologian to the Church is a matter for debate among theologians themselves. Some would stress the independence of the theologian, his obligation to pursue truth as he sees it, and his vocation within the Church as one who has to open up new understandings of faith in changing situations. Others would place more weight on the theologian's obligations toward the tradition, and would insist that even when he wants to lead the Church into new ways of thinking, he must have regard to the peace of the Church and always act in charity toward his fellow Christians. Again, some theologians lay stress on reason and experience as determining factors in their theological work. Others give more weight to the Bible and tradition. But I think that these differences are differences of emphasis rather than quite different ways of conceiving the work of the theologian or his relation to the Church. I should think that almost all theologians recognise that there is a difference between the theologian and the philosopher of religion, or between a faculty of Christian theology and a department of religious studies. Theology comes out of tradition and a community, while philosophy of religion is a more detached study of religion in general. Even the philosopher of religion, however, probably needs to have some measure of participation in religion if he is to bring any illumination to the subject.

At the present time, all human knowledge is undergoing rapid change, and this is bound to affect theology. There is no single theology today which enjoys undisputed authority among Christians. Even in the earlier part of the twentieth century, the theology of the Word of God, with Karl Barth as its principal architect, had a dominant place among the Protestant churches and in the ecumenical movement (though perhaps relatively few Anglicans were followers of Barth). On the Roman Catholic side, the revival of neo-Thomism, begun in the nineteenth century, came to its flowering in such notable figures as Jacques Maritain and Etienne Gilson. But these syntheses have fallen apart. Even Roman Catholic theology nowadays is infinitely varied. Karl Rahner writes of 'a number of theologies juxtaposed in a pluralist way, not contradicting each other, of course, but not susceptible of being positively incorporated into a higher synthesis'.[4] If indeed theology is an attempt to reflect on the unfathomable mystery of God as we have known him in Jesus Christ, then it would seem that multiplicity in theology is inevitable, for no single theology will ever grasp the mystery in its fullness.

This is not to say that everything is permitted or even that one theology is as good as another. But it does acknowledge the need for theological exploration and discussion. The truth of theology is dynamic and growing, and it is reached rather in the dialogue between different partial insights into the truth than in the construction of a 'consensus' theology, for this

251

already threatens to become a theology that is dead and incapable of further development.

Can we now try to define more precisely the roles which bishops and theologians might play and how they might be related in the theological enterprise of the Church?

Traditionally, the role of the bishop has been seen in conservative terms. His duty has been understood as that of maintaining the faith received from the apostles, of safeguarding it against errors, and of driving away strange doctrine. It must be confessed that this picture seems somewhat repressive in modern times! If indeed theology is in process of change and development, and if the bishop has a special responsibility in this area, can he discharge that responsibility simply by conserving a supposed deposit of truth? Should he not himself be a leader in theological exploration?

It is not easy to give a simple answer to these questions. I served on an advisory committee of the American Church under the chairmanship of the late Bishop Stephen Bayne when we were asked to discuss the whole question of theological freedom and responsibility in the Church. On the role of the bishop, we agreed on the following wording: 'The bishops' role is the calm enabling of the theological dialogue. They themselves need not phrase experimental formulations, though if they are theologically competent and phrase them in an expressedly experimental fashion, they need not refrain. However, the bishops' principal role would be to encourage inquiry.' [5] I would still find myself very much in agreement with this. It is not saying that the bishops' role should be a purely conservative one — on the contrary, the bishops are to enable and encourage theological discussion. But they themselves should be cautious of embracing startling innovations. They have a pastoral responsibility to all their people, and they must try to carry all their people with them. We know how at the present time some Churches have been grievously divided between so-called 'conservatives' and so-called 'progressives' — though these labels are tendentious and question-begging. I have said already that conflict and dialogue are necessary on the way to theological truth, but the sad thing is that such conflict very often leads into bitterness, division and polarisation. The bishop will no doubt have his own honest opinion on such divisive questions, but he must not be partisan and must try to prevent polarisation.

What are we to say of the role of the theologian? He can be adventurous and innovative in ways that are difficult for the bishop. Yet this always brings a certain temptation. Theologians can only too easily begin to think of themselves as the *teleioi*, those who have attained to a *gnosis* that is beyond the reach of the ordinary faithful. Theologians sometimes refer, almost with contempt, to 'popular religion' or 'unreflecting Christianity'. In Germany, where perhaps theological professors have been more venerated than anywhere else in the world, the complaint has sometimes been made that the churches there suffer from a 'papacy of the scholars'. This is certainly a danger, if academic theology is set over against the religion of the ordinary people. But surely the perception of spiritual truth is not a purely intellectual matter. The fundamental truth of Christianity itself is the truth of Jesus Christ, and this truth exists concretely in his person before it is ever transcribed into theological propositions. It needs not intellectual acumen but spiritual sensitivity to apprehend it, and a truth may be implicitly grasped on the level of prayer and worship before it becomes theologically explicit. The *lex orandi* may give direction to the *lex credendi*.

Christian theology is too important a matter to be left to the professional theologians alone. The bishops cannot do it alone, but neither can the theologians. Yet I would want to say that the enterprise needs more than even bishops and theologians working together. It needs priests and people as well. Theology is a responsibility of the whole Church, and can only be rightly done if the whole Church participates.

Now, I am not saying this in the name of some foolish egalitarianism, as if all Christians were equally qualified to 'do theology', or as if questions of theology could be settled by majority vote. (On the last point, I would agree with Hans Urs von Balthaser that 'in a Church which is essentially the little flock, it is not the majority which is right; it never has been, and today it is less so than ever.[6])

It is not a case of everybody doing the same thing, but of each individual and each group bringing a particular *expertise* for a complex task, the successful performance of which needs all their contributions. The theologian brings his *expertise*, which consists in scholarship, whether in biblical studies or the history of theology or in philosophical theology or whatever it may be. But this remains academic until the theologian is joined by the bishop and his priests, who bring their special knowledge of the problems facing the Church in mission and the cure of souls. Yet I would suggest that it is necessary to bring in still a third group, the laity, who know better than theologians or clergy the state of play in the workaday secular world. Left to themselves, theologians and bishops may fall to discussing questions which are sadly out of touch with where people are living today.

This task of doing theology together I call 'co-theologising,'[7] and it is an essential part of the rediscovered collegiality of all Christians within the Church. I can think of no task that is more urgent for the Church today than such co-theologising, thinking deeply together about the meaning and implications of Christian faith in the modern context. Bishops have a special responsibility for getting such thinking going, for they know the needs and mood of the Church and must enable and guide the dialogue. Theologians have their responsibility of bringing the treasures of their learning out of the study to the service of the Church. Both bishops and theologians need the wisdom and knowledge of the lay people if their thinking is to make an impact where it is needed.

REFERENCES

1 David L. Edwards, *The British Churches Turn to the Future*, p. 3 (S.C.M. Press, 1973).

2 Eusebius, *Ecclesiastical History*, tr. C. F. Cruse, p. 226 (Bell, 1903).

3 *Ibid.*, VI, xxvii, p. 233.

4 Karl Rahner, *The Christian of the Future*, tr. W. J. O'Hara, p. 34 (Herder & Herder, 1967).

5 Stephen F. Bayne, ed., *Theological Freedom and Social Responsibility*, p. 17 (Seabury Press, 1967).

6 Hans Urs von Balthasar, *Elucidations*, p. 95 (S.P.C.K., 1975).

7 John Macquarrie, *Principles of Christian Theology*, p. 441 (S.C.M. Press, Revised Edition, 1977).

5 - The Bishop as guardian of the faith

John Coventry, S.J.

Many modern studies have made it clear that episcopacy emerged in Christian history as a decisive pattern of ministry and government, and became universally accepted in the second century, without any awareness of definite instructions from Christ or his chosen disciples about church organisation. It emerged owing to historical and cultural factors which cannot now be traced in any detail. But, having emerged and persisted for many centuries, it can be seen to exhibit certain clear theological values. And, in that sense at least, it can be said to have emerged under the guidance of the Holy Spirit.

At different points of history episcopacy has variously blended with and related to synodal forms of the exercise of pastoral responsibility. We are now able to see that the distinction between episcopal and so-called non-episcopal Churches is less clear than it appears at first sight. The non-episcopal Churches have certainly exercised *episcope* or oversight, in matters of faith and in other matters; and they have variously commissioned episcopal persons with wider responsibilities than other ministers. What is distinctive about episcopacy is that it marks off certain ministers for life as members of a higher order of ministry, and therefore with a higher degree of responsibility. In this particular significant way a bishop embodies for the people entrusted to his charge the pastoral care of Christ for his Church.

The New Testament shows a very diverse sharing of ministries without any clear structural pattern. It is clear that, on any overall view of the development of Christian ministry, there was a trend of clerical absorption. First of all the ordained ministers absorbed lay ministries. Then bishops more and more absorbed the functions of other ministers, so that the pattern could emerge that all ministry belonged primarily to bishops and was delegated by them to presbyters and deacons. For instance: some independence of the function of teachers persisted from the New Testament through the *Didache,* Hermas, Justin, Origen and Clement of Alexandria; clerical absorption of the teaching function begins with Origen, and is total in the *Didascalia,* the early Tertullian, and in Cyprian; episcopal absorption or control of teaching is firmly established by Nicaea and is complete in the ensuing patristic period. Bishops at that time were the theologians; they were the teachers and preachers *par excellence,* and spent much of their time in these ministries. By the seventh century episcopal preaching was tailing off, and eventually the friar preachers moved into the vacuum created; but meanwhile, as the presbyters took on more of the preaching in scattered areas, the episcopal role became that of supervising their teaching. The rise of monastic life provided a context for teaching independent of episcopal-presbyteral structures. And by the high middle ages the simultaneous rise of the universities and the mendicant orders provided something of a challenge to episcopal control. The theologians who emerged in the universities were in fact if not in principle clerical; but a university faculty ran itself, and held a position analogous to the exemption from episcopal control of the religious orders.

Since the Reformation, in various ways and at different paces in different Churches, there has developed a movement of what may fashionably be called devolution — an abandoning of the idea that episcopacy contains within itself all ministries, a diversifying of function, an encouragement and co-ordination of the gifts of all members of the Church, and an involvement of as many as possible in the making of decisions. But however far the process is carried, the ministry of bishops can never become simply one ministry alongside many others. Inherent in the idea of episcopacy, as in its tradition, is the element of higher responsibility for the whole Church. Some writers have taken the view that Christ gives his whole ministry primarily to the Christian community, and that episcopal responsibility is delegated to bishops by the community. But it is not easy to see how such a view can be based on the New Testament witness. Christ did not first found a Church, which then produced a ministry of oversight out of itself. By his choosing and training of chosen followers and witnesses to his Resurrection out of the greater number of those he taught, he founded an inherently structured Church, a Church with a pastoral ministry to embody his own shepherding of the whole flock. And though episcopacy did not emerge by any simple or linear process of transmitting authority, or responsibility for the whole community, nevertheless when it emerged it was seen to be in succession to the ministry of those whom Christ himself had chosen to be guardians of his people.

CONSERVING RATHER THAN INNOVATING

The word 'apostle' means more or less the same as 'missionary', and bishops did not in fact take over this evangelising role but succeeded to the Twelve Apostles and to the missionary apostles of New Testament times in terms of their pastoral care of Christian communities. Bishops are not by tradition the preachers of the gospel in this missionary sense. Nor since the development of presbyteral preaching and the rise of the mendicant orders have they been *the* preachers within the Church, in the sense of doing the most preaching or of doing it in the most widely effective way. But preaching

256

has nevertheless been central to their ministry for a variety of interconnected reasons: because of their particular witness to the faith of the apostles; because of their overall responsibility for Christian communities; and because of the centrality in a diocese of the bishop's celebration of the eucharist.

The idea that bishops have a 'charism of truth' goes back to Irenaeus, and Cyprian can lay claim to some kind of direct guidance. If such a claim is made for the individual bishop, we may be right to see this as part of the process of absorption referred to above, namely as an institutionalising of the charism of prophecy attested in the New Testament. We would not readily admit today that any special insight into Christian truth goes with appointment to responsible office. A different belief, however, would be involved in thinking that the Holy Spirit preserves the Church in fidelity to the gospel through the corporate witness of bishops in council.

With the rise of the theologians and the development of scholarship in the universities there has arisen in the Church a certain tension between the claims and roles of intellectual force and qualification on the one side, and of overall responsibility for fidelity to the gospel on the other. The tension brings out the ambiguity of the word *magisterium*. For the teaching ministry is widely and diversely shared in the Church beyond priests and bishops: by our mothers and fathers; by teachers at different levels of schooling; by the acknowledged writers and scholars whose insights into Christian truth have in fact reshaped the thinking of successive generations. Such scholarship and systematic thought rightly claims to be judged by its peers. However, the tension that exists between these two different types of authority and of ministry can properly be seen as a desirable tension, a balance that needs to be preserved rather than as a destructive tension to be overcome. It could only be overcome disastrously, either by suppression of intellectual integrity and freedom, or by the Church abandoning any ministry of overall responsibility for the faith. The theologians do not claim any such responsibility, nor does the nature of their work suggest that it could be theirs. They have their personal sense of responsibility to the faith which they endeavour to explore and to express ever more fully, and in terms that grapple with the problems and relate to the insights of their day. But their work is of its nature pioneering and exploratory. It will often be far out ahead of the normal thinking of their fellow Christians and the normal preaching of ordained ministers. They will be meeting challenges, the very existence of which their own generation as a whole is hardly aware. And so they will be open to suspicion and even to abuse. Hence it can be urged that it is part of the responsibility of bishops to ensure that scholars have scope and freedom to fulfil their own tasks, and support in fulfilling them.

Individual bishops may, of course, be theologians of high quality, as they may be trained and professional teachers — a new field of expertise, with its independent standards, which has arisen in comparatively recent

257

times. But the role of bishops as such in handing on the faith would appear to be one of conserving rather than of innovating; a role of ensuring as far as possible that the new insights and formulation of Christian truth are in continuity with the old and can be recognised as expressions of the same faith. The tension between the pioneering work of scholars and the perspectives and categories of thought currently familiar in Christian teaching can be seen as a tension between past and present; and once more it is a tension that needs to be maintained rather than resolved, in order to give as many as possible in the Church the opportunity both to assimilate what is new and to test it against their actual experience of Christian believing.

Newman, in his preface to the third edition of his *Lectures on the Prophetical Office*,[1] sees a balance in the Church between the different 'authorities' of bishop, saint and scholar: the church leader, a man of experience, with a call from Christ to assume overall responsibility; the committed believer sharing in the *sensus fidelium*; and the man of learning. The role of the bishop can partly be seen as that of maintaining the other forces at work in the Church in balance, of ensuring that the various gifts given to others by the Spirit are allowed their full interplay in order to enrich and build up the Body of Christ. But that is not the whole of his role — to hold the ring for others. From the emergence of episcopacy onwards it was understood in the Church, and in practice exercised itself, to preserve and to hand on the authentic teaching of the apostles. It had a special ministry and special responsibility of witness to apostolic tradition. One modern writer summarises thus:

> 'It would be a mistake to limit "apostolic succession" to this episcopal college. The entire Church bears the mark of "apostolicity"; the entire Christian community is the bearer of the apostolic tradition. Yet there is a special role that this episcopal college fills. It bears witness to the present community of faith within "the great church" and so binds to one another the local communities of believers. And it bears collegial testimony to the enduring presence of the apostolic witness within the church and to the church's fidelity to that witness. In this function the episcopal college stands in historical continuity with the Twelve's function of collegial witness to the death and resurrection of Jesus.'[2]

And the same writer adds that, just as the collegial witness of the Twelve was normative of primitive Christianity's faith, so has the collegial witness of the bishops remained normative of the Church's faith in succeeding generations. The essential ideas of apostolic succession that are to be found in Irenaeus have stood the test of time: there is a linear sign of continuity in the succession of bishops to presidency in Christian communities; there is a lateral or horizontal sign of sharing the faith of the Church in the communion of Churches through their bishops with each other. In his commentary on *Ministry and Ordination,* the agreed Anglican-Roman Catholic statement, Bishop Alan Clark writes (p. 36):

258

'The chain of succession is to be seen not in a series of persons who have sacramentally received the office of bishop, or in the "handing on" of the sacramental gift already possessed by the ordained prelates, but in an unbroken "communion" of local churches, *focused in the person of their bishops,* with each and every other local church and their bishops.'

TO SPEAK AS ONE HAVING AUTHORITY

One may feel some diffidence in attempting to state the role and responsibility of bishops as guardians of the faith in a way that does justice to modern biblical and historical studies of the origin and development of the Church's ministry. But diffidence increases when one turns to consider how in practice this role is to be fulfilled. The 'hermeneutical question' as it faces us today is a complex mass of problems. These are fairly stated in *Christian Believing,* the Report of the Doctrine Commission of the Church of England (SPCK 1976).

In a personal essay published in that volume Professor G. W. H. Lampe provides a very useful schema for our thought. Revelation is an act of God, who reveals *himself* and not information about himself. Faith is man's personal encounter with and recognition of God so revealing himself in historical situations. Hence one can say that no revelation occurs until there is a grasp of it by faith; one as it were slides into the other, so that we cannot distinguish them as separable or consecutive events. But faith does not exist in a 'pure' state: man only grasps God's reality through the medium of some conceptual or imaginative pattern, which can more or less adequately be put into words. So faith and beliefs slide into each other, and one cannot get at or analyse faith apart from the beliefs in which it expresses itself. Some beliefs, or forms of expression of faith, become more and more firmly accepted by the Church: they become doctrines. So beliefs slide into doctrines, and it is impossible to draw any clear line between them.

This scheme of understanding only sets the stage for the problems that then arise. If Christ is the fulfilment, the bringing to unforeseen fullness, of the self-communication of God attested progressively in the Old Testament, then in what sense is the Old Testament a Christian book, a guide to Christians about the nature and purpose of God? Can it be read in its own right and for its own sake as a guide to God's self-revelation? The New Testament is a witness to the foundational Christian faith. But it gives us a great diversity of witness and forms of expression, theologies not a theology, each expression of belief partial and conditioned by the cultural outlook, presuppositions and personal qualities of the writer. How do we get at the writer's faith if we feel bound to relinquish its mythological expression? What are we to make of interpretations of Jesus that presuppose a world in the grip of angelic and demonic forces? What criterion could there be for deciding which beliefs are the fuller and more normative,

259

which less adequate or even wrong-headed? Can it be right, or do justice to the beliefs themselves, to harmonise or to systematise them by the use of categories alien to those who formulated them? What reliance are we to place on beliefs that do not attest a direct and personal witness to the historical Jesus and the risen Christ, but are elaborations of previous witness to him? Are we to regard the earliest witness (supposing we could unearth it) as the most reliable, or are we to understand that the later witness enshrines a deeper and fuller understanding of the meaning of Christ for men, developed under the guidance of the Spirit?

If we pass beyond the New Testament, as the Church had already done before it canonised those particular writings as expressing its faith, we encounter the problems of translating the Christian faith from largely hebraic into hellenic categories; and of answering from the New Testament questions put in other times, out of new Christian experience, framed in forms of thought which are quite beyond the horizons of the New Testament writers themselves. When the Church has broadly accepted the cultural translation, and hammered out accepted answers to the new questions, in what sense is the new corpus of doctrine expressive of the same faith? The process of translation, of course, and of answering new questions, is not confined simply to one early age of the Church but continues throughout its history, and enters into new complexities as the faith spreads out beyond its European stronghold into other continents and cultures. At the same time our generation has come to realise the existence of pluralism even within a recognisably single culture. The idea of timeless and indefinitely perfectible language, of a *philosophia perennis,* or of a single comprehensive world view, has had to be abandoned. Quite apart from the inadequacy of any human formulation of the mystery of God's presence and action in the midst of our human experience, we have come to realise the partiality and limitation of any form of human expression, its embedding and imprisonment within the particularities of its own historical situation.

In the face of such difficulties (and some others) raised about the scriptures or the creeds or the councils or the great Church writers, the question must be bluntly posed: What, then, are the guardians of the faith supposed to do? It would be foolish to imagine that one has up one's sleeve any simple answer to this question. Perhaps this essay does no more than state various facets of the problem. But one or two reflections may point a way forward.

There are no logical or intellectual criteria and guarantees that the Christian faith as we can state it today is 'the same faith' as that once delivered to the saints. There is 'only' the promise of God and the guidance of his Spirit. And this is not something to which we merely notionally assent by some act of will. It is corroborated by the corporate and cumulative experience of Christians throughout the ages, as they encountered Christ in the community that discovers and responds to him as God's self-revelation;

it is established and reinforced by the marvellous power of Christ to come to new life in successive generations of believers in different historical situations, and to irradiate their world, their history, their human experience, with meaning.

With trust in this guidance of the Spirit there is a task for the guardians of the faith to perform today. If in the past the Church has been over-confident about the expressions of Christian faith, whether by naive under-standing of scripture or by complacency about the perfection and trans-cultural nature of her creeds, today she is in danger of being reduced to silence. And a silent Church has no message, no gospel, either for the nourishment of believers or as a saving message to the world. The theologians and philosophers of religion have exposed the limitations of all expressions of Christian faith and in the process have induced a loss of nerve. What is now needed is that the Church should go beyond this stage and find a way of living with her limitations, and of carrying out in and through them the task of proclaiming the Good News of salvation in Jesus Christ. That way forward will not be easy, or open to testing by any simple criteria. It will involve holding a balance between the different gifts and ministries in the Church, and between the guidance of the Spirit attested in tradition and the voice of Christian prophecy today. The pastors of the Church will faithfully fulfil this charge entrusted to them in so far as they are sensitive to the experience and understanding of all Christian communities. But at the end of the day, in and through the difficulties and limitations, and therefore in all humility, the Church through its pastors will need to speak with a clear voice, as one having authority.

REFERENCES
[1] Attention is drawn to this pattern of Newman's by Dr Nicholas Lash in *Voices of Authority*, p. 98 (Sheed & Ward, 1976).
[2] Bernard Cooke, *Ministry to Word and Sacraments*, p. 338 (Fortress Press, 1976).

6 - The bishop's consecration and vows
Keith Rayner

CONSECRATION AS A SACRAMENT

Each of us who has been consecrated a bishop in the Church of God will have the memory of that event vividly impressed on his mind. The Church rightly makes the consecration of a bishop an act of great solemnity. It is not only a deeply significant event in the personal history of the man himself as he enters into God-given vocation from which there is no turning back; it is also an occasion of great significance for the Church, for every consecration is 'an expression of the continuing apostolicity and catholicity of the whole Church'.[1]

To describe consecration as a sacrament raises for Anglicans the problem of definition. Anglican formularies, while unambiguous about baptism and the eucharist as sacraments, are ambivalent about the status of the 'five commonly called Sacraments', of which holy orders is one. The Articles insist that they are 'not to be counted for Sacraments of the Gospel',[2] and the Prayer Book Catechism refers to 'two only, as generally necessary to salvation, that is to say, Baptism, and the Supper of the Lord'.

This is, however, essentially a question of definition, and reflects a diversity of understanding of the term 'sacrament' going back to the early history of the Church. For while by the high Middle Ages, the western and eastern churches alike had settled on seven sacraments, the name had been applied at different times and by different fathers to both a larger and a smaller number of ordinances possessing some distinctive outward sign.

The reformers tended to limit the term to those sacraments which were specifically instituted by the incarnate Christ, who himself attached a promise of grace to a particular outward sign. By this criterion, holy orders could scarcely qualify, for while Jesus' call and commissioning of the apostles indicated clearly enough his purpose of instituting a ministry for his Church, it cannot be demonstrated that he personally ordered the laying-on of hands as the outward and visible sign of a sacrament.

Nonetheless, the classical Anglican formularies refrained from any absolute denial of the sacramental status of the 'lesser' sacraments. The Second Book of Homilies, for example, in specifically referring to ordination, declared that 'neither it, nor any other Sacrament else, be such Sacraments as Baptism and the Communion are'.[3] If the emphasis lies on the pre-eminent place of the two gospel sacraments, the implication is that the others are in some sense to be understood as sacraments.

It is not hard to see why holy orders has traditionally been seen as a sacrament. The laying-on of hands in ordination is a distinctive outward sign, going back through the history of the Church to earliest times, and discernibly rooted in the New Testament. It is there associated both with the authority to exercise ministry in the name and with the power of Christ, and with a gift of God's grace for the right exercise of that ministry (I Timothy 4 : 4, II Timothy 1 : 6). In its combination of outward sign and inward grace it fulfils the nature of a sacrament.

The outward sign of this sacrament is, then, clear enough, namely the laying-on of hands with the form of words appropriate to the particular order concerned. There has often been confusion, however, as to the gift conferred. Does ordination ratify the gifts of the Spirit with which the man has already been endowed and so give public authorisation for the ministry for which God has equipped him? Or does it confer a spiritual gift which itself equips the man for his ministry? Both interpretations of the meaning of ordination have been put forward.

The fact is that both are true. Certainly the element of public authorisation is important. In ordination the Church declares to its own members and to the world at large that this man is authorised to speak and act in the name of Christ and his Church in those spheres of responsibility to which his particular order commits him. The public conveying of this authority is itself no small gift. It opens up the possibility of doing things which would not be possible for even the most spiritually gifted man who lacked this authority. This is obviously true in the areas of sacramental ministry and of government in the Church; but also in a very real sense in other respects where what he says and does carries weight because of the status he is known to have within the Church.

The man will have been endowed with natural and spiritual gifts before his ordination. Obviously the Church takes account of these gifts in the process of selection by which it determines that *this* man rather than *that* is fitted to be ordained. Just as the seven of Acts 6 were chosen and set apart with the laying-on of hands for the ministry because they were 'of good repute, full of the Spirit and of wisdom',[4] so the kind of qualities needed for a bishop (including those listed in I Timothy 3 : 1-7) will be looked for in a man before he is chosen for consecration and not simply expected to develop as a consequence of the grace of orders.

This is one side of the coin. The other side is that when God calls he also fits for the calling, and in the sphere of ministry as of salvation our justification is not by our works but by God's grace. God's call, not our gifts, has the priority. Our gifts may be an earnest of God's purpose in calling us ; they are not the ground of our being called. So it is entirely consonant with our total understanding of God and his working with men

263

that in sealing his call to ministry in the act of ordination he gives at the same time a gift of his grace to enable us to fulfil that vocation. So the author of II Timothy could unambiguously write of 'the gift of God that is within you through the laying-on of my hands'.[5] This confirms our assurance that those whom God calls and commissions through his Church to be bishops, priests or deacons, receive in the ordination not only the authority to execute their ministry but the grace to fulfil their vocation faithfully and effectively.[6]

These principles apply to ordination as to any of the holy orders of ministry, and not least to the consecration of bishops in which the sacrament of orders is conferred in its fulness.[7] In the case of the consecration of bishops there is particular importance in the canonical rule that at least three bishops join in the laying-on of hands. This has a double significance. It makes absolutely clear that there is no doubt as to the historic continuity of the apostolic office by the unbroken succession of episcopal consecration. For while, as the Anglican-Lutheran International Conversations recognised, 'the succession of apostolicity through time is guarded and given contemporary expression in and through a wide variety of means, activities and institutions'[8] and not only through the historic succession of bishops, Anglicans believe that the historic continuity of the episcopate is 'an outward and visible sign of the Church's continuing unity and apostolic life, mission and ministry'.[9] The participation of a number of bishops as co-consecrators also signifies the collegial nature of the episcopate. The new bishop is not receiving authority and grace simply to be used individually. He is being incorporated into a college of bishops to which is committed the carrying out of apostolic mission in its fullness, and he must operate not in isolation but in inter-relationship with his fellow bishops. The grouping of dioceses in provinces is one expression of this important theological principle.

What are we to make of the notion of a 'sacramental character', often spoken of in Catholic theology as being conferred in ordination, and its associated concept of the 'indelibility' of orders? There are some ways of interpreting this motion which are unacceptable to most modern thinkers, including some Roman Catholic theologians like Hans Küng, who has referred to 'the baseless notion of a sacramental "character"'[10] The problem is that in later scholastic theology the term was understood to imply a distinct ontological character imprinted on a man's soul at his ordination, which separated him from other men, and which by some theologians at least was regarded as eternal. Theologians from Augustine to Aquinas, however, did not understand the term in this sense, and as Piet Fransen has shown, the sacramental character has in fact been subject to widely different interpretations among Catholic theologians.[11]

What may be said is that at ordination, as at baptism, a man is brought into a distinctive relationship both with Christ and his Church, which gives him an abiding status in relation to both. This need not be based on any theory of ontological metamorphosis, but on the irrevocability of the gifts and call of God,[12] which reflects the fidelity of Christ's relationship with his Church. The phrase 'indelibility of orders' may not be appropriate outside the philosophical framework from which it derives. But the term testifies to the doctrine that ordination confers a status which is lifelong and which is reflected in the Church's practice of refusing to re-ordain a man who has once been duly ordained.

This raises an important aspect of the sacramental nature of holy orders. What is sacramental is not simply the act of ordination, but the subsequent life and work of the man admitted to holy orders. He is, to use O. C. Quick's term, 'a sacramental man',[13] or to use the evocative phrase of Austin Farrer (a phrase to be employed, it should be said, only with careful qualification), 'a sort of walking sacrament'.[14] It is not simply that the bishop or priest is authorised to administer sacraments, but that as a minister of word and sacrament he focuses in his person the priestly ministry of the Church, which is a sacramental body. This is no other than the ministry of Christ, who is himself the primal sacrament of God.[15]

This is why the consecration of the bishop is bound up with the self-consecration of Christ. The very word 'consecrate' calls to mind Our Lord's high-priestly prayer of John 17 in which he prays for his apostles. He himself had been consecrated by the Father for his priestly mission in the world.[16] So he prays: 'As thou didst send me into the world, so I have sent them into the world. And for their sake I consecrate myself, that they also may be consecrated in truth.'[17]

Note the flow of movement: the Father consecrates and sends the Son; the Son consecrates and sends the apostles, and for their sake he consecrates himself. So in the consecration of a bishop for the continuance of the apostolic mission, Christ consecrates the man who has been chosen, that he may lead and be the focus of the mission of Christ in his Church to the world. In ordaining and sending others the bishop continues this mission, but like his Lord he must consecrate himself for the sake of the others who are to be consecrated through him. This is to be a consecration 'in truth', which means not simply that he is to serve the cause of truth, but in M. J. Lagrange's words, that he is to be 'penetrated and interiorly charged by the truth',[18] in other words that he is to let Christ, who is the truth, fill his life. None of us has attained this ideal, but it is the goal before us all.

The sacramental nature of his consecration is the ground both of confidence and of humility in the bishop. These two are not opposite but complementary. He may have confidence because of his sacramental relationship with Christ, whose man he is. The exercise of episcopate does not depend on his natural or even spiritual qualities, and it is good for him to know that the unworthiness of the minister 'hinders not the effect of the sacrament'.[19] But that same unworthiness is the ground of his humility. The bishop will recognise that though consecrated by Christ, he falls far short of that self-consecration in truth, which is so important for the sake of those to whom he is to minister and whom he is to send on the same apostolic mission. He can only be amazed that despite his unworthiness God has called and consecrated him to so great a work.

THE BISHOP'S CONSECRATION VOWS

The examination of the bishop-designate is an important part of the rite of consecration. The questions put to the candidate reflect the Church's understanding of the office of bishop and the expectations it has of the man who is to hold the office. It is salutary for every bishop to reflect from time to time on the vows he made at his consecration and to examine himself on his fulfilment of them.

In this article we take the ordinal of the Book of Common Prayer as the starting point, but reference will be made to modern ordinals, particularly those of the Church of South India, the Episcopal Church of the United States and the projected Anglican-Methodist scheme in England.

The questions put to the candidate may be classified under five headings:

(1) *Vocation.* Does the candidate believe himself to be truly called by God? This is the first and fundamental question. Some of the newer ordinals add a second: Will he respond obediently (U.S.A.)? Is his motive the glory of God and the salvation of men (C.S.I.)? The emphasis in every case, however, is that God's call is the necessary precondition of this vocation.

The question makes no specific reference to the irrevocable nature of the bishop's calling. It must, however, be seen in the context of Jesus' words, 'No one who puts his hand to the plough and looks back is fit for the kingdom of God.' [20] Because his consecration places the bishop in a sacramental relationship with Christ and his Church, he is called to a faithfulness in the working out of his vocation which will mirror the faithfulness of Christ who was faithful to his Church to the point of death and purchased it with his own blood. [21]

(2) *The Faith.* The next three questions (out of eight in all) relate to the candidate's own allegiance to the faith of the Bible and his willingness to teach and uphold that faith. The bishop is above all the teacher and guardian of the faith. Just as the apostles were to be witnesses to Jesus and his resurrection in the unique way that could only apply to those who had known the Lord in the flesh, [22] those called to perpetuate the apostolic mission must be able to testify to the truth of the gospel from their personal study and experience. Like the apostles they are to be 'consecrated in the truth'.

In fulfilling this responsibility the bishop is charged to give a central place to holy scripture. He acknowledges that it contains 'sufficiently all doctrine required of necessity for eternal salvation'; he commits himself to the disciplined and prayerful study of scripture; he promises to drive away any teaching which is contrary to God's word. This aspect of the bishop's work cannot be too strongly emphasised. He is to steep himself in the biblical revelation and in the Christian theological tradition which transmits that revelation to our own age. In these days, when bishops tend to be over-busy about secondary things, they need strictly to set aside time for biblical and theological study. Indeed, every bishop is to be a theologian, not necessarily in the academic sense, but in the sense of being grounded in the faith of the Church and so being able to apply that faith to his own life and the lives of his people. It is his responsibility to see that the Church thinks theologically and makes decisions according to sound theological principle. Despite the sharing of many responsibilities with the clergy and laity in synods and other councils, the guardianship of the faith continues to be the special responsibility of the bishops.

Does this imply a purely conservative role for the bishop in matters of faith? The Prayer Book ordinal certainly envisages that the bishop is to conserve the common deposit of faith from corruption. That sounds conservative. But as the environmental movement reminds us, conservation can have a very positive and forward-looking meaning. Our task is not only to preserve the old faith. It is also to proclaim and interpret that faith in a world which has either not heard it or has heard it in so partial and distorted a form that it has not been able to accept it. Guarding the faith means not simply mounting the battlements to defend it; it also requires the sensitive and perceptive unfolding of its implications for living, and it involves finding new ways of expressing the faith when old formularies have lost their cutting edge. The wooden and uncritical maintenance of old categories of thought and forms of language may foster quite misleading ways of under-standing the faith, for old and unchanged forms may easily take on unintended shades of meaning when heard in a different context from that from which they sprang. This is a delicate task requiring balanced judgment and a sensitive grasp of the biblical revelation and the theological tradition of the Church.

Revised ordinals (e.g. USA and Anglican-Methodist) have recognised the need to make explicit this positive aspect of maintaining the faith. 'Will you boldly proclaim and interpret the gospel of Christ, enlightening the minds and stirring up the conscience of your people?' is a question put to the bishop-designate in the American rite. This is good. What is not so good is that he is no longer asked to commit himself to the scriptures as containing all doctrine necessary for salvation!

(3) *The Bishop's Life.* Two questions relate to the quality of the bishop's life. He promises to live 'soberly, righteously and godly' and to be gentle and merciful to the needy and the stranger.

No man is called to be a bishop because he is good enough; but the unmerited nature of his call demands of him the response of a life consecrated to Christ and so conformed to the character of Christ. Indeed these questions about the bishop's life follow naturally from the questions about his faith. There is something wrong with the faith that does not find expression in life.[23] This means that the frequent self-examination and repentance which is a duty of every Christian takes on special importance for the bishop, who bears a particular responsibility for witness to the living Christ. The chief aspect of his witness will inevitably be by the quality of his life. With his Master his prayer must be, 'for their sakes I consecrate myself'.

(4) *Discipline.* The candidate promises to set forward 'quietness, love and peace' and to correct and punish the 'unquiet, disobedient and criminous'. Discipline is a responsibility which he may not like but which he must not shirk. The mode of its exercise must be tempered by the spirit of the age. We live in a less juridical, authoritarian climate than did our sixteenth-century forebears, and the modern rites reflect this by referring to discipline in less specific terms. With fewer clergy and a less hierarchical pattern of relationships than of old, the modern bishop is able to restore the more pastoral and personal approach to discipline which typified the primitive Church. He must not, however, confuse love with weakness. Love will sometimes require stern action. Our Lord's stern treatment of those who defiled the temple was not a failure of love but a manifestation of it appropriate to the circumstances.

(5) *Mission.* 'Will you be faithful in ordaining, sending, or laying hands upon others?' This is the sole reference to the bishop's mission to those outside the Church and his pastoral ministry to those within. For the circumstances of sixteenth-century England this may have sufficed. The modern ordinals are agreed in spelling out this aspect of the bishop's responsibilities more clearly.

The promise as it stands involves more than may appear at first. It embraces the selection of candidates for ordination, provision for their training before and after ordination, and their deployment in pastoral work. These are among the most important of all the bishop's tasks.

Nonetheless too much is left out. As the leadership of the mission devolved upon the apostles in the primitive Church, so today this is an essential part of the bishop's work; and this, not only in the sense of planning strategy, but of being personally engaged in mission to the world. His very position in church and community often gives the bishop an opportunity such as few of his priests have to speak to the world in the name of Christ. This opportunity needs to be used to full advantage for the gospel's sake.

As chief pastor to the faithful, too, the bishop has a distinctive role. The American rite includes this question: 'As a chief priest and pastor, will you encourage and support all baptised people in their gifts and ministries, nourish them from the riches of God's grace, pray for them without ceasing, and celebrate with them the sacraments of our redemption?' A question such as this might well find a place in other future revisions of the ordinal.

The American rite fills an additional gap in the old ordinal, which concentrates entirely on the bishop's responsibilities as an individual. The bishop-designate is asked: 'Will you share with your fellow bishops in the government of the whole Church; will you sustain your fellow presbyters and take counsel with them; will you guide and strengthen the deacons and all others who minister in the Church?'

It is doubtful whether American bishops are the only ones tempted to excessive episcopal individualism! Such a vow might not be amiss elsewhere.

REFERENCES

[1] *Ministry and Ordination* (ARCIC Statement, 1973), para. 14.
[2] Article 25.
[3] Homily on Common Prayers and Sacraments.
[4] Acts 6:3.
[5] II Timothy 1:6.
[6] The twofold aspect of what is conferred in ordination is well set out under the terms 'authority' and 'power' by O. C. Quick, *The Christian Sacraments*, p. 142 (2nd edition).
[7] Cf. *Lumen Gentium* (Dogmatic Constitution on the Church), Vatican II, para. 21.
[8] Report, *Anglican-Lutheran International Conversations*, para. 74.
[9] *Ibid.*, para. 84.
[10] H. Kung, *Why Priests?*, p. 68.
[11] P. Fransen, 'Orders and Ordination', in *Sacramentum Mundi*.
[12] Romans 11:29.
[13] *op. cit.*, p. 142.
[14] *A Celebration of Faith*, p. 110.
[15] This theme is developed in E. Schillebeeckx, *Christ the Sacrament*.
[16] John 10:36.
[17] John 17:18-19.
[18] Quoted in A. Feuillet, *The Priesthood of Christ and His Ministers*, p. 139.
[19] Article 26.
[20] Luke 9:62.
[21] Acts 20:28.
[22] Acts 1:21-22.
[23] James 2:18.

SECTION VI

Aspects of Anglicanism

A shorter and more specialised section covered by three articles on world-wide Anglicanism.

1 - On being Anglican

Stephen Neill

ON BEING ANGLICAN

Is there anything to be said for being Anglican in the year 1977? No-one ever really wanted to be Anglican. The word Anglican has, of course, existed for a very long time; but it was used only in a geographical sense, in relation to the country called Anglia. The evidence for this is that the first use of the word Anglicanism in the great Oxford English Dictionary is from the year 1846. I have not been able to discover when the term 'Anglican Communion' was first used. Dr A. G. M. Stephenson assures me that it was used at the time of the first Lambeth Conference in 1867, and that he has some traces of earlier use. It is unlikely that any will be found earlier than the nineteenth century. It is just the fact that the English Reformers, like the Reformers on the continent, did not want or plan for a division of the Church, though they did stand out for very extensive reforms and for a measure of independence which the Pope was not willing to grant. When, then, did the idea of an English Church, separate and separable from the rest of Christendom, come into being?

WHAT KIND OF A REFORMATION?

I think that the crucial year was 1570, when the Pope most incautiously excommunicated Queen Elizabeth, set her subjects free from all allegiance to her and encouraged the idea that she might be killed. He thereby caused the members of his Church in England to be excluded from political equality for 259 years. But also his action had theological implications. He seems to have assumed that, though Elizabeth had been brought up as a Protestant, she was still in some way a member of the western church and under his jurisdiction; this neither the Queen nor her advisers were prepared to grant; from now on the Bishop of Rome could not be anything but a foreign bishop, and the idea of Henry VIII that England was an empire, with total sovereignty within itself, became the basis of the thinking of Anglicans about themselves (though Jewel's Apologia had appeared as early as 1562). What kind of a Reformation had taken place in England, and how did this Church stand in relation to the other parts of the Christian world?

There were six reformations in the sixteenth century:

1. The Lutheran reformation was basically biblical — it stemmed from

272

Luther's personal rediscovery of the meaning of certain doctrines of the Bible.

2. The Swiss reformation was doctrinal, arising from the application of the cool rational French mind to the discoveries that Luther had communicated to the Christian world.

3. The intellectual reformation, the work of the Sozzini and others like them, mainly of the Mediterranean race, tended towards unitarianism, as is seen in the long survival of the term Sozzinianism for what today we would call unitarianism.

4. The radical reformation of the Anabaptists and others maintained that theirs was not reformation but renovation, since the true church had long since died out.

5. The conservative reformation at Trent had effected many practical reforms but had not introduced a single new idea.

6. The Anglican reformation was primarily the liturgical reform. It had of course biblical, doctrinal and practical aspects. But the man who stamped his own gentle and learned character on the emerging Church of England was the greatest liturgical genius of whom we have record in the life of the Church — Thomas Cranmer. Cranmer's genius is seen at its best in the offices of morning and evening prayer and in the Litany. Out of many ancient materials he made services which were practical, useful and up to date. Every change in the Roman Breviary over the years has been in the Cranmerian direction — a sincere but perhaps unconscious form of flattery. Luther made hardly any changes in the medieval forms. The sober dignity of the first Book of Common Order in Scotland was soon forgotten. England held the palm.

WHAT KIND OF VIA?

The term *Via Media* became very popular in the early nineteenth century, though there are parallels to the idea in considerably earlier writers. The phrase has often been misunderstood as meaning that the Church of England takes a middle way as between Rome and Geneva. But this of course is not so. It is the middle way between the authoritarian Church of Rome and the radical reformers, the secretaries, who denied continuity, order and authority in both Church and State. This is by far the deepest division in the Church.

During the discussions leading up to the Report on Church Relations in England, that great ecumenical figure Nathaniel Micklem once said to me that the greatest difficulty in such discussions was the cleavage between the two views of the Church — that of the people's Church, where it was taken for granted that everyone is a Christian, unless they have contracted out; and the gathered Church where it is taken for granted that no-one is a Christian unless they have made a specific and public confession of faith in

273

Christ. He could clearly see that both were necessary, but he could see no way by which they could be reconciled in one body.

The Church of England has taken its stand resolutely on the side of the Church and as against the sects. Every resident in England still has a right to the services of the Anglican parish priest, though he is no longer required to make use of them unless he specifically desires to do so. Those who defend the establishment of the Church of England do so on the ground that the advantages to the nation accruing from an establishment of religion have so far outweighed the disadvantages accruing to the Church from the same arrangement; if the balance of advantage and disadvantage turned the other way, they would be impelled to move in the direction of disestablishment.

This Anglican decision meant that the Church of England felt itself very close to the main-line churches of the continent of Europe which had equally thrown off the constricting power of Rome, but had also accepted the role of national churches. The loss of episcopacy was not held to annihilate the unity of spirit and doctrine by which these churches were held together. As late as the early nineteenth century, Bishop Heber, by no means a low churchman, defended his right to receive communion in the great national churches of Germany, when he found himself in that country, though of course wishing to see those churches recover many things which they had lost at the time of the Reformation.

The radical difference between the two ideas of the Church came into great prominence in the time of the civil war. The Presbyterians, having played their cards very badly, failed to play a leading part. When outstanding men such as Oliver Cromwell identified themselves clearly with the independents, there really could be no truce. The Church, as Cranmer and others had made it, would disappear, and its place be taken by something very different. The conservatism of the English people brought back the king, and with him the bishops — 'no bishop no king' James I had sagely affirmed. Efforts at comprehension, better handled, might have brought back some, like the admirable Richard Baxter, without whom the Church of England was poorer. But with the independents there was really no possibility of compromise without fatal dishonesty on one side or the other. So the adjustment of limited toleration was arrived at and is with us still in England. It involved the final abandonment of the principle of one people, one ruler, one faith, one Church. This is not an ignoble ideal. It is just that it proved to be 'the high that proves too high, the heroic for earth too hard'. We have not yet arrived at the kingdom of heaven, and must therefore accept something else — an ideal of toleration, which creates a unity of mutual respect, but not of faith and of worship.

THE HOME OF REFUGEES

From the beginning the Church of England has been a hospitable

274

Church. Fortunate in having continuity denied to many other countries, and a gradually growing spirit of toleration, England has been able to absorb wave after wave of refugees — from Jan Laski and his like in the days of the persecutions, to German non-Aryan pastors, of whom so many serve with such excellence in the ranks of the Anglican clergy today. Anglicans have recognised that foreigners, even those coming to settle permanently in England, may wish to keep their own ways; hence the strange anomaly of the Huguenot congregation in the crypt of Canterbury cathedral. But many of our guests, like the great scholar Isaac Casuabon, have found in the Church of England that combination of order and freedom, which they had sought in vain in the best reformed churches of the continent. We might perhaps add the service rendered by England over many years as the home of refugee Jews, from many countries, until America took over this role in the middle of the nineteenth century; though here there was wide recognition that Jews would wish to keep their identity, and must be permitted to do so, within the limits imposed by public order. The island kingdom has always been in danger of isolation, a spirit that reached its highest point at the end of the eighteenth century during the Napoleonic wars, together with the loss of Latin as the universal language of communication among the learned. And even this was mitigated by the presence in England of the numerous refugee bishops from France, who by their modesty and devoutness gave to the English people a new picture of the Scarlet Woman. Our history has been greatly enriched by those who have come to live with us, and have brought the variety of their experiences into the life of the Church.

RADICAL QUESTIONINGS

The Church of England had accepted from the start the position of a majority church with government support. Could Anglicanism subsist in a minority position and in total separation from the State? Was it a viable form of Christian faith and not just a viable form of Christian organisation? In the heyday of the Church of England (at that time the United Church of England and Ireland), no one even asked such questions. But clearly they were of very great importance, and had in fact been answered before they had been asked.

The Episcopal Church in Scotland has never been very kindly treated by its richer neighbour to the South. Yet that small body has had a noble history. During the period of repression following on its unfortunate identification with the cause of the Young Pretender, under the most unfavourable conditions that Church had kept itself alive, and developed traditions of its own, rather different from those of the Church of England. It could not be otherwise, since that Church was living as a tiny minority in a world dominated by the Presbyterians and could expect no help at all from the State. The same question was to be asked in a rather different form when the thirteen colonies west of the Atlantic decided to assert their independence.

An attempt had been made in Virginia to reproduce the main features of the Anglican establishment, with the curious variant that even those most closely wedded to the traditions of the Church saw no necessity for — the introduction of episcopacy into the western world. But when independence came, Anglicans in that new world affirmed with great resolution, 'We intend to remain Anglicans, and neither political independence, nor spiritual freedom is to be taken as marking any desire to cut ourselves off from our home.' (This is not a quotation but a summary of many expressions of similar ideas.)

The reactions of sheer puzzlement in England make an interesting study. How can one who does not take the oath of allegiance to the king be an Anglican bishop? This would seem to violate the principle of 'no king no bishop', which is the corollary of the principle 'no bishop no king'. And archbishops without a seat in the House of Lords? This would seem to be a contradiction in terms. Only gradually did it come home to the ecclesiastics in England that history had stolen a march on them, and that things which they judged to be impossible were already enjoying a comfortable existence. What Scotland and America had begun were followed up by New Zealand and South Africa. The sensational event of the consecration of the first black bishop, Samuel Adjai Crowther, in 1864, had brought it to the attention of a great many people that African Anglicanism was already a reality. The notable success of Anglican missions in India, China and Japan was steadily changing the racial and national characteristics of the Anglican fellowship. By the end of the century it had become clear that what had begun as a single Church for one island community had developed una-wares into a world-wide communion of Churches, each claiming complete autonomy, but all bound together by subtle principles of unity.

WHAT PRINCIPLES OF UNITY?

But how in the world does such fellowship of Churches hold together? Has it any reality at all?

The great merit of the British people is that they have never learned the first principles of logic, and therefore defy all those rules of reason which make so strong an appeal to our brethren just across the English Channel. Without batting an eyelid they reconcile the irreconcilable and achieve the impossible. One of the greatest pleasures of the British visitor to the United States is that of explaining to his American friends the game of cricket in terms of that elaborated form of the children's game of rounders which the Americans call baseball. The American friend is left speechless in perplexity. It is the same with the effort to explain the Commonwealth of Nations. 'But it just couldn't exist.' Nor is it certain that it can go on existing; but for the moment it does, and, even if it does not quite fulfil the eager hopes of those who worked for its existence in becoming the greatest force on earth for the peace of the nations, it yet remains a real unity, which bridges gaps and brings together races and peoples of the most diverse origins and strangely diverse forms of government in a fellowship as strongly experienced as it is weakly defined.

It is the same with this odd formation called the Anglican Communion. Some time after its formation the World Council of Churches became aware of that mainly twentieth-century phenomenon, the World Confessional Organization. It was decided to hold a meeting of general secretaries of such organisations. The then executive officer of the Anglican Communion, Bishop Stephen Bayne, rightly refused to attend on the ground that the Anglican communion is a fellowship of Churches and not a confessional organisation. All Anglican Churches are automatically a part of the fellowship, and every Anglican in the world is the responsibility of some bishop or other though the Anglican in Siberia may not see much of his spiritual father, the Bishop of London. The admirable officer in Geneva who was a Presbyterian quite honestly could not see the difference between the World Alliance of Reformed Churches to which Churches may adhere if they wish, or the Lutheran World Federation to which a number of Lutheran churches do not belong, and this strange Anglican phenomenon; all attempts to explain this to him were in vain; 'but you *are* a World Confessional Organization, and it is no use saying that you are not'. What is to be done? Almost all Americans believe that the Church of England is a State Church and that bishops are paid by the government. Almost all Americans believe that the Archbishop of Canterbury is some kind of a Pope. And if he is not, what is he for?

Now, if we find it so difficult to explain ourselves to other people, it is possible that we have not quite understood ourselves. The question of what constitutes the unity of the Anglican fellowship became for various reasons a burning question in the middle of the nineteenth century.

The first obvious answer was the liturgical unity, which naturally characterises the fellowship born of the liturgical reformation. There were some small variations in Scotland and America; but generally speaking the Anglican wherever he might be could count on finding the familiar service in whatever church he had the opportunity of attending; and, in whatever language the service might be conducted, he would know just where he was and what was happening.

All the Anglican Churches accepted the Thirty-nine Articles of Religion as the official explanation of their position in relation to other possible understandings of the Christian faith, though the degree of assent to them has varied from Church to Church.

There was an intense sense of loyalty to the Church of England as the fount and origin of the Communion, and to the Archbishop of Canterbury as the visible representative of that unity. But there was no formal expression of that unity.

It was the case of Bishop Colenso that precipitated the demand,

277

coming particularly from the Canadian Church, that what had existed as experience and sentiment should take on some visible form. What emerged was very much less than the Synod of the whole fellowship for which the Canadian Church had hoped. The Lambeth Conference makes for itself very moderate claims; it is no more than a large committee invited to meet on the sole responsibility of the Archbishop of Canterbury, who decides *motu proprio* whether another conference is to be held, and who should attend it. It has been stated again and again that decisions of the Conference have no authority other than that which they may acquire by their intrinsic wisdom. Like most other ecclesiastical assemblies successive Conferences have weakened their influence by trying to do far too many things, and passing countless resolutions which no-one will ever read. And yet a Lambeth Conference is an impressive gathering. All attempts to bring it to an end have proved unavailing. The colonial boys, who are holding the fort in such areas as the Arctic and South-west Brazil and Sabah feel the need of it much more than the bishops of Chester and Rochester and Winchester and Worcester. The educational value of the Conference can hardly be over-estimated.

Having come so far, it was almost inevitable that the Anglican Communion should go a little further in the organisation of itself. It now has a Consultative Council meeting regularly once every two years, and with a small central headquarters in London. There is a strange contrast between the towering headquarters of the Lutheran World Federation in Geneva, and our very modest little headquarters in Belgravia; but perhaps we really have the best of the bargain.

CAN IT HOLD TOGETHER?

The Anglican fellowship has always been committed to the idea of one Church, in which all Christians will be able to find a home. This being so, it has a record of ecumenical endeavour unequalled by any other Christian fellowship in the world. When Miss Rouse and I were editing the *History of the Ecumenical Movement*, we were at times embarrassed, both being Anglicans, to find that the story was unrolling itself at certain periods simply as the story of Anglican ecumenical effort. No other fellowship has reached out more widely, with more generous sympathy and a deeper desire to understand. This being so, the Anglican Communion has had to ask poignantly the question whether it is to be regarded as a permanent part of the world Christian scene, or only as a provisional entity, provided by God to fill in the gap between primal unity and the godly union we hope may yet be in his purpose for his Church. This question was faced honestly and sincerely by the Lambeth Conference of 1948, and the answer returned was emphatically that we must face the possibility of our own demise, if it should be the will of God that what is at present Anglican should find itself absorbed into a more fully catholic union, in which everything that has been valued

278

as Anglican in separation should find its appropriate home. It was added that premature dissolution of the Anglican Communion, before its specially appointed work was done, might involve disloyalty to the will of God. By these devout and cautious expressions of opinion I think that all thoughtful Anglicans would stand today.

The pressure to consider the question came from two directions.

The Anglican fellowship was growing into a wider episcopal fellowship. It had found itself drawn to help smaller bodies which desired to be both evangelical, in the true sense of the term, and episcopal and did not know where to look for a home. In the earlier part of the nineteenth century the Waldensian Church in Italy looked to the Church of England for aid, generously provided under the inspiration of the good General Beckwith, who lost a leg at the battle of Waterloo, and whose wooden leg is reverently preserved in the Waldensian museum at Torre Pellice. Later we lost our primacy of aid to the Presbyterians. This outgoing generosity did not commend itself to all parties in the Church. When, in 1894, three Irish bishops consecrated Señor Cabrera as bishop of the Spanish Reformed Episcopal Church, the *Church Times* sent a telegram of condolence to the Pope on this aggression in his dominions. But the movement of history has been in the other direction. Parts of the Anglican fellowship have communion with a variety of bodies in various parts of the world. The question has been raised whether any specifically Anglican conference is any more needed, and whether it should not be replaced by a conference of the wider episcopal fellowship.

The question was posed in an even more acute form by the formation of the Church of South India (1947) and the Church of North India (1970). The Anglican fellowship has never claimed universal jurisdiction. By agreeing to the formation of these two churches, it declared its intention not to have any special Anglican witness in the areas for which these Churches would now be responsible, being satisfied that all those things for which Anglicans are specially concerned would be cared for by the united Churches when they came into existence. This hope has been splendidly fulfilled; these Churches are not loose federations, as was at one time feared, but real Churches, and the members of them feel themselves to be heirs of all the uniting traditions and therefore richer than they were in the days of separation. So the Anglican fellowship as such has simply ceased to exist in certain areas in which it once prospered.

In more recent times the current of ecumenical concern seems to be flowing away from such local unions, in the direction of consultation between worldwide Christian fellowships on what we have now learned to call a global basis. This may be the direction in which God is calling us to act today. Oddly enough the coming into existence of the World Council of Churches to work for the unity and renewal of the Church has caused us all to be more denominationally aware of ourselves than we were; meeting others as we now do, we learn to know ourselves. And perhaps the unit, in this situation, is a wider fellowship rather than just the local Church. So the Anglican Communion seems to have acquired a new reason for existing; it is already as such engaged in discussions, not only with Roman Catholics but with others as well.

THREATS TO UNION

It must be recognised, however, that Anglican unity is not something that can be taken for granted today as it was a century ago.

Liturgical uniformity is a thing of the past. Provinces have claimed the right to go ahead with liturgical revision, often with less consultation with others than might have been desirable. As a result the two volumes edited by Mr Buchanan contain a kenspeckle variety of rites, in which variety is more evident than unity of theological understanding or of liturgical principle. The result is that an Anglican moving from place to place never knows with what rite he is going to be confronted, and is more likely to be perplexed by the unfamiliar than cheered by the continuity of a tradition to which he has long been accustomed. This liturgical freedom was inevitable, and on the whole desirable. It does bring home to us our lack of any central point of reference through which unity can be preserved in variety and the special Anglican ethos can be maintained as a general guiding principle in the work that is being done.

The Thirty-nine Articles have been generally abandoned. In some provinces this has been done deliberately. Sometimes the Articles have been replaced by a more modern confession of faith; in others they have been replaced simply by a lacuna. No one, I think, would wish to work out today confessions of the amplitude of those produced in the sixteenth century. It might be an advantage if we had something to which we could refer as a plain setting forth of what Anglican faith and principle really are, especially now that it is impossible to point to one common liturgy as a means of testing the spirits whether they be of God.

The question of the ordination of women has, as was to be expected, proved divisive. Opinions range from the view that this is one of the great revelations of the wisdom of the Spirit, to those which regard it as the total abandonment of theological principle and Christian practice. Some provinces are threatened by schism; in many others there is grave anxiety. It is already clear that the action of some provinces in going ahead with such ordinations has brought about a shift in our ecumenical position. We may lose our communion with the Old Catholics, much valued by us all in spite of their small numbers. The Orthodox have already made it quite clear that success in negotiations with them is not to be expected if we persist in what they regard as a grave departure from Catholic practice. There is no question that our position has been shifted away from the more traditional Churches in the direction of those Protestant Churches which have been ordaining

280

women for the past century and are glad that we are at least catching up with them. It is not the business of an individual writer to pass judgment on these proceedings; it is important that we should recognise the consequences of what we do, not only for ourselves, but in our relations with others whose opinion we value, even when we do not allow them to become judges of our conscience.

On the horizon there is a threat that may prove to be even more divisive. Through the centuries it has been taken for granted that the New Testament gives decisive guidance in many matters of ethical principle. In these permissive days, when the authority of Scripture is not taken as seriously as it once was, many are asking whether traditional views are to be accepted merely because they are traditional. We no longer regard ourselves as bound by laws on usury which the Church once accepted as sacrosanct; should we not realise that in such fields as sexual morality a new freedom is being offered to us of which advantage should be taken? Abandonment of old standards might lead many Christians into crises of conscience far more serious than those arising out of a change of practice in regard to ordination; the attack might be held to touch the life of the Church on a deeper level even than of ordination or episcopacy.

So we are not living in an epoch of guaranteed peace — but then perhaps 'the peace of the Church' has never been more than a relative term.

DO WE THEN GO ON?

In view of rapid changes in the world and in the Church, some may well feel that the time has come at which we should just fold up our tents, agree that the work God has given us has been accomplished, and that we should look for other ways in which his purpose can be fulfilled. I do not myself believe that this is so.

Anglicanism does at its best create a unique combination of order and freedom, of independence and mutual loyalty. Is there here a contribution that we still have to make to the life of the world?

We have not always lived up to our own ideals. But there has been in our tradition a stream of tolerance, of willingness to listen, of belief that God's last word had not been spoken when the last book of the New Testament was complete. The new spirit of flexibility in other communions is encouraging; but perhaps we are still called to be watchdogs. Whenever new and startling views are put forward, the cry of 'the truth in danger' is raised, with the desire for heresy trials and the expulsion of the traitors. I do not believe that we shall ever again make the mistake of a heresy trial. 'Never make martyrs' is a sound principle; those who believe most profoundly in the value of truth are the most likely to accept it, and to believe that truth will shine by its own light.

We have been successful in creating a world fellowship in which

281

Christians of many races can feel at home, and in which the western dominance with which we started is every day becoming less. Happily we do not stand alone; and it is not clear that we have as yet made our final contribution in this field of international development within the limits of a not too stringent definition of the Christian faith and its demands.

It is clear that we are at the beginning and not at the end of a period of liturgical renewal. Some are happier than others with the various new rites that have been produced. It cannot be said to be certain that we have found the way in which modern man should be worshipping God. We must be ready to learn from others, and at the same time feel that the continuance of controlled experiment may lead us in unexpected ways and to fulfilments that are at present beyond our ken.

We frequently infuriate our friends by all our talk of union, which seems to lead to so little. But once again we may have a service to render in our special combination of eagerness and caution. We know that haste can lead only to superficiality, and a union made with untempered mortar can lead only to new schisms. We must rejoice in the progress of our discussions with the Roman brethren; yet at the same time we see that the road is long rather than short, and that nothing is to be gained by concealment of the deep differences that do still exist.

In this and other ways we may feel that God still has work for us to do. In spite of all the changes that have come about, there is still such a thing as an Anglican ethos. If this were lost, the world Church would be poorer. How this is to be preserved, and what forms it should take in the future it is hardly possible for us to say. But perhaps our fathers in the faith were wise when they stated it as their principle to keep the mean between the two extremes, 'of too much stiffness in refusing, and too much easiness in admitting any variation from it'. Perhaps this, rather than anything else is the true Anglican *via media*. A difficult position to maintain. But perhaps we might whisper, strictly among ourselves, that when God hath a difficult thing in hand, he gives it to his Anglicans to do.

2 - Anglican Christianity and Ecumenism

Oliver S. Tomkins

Lambeth Conferences have always been concerned about other Christians. Ecumenism may be defined as taking seriously the presence of Christ in *all* Christians and therefore the common witness of all Christians in all life, in all times and all places.

The first Lambeth Conference in 1867 expressed in its Encyclical Letter 'the deep sorrow with which it viewed the divided condition of the flock of Christ throughout the world, ardently longing for the fulfilment of the prayer of Our Lord'. The second Conference urged intercession for Christian unity, whilst the third in 1888 drew up 'the Lambeth Quadrilateral' (about which more must be said later). The fifth Conference of 1908 said in its message 'We must fix our eyes on the Church of the future, which is to be adorned with all the precious things, both theirs and ours. We must constantly desire not compromise but comprehension, not uniformity but unity'. It was the sixth Conference in 1920 which issued the moving and historic 'Appeal to All Christian People', including this fine passage 'The vision which rises before us is that of a Church, genuinely Catholic, loyal to all Truth, and gathering into its fellowship all "who profess and call themselves Christians", within whose visible unity all the treasures of faith and order, bequeathed as a heritage by the past to the present, shall be possessed in common, and made serviceable to the whole Body of Christ.'

Fine words, undeniably: but how far in Anglican practice for over a century have we been able to convince our fellow-Christians that we mean what we say? I remember an American Congregationalist saying to me with deep feeling 'The Anglican communion prays more for unity and does more to prevent it than any other body in Christendom'. The purpose of this paper is to offer one man's view of the actual and potential contribution of Anglican Christianity to ecumenism, as another Lambeth Conference affords one more opportunity for words, which may or may not issue in deeds.

Part of the answer lies in what contribution Anglicanism has made in the dedicated service of its members to the ecumenical cause. God alone knows the full answer. But in terms of what is visible to all, the Anglican Communion's record is an honourable one. Ecumenism becomes most readily visible in those various movements which, in their sum, represent the common endeavour of the Churches to witness together to the Kingdom of God. By common consent, the historic origins of what we now call 'the Ecumenical Movement' lie in the Edinburgh Missionary Conference of 1910. Here, to begin with, Anglicanism was hesitant. To the High Church strand, the Conference looked too much like one more exercise of evangelical Protestantism. But in the end, the SPG was a participant and Bishops Charles Gore and E. S. Talbot and Fr. Frere C.R. were among its members and Archbishop Randall Davidson addressed the opening meeting. After that start, there was never any doubt about the commitment of Anglican missions in the work of the International Missionary Council right up to the time of its incorporation into the World Council of Churches at the New Delhi Assembly in 1961.

Anglicans took the initiative in the second strand of the ecumenical movement. Charles Henry Brent, then Bishop of the Philippines (and later of W. New York) had been at Edinburgh in 1910 and returned convinced that the credibility of the Christian mission in the world would be greatly enhanced if Christians themselves were more evidently united in 'Faith and Order'. There followed seventeen years of single-minded devotion to that vision. The American Episcopal Church was the prime mover in the early stages. Helped by Robert H. Gardiner and George Zabriskie in particular, Brent mobilised the P.E.C. to take the initiatives which issued in the First World Conference on Faith and Order at Lausanne in 1927. There the C. of E. representatives included Charles Gore, A. C. Headlam and William Temple among the bishops and from other Provinces C. F. d'Arcy, Archbishop of Armagh, Jimmy Palmer of Bombay, Norman Tubbs of Tinnivelly, Azariah of Dornakal, and representatives of Anglicanism in China, Japan and the West Indies, though it is a comment on Church leadership at that date that few faces at Lausanne were not 'white'. For the next forty years, Anglicans played a leading part in Faith and Order out of all proportion to their numbers in Christendom — a source both of strength and of weakness for the Movement as a whole.

In the third strand, Bishop George Bell testified to the slowness of Anglicanism to commit itself to 'Life and Work'. The role which Brent played before Lausanne 1927 was played before Stockholm 1926 by a Swedish Lutheran, Archbishop Nathan Soderblom of Uppsala. Davidson allowed his chaplain, George Bell, to take part and Theodore Woods, newly Bishop of Winchester, both played a vigorous part himself and gave the Conference a *cachet* of Anglican respectability and Anglican fears of 'Pan-Protestantism' were somewhat allayed by Soderblom's success in thoroughly involving the Orthodox Churches. It was not until the Oxford Conference on 'Church Community and State' in 1937 that Anglicans (apart from the courageous George Bell) were really prepared to throw themselves into this manifestation of the Church's concern to witness in the area of social and international affairs.

This glance at the historical origins of the ecumenical movement, and the (very incomplete) list of Anglican participants in it, has been given partly to illustrate the nature of ecumenism, partly to emphasise that Anglican commitment to it has deep roots.

'Ecumenism' is more than the organised Ecumenical Movement. I think that it would be a fair analogy to say that the relationship between the two is comparable with the relationship between the Kingdom of God and the Church. Just as God rules and reigns outside the bounds of the visible Church, so the ecumenical vision is being realised wherever the Holy Spirit draws together Christians in mutual love and common service. But the Ecumenical Movement (denoted by capital initials) is to be found where the Churches corporately contribute persons — and money to enable them — in a continuing, sustained and purposeful programme of common witness. The three independent but related strands, of which we have already taken note, became steadily more intertwined. As the modern world of rapid travel and instant communication took shape in this century, it was natural for these diverse impulses also to take on a more coherent form, to issue in 1948 in the World Council of Churches. But the same contemporary forces also enabled the 'World Confessional Families' to become more self-aware. Anglicanism has shown a distinct reluctance to become as formally organised as some of the others. For nearly a century there was almost no formal means of contact between the Anglican Provinces between Lambeth Conferences. Gradually more was done. The late Bishop Stephen Bayne became the first whole-time officer after the Lambeth Conference of 1958. After the 1968 Conference the Anglican Consultative Council came into being, so that for the first time there was a regular, representative gathering to draw together the Anglican Provinces at more frequent intervals. The relevance of this fact to our theme is that we cannot understand the relation of 'Anglican Christianity and Ecumenism' unless we recognise that there is a certain polarity between the relationship of the 286 'member churches' of the W.C.C. to each other in that unique forum and the 25 Anglican Churches (each of which is a member of the W.C.C.) as they develop something of a common mind in relation to the other corporate confessional minds developing through the 'World Confessional Families'.

This polarity has been powerfully accentuated by the single biggest change in the ecumenical scene in the past fifteen years — the emergence of the Roman Catholic Church, since Vatican II, as an active participant in the ecumenical dialogue. This includes not only an intimate relationship with the W.C.C. (of which of course it is not a 'member church') but also a series of bilateral conversations with Orthodoxy, Methodists, Lutherans, Reformed, etc. Since the Church of Rome is essentially an international body, the vis-à-vis for ecumenical discourse is another international body. Yet Anglicanism continues reluctant to become as confessionally organised as are, for example, Reformed or Lutherans. But the Secretary-General of the

A.C.C. is the present chairman of the Conference of Secretaries of World Confessional Families without thereby implying that the A.C.C. considers itself to *be* a World Confessional Family. So — without being a tidy pattern — the ecumenical movement today does contain a certain tension between an emphasis upon local, regional churches (usually national in their identity) as the basic unit of ecumenical exchange and an emphasis upon global confessional fellowships as the unit.

That is why, for the remainder of this paper, we shall look at each of the three constituent strands of the Ecumenical Movement and pick out from each of them a single issue, which seems to me to be a crucial one, and then look at the ways in which Anglican Christianity, focused in the A.C.C., has been responding to that issue since the last Lambeth Conference: 1968 also happened to be the date of the Uppsala Assembly of the W.C.C.

I. MISSION

The past decade has seen a sharpening of the discussion about the meanings of mission, evangelism and dialogue with those of other faiths. A recent book by an English (though not Anglican) theologian made a distinction between 'ptolemaic' and 'copernican' theology. Just as ptolemaic cosmology saw the universe as circling round the earth, so there is a theology which sees all thought about God as circling around itself; as copernican cosmology sees the earth with other planets circling round the sun, so there is a theology which sees all systems of thought about God as different perspectives upon an Ultimate Reality beyond the full comprehension of any of them (see pp. 30-34 of *'Death & Eternal Life'* by John Hick). Such an analogy dramatically raises all the questions about the uniqueness and finality of Christ in the whole human quest for God. As Christianity finds itself in ever more inescapable encounter with the other great religious faiths and as the urgent need for world community raises the question of the basis upon which mankind must unite or perish, is it possible for Christians to affirm with the former certainty that in Christ alone is the Way, the Truth, the Life?

At the Nairobi Assembly of the W.C.C. there was considerable tension between Section I 'Confessing Christ Today' and Section III 'Seeking Community: the Common Search . . .' In the meetings of the A.C.C., at Limuru in 1971, the section on Mission and Evangelism was well aware of the questions which are put to the Church about the *form* of its unchanging mission to proclaim salvation through Christ 'to every creature'. We must be 'willing to listen as well as talk, and to learn as well as to communicate' (ACC I. p. 44). At Dublin, the ACC again faced 'dialogue' which starts from God-in-Christ, yet 'because we believe that Christ is the Light of the World, we must gladly recognise any light wherever we find it' (ACC II p. 49). At Trinidad, the ACC recognised how far all formulations of Christian theology are influenced by the cultural context in which they are developed. As the concepts of Greek philosophy, which influenced classical Christian theology, are strange for example to Indian thought, how far could the idea of *avatar* be more meaningful there?

As a larger, and growing, proportion of the Christian minority in the world comes from backgrounds of thought outside the European tradition, are we going to find that the main task of the Christian mission is so to *listen* to other minds that as Christians we can speak in ways that may be new but are more meaningful? Yet does not 'real listening' always carry with it the possibility that the hearer may himself be changed in the process? And since the relationship between 'the thing expressed' and 'the way of expressing it' is so subtle and elusive, how do we recognise whether a different way of saying it is saying something different? The problems are made more acute by the recognition amongst biblical scholars that there are diverse 'theologies' within the Bible itself.

As the Ecumenical Movement becomes more truly representative of widely different cultures, and as the Christian community engages faithfully with the entire human community, is it not likely that these are the sort of challenges which must be met by the Christian Mission?

II. VISIBLE UNITY

At the Nairobi Assembly the W.C.C. revised its Constitution so that the first of its 'functions and purposes' now reads: '(i) to call the Churches to the goal of visible unity in one faith and in one eucharistic fellowship, expressed in worship and in common life in Christ, and to advance towards that unity in order that the world may believe.'

Yet the last decade has seen a surge of doubt as to how 'visible' our unity in Christ is to be.

ACC III, meeting in Trinidad in 1973 (p. 9) noted 'the collapse of a significant number of negotiations towards Church union in which Anglicans have been involved' and lists eight such in the accompanying pages of survey. The implication is drawn that the previously accepted idea of 'organic union' had proved too inflexible, usually conceived at 'the formation of one ecclesial structure, usually within the boundaries of a single nation' (p. 17). Attention was drawn to the Ten Propositions emanating from the Churches' Unity Commission in England, in which there is no 'Scheme of Union' suggested, instead there is 'an open-ended and ongoing process — which will lead all the Churches into an ever deepening unity'.

But if unity is indeed to be *visible*, sooner or later this vagueness will have to yield to something more definite. The disenchantment with union schemes is understandable, in the light of so many failures and disappointments. Converts to the idea of open-ended process, like all converts, tend to exaggerate their former delinquency. It is suggested that the unity movement has sought to impose uniformity, to treat the Churches as though they were static pieces ingeniously to be fitted together like a jig-saw puzzle, to over-emphasise the institutional aspect of the Church to the neglect of its vitality and freedom in the Spirit. There must be something in these charges for them to stick. Yet we have seen that already in 1908 the Lambeth Fathers were saying that 'We must constantly desire not compromise but comprehension, not uniformity but unity' and the same spirit breathes through the proceedings of Lausanne 1927.

Yet there *is* something different about the ethos of the '70s. In politics and industry as well as in ecclesiastical affairs, there is a widespread rejection of inherited forms, a streak of anarchism and an impatience with the 'system'; a pluralist society is sceptical of the value of structures; a spirit of subjectivism rejects any concepts which are not verifiable in experience. The age of 'planning' is breeding its own nemesis. These are the negative aspects of an invigorating sense of new possibilities, of a broad demand for participation in decision making: of a vitality which moulds its own forms; an honesty which rejects the second-hand and prefers process to blue-prints.

Something of this temper informed the reconsideration by Lambeth 1968 of the venerable *Quadrilateral*. Instead of regarding that as the immovable four walls within which all Anglican discussion of unity must be confined, the Report (pp. 122ff) starts from Ephesians 4.3 and 13 where unity is seen *both* as a gift to be kept and a goal to be attained. Each of the four points is reaffirmed from this double perspective, 'as affirming both that which God has given and that to which he calls us'. (See Lambeth 1968 Report for full text.)

A similar readiness to live with tensions has informed the Faith and Order discussion within the W.C.C. on the stubborn task of discerning the 'nature of the unity we seek'. ACC III (pp. 15-19) sketches the reasons for a changing vocabulary to describe a widening experience. Already implicit in the New Delhi definition, in a sentence of more than Pauline length, is the tension between the 'unity of all in each place' and unity 'with the whole Christian fellowship in all places and all ages'; at Lund in 1952, Faith and Order asked the Churches to start 'to do together all that conscience does not compel us to do separately'. That they still need to be asked — though we may add the astringent rider that there is no virtue in doing together what we ought not to be doing at all. There is the tension between local unions and World Confessions (already referred to) — unity made visible not so much in geographic regions as in the 'reconciled diversity' of corporate spiritualities and theologies. There is the tension, acute in some areas of local ecumenical experiment, between day-to-day practising of a common life in Christ and loyalty to the as-yet unreconciled denominations from which the local congregation depends. Yet all these tensions are the sign, and the price, of being alive. The abiding contribution of the Roman Communion in this time of fluidity is that there the tension between what has been given and what is being discovered is a cause of deep pain. This too is a parable, a parable of the way of the Cross. Without a real dying, there can be no resurrection. In John 17, Jesus prays for our unity but he offers us his glory: and the 'glory' of Christ, in St. John, is always his Passion. Open-endedness is no way forward until it takes up the Cross.

III. THE WORLD

In the last decade nothing has hit the headlines in ecumenism like the W.C.C. Programme to Combat Racism. That too may be seen as a parable. The early ecumenical conferences were overwhelmingly 'white'; by the time of the Nairobi Assembly there were, in the 670 or so voting delegates, 107 Africans, 92 Asians, 20 from the Middle East, 9 from the Caribbean and others from areas like Latin America which are certainly not part of the rich northern hemisphere. Nearly 100 from Eastern Europe add to the non-NATO parts of the world. Such statistics only hint at the complexity of the cultural, political and economic diversity of the present ecumenical scene. The significance of the launching of the Programme to Combat Racism was that, in addition to passing resolutions, the W.C.C. *did* something about the distribution of power in the modern world. The effects were sharply divisive. ACC I, meeting on African soil, and ACC II in 1973, both revealed that the issues raised were deeply divisive also within the Anglican Communion, where the growth of autonomous Provinces in former missionary areas has altered the balance within its membership. All this is plain to see. but the PCR was significant because it brought to the surface all kinds of related issues which cut across boundaries in a bewildering way. 'White racism' had been designated in the PCR as the central issue but some felt that this had the effect of muffling protest against other heinous violations of human rights; although the grants to liberation movements were for non-military purposes, some felt that this was to condone violence; the General Synod of the Church of England even went so far as to cut £1,000 from its contribution to the W.C.C., and some felt bitterly ashamed at such pettiness. And so one might go on cataloguing the conflict. It was a source of much pain, as well as of much joy to those who felt that the Christian Churches had at last made it clear 'that they are ready to stand by the oppressed and exploited even when there is some risk to themselves' (ACC I. p. 18). By the time of the Nairobi Assembly, the PCR came to be reaffirmed by the W.C.C. and continues on its agenda.

The whole episode has a significance wider than itself, which affects the Anglican Communion as part of the wider Christian fellowship. The Church lives in a deeply divided world, itself torn by the conflicts which tear mankind. The conflicts call for decision; generalisations can no longer conceal them and the Church cannot adopt an Olympian attitude, standing above the struggle. In that situation, how can Christians demonstrate a unity which transcends the tragic elements in human affairs? We can find out only by plunging in. As we plunge, we find that we are experiencing, in new ways, the Cross as the point of intersecting forces. Within the Community of the Crucified, mutual forgiveness, mutual prayer, mutual love may come alive in unexpected ways. That, at least, is my own experience in a small way during the past ten years. I offer it here as a testimony of hope, at a time when such conflicts look like continuing to be part of living today in a torn world. The Anglican Communion reflects within itself the divisions of the humanity of which we are part. But not to seek to escape the pain is perhaps the way in which Churches corporately may bear in their body the marks of the Lord Jesus.

3 - Anglican Patterns

John Howe

This essay is a selection from among the many thoughts and considerations that may come to a secretary of the Anglican Communion. He travels, but only because he belongs to the whole of it — as much to Australia and Burma as to West Africa and the West Indies. But while he must be deeply committed and believing in the Anglican Communion he must regret its need to exist. I believe Jesus Christ intends the unity of His Church; but it is divided. Generally speaking denominations now reach out to one another, and where they agree often walk together. While the secretary's job has great responsibilities there, he is in particular appointed to and by the Churches of the Anglican Communion. In a divided Church a good deal has to be done by denominations. Our centres of decision, structures in towns or in the world, origins and histories, as well as faith and order, require it. The convictions involved in the denominations or divisions of the Church are often deep and sincere and learned. But Anglicanism, like the others, exists in its present form because of division. In some areas of theology, where one might most wish to be logical, conclusions tend to be illogical. From our standpoint in this world the Body of Christ cannot be divided — and is. Triumphalism is always out of place. Division that is comfortable must always be suspect.

Now, without prolonging justification, let us turn to Anglicanism. There are some matters, simple in themselves, which would benefit from an agreed and accepted Anglican policy. The Church is unevenly spread over the five continents. In some dioceses the area is great and the number of Christians few. But there are also areas with no Anglican diocese and with unlimited Christian work to be done. There is often the urge to push into those areas. The intention is to achieve more. The result is questionable. Frequently the resources of men and money are not available. We need in many places, I believe, to consolidate where we are already, and where as yet the work is minute in relation to the population, and is expensively disconnected in relation to the geography. To consolidate can be better than to spread. Moreover, except where governments maintain barriers, there are few places where Christian Churches, although not Anglican, are not already comparatively well established. For the few Anglicans who find themselves in those places is it not better that in this fractured world they join with a Church that is already there?

An even more practical matter concerns Provinces. But first we need clarity about the word itself. On my rough count Anglicanism uses it with seven shades of meaning. Basically we have two. A Province (with a capital letter) is used to signify a whole autonomous Church, like the Church of the Province of South Africa, or the Church of England, with one Provincial or General Synod. A few autonomous Churches have subdivisions within them, internal provinces (no capital letter), like the Church of Ireland with two, or Canada with four. These internal provinces may have an archbishop like York, or may not, like USA.

Now for my point about Provinces. An autonomous Church has it within its power to divide. But this is in effect an irreversible process. I believe that sometimes it is a desirable course, and that always the subject is approached with caution and care. But there may be need for more general thought among us about this aspect of church structure; and how Provinces best relate to the useful, but less formal, association of dioceses in 'regions'.

There is no rule of thumb about the size of a Province, numerically or geographically. Some span several countries, which while inconvenient concerning languages and national laws, is a fine expression of Christianity transcending human boundaries. None is less than a whole country. No two situations are alike, and each Province must make the final decision for itself. But with the number of Anglican Provinces increasing, and with a new autonomous Church being properly a matter concerning the whole family, some discussion outside the Province at an early stage before it decides to divide may be a good procedure, especially in relation to mission, training and resources.

Also practical, but with every sort of implication, is consideration of the world we are in. In one country an Archbishop has died violently, in another the killing for political reasons of a Cardinal is reported. These events focus our attention. But in various countries besides the conspicuous leaders and martyrs of the Churches, Christian men and women for their faith are imprisoned and tortured or simply vanish for ever out of human knowledge. Conditions may improve. We tend to assume crises will pass. In some countries this may happen, but the appearance of the world indicates that they will be replaced by others. To this picture must be added that part of the pattern where countries with a long Christian past have allowed the gospel to become modified by traditions so that to respond to the gospel is in fact to be discordant with the way of life. All is less well than it seems. To opt for the gospel and the apostolic tradition has become a matter of challenging the national tradition.

Increasingly, it seems to me, the faith of the Christian is being put to the test. If there ever were a comfortable Christian road it is getting narrower. Commitment to Christ and his Church will matter increasingly, and then quite often the Christian will not be a popular person.

For this generation turmoil is permanent in one part of the world and another. When Christianity is too closely linked to politics, or social history or culture, it becomes distorted, then breaks down. As the gap opens we have to separate and re-assess the essentials of the gospel requirement.

This, I believe, is one aspect, and not an unhopeful one, of the world in which Anglicanism is set.

A long development in the Anglican Communion has become much clearer in the last decade or two. Within the world family not only have more parts of the Church become autonomous, but the implications of autonomy are more fully understood. Some Churches have more influence than others, not least the Church of England, but also the Churches of Africa grow and the older Churches of the west decrease in strength. This shakes up the old balance and makes easier the appreciation of the fact that beyond their geographical diversities the twenty-five autonomous Churches of the Anglican Communion form a family of equals.

The process by which they work together is not imposed by law since there is no over-arching canonical authority. Instead, on major matters, the Churches consult together, and then in the further light of its own circumstances and needs each Church (General Synod) makes its own decisions and rules. A common faith and practice, and a common regard and affection are necessary, and will always be so. By this means a procedure with much decentralisation has not become a recipe for disintegration.

On the one hand the process is helped by the comparative ease of communication, and of meeting from time to time. The aim of communicating is not only to consult on major matters of faith, which come comparatively rarely, but also for sharing pastoral and spiritual experience, and for the slowly increasing recognition that mission everywhere concerns everyone — and is indeed ecumenical, for the whole household of God. (An implication is that modern means of travel should not be ignored; but travel without adequate purpose is always a misuse of money.)

On the other hand the practice of general consultation and local decision is not fully developed yet. So one may find similar researches are repeated unnecessarily, or that in deference to the larger family the implications of local factors and culture may be ignored. It may be felt that in twenty years' time the decisions about the ordination of women to the priesthood might have been handled more expertly, though that is not to imply that they could have been postponed, or that results would have been different. There has been much study and concentrated thought in the Anglican Communion, but there is a case for suggesting that even more consulting together, and more sharing of thought and study would have been to advantage. And without much doubt there could also have been more consultation with

Churches of other denominations not least with non-episcopal denominations. Whether that view is held or not, I believe that in a divided Church Anglicans have to make their own decision in obedience to truth as they see it. The decision cannot in effect be passed across to someone else. The case is strong for supposing that the Anglican family's process of decision-making can become much more mature and observant, but that concerns the probable future of the process, not contemporary decisions. It is of immediate importance that we should not stay where we are.

A subject akin to this concerns a present tendency that is good, namely the possibility of approaching one another more by converging than by a sort of quantum-jump.

Although uniformity need not be 'monolithic', diversity can be excessive. I believe the styles of expression, the comprehensiveness, contained within Anglicanism have been, despite equal sincerities, at times a hindrance to what the gospel was about — even though the opposite was intended. One example that I must think about frequently in my travels is differences put under the heading of churchmanship. The word is inadequate for good theologies that go deep. In England, and the places influenced in the past by its history, there was for a long while no one service for which the faithful gathered. The tendency was to belong to the Mass party or the Mattins party with the appropriate theology, manners of communication, drinking habits and so on. The other side was not well thought of. I take no sides, but say 'the pity of it'.

In the days of 'mission overseas' each, with a truly impressive zeal, set up dioceses overseas where it had a clear run. And today we often have Provinces or dioceses uniformly following one tradition or another. As Provinces have become indigenous, and people travel much more, the unsatisfactoriness has become more apparent. I have two points. First, in a Communion where the fundamental wish of all must be to do what Christ wants, the measure of impediment in this situation is deserving of grave and sympathetic thought — for every country. Second, whatever we may deserve, there are today signs for hope and encouragement. It is not only that differences are less than they were, but the growing appreciation — not least through the encounters of the Church in the third world — that so much is held in common, that we have a lot we can learn with thankfulness from one another, and that quite a number of things for which once people would almost go to the stake do not matter very much after all. Probably not too late we are compelled by today's world to ask what the gospel says, and what the Church is for.

As we seek to answer we converge. It is not only the way out of past excessive diversities, but the measurement we have to apply to assumptions, and to politics, and to philosophies of liberation, and of human purpose. If Christians are to tell mankind what the gospel is about and expect a hearing then among the Christians themselves there has to be collaboration. 'Our divisions hinder this witness, hinder the work of Christ, but they do not close all roads we may travel together. In a spirit of prayer and of submission to God's will we must collaborate more earnestly in a greater common witness to Christ before the world in the very work of evangelisation.' (The *Common Declaration* of the Archbishop of Canterbury and Pope Paul VI, 1977, quoting Pope Paul's *Evangelization in the Modern World* para. 77.)

And so we are led to a second critical area where one may discern convergence as a fundamental influence — the quest for Christian unity. The vastness of the quantity of ecumenical literature is distressing: the scholarly research, the brain-teasing analyses, the articles, the reports of conversations. On to my desk comes another WCC document or another study from Anglican/Orthodox discussions. One wants to say 'And so little is accomplished', or who beyond a select group will read it? And yet I find it difficult to suppose that the concern for unity would persist if the writing and talking died away. Not that all the writing matters, or that none of the talking conceals a tiny hope that nothing revolutionary will happen. Some parishes do not fence themselves in as they did. Churches in Asia and Africa hear the World Council and other bodies talking in a language they appreciate and seldom hear elsewhere. Vatican II has brought the Roman Catholic Church to the middle of the ecumenical stage.

Little of all this is directly traceable to one piece of writing, or even several, and big endeavours of official unity discussions often issue in little more than a rather disappointing ecumenical mouse. Devising paths to unity does not have much success. Yet all this effort and concentration seems to provide the context in which the Holy Spirit is prepared to work, and as we have seen, little by little, things happen. It may not be fast enough for ecumenists or for God, but as an ingredient it seems to be the best that is available.

The effect is of a convergence towards unity. No one plan is dominant, and most are lost in the general process. In connection with the Anglican/Roman Catholic talks some people have felt there can be no further progress until the validity of Anglican Orders is acknowledged, or a particular position of one Church or the other is revoked. I suspect our progress to unity will not be by singling out this or that, however important it may be, nor by devising what some call the terms for a merger. Rather, as a whole joint process moves forward new positions and relationships will supersede the old. In short, convergence towards truth is more likely and profitable than confrontation or negotiation over particular issues. Many particular issues will be superseded, and moreover the course of events will be influenced by what happens in local churches, and parishes, and in the lives of people. Especially in parts of the world where secular influences are strong, churchgoing people wish their relationships with their neighbours to relate to the gospel of love and justice and not to be bound only by norms of their denomination. It is true the attitudes within denominations change, but for

295

some there is too much caution, or it is felt that a local situation and its possibilities are not perceived adequately at the centre.

Another subject that needs careful consideration is the way people understand the Bible. The kinds of unity and collaboration that characteristically are associated with the World Council of Churches and local or national Councils of Churches are seen by some to divert the over-riding biblical message in the interests of well-meant ecclesiastical concern. In broad terms, one approach is associated with conservative biblical scholarship, and the other with critical biblical studies, and some kinds of evangelical theology. Across the world there is a good deal of diversity in the content of conservative biblical expositions, and in attitudes to membership in the Churches. Also here, too, there are influences both for change and for inspiring evangelisation in others which commend themselves by their own quality. But the point to be made is that the attitude we have been describing relates to a proportion of the world's Christian population that is both considerable and must be considered. It is capable of being divisive, and is; but also it is increasingly capable of contributing constructively as the whole Christian attention intensifies its focus on what the gospel is about, and what the Church is for.

These notes began with an apologia for the existence of denominations, a state of affairs that is made inevitable by the divided condition of the Church. There is some satisfaction and hope that writing about the Anglican Communion cannot be done without considerations of ecumenism. The implication is not that theological beliefs may be taken lightly, but the opposite — the fundamental need to understand and learn what God wishes for his one, whole creation.

In this context, too, we may be glad at the increasing universality and internationalism that one sees in the Churches and not least in the Anglican Communion. Of different cultures we have much to learn from other continents and to profit thereby. For example, the west has long traditions which include in-built assumptions as to the meanings of biblical words. But the assumptions, particularly those that arise out of a culture, can be misleading. For example, parables that build on family relationships may be better understood from the in-built assumptions of some African communities. The very point was made at the WCC meeting in Nairobi in 1975 about the word 'son' (which has such great implications) in the Prodigal Son: in different cultures and continents the word is diversely understood. We have much to learn from one another, and all may never be understood; to listen and learn is vital.

Within this whole field of communication it is necessary at a Lambeth Conference or an Anglican Consultative Council meeting for those whose own language happens to be English to remember how many people are speaking in their second or third language. In the Anglican world now — half of which by diocese is not in the Commonwealth — the language of the people in the congregations in the growing Churches is seldom English, and our General Synods operate in a number of tongues: French, Japanese, Portuguese, Spanish, Swahili.

These one or two illustrations in the field of communication that relate directly to the Anglican family are touched upon to indicate a big field for our appreciation of God's work and our thoughts about what God wants. By grace rather than by design we have become an indigenous, international and inter-cultural family. Some other Churches are more numerous, though I believe that only the Romans are more widespread. And all are small compared with the multiplying population of the world.

Given our situation, the question is: What does Christ want the Anglican Communion to do?